MOST USEFUL SHORTCUT KEYS

Copy	Ctrl+C
Cut	Ctrl+X
Paste	Ctrl+Y
Repeat the last action	F4
Undo the last action	Ctrl+Z
Redo undone action	Ctrl+Y
Save	Ctrl+S
Print	Ctrl+P
Open	Ctrl+O
New	Ctrl+N

Show Spelling dialog box	F7
Show task pane	Ctrl+1
Close workbook	Ctrl+W or Ctrl+F4
Close Excel	Alt+F4

NAVIGATION AND VBA

Navigation

Show active cell after scrolling	Ctrl+Backspace
Move to edge of current data region	Ctrl+Arrow key
Move to beginning of row	Home
Move to cell A1	Ctrl+Home
Move down one screen	Page Down
Move up one screen	Page Up
Move to the next sheet in the workbook	Ctrl+Page Down
Move to the previous sheet in the workbook	Ctrl+Page Up

VBA

Show Macro dialog box	Alt+F8
Open Visual Basic Editor	Alt+F11
Run Sub/ UserForm	F5
Step into and step through macro	F8
Help on selected word	F1

CELL SELECTION AND FORMATTING

Select Cells

Select current data region	Ctrl+A
Select entire column	Ctrl+Spacebar
Select entire row	Shift+Spacebar
Select entire worksheet (If active cell is not in a data region)	Ctrl+A
Select entire worksheet (If active cell is within a data region)	Ctrl+A, Ctrl+A again
Hide selected rows	Ctrl+9
Hide selected columns	Ctrl+0 (zero)

Format Cells

Display Format Cells dialog box	Ctrl+1
Apply General number format	Ctrl+Shift+~
Apply/remove bold format	Ctrl+B
Apply/remove italic format	Ctrl+I
Apply/remove underlining	Ctrl+U
Apply/remove strikethrough	Ctrl+5
Create new dynamic list	Ctrl+L

DATA ENTRY AND EDITING
Enter and Edit Data

Enter a SUM formula . . . . . Alt+=
Enter the current date . . . . Ctrl+;
Enter the current time . . . . Ctrl+Shift+:
Cancel cell entry . . . . Esc
Enter same entry in
   all selected cells . . . . Ctrl+Enter
Copy the entry from
   the cell above . . . . Ctrl+'
Fill entry down . . . . Ctrl+D
Fill entry right . . . . Ctrl+R
Display Find and
   Replace dialog box . . . . . Ctrl+F or Ctrl+H

Create names from
   row/column labels . . . . Ctrl+Shift+F3
Open the active cell
   for editing F2
Line break in cell entry . . . . . Alt+Enter
Show formulas in
   worksheet . . . . Ctrl+`
                     (grave accent)
In an empty cell,
   display Insert
   Function dialog box . . . . . . Shift+F3
In a formula, display
   Function Arguments
   dialog box . . . . Shift+F3

CUSTOMIZE DIALOG BOX

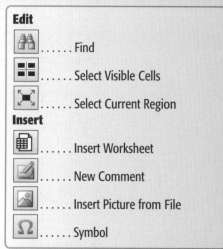

Edit

. . . . . . Find

. . . . . . Select Visible Cells

. . . . . . Select Current Region

Insert

. . . . . . Insert Worksheet

. . . . . . New Comment

. . . . . . Insert Picture from File

. . . . . . Symbol

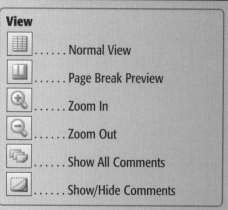

View

. . . . . . Normal View

. . . . . . Page Break Preview

. . . . . . Zoom In

. . . . . . Zoom Out

. . . . . . Show All Comments

. . . . . . Show/Hide Comments

Tools

. . . . . . Run Macro

. . . . . . Record Macro

. . . . . Visual Basic Editor

. . . . . . Camera

Data

. . . . . . AutoFilter

. . . . . . PivotTable and
        Pivot Chart Report

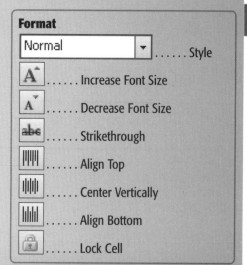

Format

Normal   . . . . . . Style

. . . . . . Increase Font Size

. . . . . . Decrease Font Size

. . . . . . Strikethrough

. . . . . . Align Top

. . . . . . Center Vertically

. . . . . . Align Bottom

. . . . . . Lock Cell

the Unofficial Guide® to Excel® 2003

Julia Kelly

WILEY

Wiley Publishing, Inc.

Unofficial Guide® to Excel® 2003

Published by
Wiley Publishing, Inc.
111 River Street
Hoboken, NJ 07030-5774
www.wiley.com

For general information on our other products and services or to obtain technical support please contact our Customer Care Department within the U.S. at (800) 762-2974, outside the U.S. at (317) 572-3993 or fax (317) 572-4002.

Wiley also publishes its books in a variety of electronic formats. Some content that appears in print may not be available in electronic books. For more information about Wiley products, please visit our web site at www.wiley.com.

Library of Congress Control Number: 2005937343

ISBN-13: 978-0-471-76321-5

ISBN-10: 0-471-76321-7

Manufactured in the United States of America

10 9 8 7 6 5 4 3 2 1

Page creation by Wiley Publishing, Inc. Composition Services

For Michael, my one-and-only.

Acknowledgements

I want to thank my resilient and hard-working agent Margot Maley Hutchison, at Waterside Productions, for keeping me working; I'm also grateful for the cheerful expertise of the entire editorial staff behind this book, including Acquisitions Editor Jody Lefevere, Project Editor Cricket Krengel, Technical Editor Namir Shammas, and all the creative and meticulous others without whom this book would not be the delightful tome you hold in your hands. Last but not least, I want to express my appreciation to clients who've brought me intriguing Excel problems over the years, and whose solutions frequently end up as examples in my books.

Credits

About the Author

Julia Kelly lives in rural north Idaho with horses, cats, small garden dogs, assorted wild animals, free-range chickens, and bird dogs who've finally learned not to "retrieve" the free-range chickens.

Contents

Sometimes I watch people work in Excel — people who are very proficient in Excel, and have been using it for years — and I get frustrated with how slowly and inefficiently they work. When I can't stand it any longer, I show them a simple thing like Format Painter or AutoFill double-click, and they are always surprised and tell me "I didn't know you could do that." That's the sort of thing I want you to get from this book — even if you just skim the book for tips and tricks.

I write the sort of books that I like to use (quick references); in fact, I refer to my own books when I haven't used a specific feature in a year or two and I want the answer fast. My intention with this book was to write an easy-to-use insider's guide to the best, quickest ways to do the things that most people need to do (and brief introductions to some features that fewer people need to use, but enough to show you what those features are capable of).

I don't intend this book to be a compendium of every single feature in Excel — there are much fatter books that do that job admirably. For example, there are a great many more functions in Excel than I cover in this book. Many of them have been around since the dinosaurs and have since been replaced by features that are altogether easier to use than the original functions were. Many other functions are useful only to individuals in high-end mathematics, science, and engineering fields; other books do cover them (see the Appendix for some titles), but not this book.

I intend this book to be an easy-to-use quick reference for when you're at work and you need to quickly know or be reminded of how to do something; to show you the best, easiest, most efficient ways of doing everything; and possibly show you how you can make your work easier and faster using techniques that you didn't know you could use.

Special Features

Every book in the Unofficial Guide series offers the following four special sidebars that are devised to help you get things done cheaply, efficiently, and smartly.

1. **Hack:** Tips and shortcuts that increase productivity.

2. **Watch Out!:** Cautions and warnings to help you avoid common pitfalls.

3. **Bright Idea:** Smart or innovative ways to do something; in many cases, this will be a way that you can save time or hassle.

4. **Inside Scoop:** Useful knowledge gleaned by the author that can help you become more efficient.

We also recognize your need to have quick information at your fingertips and have provided the following comprehensive sections at the back of the book:

1. **Glossary:** Definitions of complicated terminology and jargon.

2. **Recommended Resources:** Suggested titles and Web sites that can help you get more in-depth information on related topics.

3. **Creative Worksheets:** Real-world worksheets that go well beyond the average worksheet by combining Excel features, objects, controls, formulas, and macros. Use them for creative inspiration.

4. **Index**

First Things First

GET THE SCOOP ON...
Starting Excel ▪ The Excel environment ▪ Getting help ▪
Opening workbook files ▪ Searching for a file ▪ Using
hyperlinks to open files ▪ Saving workbook files ▪
Creating and using templates ▪ Closing workbook files

PART I

Getting In and Out

Chapter 1

This chapter covers all the most basic procedures in Excel. Starting, quitting, opening and closing files, using hyperlinks, creating templates, and saving files are all the same as in other Office programs, and in fact, you can use the information learned in this chapter in other Office programs.

Even if these procedures are familiar to you, you'll get my spin on them and possibly pick up a few tips about things you didn't know about before.

Starting Excel

Starting Excel is the same as starting any other program: You click the Windows Start button and look for Excel in the Start button's nested Programs menus. When you first use Excel, this is the only way to start the program, but when you use Excel often, there are better, faster ways to start it.

One faster, more efficient way to start Excel is to put a shortcut icon for Excel on your Windows taskbar Quick Launch toolbar.

Starting with the Quick Launch toolbar

When I want to start Excel with a new workbook, I use the icon on my Quick Launch toolbar on the taskbar (shown in Figure 1.1).

3

Inside Scoop

If your Quick Launch toolbar isn't visible at the left end of the taskbar, right-click the taskbar, point to Toolbars, and click Quick Launch.

Excel

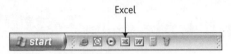

Figure 1.1. The Quick Launch toolbar on my taskbar

To put the Excel shortcut icon on the Quick Launch toolbar, open the Programs list on the Start menu. Click and drag the Excel icon down to the Quick Launch toolbar and drop it in position.

Some programs put their startup icons on the Quick Launch toolbar for you when you install the program, whether you want the icon there or not. To delete an icon from the Quick Launch toolbar, right-click the icon and click Delete.

The Excel environment

If you're new to Excel, you'll find a lot of unfamiliar terms and objects in the Excel landscape. The next figure shows the default Excel window and many of the terms and objects I refer to in procedures throughout the book.

In later chapters, I show you how to customize your Excel window to suit your preferences, doing things like changing the toolbars (Chapter 19), splitting and freezing your worksheet (Chapter 2), and changing your screen display (Chapter 19).

But when you first start Excel, you see the window that appears in Figure 1.2.

Task panes

The task pane (shown in Figure 1.3) is a vertical pane of information that appears on the right side of your Excel program window when you perform certain operations. It's a new feature in Excel 2003, and is, quite frankly, overkill—in many cases it's just a different and more unwieldy method of performing tasks that were previously performed in a dialog box, and is usually unnecessary clutter in your workspace. When you perform an operation that requires the task pane, such as getting help,

Bright Idea

If you don't like the Quick Launch toolbar, click and drag the Excel icon from the Programs menu and drop it on your desktop instead to create a desktop startup icon. To avoid cluttering your desktop with myriad icons, you can create a new folder on the desktop and drop many icons in the folder.

searching for files, or inserting clip art in a worksheet, it appears automatically; and when you don't need it, you can click the X button in its upper-right corner to close it and regain that worksheet space.

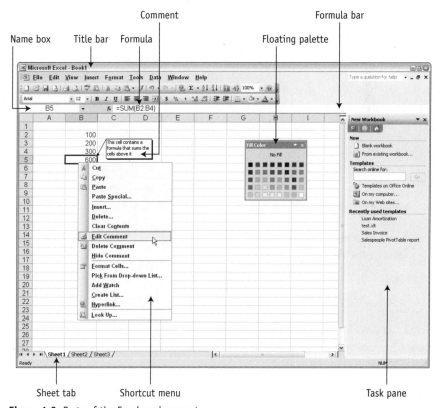

Figure 1.2. Parts of the Excel environment

Inside Scoop

When you hold the mouse pointer over a toolbar button, a ScreenTip — a small label — appears that tells you the name of the button. If you don't see ScreenTips, choose Tools ⇨ Customize, and on the Options tab, select the Show ScreenTips on toolbars check box.

Figure 1.3. A task pane

Task panes have list boxes and text links that help you perform a specific task, and they're fairly straightforward.

Inside Scoop

Every time you start Excel, the Startup task pane appears. Turn it off by choosing Tools ⇨ Options. On the View tab, deselect the Startup Task Pane check box.

When you want to use a specific task pane, open it by choosing View ⇨ Task Pane, and then choose the task pane you want from the Other Task Panes list; if a task pane is already open, click the small triangle in the upper-right corner of the task pane to choose a different task pane.

The Formula bar

The Formula bar, shown in Figure 1.4, is the long, open box that appears above the column letters in the worksheet, and is part of the worksheet.

The box at the left end, the Name box, shows either the address of the selected cell or the name of the selected cell or range (if the selection is named). I tell you more about naming cells and ranges in Chapter 4.

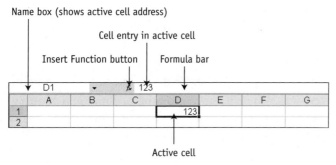

Figure 1.4. The Formula bar

The *fx* button is the Insert Function button; it opens the Insert Function dialog box (which is discussed in Chapter 5).

The Formula bar displays the underlying data in the active cell, whether the actual cell data is a formula or a value. The data displayed in the cell, the *displayed value*, is the result of formatting the value in the cell and can be entirely different from the actual value in the cell, as shown in Figure 1.5. Regardless of what is displayed in the cell, the data you see in the Formula bar is the data Excel calculates. I tell you about formatting in Chapters 6 and 7.

Inside Scoop

If you don't see the Formula bar, it's been turned off. Choose View ⇨ Formula Bar to turn it on.

Inside Scoop

I've never used either the X or the check mark button because pressing Enter and Esc are so much quicker when your hands are already on the keyboard.

Actual calculated cell value

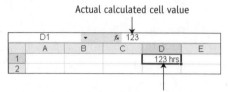

The displayed value after formatting the cell

Figure 1.5. Displayed versus actual value

You can type data directly in a cell, or you can select the cell and then click in the Formula bar to type your entry. Usually, typing data directly in the cell is most efficient, but sometimes it's easier to edit an entry in the Formula bar. When you *open* a cell for entry or editing — when you begin to type an entry or double-click a cell to edit its data — an X and a check mark appear between the Name box and the Formula bar. The X button cancels your editing operation (the same as pressing Esc) and the check mark button enters the data (same as pressing Enter).

Menus

Of course, you no doubt already know what the menu bar is and how to use menu commands: You click the menu button and then click the command on the dropped menu. What you need to do now is make sure you have Microsoft's personalized menus turned *off.*

With XP, Microsoft assumed that long lists of commands on the drop-down menus were confusing to users, so it created *personalized menus* that show only the commands you use the most or have at least used once. Alas, it is not an improvement. Users want consistency — I know I do, and if you search the Web for *personalized menus,* you'll find lots of other folks who share my distaste for them. Users want to be able to find a command quickly even if they have never used it before. Many don't realize that they must click the tiny double arrow at the bottom of the personalized menu to show the rest of the commands, and the menu behavior switches from personalized to full while you use it, and, well, I won't go on. It was a bad idea.

Inside Scoop

The personalized menus setting applies to every Office program, which is a good thing because you don't have to turn the personalized menus off in each program. Turning it off in one program turns it off in all programs.

To restore normal menu function to personalized menus, right-click in the toolbar area and click Customize. In the Customize dialog box, click the Options tab, shown in Figure 1.6. Select the Always show full menus check box, and click Close. (If, when you right-click in the toolbar area, you don't see the shortcut list of toolbars and the Customize command, click Tools ➪ Customize instead.)

Figure 1.6. Turn off personalized menus.

Toolbars

Two toolbars appear when you first start Excel: Standard and Formatting. You use the buttons on these two toolbars more than any others, but there are many that you won't use. Chapter 19 shows you many handy button-related skills.

However, right now, I'm sure you will find it helpful to learn what some of the many buttons you see are for. So, take a look at Tables 1.1 and 1.2 to help you sort out the buttons on the Standard and Formatting toolbars.

Bright Idea

If you haven't used a button for a while and you can't remember what it does, position your mouse pointer over the button. A ScreenTip displays the button's name.

Table 1.1. Standard toolbar buttons

Button Face	Button Name	Function
	New	Opens a new workbook
	Open	Opens an existing workbook
	Save	Saves the active workbook
	Permissions	Sets permissions for forwarding, editing, or copying workbook
	Print	Prints the active worksheet
	Print Preview	Previews the printed page
	Spelling	Opens the spell checker
	Research	Opens the Research task pane
	Cut	Cuts selected data for pasting
	Copy	Copies selected data for pasting
	Paste	Pastes cut or copied data
	Format Painter	Copies formatting from one area to another
	Undo	Undoes previous actions
	Redo	Reverses Undo actions

Button Face	Button Name	Function
	Insert Hyperlink	Inserts a hyperlink
Σ ▾	AutoSum	Writes a SUM formula
A Z ↓	Sort Ascending	Sorts table in ascending order
Z A ↓	Sort Descending	Sorts table in descending order
	Chart Wizard	Starts the Chart Wizard
	Drawing	Displays the Drawing toolbar
100% ▾	Zoom	Changes worksheet magnification
	Help	Opens the Help task pane

The buttons and bars move around

Lost your button because your toolbars are displayed on a single row? Click the down arrow at the right end of a toolbar to choose a button that isn't displayed because of a lack of space. When you click a hidden button, it replaces a displayed button that you haven't used in awhile.

I prefer my toolbars stacked on top of each other in separate rows, with all buttons visible so I don't have to search for them when I need them. To rearrange the toolbars on separate rows, drag the vertical dots on the left end of a toolbar to move the toolbar to a new row.

If you drag a toolbar and find it floating on the worksheet, double-click the toolbar title bar to redock it at the top.

Table 1.2. Formatting toolbar buttons

Button Face	Button Name	Function
Arial ▾	Font	Displays list of available fonts
10 ▾	Font Size	Displays list of font sizes
B	Bold	Boldfaces selected data
I	Italic	Italicizes selected data
U	Underline	Underlines selected data
≡	Align Left	Aligns data to left in selected cells
≡	Center	Centers data in selected cells
≡	Align Right	Aligns data to right in selected cells
	Merge and Center	Combines adjacent cells into a single cell
$	Currency Style	Formats numbers in accounting style, not currency style
%	Percent Style	Formats numbers in percent style
,	Comma Style	Formats numbers in comma style
.00	Increase Decimal	Increases number of decimals displayed
.00	Decrease Decimal	Decreases number of decimals displayed
	Decrease Indent	Decreases indent (moves entry left within the cell)
	Increase Indent	Increases indent (moves entry right within the cell)

Button Face	Button Name	Function
[icon]	Borders	Applies borders or displays a palette of border options
[icon]	Fill Color	Applies cell color or displays color palette
[icon]	Font Color	Applies font color or displays color palette

The Status bar

The Status bar is the bar along the bottom of the Excel program window (shown in Figure 1.7). It usually reads Ready at the left end and probably reads NUM near the right end.

Figure 1.7. The Status bar displaying several indicators and AutoCalculate

The word Ready at the left end means Excel is waiting — ready — for you to do something; when you are doing something, such as typing or copying an entry, the word Ready changes to a directive that tells you what to do next because Excel assumes that you don't know what to do next. You rarely notice any of these words at the left end of the Status bar, nor do you need to, but someone always wonders about those words.

The word NUM at the right end, however, is more informational. It means the Number lock on your keyboard's keypad is turned on, and when you type numbers, you get numbers.

Inside Scoop

If you don't see the Status bar at the bottom of the program window, choose View ⇨ Status bar.

Watch Out!

If you attempt to type numbers on your keypad and all you get is the active cell bouncing around, the problem is that your Number Lock is turned off (you won't see NUM in the Status bar, either). Press the Num Lock key to fix it.

Most of the Status bar indicators appear briefly, and chances are you'll never notice them unless you have a problem (such as an unexpected Caps Lock entry). Other Status bar indicators you might see near the NUM indicator are

- **CAPS.** Caps Lock is on (everything you type is capital letters); press Caps Lock to turn it on or off.

- **OVR.** Overwrite mode is on (each character you type overwrites an existing character instead of pushing existing characters to the right); press Insert to turn it off. If you want to turn it on, which is unlikely, press Insert while you are editing a cell's contents.

- **FIX.** Fixed decimal entry is on. This is a very useful feature in the right circumstances; you learn more about it in Chapter 3.

- **SCRL.** Scroll Lock is on (you can move around the worksheet with arrow keys without moving the active cell, just like using the mouse and scroll bars); press Scroll Lock to turn it on or off.

- **END.** End key is pressed and Excel is waiting for the second part of an End+ key combination; End+arrow key moves the active cell to the farthest reaches of the worksheet or to the beginning or end of a row or column of data.

- **EXT.** Extended mode is on (Excel extends your current selection of cells in the direction of the arrow key); press F8 to turn Extended mode on or off (but Shift and the arrow keys are a simpler way to do the same thing).

The most useful item in the Status bar is the AutoCalculate box, which calculates numbers in all selected cells whenever you have two or more cells selected. You learn more about it in Chapter 4.

Getting help

The fastest way to get help is to look it up in the index of a good book (like this one), but if someone else is using the book, or you want the answer to an obscure question that's not covered in your book, you can look up a topic in Excel's help files.

The best ways to get help from Excel are

- **The Ask A Question box.** The easiest and fastest way for general questions

- **The ? button.** Specific help about the options in a dialog box

Inside Scoop

When searching help files, a few well-chosen words yield better results than complete sentences or questions.

The Ask A Question box

The Ask A Question box is in the upper-right corner of the file window next to the Minimize Window, Restore/Maximize Window, and Close Window buttons. It reads "Type a question for help," as you can see in Figure 1.8.

Figure 1.8. The Ask A Question box

Click in the box, type a word or phrase about which you want help, and press Enter. The Search Results task pane opens with links to narrow your search, as shown in Figure 1.9.

If you're connected to the Internet when you ask for help, Excel goes online to Microsoft for help (and you generally get far too many options on superficial, vaguely connected topics). If you're not connected to the Internet, Excel searches its local help files for the answers (which is much faster and more direct). But even if you're connected—and most high-speed connections keep you constantly connected—you can choose which help source (local or online) you want; I only use the local, offline help files because it's faster and more direct.

Specify the help source you want to use in the Search box at the bottom of the Search Results task pane (shown in Figure 1.10).

When you click a link in the task pane, another help window, like the one shown in Figure 1.11, opens with specific help about your question.

Hack

Unfortunately, you cannot bookmark help files any more. When you think you may need a difficult-to-find Help topic in the future, select and copy the Help window text, and then paste it into a Word document or an Outlook note (or any other quick-access file) and save it where you can find it easily.

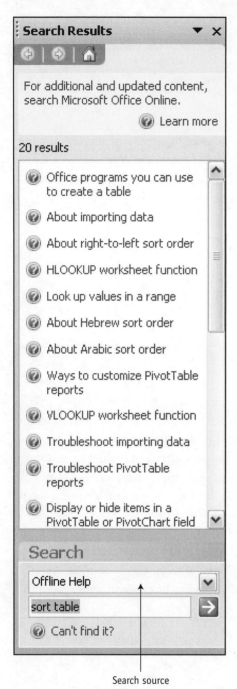

Search source

Figure 1.9. The Search Results pane

Figure 1.10. Specify a help source in the list box at the bottom of the Search Results task pane.

Click an arrow link to open the topic

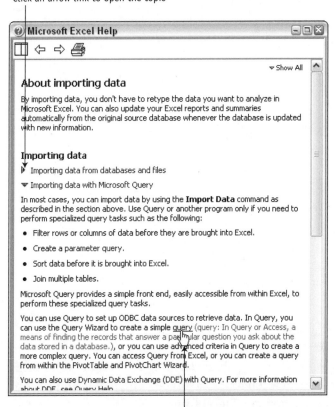

Click blue words for definitions

Figure 1.11. A help window

If you don't see the specific help you need, try typing different words or phrases in the Search Results pane to direct your search differently. Often the help file you need is there in your computer, but difficult to find because the Search function in Microsoft's help files are not very flexible.

The dialog box ? button

The other quick source of help, clicking the ? button in the upper-right corner of a dialog box, is much more context-specific and gets you the answers you need quickly and directly. If an option in a dialog box mystifies you, click the ? button to get a help window that describes each specific item in the dialog box.

Some dialog boxes have help links with even more specific help. For example, the Insert Function dialog box shown in Figure 1.12 has a help link at the bottom that pulls up a help file about the specific selected function.

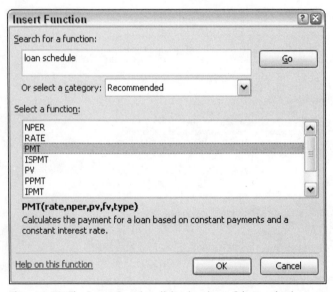

Figure 1.12. The Insert Function dialog box has a ? button in the upper-right corner and a separate Help on this function link in the lower-left corner.

That silly Office Assistant

The Office Assistant, that cloying character that shows up and bounces around on your worksheet when it thinks you need help, is nothing more than the Ask A Question box in cartoon form.

CHAPTER 1 ▪ GETTING IN AND OUT

Watch Out!

If you uninstall the Office Assistant from Excel, it disappears from all of your Microsoft Office programs — which is a good idea if you don't like the animations. It saves you the trouble of having to repeatedly uninstall it in each separate program.

To remove the Office Assistant completely, which is my choice, you must uninstall it with the Add/Remove Programs feature in the Windows Control Panel:

1. Open the Control Panel and click Add/Remove Programs.

2. Select Microsoft Office 2003, and click Change.

3. In the Setup dialog box, click Add or Remove Features, and click Next.

4. In the next dialog box, select the Choose advanced customization of applications check box, and click Next.

5. In the next dialog box, click the plus symbol next to Office Shared Features — that's where you find the Office Assistant.

6. Click the button next to Office Assistant, and choose Not Available from the menu that appears (as shown in Figure 1.13).

7. Finally, click Update at the bottom of the dialog box and it's gone.

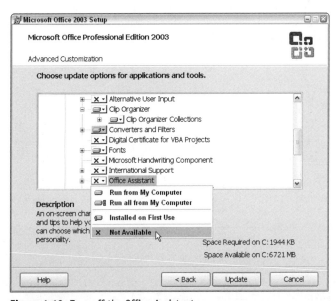

Figure 1.13. Turn off the Office Assistant.

Excel, heal thyself

If Excel begins to behave strangely, you may have a corrupt program file (yes, it still happens, although rarely). There are two easy fixes you can try; they may or may not help, but they're fast and worth a shot.

The first fix is the Help ⇨ Detect and Repair command. It's self-explanatory — close your open workbook files, set it to working, and give it a few minutes.

The second fix is to reinstall Excel (and any other Office programs you want to reinstall while you're at it):

1. Close all programs, then choose Start ⇨ Settings ⇨ Control Panel ⇨ Add/Remove Programs.

2. Choose Microsoft Office 2003 (or Excel 2003 if it's installed separately) and click Change.

3. In the Maintenance Mode Options dialog box, click Reinstall or Repair, and then follow the steps to repair or reinstall Excel.

Don't worry about losing data if you reinstall Excel; as long as your workbook files are saved and closed before you start the process, reinstallation won't affect them.

Searching the Microsoft Knowledge Base

When you have serious problems in Excel, or in any Microsoft program, the Microsoft Knowledge Base is sometimes a good source of solutions. For me, it's a last resort because, although the Knowledge Base is an extensive database of articles about bug fixes, known problems, workarounds, and so forth, it's not fast. You'll find lots of articles that don't apply to your problem at all, and it takes some time to plow through all the article titles to find applicable information (if it exists). Occasionally, however, it's got the information you need, for example, if you install a new antivirus program and suddenly a Microsoft program goes out of kilter — and it's free.

To use the Microsoft Knowledge Base, go to `http://support.` `microsoft.com`. When you get there, click the Search the Knowledge

Hack
If you find a helpful article in the Knowledge Base, bookmark the Web page in your browser or print it for future reference.

Bright Idea

As long as you're in the Microsoft site, take a look around for updates and extra features to download.

Base link and follow the instructions for your software program and question.

Opening workbook files

When you start Excel, a new unsaved workbook file opens. To open another new workbook, click the New button on the Standard toolbar. The workbooks, by default, are named Book1, Book2, and so on, which indicates their unsaved status.

Quite often, however, there are existing workbooks that you want to open. If Excel is not already open, you can open both the file and Excel at the same time. If Excel is already open, you can use the Open button on the Sandard toolbar or, if you've used the file recently, you'll find the file listed at the bottom of the File menu.

When Excel is closed

I use a few different methods, shown in Figure 1.14, to open existing workbook files, depending on where the file is saved, whether Excel is already open, and when I last used the file:

- If I've used the file recently, I open it from the Start menu Documents list (My Recent Documents in the new Windows XP Start menu).

- If it's a file I haven't used in a while, I navigate through folders to find the file icon. I have shortcut icons on my desktop to the folders I use most often, which saves me considerable navigation time (for example, I don't have to start at My Computer and work my way down).

- If it's a file I use a lot, such as my Checkbook Balance workbook (see Appendix B to learn about that workbook), I keep a shortcut icon to that file right on my desktop where it couldn't be any more convenient.

Documents menu

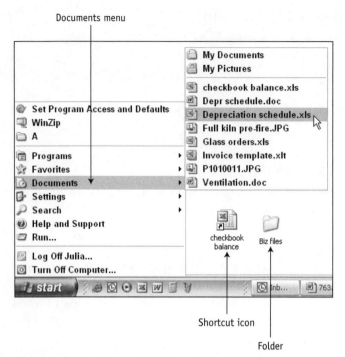

Shortcut icon

Folder

Figure 1.14. Opening an existing file

To put an icon to a specific file on your desktop, open the folder where the file is stored, right-click and drag the file icon onto the desktop, and choose Create Shortcut(s) Here from the shortcut menu that appears when you drop the icon. To put a shortcut to a folder on your desktop, do the same thing — open the folder where the folder you want is stored, and right-click and drag the folder icon onto the desktop.

When you want to delete a shortcut icon from a cluttered desktop or because you no longer regularly use the file, right-click the icon and click Delete. Confirm you want to delete the shortcut (the file or program remains unaffected; all you delete is the shortcut icon on the desktop), and it disappears from your desktop.

Bright Idea

A shortcut icon label is not connected to the file — you can change it to anything you want. To change the icon label to something shorter or more intuitive, click the label twice (not a double-click), type a new name, and press Enter.

When Excel is already running

If you've used a file recently, you find it listed at the bottom of the File menu (as shown in Figure 1.15). You can show up to nine recently used files there; Excel lists each file you open or save and pushes the least recent file off the list. I like to show four files, because it's long enough to be useful but short enough to keep the menu from becoming unwieldy.

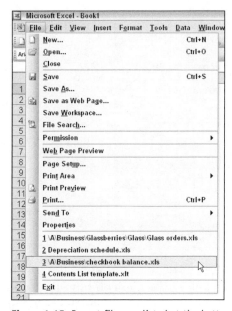

Figure 1.15. Recent files are listed at the bottom of the File menu.

To change the number of files displayed, choose Tools ⇨ Options. On the General tab, set the number of files you want in the Recently used file list box, shown in Figure 1.16.

The most common way to open workbooks from within Excel, especially if you haven't used the file in a while, is to click the Open button on the Standard toolbar and navigate to the file in the Open dialog box. You can then double-click the Excel file you want to open.

Hack

If your Open or Save dialog box suddenly maximizes to fill the screen, you probably inadvertently double-clicked the title bar. To return the dialog box to a normal size, double-click the title bar.

Hack

Excel's Open and Save dialog boxes default to the My Documents folder. To change the default folder, choose Tools ⇨ Options. On the General tab, in the Default file location box, type the path to the new default folder (beginning with the drive letter).

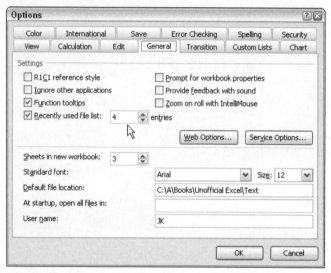

Figure 1.16. Set the length of your recently used file list.

To make the Open dialog box a lot more convenient, you can put shortcuts for the folders you use most often in the My Places bar on the left side of the dialog box:

1. In the Open dialog box, navigate to the folder that contains the folder you use most often.

2. Click to select the folder icon you want to add to the My Places bar, and then click the Tools button (as shown in Figure 1.17).

3. Click Add to My Places.

The folder is placed in the My Places bar and saves a ton of time navigating in the Open dialog box. These folders also appear in the My Places bar in the Save dialog box.

To remove a folder icon from the My Places bar, right-click the icon and click Remove. You can't remove built-in icons, such as My Computer, but you can add your own folders, and that's personalization that works.

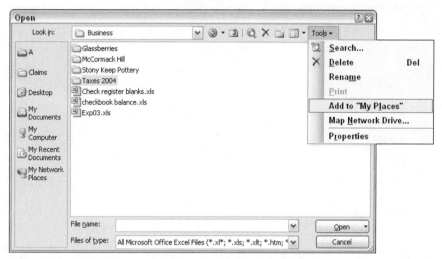

Figure 1.17. Add a folder to the My Places bar for faster navigation.

Opening several files at once

You can open several files at the same time from the Open dialog box: Ctrl+click or Shift+click to select the files (as shown in Figure 1.18), and then click Open.

Ctrl+click (click an initial item, then press Ctrl while you click more items) selects each individual item you click, and is best when you want to select multiple nonadjacent items; Shift+click (click an initial item, then press Shift while you click another item) selects all the items in between the initial item and the item you Shift+click. Both work in all Office programs and for all kinds of items — cells, sheet tabs, paragraphs in Word documents, files in folder windows, and so forth.

Multiple windows

In Excel 2003, it's difficult to open files in separate Excel windows. Unlike earlier versions of Excel (and the other Office 2003 programs), when you open multiple files, Excel 2003 opens them all in the same

Inside Scoop

You can also "lasso" several adjacent file icons with the mouse to select and open all the files at once.

program window, which makes it awkward to have two files open side by side (something I often want to do for ease of copying between workbooks, and so forth). Sure, you can use the Window ⇨ Arrange command to arrange the open windows in one program window, but in practice that's cumbersome.

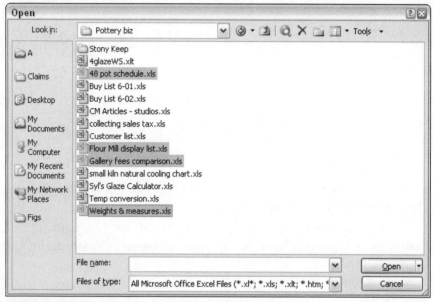

Figure 1.18. Ctrl+click to select and open multiple files at once.

In Excel 2003, the only way to open files in their own Excel program windows is to start up another instance of Excel and open the second file in the new program window. Use any method you like to start Excel again; I use the icon on the Quick Launch toolbar. With multiple program windows open, you can resize and reshape each workbook to your heart's content, or open one while you minimize the other; I find separate Excel windows are much more flexible than multiple workbook windows in a single program window.

Watch Out!

When you open a second Excel program window, you may be warned that the file Personal.xls is locked for editing. Unless you want to save macros to the hidden Personal.xls file, that's no big deal. Go ahead and click the Read Only button; the file will function and save normally.

Multiple taskbar buttons

One more thing that happens when you have more than one file open, whether or not they're in multiple program windows, is that in Windows XP you may have a single Excel button on the taskbar and you need to do extra clicks to switch between open files. I like each of my open files to have its own taskbar button so I can see at a glance which files are open and switch to a different file with a single click.

To make separate taskbar buttons in Windows XP, right-click the taskbar and click Properties. On the Taskbar tab, shown in Figure 1.19, deselect the Group similar taskbar buttons check box.

Figure 1.19. Set separate taskbar buttons.

Searching for a file

When you absolutely can't remember where you saved a file, or if you saved it at all, try searching for it. All the Office 2003 programs share a good Basic File Search task pane.

Choose File ⇨ File Search to open the task pane, shown in Figure 1.20. The Search Tips link in the task pane opens a remarkably useful help file that covers all the options by which you can search for a file.

You can type words to search for in the Search text box — part of the filename, words in the file text, keywords you saved in the file's

Properties—but you don't have to type any search words at all if you're just searching for all the Excel files.

To find only Excel files, open the list in the Results should be box and select the Excel files check box.

Search Tips   Where to search

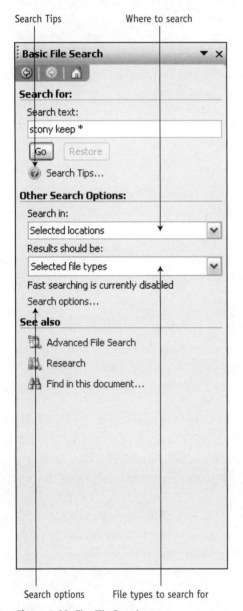

Search options   File types to search for

Figure 1.20. The File Search pane

Inside Scoop

If you select a check box that has a plus to one side of it only one time, Excel searches that folder and none of its subfolders, which is usually far too limiting. Select the check box a second time (the icon changes to multiple boxes) to search all the subfolders in that folder.

To speed up your search, limit it to as specific a location as possible. Open the Search in list under Other Search Options (see Figure 1.21), and deselect the Everywhere check box to clear all the subsidiary check boxes. Click the small plus symbol next to a drive or folder to expand a list of subfolders for searching, and select the check box for each location or folder you want to search.

Figure 1.21. Expand the list by clicking the plus symbols, and selecting the check boxes to search.

To start the search, click Go. Found files are listed in the Search Results task pane (see Figure 1.22).

Bright Idea

Narrow your searches by using two or more words in the Search text box, or expand your searches by using wildcard characters.

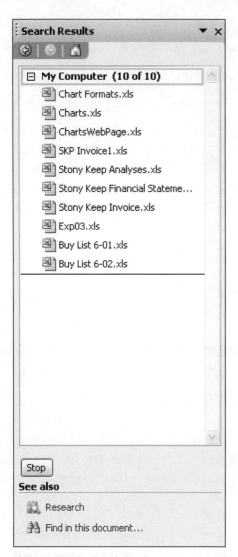

Figure 1.22. The Search Results pane

Point to the file you want and click the arrow that appears (as shown in Figure 1.23).

To open the file in Excel, click Edit with Microsoft Office Excel. To create a copy of the file with a different name, click New from this file; an unsaved copy of the workbook opens with the original filename and a sequential copy number in the title bar.

If the search doesn't find the file you want, click Modify and search again.

Figure 1.23. File-opening options

You can set more stringent conditions for the search by clicking the Advanced File Search link. For example, you can limit your search for

---

Wildcard searches

You can use wildcard characters to expand a search for related words or phrases. Wildcard characters are placeholders for unknown characters in a word and allow the search to find any word that matches the characters you typed and has any character(s) in the wildcard position(s). The wildcard characters are *, ?, and ~.

The wildcard character * allows you to search for words with any multiple of unknown characters. For example, a search for north* will find northwest, northeast, and northern.

The wildcard character ? allows you to search for words with any single unknown character. For example, you can search for any year in the 1990s by using 199? and it will find 1993 and 1999 but not 1989 or 1973. To find any year in the twentieth century, you can use two ? characters: 19??.

What if you want to search for a word or phrase that contains an actual * or ? character? That's where the ~ (tilde) character comes in. For example, to find the word Questions?, search for Questions~?.

Excel files in a specific folder to those created after May 2005 by choosing Creation date in the Property box, choosing on or after in the Condition box, and typing a date in the Value box (see Figure 1.24).

Figure 1.24. Set stringent search conditions in the Advanced File Search task pane.

Set as many conditions as you need and click Add to add each one. After you click Add, the Go button reappears so you can run the search again.

Using hyperlinks

Hyperlinks are a really fast way to open another file or a Web page, and they're easy to create. A hyperlink is text you can click to open a different Web page in your browser — you've probably used them quite a lot while

Inside Scoop

Speed up basic file searches by indexing your files. To turn on indexing, choose File ⇨ File Search. In the Basic File Search task pane, click the Search Options link. In the Indexing Service Settings dialog box, select the Yes, enable indexing service and run when my computer is idle option, and click OK.

Bright Idea

The URL may be useful, but if you want a more user-friendly name for the hyperlink, right-click the link and click Edit Hyperlink. In the Edit Hyperlink dialog box, type the display name you want in the Text to display box.

surfing the Internet — and you can create them in worksheets to open both Web pages in your browser and other files in your computer.

To create a hyperlink to a Web page, type the URL in a cell and press Enter. For example, if you type **www.google.com** in a cell and press Enter, your entry turns blue and is underlined (as shown in Figure 1.25), and when you click the new hyperlink, your browser opens to the Google search Web site.

Figure 1.25. A hyperlink typed in a cell

To create a hyperlink to another file on your computer or on your network, use the Insert Hyperlink dialog box:

1. Choose Insert ⇨ Hyperlink.

2. Click Existing File or Web Page in the Link to pane and Current Folder in the Look in pane (see Figure 1.26). The usual navigation tools appear above the list of files.

Figure 1.26. Create hyperlinks to other files in your computer or network.

3. Navigate to the file you want and click it (the URL appears in the address box).

4. Type a user-friendly display name in the Text to display text box, and if you want an explanatory ScreenTip to appear when the mouse is over the hyperlink, click ScreenTip and type the text.

If you need to select the cell after the hyperlink is created (so that you can add color to it, for example), click the hyperlink and hold down the mouse button for a moment; the mouse pointer changes from a hand to a white cross, and the cell behind the hyperlink is selected.

To remove a hyperlink, right-click the hyperlink and click Remove Hyperlink. The hyperlink text remains but is no longer active; press Delete to remove the text.

Saving workbook files

Saving an Excel workbook is like saving any other file: Click the Save button on the toolbar. If the file has never been saved, the Save As dialog box opens. Type a filename in the File name box, choose a folder in the Save in box, and click Save. If you're saving a file that's already been saved, click the Save button on the Standard toolbar to save the changes.

By default, Excel tries to save every workbook in the My Documents folder. Saving workbooks to your own more accessible folder makes more sense.

If you don't want to use the default My Documents folder, and you don't want the extra trouble of navigating to your own folder each time you save a new workbook, change the default folder:

1. Choose Tools ⇨ Options.

2. On the General tab, in the Default file location box (shown in Figure 1.27), type the path to your folder. If you're not used to typing paths, the easiest way to find the path to your folder is to open the folder window. The path to the folder is in the Address box at the top of the folder window.

3. Copy that path and paste it in the Default file location box.

The Save As dialog box opens with your file in the Save in box, and the Open dialog box opens with your file in the Look in box.

Watch Out!

If you completely mess up a workbook, don't save it because you'll overwrite all the good data that was in it when you started. Instead, close the workbook without saving it, then reopen it and start again.

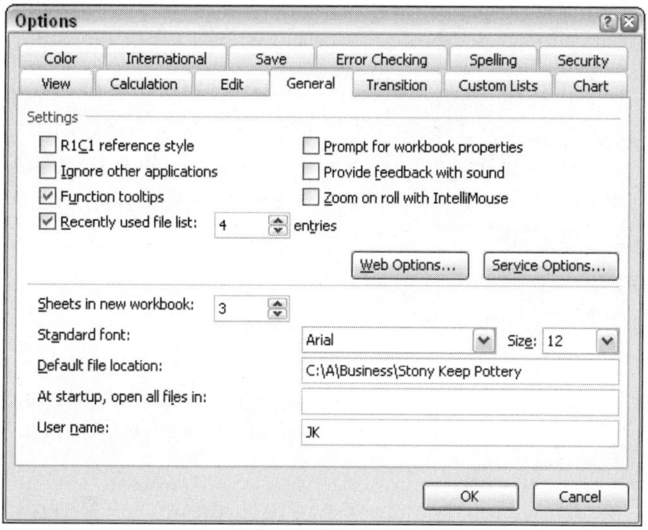

Figure 1.27. Change the default folder.

Setting workbook properties

At one time, Workbook properties, in particular the Keywords property, were important for speedy file searches. They're not as important now that file searching searches for words anywhere in the file, including keywords. But you can still use keywords to your advantage by setting a Keywords property that is unique to a particular file or set of files, regardless of whether the keyword appears in the file text. To set file properties, choose File ⇨ Properties. The Properties dialog box for your file will open as shown in Figure 1.28.

Bright Idea

Set several keywords for a file, using every word you might happen to think of two years from now when you're trying to find the file again.

Inside Scoop

File Properties provide detailed information in folder windows. In a folder, choose View ⇨ Details. Right-click the header row and click the properties to display. Click More to show properties not on the first list. (Don't bother displaying the keywords property — it doesn't work. It's a bug.)

Figure 1.28. Setting file properties

You can set workbook properties any time you have the workbook open; just be sure you save the workbook again after you set the properties.

AutoRecover

Excel is set up to automatically save your data every ten minutes, so if your system crashes for any reason, there's a backup file with all but the last few minutes of data saved. If your system does crash, when you start Excel again, you are offered saved backup copies of all the files that were open at the time of the crash. You can open a backup file (you must save it again), or you can open the original and see what, if anything, was lost.

Watch Out!

The saved backup files are not really saved copies of your files; they're only temporary in case of a crash. You still need to save your workbooks in the normal way.

Bright Idea

If you create (and save) a workbook with formulas and macros that you want to use repeatedly without saving new data in it (such as the Checkbook Balance workbook in the Appendix B), don't save it at all. Ever. Every time you open it you find it ready to use again.

If you don't want Excel to save backups of your files automatically, choose Tools ⇨ Options, and click the Save tab (shown in Figure 1.29). Deselect the Save AutoRecover info every check box. You can also change the time period for saves if, for example, you want AutoRecover backups saved more often.

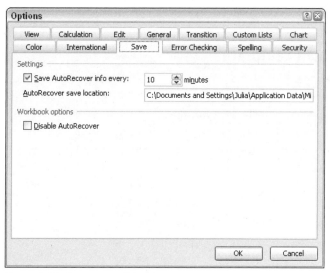

Figure 1.29. Set or turn off AutoRecover.

Creating and using templates

A *template* is a foundation workbook you use to create other workbooks, and if you create the same sort of workbook repeatedly (for example, an invoice), it's a timesaver because all the setup work is done; all you add is data.

You set up a template with all the formatting, formulas, macros, and workbook/worksheet settings you need in the finished file, and then save it as a workbook template instead of a workbook. When you open the template, what you get is a ready-to-use copy of the workbook rather than the template itself.

Reuse existing workbooks

I have to admit, I often don't bother creating templates, instead I just reuse an existing workbook by changing the data, but if I forget to save it as a new file, I lose all the data in the original file. A lot of you probably do that, so now there's a link on the New Workbook task pane (which opens when you choose File ⇨ New) called From existing workbook. It allows you to open an unsaved copy of an existing workbook so you don't lose the original. You just have to remember to choose File ⇨ New and click the link to open the workbook copy (this is the safest way to make a copy of an existing workbook as if the existing workbook was a template).

Creating your own templates

To save a workbook as a template, choose File ⇨ Save As and, in the Save As dialog box, click Template in the Save as type drop-down box (as shown in Figure 1.30). A workbook template file has the extension .xlt instead of .xls. When you choose Template, the Save in folder switches to the Templates folder and tries to save your template in the deeply buried Microsoft/Templates folder.

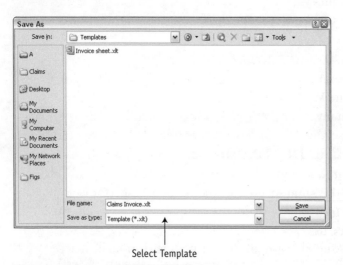

Select Template

Figure 1.30. Saving a workbook as a template

Watch Out!

If you have file extensions (.xls and .xlt) hidden, you won't know a template is open unless you include the word template in the filename. To show the extensions, open any folder and choose Tools ⇨ Folder Options. On the View tab, deselect the Hide extensions for known file types check box.

When you allow Excel to save the template in the Templates folder, you must open a fresh copy of the template by choosing File ⇨ New, clicking On My Computer in the New Workbook task Pane, and double-clicking the file icon on the General tab of the Templates dialog box. But if you need to modify the template, it's difficult to find, as deeply buried as it is.

My preferred way to handle saving templates is to navigate to the folder of my choice in the Save in box. That way I know exactly where the template is and I can easily open the template file if it needs modification.

My opening procedures depend on what I want to do. If I want to modify the template, I open it using Excel's Open dialog box; the template opens — it reads ".xlt" in the filename — and I can modify it and save it again. If I want to open a copy of the template — an unsaved workbook ready for data — I can either double-click the template file in the folder window where it's saved, or choose File ⇨ New, click the From existing workbook link in the New Workbook task pane, and navigate to the folder where I saved the template.

Using Excel's prebuilt templates

Excel also has several prebuilt template files, both installed with Excel and available on the Web. To get to them, choose File ⇨ New, and then click either the On my computer link or the Templates on Office Online link. If you choose the On my computer link, click the Spreadsheet Solutions tab in the Templates dialog box that appears, and double-click a template.

Bright Idea

Microsoft's Loan Amortization template (File ⇨ New, On my computer, Spreadsheet Solutions tab), is definitely worth checking out. I used to show others how to create that worksheet themselves, but Microsoft realized it was useful and now provides a prebuilt, bulletproof workbook template.

I've never used a prebuilt template because I prefer to build my own, but they're worth a look because they are good examples of items and features you may want to include in your own templates. For example, Figure 1.31 shows an online template for a 2006 calendar on multiple worksheets—you open the Microsoft templates page, find a template you like, and click the link to download it. And ready-to-use is certainly faster than building your own.

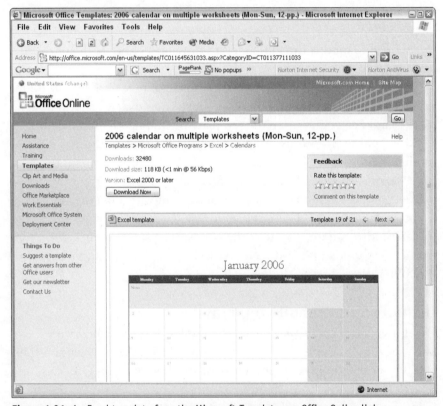

Figure 1.31. An Excel template from the Microsoft Templates on Office Online link

Changing Excel's default templates

Whenever you open a new workbook, you get a copy of Excel's default workbook template filled with copies of Excel's worksheet template. If there's something in a new workbook or worksheet that you change every time, such as gridline color, column width, or font size, you can create the settings you want in the default workbook so that every new workbook opens with your changes already in place.

Some settings, such as number of worksheets in a new workbook and font and font size, are easiest to set in the Options dialog box. Choose Tools ⇨ Options to open the dialog box and click the General tab.

You can create other more personalized settings, such as changing gridline color or placing a company logo on every worksheet, in the default workbook template (book.xlt) or the default worksheet template (sheet.xlt).

Change the default workbook template

To make changes in the default workbook template, open a new workbook (the default workbook template is applied). Make your changes, and then save the workbook as a template named book.xlt in the XLSTART folder, as shown in Figure 1.32.

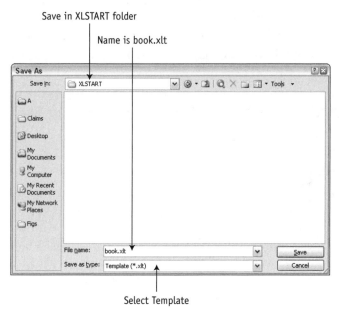

Figure 1.32. Saving a new default workbook template

Watch Out!

If someone else uses your computer, they may be dismayed to find that new Excel workbooks are based on your modified default workbook template, so you should be prepared to either tell them about the change or delete the new default workbook.

To locate the XLSTART folder, open the Save in list and start at your drive letter. Navigate through the folders until you get into the XLSTART folder. In my computer, the path is C:\Documents and Settings\Julia\ Application Data\Microsoft\Excel\XLSTART. Yours will likely be found in a similar location.

Change the default worksheet template

Customization in the workbook template, book.xlt, appears in every new workbook, but if you add a new worksheet to the workbook, you get a copy of the default sheet template, regardless of the customization in book.xlt. For customized new worksheets, you must also create a new worksheet template.

To customize the worksheet template, open a new workbook and delete all but one worksheet. Customize the remaining worksheet and save the workbook as a template named sheet.xlt in the XLSTART folder.

Your new templates won't affect existing files, but all new workbooks and worksheets will have your new templates applied.

To return to either of Excel's default templates, open the XLSTART folder and delete the book.xlt or sheet.xlt template that you created. When your template is gone, Excel generates new default workbooks based on its own internal settings.

Closing workbook files

Closing workbook files is just like closing files in other Office programs: The fastest way to close a workbook file is to click the Close Window button in the upper-right corner of the workbook window. The Close Window button is below the Close button for the program (see Figure 1.33). When you position the mouse over the Close Window button, Close Window appears in a ScreenTip.

Figure 1.33. The lower button closes the workbook window; the upper button closes Excel.

Hack

You can close all open workbooks with a single command. Press and hold Shift while you choose File ⇨ Close All (the Close command on the menu changes to a Close All command when Shift is pressed).

Hack

If you're a keyboarder rather than a mouser, you can quit Excel by pressing Alt+F4.

Quitting Excel

When you finish using Excel, or when you need to shut down or restart your computer, click the Close button in the upper-right corner of the Excel window. Be sure you click the Close button in the program window—the button in the Excel title bar, whose ScreenTip reads Close—rather than the Close Window button in the workbook window (the button below it, whose ScreenTip reads Close Window).

Just the facts

- Start Excel from the Start menu or a shortcut icon on the Quick Launch toolbar.
- Get help from the Ask A Question box; use Offline Help as a source for fast help.
- Click the ? in the upper-right corner of any dialog box for an explanation of dialog box options.
- Go to the Microsoft Knowledge Base when all else fails.
- Open existing files from the Start menu Documents list or from a folder window, and start Excel at the same time.
- Search for files using Excel's Basic File Search task pane.
- Use hyperlinks to open Web pages or other files in your computer or network.
- Use templates to create ready-to-use workbook files with all formulas, formatting, and macros in place.
- Close files with the Close Window button in the upper-right corner of the workbook window.
- Quit Excel with the Close button or pressing Alt+F4.

GET THE SCOOP ON...
Worksheet basics ▪ Selecting worksheets ▪ Naming work-
sheets ▪ Rearranging worksheets ▪ Adding and deleting
worksheets ▪ Changing the default number of worksheets
▪ Hiding worksheets ▪ Moving around in a worksheet ▪
Selecting cells ▪ Freezing panes ▪ Splitting panes ▪
Multiple windows ▪ Zooming a view

All About Worksheets

In the early days of spreadsheet programs, there wasn't much to learn about worksheets because there was only one in each file. An entire Excel file consisted of a single worksheet, and there was no need to name it or move it or rearrange it or delete it, nor could you add another. Then someone thought, "Wouldn't it be a great idea to have more than one worksheet?" and the next version of Excel had a default 16 worksheets in each new file. That was a lot of worksheets (allegedly the idea was one for each month and one for each quarter), and when Microsoft discovered that users were deleting them en masse, it calmed the corporate worksheet frenzy so that by Excel 2000 there were only the three default worksheets in each file that we have today.

With the ability to add new worksheets, files became workbooks for holding the surfeit of worksheets, and there were more and more features added for rearranging them, adding, deleting, and naming them, navigating through them, and coloring their sheet tabs. Now there are enough things you can do with worksheets to fill a whole chapter and more about them (more things you can do with worksheets, such as protecting them, appear in other chapters).

Chapter 2

Worksheet basics

The *worksheet* (shown in Figure 2.1) is the basic document in which you do work in Excel, including entering, calculating, and organizing data. One or more worksheets are contained in each *workbook*, which is an Excel file. Three worksheets are in each workbook by default, but the number you end up with is your choice—you can add and delete worksheets as needed.

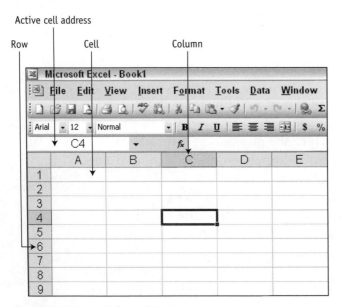

Figure 2.1. Elements of a worksheet

These are the basics you need to know about worksheets:

■ Each worksheet is divided into a grid of rows and columns. The rows are identified by numbers down the left side of the worksheet, and the columns are identified by letters across the top of the worksheet.

■ The grid units are called *cells*. Each cell has an address—a location on the worksheet—given by its row number and column letter.

Hack

If your list of data is longer than 65,536 rows or wider than 256 columns, you can either break the list onto multiple worksheets or enter the list in an Access table, which has no size limits.

When a cell is selected, its row number and column letter are highlighted, and its address is displayed in the Name box.

■ You can enter data into any cell you want, in any order that's efficient for you. You can enter data in one cell at a time or into several cells at once (see Chapter 3 for specific data entry techniques).

■ A worksheet has a total of 256 columns and 65,536 rows, and cannot be expanded beyond those limits.

Selecting worksheets

A workbook can contain a single worksheet or hundreds of worksheets, limited only by your system memory and your patience. By the way, worksheets are also called *sheets*; the name worksheet distinguishes them from chart sheets (covered in Chapter 12).

Selecting a single worksheet

Select a single worksheet by clicking its sheet tab. Clicking a sheet tab brings that worksheet to the top of the virtual stack of worksheets in the workbook (shown in Figure 2.2). The selected sheet tab turns white with bold font, while unselected tabs remain gray with normal font (unless you color the sheet tabs, which is covered later in this chapter). The selected worksheet is called the *active* worksheet.

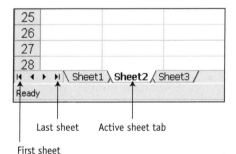

Last sheet   Active sheet tab

First sheet

Figure 2.2. Click sheet tab to bring a worksheet to the front.

Bright Idea

Create a single workbook to hold many worksheets that contain similar data, such as all your invoices for a month or a year, all the complex formulas you've used in other files, or custom styles or formatting you've created for other workbooks and want to reuse to standardize your presentations.

When you have a great many worksheets in a workbook, some of the sheet tabs may be hidden on the left or right end of the sheet tab bar. Use the buttons on the sheet tab scroll bar (shown in Figure 2.3) to bring the hidden tabs into view one at a time or to jump to the leftmost or rightmost tab.

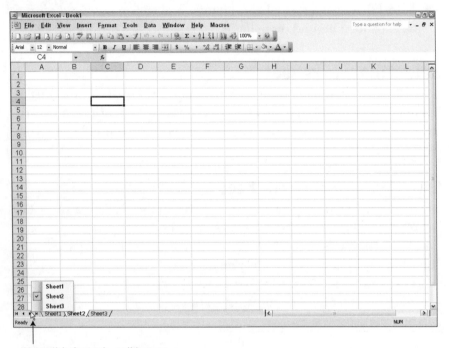

Right-click sheet tab scroll buttons

Figure 2.3. If some of your sheet tabs are hidden, right-click the sheet tab scroll buttons to see a list of all your worksheets.

Selecting several worksheets

If you need to move, add, or delete several worksheets, it's quickest to select them all and perform the operation on all of them at the same time.

To select several worksheets in a row, click the first tab, then Shift+ click the last tab. To select several worksheets that are not next to one another, click the first tab, then Ctrl+click the remaining tabs. When more than one worksheet is selected, the word [Group] appears in the program title bar — a useful reminder if a selected sheet tab is hidden at the end of the sheet tab bar. When several worksheets are selected, the *active* worksheet — the one on top — is the worksheet with the bold-faced name (as shown in Figure 2.4).

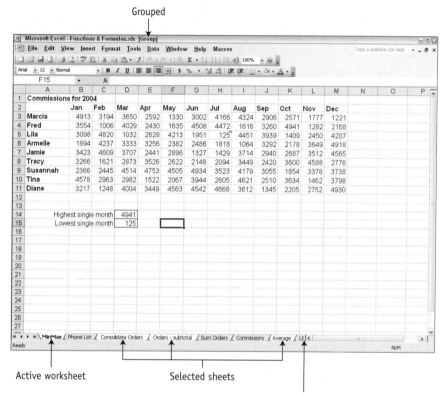

Figure 2.4. A group of worksheets is selected.

Shoot multiple worksheets

Here's an efficiency trick I use a lot: To create several identical worksheets — for example, to change the font or font size or add specific borders, data, or formulas — select several worksheets and enter the formatting, data,

Hack

If you create a set of identical worksheets and forget to select the group of worksheets before formatting them, all is not lost. Make copies of the worksheet you formatted (see how later in this chapter).

Watch Out!

If you have only two or three sheets selected, clicking one of them doesn't deselect the others; it merely activates the sheet you clicked. If you have only three sheets in the workbook and they're all selected, to deselect them you must right-click one of them and click Ungroup Sheets.

and formulas that you want them to share. Everything you do to any one of the selected worksheets is done in all of the selected worksheets.

Deselecting a group of worksheets

When you finish working with a group of worksheets, you need to deselect them (unless you've deleted the group, which leaves you with just one of the remaining sheets selected anyway). To deselect the group, click any tab in the workbook other than the active tab (the active tab is the one with the name in bold font).

Naming worksheets

No two worksheets can have the same name, and the default worksheets are named with sequential numbers, as in Sheet1, Sheet2, and so on. In a workbook in which I'm just experimenting, messing around, and only using the first worksheet, I don't bother naming the worksheets; but in a workbook with many worksheets or one that I need to send to someone else, the worksheet name is all-important as a means of finding the data I want quickly.

To rename a worksheet, double-click the sheet tab and type the new name (as shown in Figure 2.5), then press Enter or click in the worksheet.

25			
26			
27			
28			

◄ ◄ ► ►│ \ Sheet1 \ **my new worl** \ Sheet3 /

Ready

Figure 2.5. Renaming a worksheet

Watch Out!

Although you can use other characters such as periods, semicolons, apostrophes, and quote marks in a sheet name, those characters can add an element of unpleasant unpredictability in formulas and VBA code.

Worksheet names can have up to 31 characters but cannot use the characters :, \, /, ?, or *. Don't worry about remembering them, however; if you try to type a forbidden character in a sheet name, the character simply won't type.

Sheet tab colors

Coloring sheet tabs is more than just giddy fun; it allows you to color-code the contents of a workbook.

To color a sheet tab: Right-click the tab and click Tab Color on the shortcut menu. Click a color in the Format Tab Color dialog box.

When sheet tabs are colored, all the unselected tabs show full color; selected tabs are white with bold font and a stripe of color at the bottom of the tab (as shown in Figure 2.6).

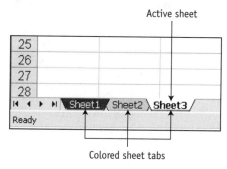

Figure 2.6. Coloring sheet tabs

Rearranging worksheets

Eventually you may want to rearrange the worksheets in a workbook. You can move a worksheet to a new location in the same workbook, make a copy of a worksheet in the same workbook, and move or copy worksheets into another workbook.

Moving worksheets

The quickest way to move a worksheet is to click and drag the sheet tab to a new location among the other sheet tabs. When you drag a sheet tab, a small triangle appears above and between sheet tabs; drag the mouse with the little sheet icon along the row of tabs and drop it when the triangle is between the sheets where you want to move your sheet (see Figure 2.7).

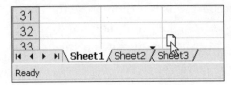

Figure 2.7. Drop the sheet tab when the small triangle is in position.

Copying worksheets

When you copy a worksheet, you create an identical copy of the work-sheet except for the sheet name, which gets a sequential number in parentheses appended to it.

The quickest way to copy a worksheet is to drag the tab — as if you are moving it — and press Ctrl when you drop it. When you press Ctrl, the mouse with the little sheet icon displays a small plus symbol to indicate a copy (see Figure 2.8).

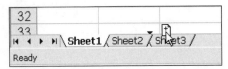

Figure 2.8. The small plus symbol indicates a copy.

Moving or copying worksheets to another workbook

Moving or copying sheets to another workbook is almost as easy as moving or copying within a workbook: Open both workbooks and drag the sheet

---

Create a new workbook from a worksheet

You can create a new workbook from a single worksheet by drag-ging the sheet tab into the program window. Click the Restore Window button to the right of the Ask A Question box to make the workbook resizable within the Excel program window. Drag the workbook window borders so you can see a bit of blank program window, then drag the sheet tab out of the workbook and drop it in the Excel window outside of the workbook. A new, unsaved work-book is created with the sheet you dragged. (Press Ctrl when you drop the sheet tab if you want to create a new workbook with a copy of the worksheet.)

Inside Scoop

When you move or copy a worksheet to a new workbook, all the cell/range names, styles, and custom formats in the sheet move with it into the new workbook and are available to all the sheets in the new workbook.

tab from one workbook to the other (press Ctrl to drop a copy of the sheet). To see both workbooks so that you can drag from one to the other, you need to arrange the workbook windows (see how later in this chapter).

Dragging between two workbooks is easier, but if you don't want to arrange the windows to see both workbooks, you can still move or copy sheets the long way:

1. Right-click the tab for the sheet you want to move or copy, and click Move or Copy. The Move or Copy dialog box is shown in Figure 2.9.

2. In the To book box, select the name of the workbook into which you want to move or copy the sheet.

3. In the Before sheet box, click the name of the sheet where you want to position the moved/copied sheet (it doesn't matter where you position the sheet — you can move it by dragging it within the new workbook later).

4. To copy the sheet, select the Create a copy check box.

Figure 2.9. Moving or copying a sheet to another workbook

Inside Scoop

In every Office program, you don't have to hold down Ctrl while you drag to copy an item; you only need to press Ctrl while you release the mouse to drop the item you're copying.

Adding and deleting worksheets

To add a new worksheet: Right-click a sheet tab and click Insert. In the Insert dialog box, double-click the Worksheet icon (shown in Figure 2.10).

Default worksheet

A worksheet template I created

Figure 2.10. Adding a new worksheet

To add several worksheets at a time, select as many worksheets as you want to add before you right-click a sheet tab and click Insert.

To delete a worksheet, right-click the sheet tab and click Delete. To delete several worksheets at one time, select all the worksheets you want to delete before you right-click a sheet tab and click Delete.

Create your own worksheets

When you open the Insert dialog box, there are several icons for sheets you can insert. All but the worksheet icon are not generally useful; but you can create your own special worksheet templates that you can add as needed from the Insert dialog box. First, delete all but one worksheet from a workbook, and set up the remaining worksheet as your template. Then choose File ⇨ Save As and save the file as a template in the Templates folder. Close the workbook. Open a new workbook, right-click a sheet tab, and click Insert; your new worksheet template is there!

Watch Out!
You can't undo a deleted sheet. If you inadvertently delete a worksheet, quickly close the workbook without saving it. When you reopen the workbook, the deleted sheets are back in place.

Changing the default number of worksheets

If you find yourself consistently adding or deleting worksheets in new workbooks, save yourself the effort and change the number of worksheets in new workbooks. Choose Tools ⇨ Options, and on the General tab (shown in Figure 2.11), change the number in the Sheets in new workbook box.

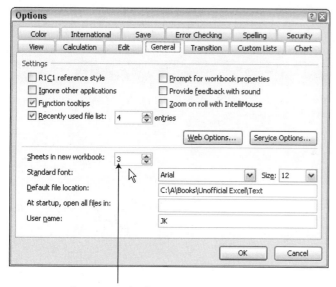

Type new number here

Figure 2.11. Change the number of worksheets in new workbooks.

Hiding worksheets

Sometimes I create a workbook for a client who isn't terribly adept in Excel. As part of my "bulletproofing" process, I place data that I don't want clients altering on a separate worksheet and then hide that worksheet; because the clients aren't terribly proficient, they never know there's a hidden worksheet (or how to unhide worksheets). They just think the workbook is amazing.

Inside Scoop

You can also limit users' mobility in a workbook by hiding the sheet tabs, so they only have access to one visible sheet. To hide sheet tabs, choose Tools ⇨ Options; on the View tab, deselect the Sheet tabs check box. To show sheet tabs again, select the check box.

To hide a worksheet, click the sheet tab to make it the active worksheet, and then choose Format ⇨ Sheet ⇨ Hide.

To unhide a worksheet, choose Format ⇨ Sheet ⇨ Unhide, and then click the name of the worksheet in the Unhide dialog box and click OK.

Moving around in a worksheet

There are many ways to move around in a worksheet and get from cell to cell. Table 2.1 lists all the ways I use (but is by no means comprehensive).

Table 2.1. Moving around a worksheet

To Move	Do This
Down one cell	Press Enter
Right one cell	Press Tab
One cell up, down, left, or right	Press the arrow keys
To the beginning of a row	Press Home
To the upper-left corner of the worksheet	Press Ctrl+Home
To the lower-right corner of the used area of the worksheet	Press Ctrl+End
To the beginning or end of a data row	Double-click the left or right border of the active cell in that row
To the top or bottom of a data column	Double-click the top or bottom border of the active cell in that column
Scroll up or down	Use the mouse wheel or drag the vertical scroll bar; drag the scroll bar to the end of its channel to go to the bottom of the worksheet used area

To Move	Do This
Scroll side to side	Drag the horizontal scroll bar; drag the scroll bar to the end of its channel to go to the right end of the worksheet used area
To a specific named range	Select the name in the Name box list
To return to the active cell after scrolling	Press Ctrl+Backspace

Selecting cells

Selecting cells and ranges of cells is elementary to entering data. Table 2.2 lists all the methods I use for selecting cells.

Table 2.2. Selecting cells and ranges

To	Do This
Select a cell	Click the cell
Select a rectangular range	Click and drag over the cells, or click the cell at the start of the range, then Shift+click the cell at the end of the range
Select a contiguous table of data around the active cell (the current region)	Press Ctrl+A
Select a specific named range	Select the name in the Name box list
Expand a selected range by one cell, row, or column	Press and hold Shift and press an arrow key
Select a column	Click the column letter
Select a row	Click the row number
Select all the cells in the worksheet	Click the gray box above the row numbers and left of the column letters
Select multiple separate cells	Click the first cell, then Ctrl-click the remaining cells
Select a column of cells in a long table of data	Click the top cell, then press Shift and double-click the bottom border of the top cell

The worksheet used area

You can go to the end of a worksheet's used area by pressing Ctrl+End; this takes you to the farthest reaches in which you've ever worked in that worksheet, whether or not there is still data in those farthest reaches. Your scroll bars stretch to those reaches of emptiness, so if you ever wonder why your current table is small but the scroll bars are really short, it's because the scroll bars still correspond to the worksheet used area. I like to view the end of a long table quickly by dragging a scroll bar right to the end of it's scroll channel, but if the worksheet used area is much bigger than I'm working in, it's no longer an efficient means of scrolling quickly.

I always reduce the used area of a worksheet when it grows larger than I currently need: Delete all the rows and columns between the end of the used area and your current working area, then save and close the workbook. When you reopen the workbook, the used area is reduced to what's really in use and the scroll bars are longer and more efficient.

Freezing panes

Freezing panes is a procedure I use quite often. When you work on a very long or wide list, the column and/or row headings disappear when you enter data at the end of the list. But you can keep your column headers in view no matter where you are in the list if you freeze the rows that hold the column headers; and you can keep row headers in view if you freeze the column that holds the row headers.

To freeze rows, select the row below the row you want to freeze by clicking its row number (see Figure 2.12) to select the entire row, then choose Window ➪ Freeze Panes.

When you scroll up and down the list, the header row stays in view.

	A4	▼	ƒx	12/2/2004		
	A	B	C	D	E	F
1	Coffee Orders for December 2004					
2						
3	Date	Product	Price/lb	Lbs	Total	
4	12/2/04	Santo Domingo	9.50	100	950.00	
5	12/2/04	Antigua	10.50	100	1,050.00	

Figure 2.12. Select the row below the row you want to freeze.

Hack

When you have frozen panes, you can get back to the upper-left corner of the unfrozen pane quickly by pressing Ctrl+Home.

To freeze columns, select the column to the right of the column you want to freeze by clicking on its column number to select the entire column, and choose Window ⇨ Freeze Panes.

You can freeze both columns and rows by clicking a single cell just below the row and to the right of the column you want to freeze (as shown in Figure 2.13).

To unfreeze panes, choose Windows ⇨ Unfreeze Panes.

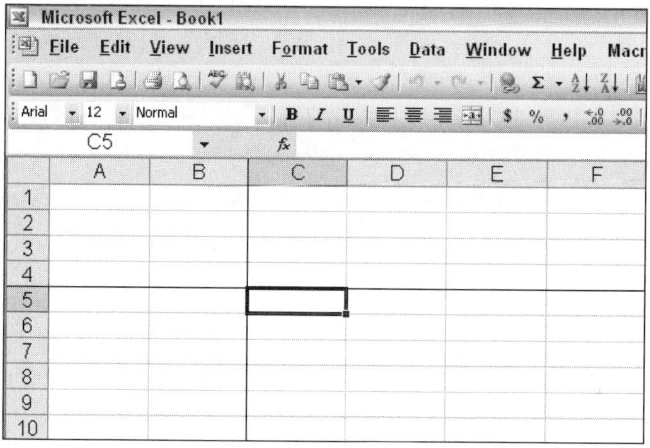

Figure 2.13. Freezing rows and columns with a single cell

Splitting panes

Splitting panes is the fastest way to look at two separate areas of the same worksheet at once, although I find multiple windows to be more effective.

To split panes so that you can scroll through rows in two parts of the worksheet (see Figure 2.14), drag the split box above the vertical scroll bar down into the worksheet to create a horizontal split bar across the worksheet. To split panes so that you can scroll through columns in two parts of the worksheet, drag the split box to the right of the horizontal scroll bar across into the worksheet to create a vertical split bar across the worksheet.

Drag horizontal split box from here

Horizontal split bar

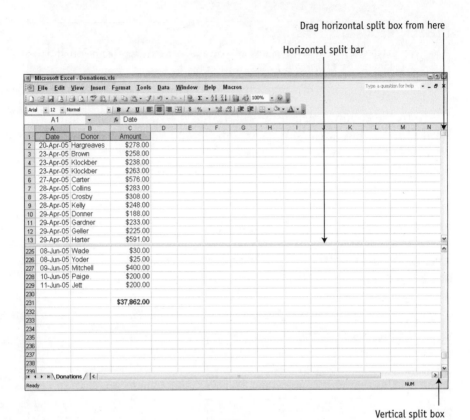

Vertical split box

Figure 2.14. Drag a split box into the worksheet to create a split bar across the screen.

To move a split bar, drag it. To remove a split bar, double-click it.

You can split a worksheet into four panes by using both split bars (or by choosing Window ⇨ Split), but there's not much point in it and it's confusing to maneuver in.

Split panes versus multiple windows

The biggest differences between split windows and multiple windows are that in split windows, you only have one set of row numbers and column letters, while in multiple windows you have row numbers and column letters in every window (which can crowd a small monitor). Split panes can only be used within the same worksheet, while several multiple windows can be opened into the same worksheet, different worksheets in the same workbook, and different workbooks.

Multiple windows

A better way to work in two parts of the worksheet simultaneously is to use multiple windows, but more than that, you can work in different worksheets and different workbooks with multiple windows.

Opening windows in the same workbook

To open multiple windows in the same workbook, as shown in Figure 2.15, choose Window ⇨ New Window.

Two windows, same workbook

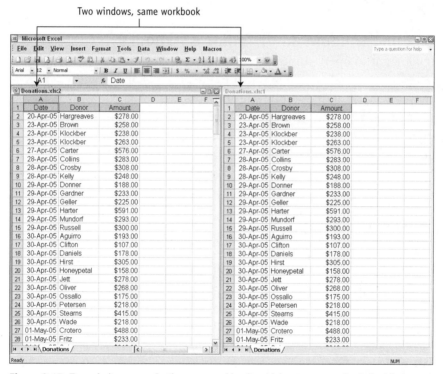

Figure 2.15. Two windows open in the same workbook, which you can see in their title bars

You won't see much of a change, other than in the title bar, which will read *workbook name:2*, indicating a second window into the active workbook. These are not copies of the workbook, they are merely windows into

Watch Out!

Limit your number of open workbooks when you open multiple windows, or you may be overwhelmed with the number of windows that open.

Inside Scoop

No matter which arrangement you choose, you can reshape any window by dragging its borders, and reposition any window by dragging its title bar.

the same workbook that allow you to view different parts of the same workbook at the same time. To see both (or all) windows, as shown in Figure 2.15, choose Window ⇨ Arrange, and choose an arrangement. Vertical is the most useful, I think, but try all four arrangements to see what works best for your task.

Opening windows in different workbooks

If you want to open windows in two different workbooks — for example, to move or copy sheets from one into the other by dragging sheet tabs — all you need to do is open both workbooks, and then choose Window ⇨ Arrange and choose an initial arrangement. Figure 2.16 shows windows in two different workbooks, as you can see by their title bars, and the windows are resized and reshaped for convenience.

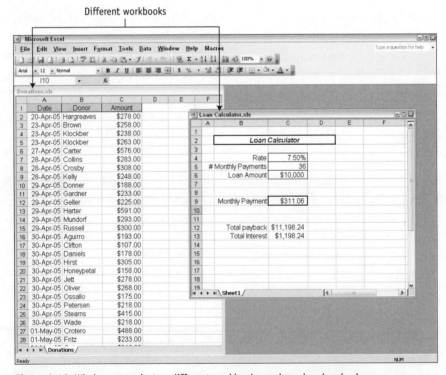

Figure 2.16. Windows open in two different workbooks, reshaped and resized

Closing windows

To return any window to full size within the program window, double-click the window title bar. All open windows remain open but hidden behind one another (and you can switch between them by clicking the taskbar buttons). Click the Window menu to see a list of all the windows that are open after they are maximized.

To close a window, click its Close button. If the window is a workbook, the workbook closes; if the window is a duplicate of a single workbook (the title bar reads workbook name:2), the workbook remains open but the duplicate window into it closes.

Comparing side by side

A new multiple-windows feature in Excel 2003 is Compare Side by Side. It allows you to scroll through two or more worksheets or workbooks at the same time for visual comparison, which is useful when you need to compare similar worksheets, and saves you having to scroll through each window separately. With Compare Side by Side turned on, scrolling either the vertical or horizontal scroll bar in one window scrolls both windows identically, as shown in Figure 2.17.

To turn on side-by-side scrolling in two windows, open both workbooks — or a new window in one workbook if you're comparing worksheets within the same workbook — and display them in separate windows. Then choose Window ➪ Compare Side by Side.

When side by side is turned on, a toolbar appears with three buttons:

- Synchronous Scrolling turns side-by-side scrolling on and off.

- Reset Window Position repositions open windows to a horizontal arrangement.

- Close Side by Side turns off side-by-side mode and returns the windows to their original positions.

If you want to rearrange the windows while side-by-side scrolling is turned on, choose Window ➪ Arrange and choose a different arrangement; changing the arrangement doesn't affect side-by-side scrolling.

Watch Out!
Comparing side by side is new and still just a little buggy. If you start switching between views and turning side by side on and off, you may get unexpected and useless results of all kinds. Close all open workbooks, reopen them, and start again.

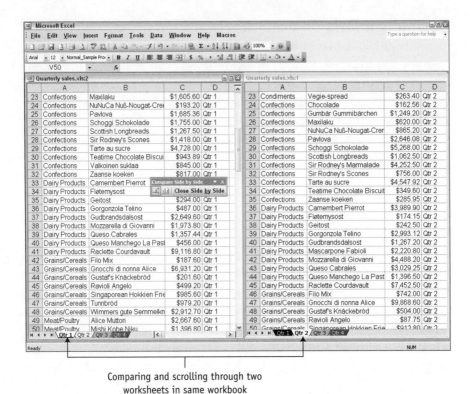

Comparing and scrolling through two
worksheets in same workbook

Figure 2.17. Two different worksheets (Qtr 1 and Qtr 2) opened in Compare Side by Side view

Zooming your view

Zooming your view lets you zoom out for an aerial view or zoom in for a
magnified view (see Figure 2.18). When you open a workbook, the zoom
setting is 100%, but depending on the size of the font in your worksheet
or the resolution of your monitor, 100% may be either too small to read
comfortably or too big to see enough of your worksheet. Zooming your
view in or out does not affect the printed worksheet at all.

The quickest way to zoom to a different standard zoom setting is to
click the arrow on the Zoom button on the Standard toolbar, then click

Bright Idea

If you have named ranges of cells, you can see the ranges easily by zooming
out to 39% or less. The range name is displayed across the range, rather like
city names on a map. See Chapter 4 for more about naming ranges.

one of the preset zoom settings. The Selection entry on the Zoom button list zooms to fill the workbook window with the selected range.

Often the most convenient zoom is a customized zoom setting that works best for you. In one of my templates the text is very small, so I keep it zoomed to 120% to read it easily (workbooks saved with a zoom setting keep that zoom setting when reopened). To set a custom zoom setting, click in the Zoom box, type the percentage you want, and then press Enter.

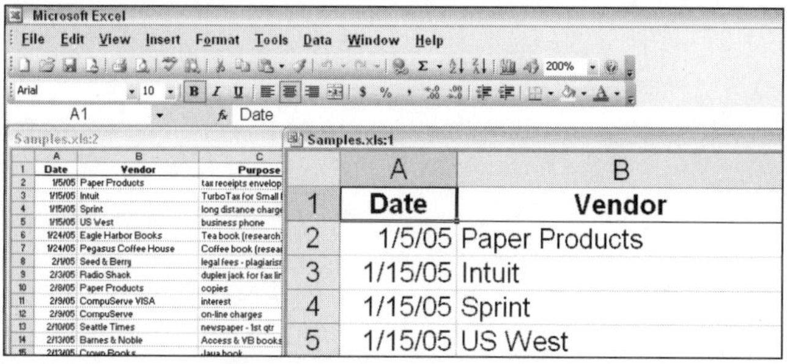

Figure 2.18. Two windows in the same worksheet, with a different zoom factor in each window

Just the facts

- Select a worksheet by clicking its sheet tab.
- Name a worksheet by double-clicking its sheet tab and typing a new name.
- Move a worksheet within a workbook or to another workbook by dragging its sheet tab.
- Add a worksheet by right-clicking a tab and clicking Insert.
- Delete a worksheet by right-clicking a tab and clicking Delete.
- Split panes in a worksheet by dragging a split box into the worksheet.
- Open multiple windows in the same workbook by choosing Window ⇨ New Window and then Window ⇨ Arrange.
- Open multiple windows in more than one open workbook by choosing Window ⇨ Arrange.
- Change the zoom setting by selecting one in the Zoom button list or by typing a number in the Zoom box.

PART LI

Getting the Data In

PART II

GET THE SCOOP ON...
Entering data directly ▪ Data entry techniques ▪ Creating
a dynamic list ▪ Creating a data entry form ▪ Validating
data during entry ▪ Editing cell entries ▪ Finding and
replacing data ▪ Moving and copying data ▪ Inserting,
deleting, and rearranging ▪ Breaking a column into
multiple columns ▪ Adding worksheet comments ▪
Checking your spelling

Entering and Editing Data

Chapter 3

N ow we get into the bottom-line basics of Excel: entering data into worksheets. Entering data can be as simple as clicking a cell, typing, and pressing Enter; but when you have a lot of data to enter, you can make the process faster and easier by taking advantage of some exquisite data entry features and tricks, including AutoComplete, AutoFill, custom lists, and keystrokes that even inveterate mousers like myself can't do without.

In this chapter, I talk about raw data, by which I mean text and number values rather than formulas. Writing formulas is covered in Chapters 4 and 5, and importing data from other programs is covered in Chapter 18.

In addition to entering raw data, I show you how to move data around after it's entered, get it entered correctly to begin with using data validation, edit data, and correct mistakes.

I also show you how to separate, or *parse*, a single column of data into multiple columns, insert and delete rows, columns, and cells into a worksheet, add comments to a worksheet, and use AutoCorrect to speed up data entry.

Entering data directly

Entering data directly into cells in a worksheet (that is, without using a data entry form) is a subject rife with possibilities and tweaks and techniques for doing things faster.

Entering numbers is just like entering text, and when an entry consists of nothing but numbers, Excel assumes the entry is a calculable number. Leading zeroes are removed, the number is included in calculations, and number formatting is available. If, however, the entry contains any letters, Excel assumes the entry is text and ignores it in calculations.

Punctuation for automatic formatting

Some punctuation marks control how Excel interprets your entry and whether or how the data is calculated, and you can use these punctuation marks to tell Excel how you want the data interpreted without specifying formatting for the cell (you can always specify different formatting after the data is entered — see Chapter 7 about formatting data).

Punctuation for numeric formatting

If you type the following punctuation marks when you enter numeric data, the data is simultaneously formatted:

- A minus sign before the number, as in –100, makes the number negative.
- Enclosing a number in parentheses, as in (100), makes the number negative.
- A percent symbol at the beginning or end of the number, as in %25 or 25%, makes the number a percentage.
- A currency symbol at the beginning of the number, as in $100, makes the number currency.
- A single decimal point, as in 100.10, makes the number a decimal (but two decimal points, as in 100.10.10, makes the number text).

Watch Out!

If you don't see what you expected when you enter data, it's often because the cell was previously formatted as something different and the new entry gets the previous format no matter what punctuation marks you type. Choose Edit ⇨ Clear ⇨ Formatting to return the format to General.

Hack

If you've got many numbers mistakenly entered with apostrophes, you can convert them all back to numbers at once: Enter 1 in a cell, then select and copy the cell; select the range of cells to convert; choose Edit ⇨ Paste Special, choose Multiply, and click OK. (Then delete the 1 in that first cell.)

- One or more commas separating groups of three numbers (hundreds), as in 1,100,100, specifies a number (but 1,100,10 is text because it's not a real number).

- An equal sign (=) starts a formula. See Chapter 4 for more on formulas.

- An apostrophe (') typed at the beginning of a number tells Excel the number is text; it's not calculable and retains leading zeroes.

Punctuation for date or time formatting

Excel calculates dates and times as serial numbers, but if you see a serial number in a cell, you'll be hard pressed to identify the date it represents because there are many formats for dates and times.

There are several date formats, and when you enter any number that Excel can possibly interpret as a date, you get a date. Dates and times are calculable numbers that are covered more fully in Chapter 7.

If you type the following punctuation marks when you enter data, the data is simultaneously formatted:

- Forward slashes in numbers that might be dates, as in 7/4 or 1/1/06, create dates.

- Dashes in numbers that might be dates, as in 7-4 or 1-1-06, create dates.

- You can type the month name or abbreviation, as in jun 4, to enter a date.

- If you don't type a year, Excel assumes (and calculates) the current year on your computer clock.

Inside Scoop

When you enter a date in a cell, it's usually automatically formatted as a date and you see the date format in both the cell and the Formula bar. If you want to see the serial number that Excel is really calculating, format the cell as General (more on formatting data in Chapter 7).

Watch Out!

If you enter a date with just numbers and punctuation, Excel may misunderstand which number is the month and which is the day. To be sure of your entry, either type the month name, as in 4/jul or 4/jul/05 or 4 jul or jul 4, or format the cells with a date format before you enter dates.

When you type time entries, all you do is type the hour and minute numbers separated by a colon (:), as in 10:30. You can enter times in a 24-hour format, in which 11:00 PM is entered and displayed as 23:00, or you can enter times in a 12-hour format, in which 11:00 PM is entered as 11:00 pm or 11:00 p or 11 p, and displayed as 11:00 PM. Whatever your displayed time might be, you can see what time Excel is using to calculate by selecting the cell and looking at the Formula bar (see Figure 3.1).

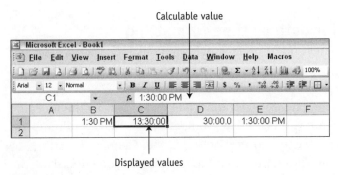

Figure 3.1. No matter what the displayed value shows, the calculable value is found in the Formula bar.

You can enter time components in hours, minutes, seconds, milliseconds, and even smaller, by separating each component with a colon. A time entry must have an hour component; to enter a time of less than an hour (for example, 22 minutes), enter 0:22.

Data entry techniques

Different situations call for different data entry techniques, but all the techniques I show you are those that I use all the time. Being a mouser

Inside Scoop

If you want to display a number with text, as in 6.5 hours or 10 years, don't type the text (because then it's noncalculable). Instead, type the number and then format the cell to display the text automatically (see Chapter 7 to learn how).

myself, I won't waste your time and mine on esoteric keystrokes that you can always look up in the help files, but I'll give you the keystrokes that I use often. In addition to scattering this handful of useful keystrokes into separate sections, I list them for you in Table 3.1.

Table 3.1. Keystrokes I can't live without

Keystroke	What it does
Ctrl+C	Copies the current selection
Ctrl+X	Cuts the current selection
Ctrl+V	Pastes the most recent cut or copy
Ctrl+Z	Undoes the last action; if pressed repeatedly, it undoes each preceding action
Ctrl+'	Copies the entry in the cell above
Ctrl+;	Enters the current date
Ctrl+Shift+;	Enters the current time
Ctrl+D	Copies the cell at the top of a selection into all the selected cells below
Ctrl+Enter	Enters the same entry in all selected cells
Esc	Clears the currently open cell before you press Enter
F4	Repeats the last action; if pressed repeatedly, it continues to repeat the same action

Enter data in a single cell

To enter data in a single cell, click the cell to select it, type the data, and press Enter. Done.

You can also "lock in" your entry by clicking any other cell in the worksheet, or by pressing Tab to move to the right, which is the best way to enter data in a table row.

Inside Scoop

If you are a hard-core keyboarder, type **keyboard shortcuts** in the Ask A Question box and you find more keystrokes than you thought existed.

Enter data in a table

Here is why using the Tab key to enter data across a table is the best way: If you enter data in a multicolumn table and move along each row before starting the next row, using the Tab key to move to the next cell on the right automatically starts the table-entry feature. This feature doesn't have a clever name, but it works like this: Type data in the leftmost cell in the row, press Tab to move to the right, type data, and so on until you reach the end of the row. Then press Enter. Instead of moving down one cell, pressing Enter moves the active cell back to the beginning of the row, but in the next row down (as shown in Figure 3.2).

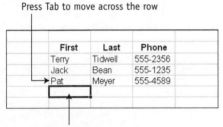

Press Tab to move across the row

Press Enter to start a new row

Figure 3.2. Use Tab and Enter to move in a table.

The table

A *table*—a concept that is integral to many Excel features—is a rectangular region of data that contains no fully blank rows or columns. A table can have many empty cells, but a completely empty row or column delineates the perimeter of the table. Many of Excel's most useful features, including AutoFilter, AutoComplete, Pick From List, PivotTables, Charts, sorting, and subtotaling, to name but a few, expect to find your data in a contiguous table.

The terms *list* and *table* have always been used interchangeably, in both this book and Excel's help files. A new feature in Excel 2003 is also called a *list*, but it's more intricate than a simple list of data. I call the new list a *dynamic list* to differentiate it from the simple list, which is a range of data with column headings (more about dynamic lists later in this chapter).

Watch Out!

If you click to select a different cell while entering data in a table, you temporarily break the table-entry feature; to get it working again, just click at the beginning of the row and start using the Tab key again to move from cell to cell.

Enter numbers with a fixed decimal

If you enter a long list with at least one column of decimal entries (for example, prices), you'll be typing the decimal point in every one of those numbers. To avoid the extra typing and the potential for misplaced decimals, I turn on fixed-decimal entry. With fixed-decimal entry, all I type are the numbers; the decimal inserts itself at the correct place (see Figure 3.3).

All you type are the numbers

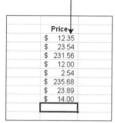

Figure 3.3. Fixed-decimal entry adds the decimal point automatically.

To turn on fixed-decimal entry, choose Tools ⇨ Options, and on the Edit tab, select the Fixed decimal check box (you can change the decimal places number if you need to, but the default 2 is correct for currency). Fixed-decimal is an application-level setting; it turns on for all workbooks and stays turned on until you turn it off (by deselecting the Fixed decimal check box).

I think even the clicking involved in toggling the fixed-decimal on and off is too much work, so I created a macro and custom toolbar button that toggles fixed-decimal on and off with a single click. My toolbar macro and button are in Chapter 21.

Hack

When you turn on fixed-decimal entry, the word FIX appears at the right end of the Excel Status bar. It's unobtrusive and you may never notice it; I usually test the fixed-decimal state by entering 123 in a cell, and then toggle the fixed-decimal state.

Enter fractions

To enter a fraction in a cell, leave a space between the whole number and the fraction, as in **5 3/16**. When you press Enter (or "lock" the entry in the cell by any means), the fraction you typed appears in the cell and the decimal equivalent appears in the Formula bar (see Figure 3.4); the decimal equivalent is what Excel uses in calculations. If you want to display the decimal equivalent for a fraction, enter the fraction and then format the cell as General (more about formatting data in Chapter 7).

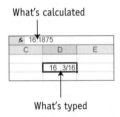

What's calculated

What's typed

Figure 3.4. Type the fraction for a fractional display.

If you want to enter just a fraction, as in ¼, type a zero first, as in **0 1/4**, or Excel enters a date instead of a fraction.

Start a new line in a cell

Quite often an entry is longer than the cell width, and you want to see the entire entry without stretching the column width from here to London. To break the line where you want it broken, and format the cell with Wrap Text format at the same time, press Alt+Enter at the breakpoint in the entry. You can break a line as many times as you want; each line break starts a new line and makes the row taller (see Figure 3.5).

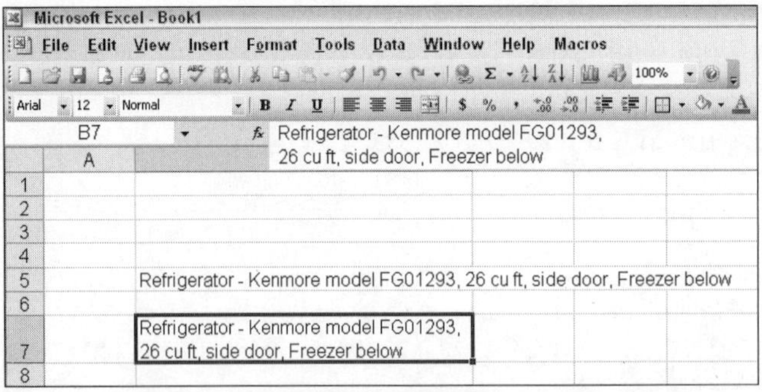

Figure 3.5. Text is automatically wrapped when you add a line break.

Hack

To separate a long entry into two cells (instead of increasing row height for wrapped text), open the cell, drag to select the second segment of text with your mouse, press Ctrl+X to cut, and press Enter; then press Ctrl+V to paste the cut segment in the new cell.

To remove a manual line break and let the line break where the column width dictates, open the cell for editing, place the insertion point at the end of the broken line (it's easiest to do this in the Formula bar), and press Delete.

You may still need to change the column width and the row height to make the cell look the way you want it, or remove the Wrap Text formatting to return the row height to normal; see Chapter 6 about formatting columns and rows, and using Wrap Text.

Make the same entry in several cells

Sometimes the data requires entering the same data in several cells in a table. For example, when I do my business expenses at the end of the year, I have many receipts from the same vendors. I sort the receipts and then enter all the receipts from one vendor at a time so I can enter the receipt data faster. Then I enter all the Vendor column entries (such as Office Depot) at once, and most of the Purpose entries (such as Office Supplies) at once, which reduces my time and tedium (see Figure 3.6). I use all of the techniques listed here at random just to break up the monotony of data entry.

	A	B	C	D	E
16	14-Aug-05	Office Depot	boxes to move office	Office Supplies	$42.57
17	05-Dec-05	Office Depot	supplies	Office Supplies	$265.97
18	05-Jan-05	Papers'n'Stuff	tax receipts envelope	Office Supplies	$2.32
19	08-Feb-05	Papers'n'Stuff	copies	Office Supplies	$1.89
20	07-Mar-05	Papers'n'Stuff	copies	Office Supplies	$1.82
21		Papers'n'Stuff		Office Supplies	
22		Papers'n'Stuff		Office Supplies	
23		Papers'n'Stuff		Office Supplies	
24		Papers'n'Stuff		Office Supplies	
25		Papers'n'Stuff		Office Supplies	
26		Papers'n'Stuff		Office Supplies	
27		Papers'n'Stuff		Office Supplies	
28		Papers'n'Stuff		Office Supplies	
29		Papers'n'Stuff		Office Supplies	
30					

Figure 3.6. One way to speed up data entry

To enter the same data in several cells:

■ Instantly enter the same data in several cells: Select several cells (drag to select a range, or Ctrl+click or Shift+click several cells), type the entry, and press Ctrl+Enter (see Figure 3.7).

■ Repeat the entry in the cell above: Press Ctrl+'.

■ Repeat an entry into several cells below the entry: Drag to select the cell with the entry and several cells below; press Ctrl+D.

■ Repeat an entry into several cells to the right of the entry: Drag to select the cell with the entry and several cells to the right; press Ctrl+R.

abc			
		abc	
		abc	
abc			abc
abc			abc
abc		abc	
abc			

Figure 3.7. Ctrl+click several cells and then press Ctrl+Enter to fill the same data in all selected cells.

Other ways to repeat the same entry include AutoFill, AutoComplete, and Pick From List, which are explained in the next few sections.

AutoFill a text entry

To fill a list with identical entries, make the entry in the first cell, and then drag the fill handle (the small black box in the lower-right corner of the cell shown in Figure 3.8) in any direction to fill the entry into all the cells you drag over.

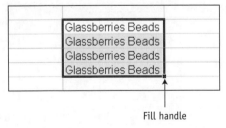

Fill handle

Figure 3.8. Drag the fill handle to fill the other cells with the entry.

If the initial entry is text, the dragged cells are filled with identical entries. If the initial entry is part of a standard list such as weekday names or month names, a list of the names is filled instead of the initial entry. You can take advantage of the AutoFill list behavior by creating your own custom list (for anything from employee names to product part numbers), which is covered later in this chapter.

If you want to fill a range with a single entry, for example, "Monday" instead of a list of weekday names, use the other multicell entry techniques listed in the previous section.

AutoFill numbers

When you use the fill handle to fill cells with numbers, even number-type entries that are formatted as text, AutoFill usually fills a number series instead of identical copies. I say *usually* because if you enter a single number, such as 45, and drag the fill handle on that cell, AutoFill repeats the number 45. But if you AutoFill a number that's formatted as text, such as a part number or a telephone number, AutoFill fills a simple number series. Why? I don't know — perhaps there's a reason, or perhaps not. At any rate, be forewarned that AutoFill does not always do what you expect with regard to numbers.

If the AutoFill Options button appears when you release the mouse button to drop the fill handle, you can click the button and use the button's list to control whether a number is copied or a series is filled. Personally I don't like the interference of the AutoFill Options button because I know how to fill what I want, so I keep it turned off.

If you want to fill a simple series, such as consecutive numbers to number a list, type the first two numbers (for example, 1 and 2, or 23 and 24), then select both cells and drag the AutoFill handle to continue the series as far as you need it (see Figure 3.9). While you drag the fill handle, take a look at the mouse character — it shows you the numbers as you drag over the cells, which makes it easy to know when to stop dragging the fill handle.

AutoFill continues any number series you start it with; for example, if you start with the numbers 1 and 4, AutoFill continues the series in increments of 3. If you want to get fancy with series-filling, right-click and drag

---

Hack

To turn off the AutoFill Options and Paste Options buttons, choose Tools ⇨ Options. On the Edit tab, deselect the Show Paste Options buttons check box. You may need to close and restart Excel for the change to take effect.

the fill handle and select one of the commands on the shortcut menu that appears when you drop the handle. Interesting things can happen when you select the Growth Trend command (for example, the series 1 and 4 fills by multiplying each preceding number by 4). The Series command on the shortcut menu gives you more intricate options for series filling.

Enter and select the first two numbers,

then AutoFill the series.

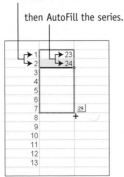

Figure 3.9. AutoFilling numbers

If you start your series with a date, AutoFill fills the series with dates incremented by day; if you need a series incremented by months or years instead, enter the date, then right-click and drag the fill handle and select Fill Months or Fill Years on the shortcut menu (shown in Figure 3.10).

Repeat an entry in the column

Two more useful techniques for repeating an entry that already appears anywhere within the column are AutoComplete and Pick From List. Both repeat an entry from anywhere within the column.

AutoComplete

When you begin typing an entry, AutoComplete fills in the remaining characters for you if it recognizes the first few characters you type (see

Inside Scoop

I can't overstate the importance of having identical entries in a list spelled identically — for successful sorting, filtering, consolidation, PivotTables, and pretty much every data organization technique. Using any of Excel's repetitive-entry features ensures that like entries are spelled identically.

Figure 3.11). If the entry is what you want, press Tab or Enter and move on. If the entry is not quite what you want, keep typing.

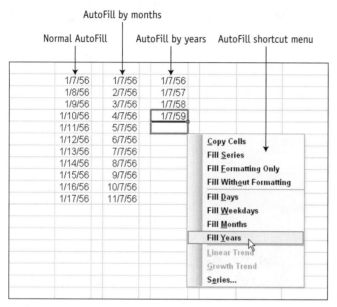

Figure 3.10. Change the AutoFill date-filling behavior with the shortcut menu.

	A	B	C	D	E
1	Date	Vendor	Category	Amount	
2	1/5/05	Paper Products	Office Supplies	$2.32	
3	1/15/05	Sprint	Telephone Charges	$36.80	
4	1/15/05	US West	Telephone Charges	$14.87	
5	1/24/05	Eagle Harbor Books	Books/Publications	$14.00	
6			Office Supplies		
7					

Figure 3.11. AutoComplete fills in an entry that's already somewhere else in the list; if you don't want that entry, keep typing.

If you find AutoComplete annoying, which some people do (but not me), you can turn it off like this: Choose Tools ⇨ Options; on the Edit tab, deselect the Enable AutoComplete for cell values check box.

Pick From List

If you have two entries in which the first several characters are the same, save yourself time by right-clicking the cell and clicking Pick From List; a list opens to display all the entries in the column, and you click the one you want to enter (see Figure 3.12).

Bright Idea

When you have two or more entries that have the same first several characters, you can repeat those entries even more quickly by setting up AutoCorrect entries for them. For more, see the AutoCorrect section.

	A	B	C	D	E
48	05-Dec-05	Office Depot	supplies	Office Supplies	$265.97
49	23-Dec-05	Sprint	long distance charge	Telephone Charg	$48.18
50	28-Dec-05	GTE	business phone	Telephone Charg	$22.20
51	29-Dec-05				
52		B&N			
53		Buddy's Books			
54		Custom Printing			
55		Dept of Licensing			
		Eagle Books			
56		GTE			
		Office Depot			
57		Papers'n'Stuff			

Figure 3.12. Pick an entry from a list of entries in the column.

AutoCorrect

I purchase lots of items at Office Depot and Office Max. When I do my tax numbers each year, instead of typing the entire "office d" or "office m" to let AutoComplete finish the entries, I use a much faster AutoCorrect entry: I type "od" or "om" and let AutoCorrect do the work for me. The results are the same as using AutoComplete, but with less effort on my part.

Not only does AutoCorrect correct your spelling as you type (built-in corrections include "the" for "teh" and "back" for "bcak"), but you can add personalized corrections to the list. The most useful aspect of AutoCorrect is that you can use it to enter long names or phrases when you type a short acronym. For example, if you need to repeatedly type **Lake City High School Alumni**, you can create an AutoCorrect entry that enters the long phrase when you type **lch** (see Figure 3.13)

To create an AutoCorrect entry:

1. Choose Tools ⇨ AutoCorrect Options.

2. On the AutoCorrect tab, in the Replace box, type your short acronym.

3. In the With box, type the replacement entry.

4. Click OK.

Hack

One new feature of AutoCorrect in Office 2003 that I don't like is the AutoCorrect buttons that appear after AutoCorrect corrects an entry. To turn them off, open the AutoCorrect Options dialog box. On the AutoCorrect tab, deselect the Show AutoCorrect Options buttons check box.

Figure 3.13. Creating an AutoCorrect entry for a long phrase

Remember that AutoCorrect entries are available and active in all your Microsoft Office programs, and may make unexpected corrections when, for example, you type in a Word document. In any Microsoft Office program, you can either delete the entry and re-create it when you need it again, or press Ctrl+Z to undo the correction and continue typing.

To delete an AutoCorrect entry, choose Tools ➪ AutoCorrect Options. On the AutoCorrect tab, type the acronym in the Replace box (if you can't remember the correct acronym, type the first letter or two and scroll

Inside Scoop

In the AutoCorrect Options dialog box there's a tab for Smart Tags. Smart Tags don't always work; when they do work, they give you more options than you usually need. I turn them off: On the Smart Tags tab, deselect the Label data with Smart Tags check box.

for the entry). When you see the entry in the With box, click Delete. The entry is deleted in all your Microsoft Office programs.

Create a custom list

Earlier in this chapter I told you about AutoFilling data such as day names or month names; these are built-in lists, and AutoFill fills the list of names for you. You can create a custom list of words or names of your own, perhaps for employee names, product names, or part numbers.

To create a custom list, type the list entries in a column, then select the entire list; choose Tools ⇨ Options, click the Custom Lists tab, and click Import. The imported list appears in the Custom Lists window.

When you type any item in the custom list and drag the fill handle from that cell, the list is AutoFilled beginning with your entry (and uses the capitalization style you typed in your initial entry, even if that is not the capitalization style you used when you created the custom list). The list is repeated as you continue to drag the fill handle.

Delete data

To delete data, click the cell and press Delete. To delete data from several cells, select all the cells and press Delete. To delete data from an entire worksheet, click the gray box at the intersection of the row numbers and column letters, and press Delete.

Mix your techniques and technologies

When I have a project that requires a high volume of data entry, I mix techniques and technologies to get the fastest, most accurate data entry I can. In addition to the data entry techniques elucidated in this chapter, I often use a voice recognition program to read data rapidly into a Word document, do any editing and formatting I need in Word (because it's usually much faster for text editing), then copy the data from Word into Excel. I also use an optical character recognition program to convert data from a scanned fax if it's clear enough, and I always ask clients to send me data in electronic format if possible, because any data that's already electronic can be imported into Excel without introducing new typographical errors. See Chapter 18 for more about importing data.

Bright Idea

Make a Clear All macro and toolbar button to clear everything — data, formats, and comments — with just one click. See Chapter 19 to learn about toolbar buttons, and Chapter 21 to learn about macros and how to record my simple Clear All button.

When you delete data, the formatting and comments in the cells are untouched. To clear selected cells of everything, choose Edit ⇨ Clear ⇨ All.

Undo an action

If you've done a number of things in a worksheet — entering data, formatting, deleting data or objects, whatever — and you decide that you've done it all wrong and want to change what you did, you can just undo those things without the bother of deleting data, unformatting, and remembering what exactly you did nine actions back.

You can undo the last 16 actions you performed in Excel — in the reverse order in which you performed them — by pressing Ctrl+Z repeatedly or by clicking the Undo button on the Standard toolbar (shown in Figure 3.14). On the Undo button there's a down arrow you can click to see a drop-down list of the last several things you did; click any item on that list to undo every action back to and including that item.

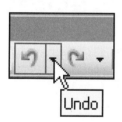

Figure 3.14. The Undo and Redo buttons on the Standard toolbar

If you change your mind about undoing something, you can redo what you undid by clicking the Redo button on the Standard toolbar (Ctrl+Y is the keystroke for Redo).

Creating a dynamic list

A dynamic list is one of the more noticeable new features in Excel 2003. I call it a dynamic list to differentiate it from a normal list, which is just columns of data with column headings at the top. Excel doesn't have a

Inside Scoop

A dynamic list is a good source for chart data, because as you add rows of data to the bottom of a dynamic list, the chart data source expands and the data is automatically included in the chart.

fancy name for it — imagine that! — and just calls it a list, which is a little confusing because Microsoft and everyone else have always used the term *list* for a regular list.

At any rate, the new dynamic list has some features automatically added for you, including AutoFilter buttons, a SUBTOTAL formula at the bottom, and a new data row at the bottom so the list automatically expands to include all your data. You can turn AutoFilter on and off yourself on any table or list, write your own SUBTOTAL formula, and insert new rows in a table any time you like, but when you create a dynamic list, all these things are done for you.

To create a dynamic list the easy way, create a normal list (at least a couple of rows of data and some column headings at the top), click in any cell in the list, choose Data ⇨ List, and click OK in the Create List dialog box.

The new dynamic list has a border (so you can tell it's a dynamic list), bold column headers, AutoFilter buttons on the column headers, and a toolbar (see Figure 3.15).

Date	Product	Price/l	Lbs	Total
12/2/05	Santo Domingo	9.50	100	950.00
12/2/05	Tanzania	10.50	100	1,050.00
12/4/05	Tanzania	10.50	200	2,100.00
12/4/05	Tanzania	10.50	150	1,575.00
12/4/05	Tanzania	10.50	45	472.50
12/4/05	Santo Domingo	9.50	55	522.50
12/5/05	Celebes	9.25	90	832.50
12/5/05	Celebes	9.25	80	740.00
12/5/05	Santo Domingo	9.50	60	570.00
12/5/05	Santo Domingo	9.50	95	902.50
12/7/05	Coatepec	10.25	150	1,537.50
12/7/05	Tanzania	10.50	100	1,050.00
12/8/05	Chanchamayo	11.00	200	2,200.00
*				
Total				14,502.50

List
List ▾ | Σ Toggle Total Row

Figure 3.15. The new dynamic list adds features to your list automatically.

Inside Scoop

When the Total row is displayed, right-click in the Total cell. An arrow appears to the right of the cell. Click the arrow and select a different function if you want to change the formula to a different calculation.

On the toolbar, click the Toggle Total Row button to display or hide the total row with the SUBTOTAL formula. I have more to say about the SUBTOTAL function in Chapter 5 and AutoFilter in Chapter 8.

If you want to change a dynamic list back to a normal list, click the List button on the List toolbar and click Convert to Range.

The only thing that a dynamic list can do for you that you cannot do yourself is publish your list to a SharePoint site. A SharePoint site is a shared-data Web site on a server that runs Windows SharePoint Services, and is beyond the scope of this book; if you type SharePoint in the Ask A Question box, you can find lots of information about it in the Microsoft Office Online help files.

Creating a data form

Usually it's easier to enter data in a table by entering the data directly in the table, but if the table is too wide to fit within your workbook window, or if you're editing data in a large table that's already filled with entries, keeping track of your place in the table can become difficult (and it's not unusual to edit a cell in the wrong row).

To keep your data intact in these situations, create a data form. A data form displays named fields (columns) for a single record (row) at a time.

To create a data form, click in a cell in the table, and choose Data ⇨ Form. An instant, temporary data form is created (see Figure 3.16).

The column headings are listed on the left, and a single row of data is displayed. There's a box for each cell in the row of data—you can enter or edit data in the boxes using any entry/editing technique you like.

To start a new record at the bottom of the table, click the New button. To finish entering a new record, click the New button again, or press Enter.

Inside Scoop

To remove the border around a dynamic list (to make it look like a normal list when you're not working in it), right-click any cell in the list, click List, and then click Hide Border of Inactive Lists.

To scroll through the records, click and drag the vertical scroll bar, click the scroll bar buttons, or press the up- and down-arrow keys. To delete a record, click Delete.

To locate specific records for editing, click the Criteria button and type a criterion in a cell (for example, to find entries in which the last name begins with "S", type **s** in the Last Name field and press Enter). When you press Enter, the form switches into query mode, and you can scroll through the records that match your criterion by clicking the Find Next and Find Prev buttons.

To close the form, click the Close button.

Figure 3.16. A data form allows you to enter or edit data in a single row at a time.

Validating data during entry

It's all too easy to inadvertently enter inaccurate data, which renders the data worthless. You can spare yourself the time spent fixing some kinds of data entry errors if the data is entered into the worksheet correctly to begin with. Data validation can help you avoid several kinds of incorrect data entry—especially helpful if someone else is entering data in your workbook—by demanding that each entry meets validity criteria that you set. For example, if a cell needs a valid date entry, or a calculable numeric entry rather than text, Excel can scream (or politely whisper) "No, that entry is incorrect. Try it again" and refuse to accept the invalid data.

To set up data validation:

1. Select the cell or range in which you want to validate data.

2. Choose Data ⇨ Validation. The Data Validation dialog box appears, as shown in Figure 3.17.

3. On the Settings tab, select the data type for acceptable entries in the Allow box.

4. Select limiting criteria in the Data box. The settings in the Data box (if any) change according to your selection in the Allow box.

5. Set limiting values in the boxes below the Data box. You can type a limiting number, a formula, or a cell address. Table 3.2 lists some useful validation settings.

6. Click the Input Message tab and type a title and message for a message that appears when the cell is selected (this is optional).

7. Click the Error Alert tab, select a style, and type a title and a message for an error message that appears when invalid data is entered (see Figure 3.18). In the Style box, a Stop error prohibits invalid data entry, while Warning and Information errors allow invalid entries after the user clicks Yes or OK in the error message.

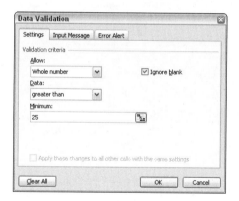

Figure 3.17. The Data Validation dialog box

Figure 3.18. Data validation message

Bright Idea

Instead of permanently specifying your criteria value in the Data Validation dialog box, click in the Minimum and/or Maximum boxes and then click in a worksheet cell. Type your criteria value in that cell; if you want to change the criteria value, edit the value in the cell.

Table 3.2. Useful validation examples

For	Allow	Data	Value
Credit card numbers	Text	Equal to	16
Credit card expiration date	Date	Greater than or equal to	=TODAY()
Specific entries	List	n/a	Drag to select a range of entries on the worksheet and enter the valid entries in those cells (you can delete the worksheet entries after you create the validation list)

To remove data validation, select the cells in which you want to remove validation, choose Data ⇨ Validation, and click Clear All. To clear validation from all the cells where this particular validation setting is applied, select the Apply these changes to all other cells with the same settings check box before you click OK.

Editing cell entries

If you are in the middle of typing an entry and haven't locked the entry in yet, press Esc to erase everything in the cell.

There are three ways to edit an existing entry:

- Double-click the cell to open it and edit the characters in the cell.
- Select the cell and press F2 to open the cell for editing, then edit the characters in the cell (this technique keeps your fingers on the keyboard).
- Click in the cell and edit the entry in the Formula bar (very useful if the font in the cell is small and difficult to work in).

Inside Scoop

To locate validated cells on a worksheet, choose Edit ⇨ Go To and click Special. In the Go To Special dialog box, click Data Validation, then click All, and click OK. All cells with validation settings are selected.

Whether you are editing in the cell or in the Formula bar, you can use the arrow keys to move through the characters one character at a time, the Backspace and Delete keys to delete one character at a time, or the mouse to select several characters to cut, copy, or delete all at once.

Finding and replacing data

If you need to find a specific cell in a large worksheet, let Excel find it for you; if you need to replace something throughout the worksheet, let Excel make all the replacements for you.

This is especially useful if you are reusing a worksheet for a new month, a new year, or a different employee name: You can replace 2004 with 2005, January with February, or Dave Smith with Mary Jones. But you can also find a cell (or all cells) with a specific formula by searching formulas for all or part of the function name, find cells with a text string but only if specific letters are capitalized, or remove your username from all the comments in a worksheet. In short, you can find and/or replace pretty much anything in a worksheet except for worksheet headers and footers (if you hard-code the year in your annual tax worksheet headers, like I do, you have to remember to open and change the headers manually every year).

Find a string

Most often you only want to find text strings in a cell (text strings are any characters typed in a cell, numbers as well as letters). To find a simple text string, press Ctrl+F, and type the characters in the Find what box on the Find tab.

Inside Scoop

You can also limit your search to cells with specific formatting. Click the arrow on the Format button, click Choose format from cell, and click a cell that has the formatting you want to find. Then click Find All or Find Next.

In a simple Find procedure, Excel finds all cells that have the characters you type within any other text string (so, for example, *we* finds
Wellington and Hollowell as well as *we*).

To find each single instance of the characters, click Find Next repeatedly. The active cell jumps to each found cell one by one.

To find all instances of the characters, click Find All. A found-cells
pane opens in the Find and Replace dialog box, listing the location of
each instance of the string. When you click a line in the found-cells pane,
the active cell jumps to that cell.

To refine and narrow your search, click Options and set more stringent search criteria (see Figure 3.19). You can restrict the search to
strings in which the characters have specific capitalization (select the
Match case check box), or comprise the entire cell entry (select the
Match entire cell contents check box), or search the whole workbook
(select Workbook in the Within box). You can also search formulas or
comments instead of displayed values by selecting Formulas or
Comments in the Look in box.

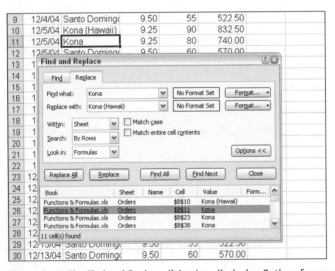

Figure 3.19. The Find and Replace dialog box displaying Options for search
criteria and the found-cells pane

Inside Scoop

The Name column in the pane lists named ranges where found cells are located.
Naming cells and ranges is useful in many ways; see Chapter 4 to learn more.

Replace a string

Replacing a string is just like finding a string, but you run the procedure from the Replace tab in the Find and Replace dialog box. You can either press Ctrl+F and then click the Replace tab, or press Ctrl+H to open the same dialog box with the Replace tab displayed.

Type the characters you want to replace in the Find what box, and the replacement characters in the Replace with box. You can replace cell formatting without changing the cell contents by replacing characters with the same characters and setting up a replacement format in the Replace with line (see Figure 3.20). Changing formatting alters the formatting in the whole cell, not just the characters (you can format individual characters manually; see Chapter 6 to learn more).

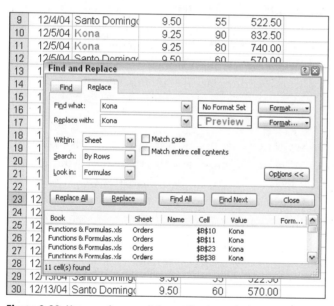

Figure 3.20. You can change cell formatting by replacing the same characters with a different format.

Bright Idea

If you want to find and replace a whole word rather than characters, type a space character in the appropriate position in both the Find what and Replace with boxes. The space character ensures that you don't end up with unintentional run-together words.

Hack

If you click Replace All and find that the procedure made changes you didn't intend, press Ctrl+Z to quickly undo the Replace All, then set up a better Replace All procedure and run it again, or replace strings one by one.

To replace characters one by one, click Replace repeatedly. The active cell jumps to each new cell before it makes a replacement; if you don't want to replace the characters in the current cell, click Find Next to ignore the currently selected cell and move to the next cell.

If you click Replace to replace strings one by one and you see a message that says Microsoft Excel cannot find a match, it just means that you have to help Excel find an initial match before it begins replacing (this is a bug, but it's one Microsoft created a Help file for instead of fixing). Click Find Next, then click Replace repeatedly. Interestingly, this doesn't happen when you click Replace All (like I said, it's buggy).

To replace all occurrences of your text string in cell values and in formulas (called a global search-and-replace), click Replace All.

Moving and copying data

The fastest way to move or copy data on the same worksheet is to drag it. Select the cell or range you want to move or copy, then hover your mouse over one border of the selected range (it doesn't matter which border). When the mouse is a four-headed arrow (shown in Figure 3.21), you've got the border; drag the border to a new location.

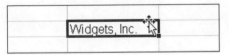

Figure 3.21. When the mouse pointer becomes a four-headed arrow, you've got the cell border.

To move the range to the new location, just release the mouse button to drop the range. To copy the range to the new location, press Ctrl while you release the mouse button (the small plus symbol on the mouse icon tells you that you are dropping a copy).

Hack

If your mouse pointer doesn't become a four-headed arrow when it's over a cell border, you have drag-and-drop turned off. Choose Tools ⇨ Options, and on the Edit tab, select the Allow cell drag and drop check box.

Inside Scoop

The small yellow box that appears next to the dragged range border while you drag is a *range tip* that shows you the cell or range address where the dragged range is located before you drop it. You can ignore it.

Between workbooks and worksheets

You can drag ranges between worksheets and workbooks, too:

- To drag a range to a new workbook, show both workbooks side by side and drag the range from one to the other.

- To drag a range to another worksheet in the same workbook, press Alt, drag the range down to the sheet tab for the worksheet you want, and when the worksheet opens, drag the range into position on the new worksheet.

The next-fastest way to move or copy data is to use keystrokes. These keystrokes are a part of every Excel aficionado's repertoire, because they are so common and they allow you to work quickly with one hand on the mouse and one hand on the keyboard:

- **Ctrl+X.** To cut cells, select a cell or range and press Ctrl+X.

- **Ctrl+C.** To copy cells, select a cell or range and press Ctrl+C.

- **Ctrl+V.** To paste cut or copied cells, select the upper-left corner cell of the paste range and press Ctrl+V.

- **Ctrl+Z.** To undo mistakes, no matter what you've done (almost), press Ctrl+Z.

My third choice for quick cutting, copying, and pasting is the right-click method. Select the cell or range, right-click in the selection, and click Cut or Copy. Then right-click the cell where you want to paste the item and click Paste.

Paste items

The fastest way to paste a cut or copied item is to press Enter. Cut or copy your item using any method you like, then click the cell where you

Watch Out!

If you copy and paste cells with formulas, you may get unexpected results because relative formula references change when you copy cells, although not when you move cells. For more about relative references and moving/copying cells, see Chapter 4.

want to paste it and press Enter. Everything — contents, formulas, and formatting — is pasted.

The next fastest ways, in no particular order, are: Press Ctrl+V, and right-click-and-click-Paste. The difference between these two methods and pressing Enter is that when you press Enter, you only get one paste. When you use the right-click or keystroke method, you can paste the same item repeatedly.

When you cut or copy anything — in any Microsoft Office program — the cut and copied selections are stored in the Office Clipboard, a hidden storage cache. To see, and choose from, all your cut and copied data, choose Edit ⇨ Office Clipboard. From the Clipboard pane (shown in Figure 3.22), you can click to paste anything repeatedly and in any order you want (just click the paste cell and then click the item in the task pane).

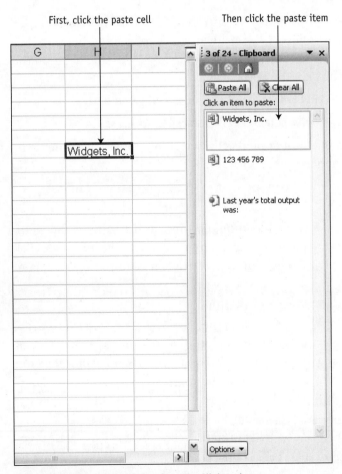

Figure 3.22. Paste copied items from the Clipboard pane.

Inside Scoop

Any item you cut appears in the Clipboard task pane, but when you paste it from the task pane, the item is copied to the paste location, not moved. To move an item rather than copy it, use the border-drag or keystrokes method rather than the Clipboard task pane.

When you want more than a simple paste, there's a useful new feature in Excel 2003: the expanded Paste button on the Standard toolbar. When you copy an item and then click the arrow on the Paste button, you get a list of paste options, as shown in Figure 3.23.

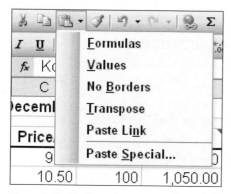

Figure 3.23. The Paste button options for copied data

The most useful item in the list is the Values option. Pasting Values is something I do quite often. It used to be hidden several mouse clicks away, and most users were never aware of it.

Why use paste values? Here's a good reason: When I create a list of formulas to join the contents of two cells (such as creating a column of full names from two separate columns of first names and last names), I want the new column of names to be values, not formulas, so I can delete the columns of first and last names without losing the formula results. By copying the column of formulas and then pasting the resulting values in their place, the formulas are replaced with their results, and the columns of first and last names can be safely deleted. To do this, select the cells with formulas and copy them. Then click the arrow in the Paste button and click Values without choosing a new paste location. Last, press Esc to remove the blinking border.

If you cut a selection and then use the Paste button options, there's only one option available: Paste Link. Pasting a link creates formulas in

Hack

When you paste items, you may see a Paste Options button next to the pasted item. If you click the button, you get a list of paste options. It's unnecessary worksheet clutter. To turn it off, choose Tools ⇨ Options. On the Edit tab, deselect the Show Paste Options buttons check box.

the paste area that reference the cut cells (for example, if you cut cell A1 and Paste Link it in another cell, the formula =A1 is pasted), and the cut cells are not moved. Linked cells display the values in the original (source) cells, and if you change a source cell's value, its linked cell changes, too.

Inserting, deleting, and rearranging

Worksheets are never written in permanent ink; one thing you will need to do eventually (perhaps often) is insert and delete rows, columns, and cells.

You may have entire rows or columns of data in a table that you want to delete, but if you only delete the data, you end up with a blank column or row that breaks your table in half. What you really need to do is delete the row or column itself from the worksheet, not just the data.

On the other hand, you may need to insert a column or row because you want to add data that belongs in the middle of the table.

Delete a row or column

To delete a row, select the row to be deleted, right-click the row number, and click Delete; to delete several rows, click and drag to select all the row numbers, then right-click in the selected rows and click Delete.

To delete a column, select the column to be deleted, right-click the column letter and click Delete (as shown in Figure 3.24); to delete several columns, click and drag to select all the column letters, then right-click in the selected columns and click Delete.

Inside Scoop

Deleting rows and columns doesn't make your worksheet any smaller; the worksheet still has 256 columns and 65,536 rows. When you delete a row or column, a new row or column is added at the bottom or right side of the worksheet.

A3	▼	f_x

	A	B⤵	C
1			
2			
3			
4			
5			
6			
7			

Figure 3.24. Right-click column letters (or row numbers) to delete entire columns (or rows).

Insert a row or column

To insert a row, right-click a row number and click Insert (the row number you right-click is pushed down to make room for the new row); to insert several rows, click and drag to select the number of row numbers you want to insert, then right-click in the selected rows and click Insert (the row numbers you selected are pushed down to make room for the inserted rows, as shown in Figure 3.25).

Right-click the row number

Right-click the column letter

A5	▼	f_x					
	A	B ↓	C	D	E	F	G
1	Date	Vendor		Purpose	Category	Amount	
2	05-Jan-05	Papers'n'Stuff		tax receipts envelope	Office Supplies	$2.32	
3	15-Jan-05	Sprint		long distance charge	Telephone Charg	$36.80	
4	15-Jan-05	US West		business phone	Telephone Charg	$14.87	
5							
6	24-Jan-05	Eagle Books		Tea book (research)	Books/Publicatio	$14.00	
7	24-Jan-05	Peg's Coffee House		Coffee book (researc	Books/Publicatio	$14.00	

Figure 3.25. Inserting rows and columns

To insert a column, right-click the column letter and click Insert (the column you right-clicked is pushed to the right to make room); to insert

Inside Scoop

You can repeatedly insert or delete rows, columns, or cells quickly by pressing F4: Insert or delete a row, column, or cell the normal way, then select the next row, column, or cell and press F4; continue pressing F4 to repeat the procedure as many times as you need.

several columns, click and drag to select all the column letters, then right-click in the selected columns and click Insert (the selected columns are pushed to the right to make room).

Inserted rows and columns always pick up the formatting of the surrounding rows and columns.

Insert and delete cells

When you need to insert or delete individual cells in a table, you can do it without affecting tables on the rest of the worksheet. When you insert cells in a table, the surrounding cells move down or to the right to make room, depending on what you select in the dialog box. When you delete cells in a table, the surrounding cells move up or left to fill in the blanks, again depending on what you select in the dialog box.

To insert cells, select the cells to be moved to make room, then right-click the selection and click Insert. In the Insert dialog box, select the option you want for moving the existing cells (see Figure 3.26).

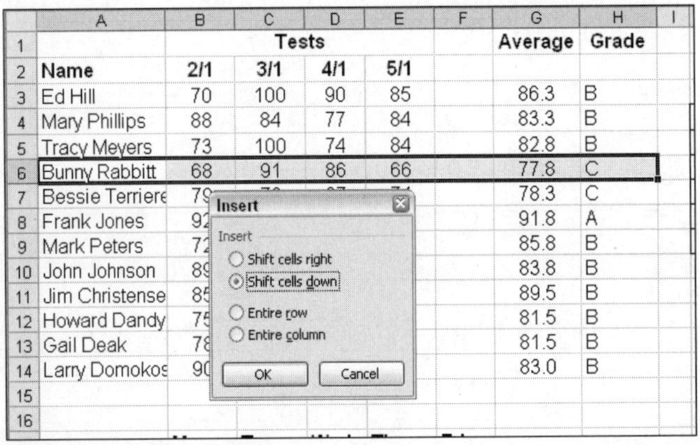

Figure 3.26. By selecting Shift cells down, the selected cells are moved down to make room for the inserted cells.

To delete cells, select the cells you want to delete, then right-click the selection and click Delete. In the Delete dialog box, select the option you want for moving the remaining cells to fill in the blanks.

Rearrange rows, columns, and cells

Suppose you just need to rearrange the columns in a table. Perhaps you have all your tax data for the year entered and decide to switch the

Vendor and Purpose columns. You can select a row or column of table data or individual cells or entire worksheet rows and columns, and insert them in a new position within existing data.

To rearrange rows, columns, or cells, select the data you want to insert elsewhere. Drag the selection border as if you were moving it (look for the four-headed arrow mouse to click the border), and press Shift while you drag the border. A hatched-line insert bar appears (see Figure 3.27) and bounces around between cells as you drag the border. When the insert line is where you want to insert your selection, release the mouse button to drop the cells.

When you drop the inserted cells, the cells around the insertion move down or right to make room.

Hatched insertion line

B	C	D
Vendor	**Purpose**	**Category**
Paper Products	tax receipts envelope	Office Supplies
Intuit	TurboTax for Small B	Tax preparation
Sprint	long distance charge	Telephone Charge
US West	business phone	Telephone Charge
Eagle Harbor Boc	Tea book (research)	Books/Publications
Pegasus Coffee H	Coffee book (resear	Books/Publications

Figure 3.27. The hatched insert line shows where cells will be inserted.

Breaking a column into multiple columns

Sometimes I enter a list of names in a worksheet and type both first and last names in the same cell (or at least I used to; now I know better). The names are more useful when they're separated into two columns, one for first names and one for last names.

Instead of deleting and retyping the names cell by cell, Excel can separate, or parse, the data into two columns for me. All I need to do is tell Excel where to break the entries.

To parse cells:

1. Select the cells. Leave an empty column on the right so the new column you're about to create has somewhere to go.

2. Choose Data ⇨ Text to Columns.

3. In the Convert Text to Columns Wizard – Step 1 of 3, select the Delimited option and then click Next. (Delimiters are characters that separate data, such as spaces, commas, and tabs.)

4. In Step 2 of 3, choose a delimiter. With names, the delimiter is most likely a space, but try selecting different check boxes—when you select the correct delimiter for your data, a vertical line appears between data columns in the Data Preview window, as shown in Figure 3.28. Click Next.

5. In Step 3 of 3, you can set formatting for each column of data. It's faster to let Excel handle this step—you can reformat data later if you need to. Click Finish.

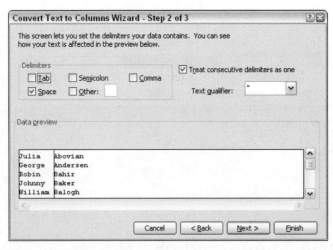

Figure 3.28. The vertical line shows where the data will be separated into columns.

The column is separated into two columns, with the new column started at the delimiter (see Figure 3.29).

If the column is parsed into extra columns because of multiple delimiter characters in some cells (such as a middle name in a list of names), you can manually move data and cells around in those few rows until you have what you need.

	A	B	C	D
1		**FullName**		
2		Julia	Abovian	
3		George	Andersen	
4		Robin	Bahir	
5		Johnny	Baker	
6		William	Balogh	
7		Dick	Bedrosian	
8		Jim	Christensen	
9		Howard	Dandyn	
10		Gail	Deak	
11		Larry	Domokos	
12		Richard	Dyhr	
13		Leo	Fabin	
14		Colleen	Fairfax	
15		Elvin	Gilroy	
16		Ardith	Gledan	
17		Irene	Hassan	
18		Ron	Kajetan	
19		Judy	Karayan	
20		Denny	Keleos	
21		Mick	Kirkegar	
22				

Figure 3.29. A FullName column parsed into First Name and Last Name columns

Adding worksheet comments

Comments are a terrific way to add explanatory information to a worksheet without having the information appear in the worksheet (unless you want to display it). I have accountant friends who use these all the time as reminders of source data for cell contents; I often use them to remind me of what a complex formula does, especially if I don't look at the worksheet for a year or so.

A comment floats on top of the worksheet instead of appearing in the worksheet. It appears when you hover the mouse over the cell, whether the cell is selected or not (see Figure 3.30).

A small, red triangle appears in the upper-right corner of a cell that has a comment.

Inside Scoop

If you want to change the username (or delete it entirely) choose Tools ⇨ Options. On the General tab, your username appears in the User name box.

To add a comment, right-click the cell and click Insert Comment. Type your comment text and click a different cell.

To edit an existing comment, right-click the cell and click Edit Comment. When the comment opens, edit the text and click a different cell.

To delete a comment, right-click the cell and click Delete comment.

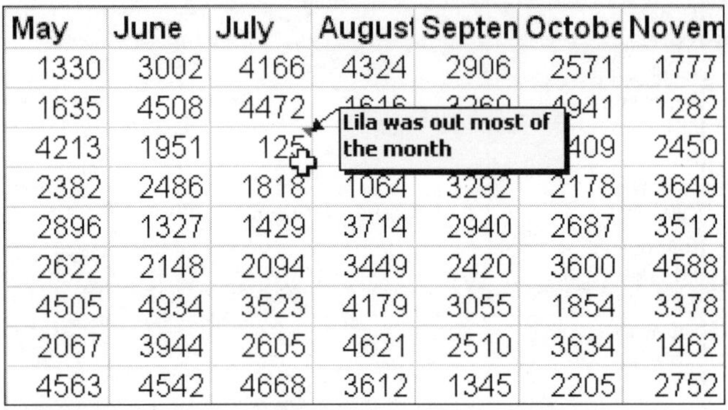

May	June	July	August	Septen	Octobe	Novem
1330	3002	4166	4324	2906	2571	1777
1635	4508	4472	1616	3360	4941	1282
4213	1951	125			409	2450
2382	2486	1818	1064	3292	2178	3649
2896	1327	1429	3714	2940	2687	3512
2622	2148	2094	3449	2420	3600	4588
4505	4934	3523	4179	3055	1854	3378
2067	3944	2605	4621	2510	3634	1462
4563	4542	4668	3612	1345	2205	2752

(Comment shown over the table: "Lila was out most of the month")

Figure 3.30. A comment adds and hides extra information.

When you create a comment, it opens with your username in bold font (see Figure 3.31). That's great if you are sharing this workbook with other users and you and the other users want to explain your entries, but if you don't need to identify the commenter, you can delete the username.

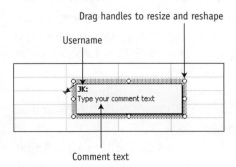

Drag handles to resize and reshape

Username

JK:
Type your comment text

Comment text

Figure 3.31. Creating a new comment

Viewing comments (or not)

You can see all the comments in every open workbook if you choose Tools ⇨ Options, and click the Comment & indicator option in the Comments section of the View tab. If you display all comments, you can relocate them on the worksheet by dragging them to new positions. They retain the new position whenever they are all displayed, but when you return the display option to Comment indicator only, the comments return to opening above the right corner of the cell. You can also hide comments completely by selecting the None option in the Comments section of the View tab. These settings won't do you any good if you share your workbook with another user, because comment display settings are application-specific and respond to the setting in the user's Excel program.

Comments open with a default size and shape, which may not fit your text. You can change the size or shape during inserting or editing (when the border around the comment is hatched or dotted) by dragging one of the handles on the sides or corners of the comment.

Checking your spelling

Adding spelling corrections to the AutoCorrect list works well for words you consistently misspell, but when you aren't aware that a word is misspelled, or flying fingers on the keyboard inadvertently misspell a word that's not in the AutoCorrect list, Excel can find many of those errors by checking your spelling for you.

To spell check the entire worksheet, click a single cell. To highlight a section of the worksheet, drag to select the cells you want to check. Then click the Spelling button on the Standard toolbar.

When the spell checker finds a word it doesn't recognize (see Figure 3.32), it displays the Spelling dialog box.

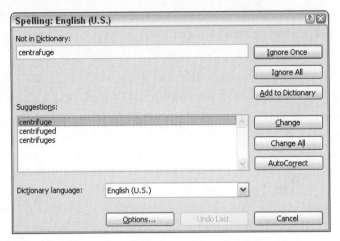

Figure 3.32. The Spelling dialog box found a misspelled word.

Your options are:

- **Ignore Once.** Ignore this instance because in other instances this spelling may be incorrect.

- **Ignore All.** Ignore this misspelling every time because it's always correct in this worksheet.

- **Add to Dictionary.** Add this spelling to the dictionary because this spelling is always correct everywhere and you don't want the spell checker to catch it any more.

- **Change.** Change to the spelling highlighted in the Suggestions list, just this once. If the spelling you want is not in the Suggestions list, change the spelling in the Not in Dictionary box and then click Change.

- **Change All.** Change to the spelling highlighted in the Suggestions list everywhere in the worksheet. If the spelling you want is not in the Suggestions list, change the spelling in the Not in Dictionary box and then click Change All.

Hack

If you inadvertently add a misspelled word to the dictionary, you can open the dictionary and delete the word. The dictionary is named CUSTOM.DIC; use Windows Search to find the filename on your hard drive. Open the file, delete the word, choose File ⇨ Save, and close the file.

- **AutoCorrect.** Change the spelling to the highlighted word in the Suggestions list, and add the misspelling and changed spelling to the AutoCorrect list.

The Options button opens another dialog box with dictionary and language options that you will probably never need to use.

Just the facts

- Enter data by clicking a cell, typing data, and pressing Enter or Tab or clicking another cell. Use punctuation to format data as you enter it.

- Use AutoFill, AutoComplete, Pick From List, custom lists, and AutoCorrect to enter complete entries quickly.

- Validate data as it's entered to prevent many errors.

- Use Find and Replace to change data throughout the worksheet.

- Drag data to move or copy it across a worksheet, to another worksheet, or to another workbook.

- Insert and delete cells, rows, and columns to remove or add data in the middle of a table.

- Insert worksheet comments to add extra information that hides in the worksheet.

- Check your spelling to keep your worksheets looking professional.

GET THE SCOOP ON...
Simple calculations and quick answers ■ Cell references ■
Writing formulas ■ Moving and copying formulas ■
Linking workbooks with formulas ■ Cell names ■ Editing
formulas ■ Auditing formulas ■ Locating worksheet errors

Working Data Magic with Calculations

O nce data is entered in a workbook, you're ready to perform calculations on it (after all, calculations are why Excel exists). To perform calculations in a worksheet, you write formulas; to perform complex calculations, you use functions in your formulas (*functions* are built-in mathematical equations that save you time and effort, and are covered in Chapter 5).

This chapter is full of basic calculation information: getting fast answers without formulas, writing your own formulas, using cell references and cell names for better calculation control, and fixing errors. It could just as well have been titled "Calculations 101."

Simple calculations, quick answers

To get really quick answers without writing a formula yourself, you have two options: AutoCalculate, which calculates cells in the worksheet temporarily but doesn't write formulas; and AutoSum, which writes very simple formulas in the worksheet very quickly.

AutoCalculate

AutoCalculate is a handy tool that I use often to calculate cells on the fly while I work. The AutoCalculate box is near the right end of the Excel Status bar, shown in Figure 4.1.

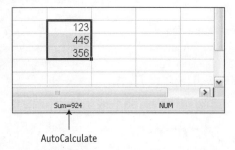

AutoCalculate

Figure 4.1. AutoCalculate is always at work. All you need to do is select two or more cells.

To use AutoCalculate, select the cells you want to calculate (two or more) and look at the AutoCalculate box.

AutoCalculate sums cells by default, but it can also average cells, count entries, count numeric entries, and tell you the maximum or minimum number in a range.

To change the calculation function, right-click anywhere in the Status bar and select a different function (see Figure 4.2). You can turn AutoCalculate off by selecting None, but it's so unobtrusive that many people never even notice it, so why bother turning it off?

If there's no display in the AutoCalculate box (and it's not turned off), that's because you only have one cell selected, or you don't have appropriate data selected for the current AutoCalculate function. For example, if you only have text cells selected, only the Count function works.

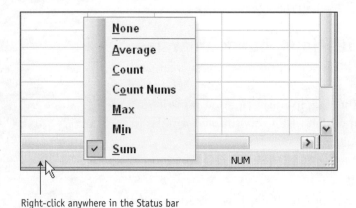

Right-click anywhere in the Status bar

Figure 4.2. Changing the AutoCalculate function

AutoSum

To enter a formula in the worksheet that calculates a group of numbers without actually writing the formula yourself, use the AutoSum button on the Standard toolbar.

AutoSum can write sum and average numbers, count all entries, and display the maximum and minimum numbers in a range.

To use AutoSum, click a cell directly below a column of numbers you want to sum, then click the AutoSum button (shown in Figure 4.3).

Figure 4.3. The AutoSum button on the Standard toolbar

Make sure that the moving border surrounds the cells you want to sum (see Figure 4.4), and press Enter.

Novem	December		
1777	1221		
1282	2168		
2450	4207		
3649	4918		
3512	4565		
4588	2776		
3378	3738		
1462	3798		
2752	4930		
	=SUM(M3:M11)		
	SUM(**number1**, [number2], ...)		

Figure 4.4. The moving border surrounds the cells that will be summed.

Hack

AutoSum can write a formula anywhere and calculate any cells you select. Click the cell where you want the formula, click AutoSum, and then drag or Ctrl+click all the cells you want to calculate.

Sum is the function most people want to use with AutoSum (and it's the function most people use in a workbook), so the default calculation is sum. To use AutoSum with a different calculation, when you click the AutoSum button, click the arrow on the button and select a different function (see Figure 4.5).

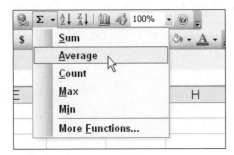

Figure 4.5. Change the AutoSum function.

Use the calculator

For calculations on the fly that don't require any worksheet data, use the Windows calculator (see Figure 4.6). You've probably seen and used the calculator—it's available in the Start ⇨ Programs ⇨ Accessories menu. The calculator is a plain-Jane sort and fairly limited, but its simplicity is what makes it convenient, and it's what I use when I want to calculate something simple without typing data into a worksheet.

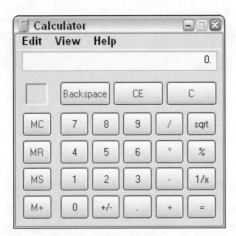

Figure 4.6. The Windows calculator

Inside Scoop

You can make the calculator much more high-tech by choosing View ⇨ Scientific (I leave it to you to understand the higher-level mathematics available there). By the way, if you want to do a quick square root, it's on the small Standard calculator, but not on the Scientific calculator.

You can open the calculator from an Excel toolbar button. Right-click in the toolbar area, click Customize, and click the Commands tab; in the Categories list, click Tools; in the Commands list, drag Custom (the one with the calculator icon) to your toolbar. Read more about toolbars and buttons in Chapter 21.

About cell references

A *cell reference* is the cell's address on the worksheet in terms of its column letter and row number. You can tell what any cell's reference is by either looking at the row and column that intersect at the cell or by selecting the cell and looking at the Name box (see Figure 4.7).

Name box

B4	▼	*fx*	3554
	A	B	C	D
1	Commissions for 2004			
2		Januar	Februa	March
3	Marcia	4913	3194	3650
4	Fred	3554	1006	4029
5	Lila	3098	4820	1032
6	Armelle	1894	4237	3333

Figure 4.7. The Name box shows the selected cell address or name.

If you click in the upper-left corner of the worksheet, the Name box reads A1, which is that cell's address: the combination of the column letter, which is A, and the row number, which is 1.

Inside Scoop

To reference an entire column, use the column letter, as in B:B for column B. To reference several columns, use the first and last column letters, as in B:D. Do the same to reference entire rows.

When you write formulas that include cells, the cells in the formula are identified by their references. For example, in Figure 4.8, the formula =A1+B1 sums the values in cells A1 and B1.

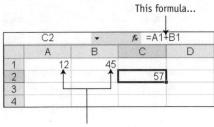

Figure 4.8. Formulas use cell references.

A *range* reference is a rectangular range of cells that are identified by the references of the range's upper-left corner cell and lower-right corner cell. The references are separated by a colon (:), as in the range reference A1:B6 (see Figure 4.9).

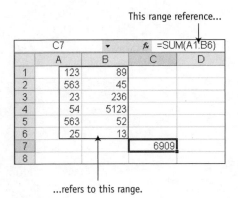

Figure 4.9. This SUM formula uses a range reference.

Cell reference types

Cells can have different types of references, depending on how you want to use them in the formula. First, I explain the terminology and how to create the different types; then I show you how they work with actual examples (at which point they'll make more sense).

For any cell, there is only one reference but four reference types: relative, absolute, and two mixed types. Dollar signs ($) in the reference determine the type:

- A1 is called relative.
- $A$1 is called absolute.
- $A1 and A$1 are called mixed.

An *absolute* cell reference is a fixed geographical point, like a street address, such as 123 Cherry Street.

A *relative* cell reference is a relative location, as in "one block west and two blocks south."

The *mixed* cell reference is a mixture of absolute and relative locations, as in "three blocks east on Hampden Avenue." A mixed cell reference can have an absolute column and relative row, as in $A1, or a relative column and absolute row, as in A$1.

The dollar signs designate the row and/or column as absolute, or unchanging, within a reference. When you write formulas, the meetings of absolute, relative, and mixed become more clear (see Figure 4.10).

Figure 4.10. The four reference types

Changing reference types

If you need to change a cell reference type in a formula, there's a much faster way than typing dollar signs ($).

The fastest way to change cell reference types is to cycle through the four types until you find the one you want: Double-click the cell containing the formula, and within the formula, click in the cell reference you want to change (see Figure 4.11). Press F4 until the reference changes to the type you want (pressing F4 repeatedly cycles through all the possible reference types).

When the reference type changes to the type you want, you can either click in another cell reference to change it or press Enter to finish.

Click in reference and press F4

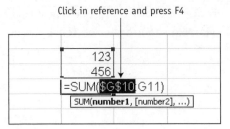

Figure 4.11. Open the cell, click in the reference (in the cell or in the Formula bar), press F4 to cycle, and press Enter.

Writing formulas

You'll probably need to do more calculations in your workbooks than AutoSum can do for you, which means learning how to write formulas.

Arithmetic operators

A simple formula might consist of adding, subtracting, multiplying, and dividing cells. Excel's arithmetic operators are detailed in Table 4.1.

Table 4.1. Arithmetic operators

Operator	Description
+ (plus sign)	Addition
– (minus sign)	Subtraction
* (asterisk)	Multiplication
/ (forward slash)	Division
^ (caret)	Exponentiation
() (parentheses)	To group operations, such as =(2+3)*4, which gives a different result than =2+3*4

Bright Idea

Here's a formula that uses arithmetic operators and a simple function to calculate the circumference of a circle, πr^2: =PI()*ref^2. Specify a cell in the *ref* argument and type the radius of the circle in that cell; then you can use this formula repeatedly by changing the radius entered in the *ref* cell.

Cell references versus static entries

Occasionally you'll want to write formulas that include a static (constant, not calculated) entry such as a sales tax rate or a product name, but it's more efficient to write formulas that only use cell references. For example, if you want to write a formula that totals prices and calculates sales tax, you can write a formula like =SUM(F6:F17)*.07, but when the tax rate changes, you must open all the formulas that use the sales tax rate and change it in every formula. However, if you put the tax rate in a cell and reference that cell in your formulas, you need only to change the tax rate in the cell, and all the formulas that reference the tax rate cell are instantly updated.

All formulas can calculate cells in the same worksheet, on different worksheets, and even in different workbooks (which links the workbooks and worksheets together).

Some simple formulas have to be written by you; there's no easy automatic feature to write them for you. But writing your own simple formulas is, well, simple. For example, a subtraction formula has to be written by you.

Simple formulas

To write a simple formula that calculates two cells (for example, subtracting one cell from another), click the cell where you want to display the results, type an equal sign (=), click one of the cells you want to use, type your arithmetic operator, click the second cell you want to use, and press Enter. The simple formula is entered, as shown in Figure 4.12.

When you build a formula by clicking cells and dragging ranges, the cells have relative references. What the formula in Figure 4.12 really does is subtract the cell *two cells above* from the cell *three cells above* the current

Watch Out!
Always click a cell to enter it in a formula; typing cell references is laborious and error prone.

Hack

You can quickly show all the formulas in a worksheet if you press Ctrl+` (the grave accent on the same key as the tilde (~). Press Ctrl+` again to hide the formulas.

cell because of the relative references. The advantages and disadvantages of using relative references become clear when you copy formula cells to a new location.

	D5	▼	ƒ*x*	=D3-D2	
	A	B	C	D	E
1					
2			Start Date	2/7/2005	
3			Finish Date	3/18/2005	
4					
5			Days to complete	39	
6					
7					
8			This cell is formatted		
9			General to show the		
10			difference between the		
11			date serial numbers.		
12					
13					

Figure 4.12. This formula subtracts one date (in cell D2) from another date (in cell D3) to how the number of days between; there's no quick automated tool for subtraction.

Moving and copying formulas

You use all the same techniques for moving and copying formula cells as for nonformula cells, but sometimes with different results.

When you *move* a formula cell, the formula moves intact and the cell references stay the same regardless of the reference types of the input cells. But when you *copy* a formula cell, bad things can happen if you're not prepared for them (see Figure 4.13).

Copy a formula cell

When you copy formulas, the reference type comes into play. Absolute references do not adjust when you copy a formula; they always calculate the same input cells.

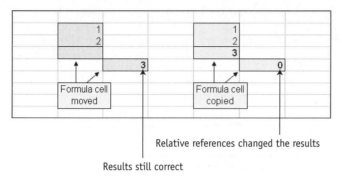

Figure 4.13. Moving and copying cells with relative references

Relative references, on the other hand, give the input cells' locations relative to the formula cell, and when you copy a formula cell to a new location, relative references continue to refer to locations relative to the formula cell. This behavior is quite handy when you expect it, and frustrating if you aren't aware of it.

To copy a formula cell with relative references and keep the formula intact, change the references to absolute before you copy the cell. You can also open the cell, drag to select the formula, copy the formula, press Enter to close the cell, and then paste the copied formula in a different cell, but changing the references is less work and more permanent.

If you want to use the same formula with relative references elsewhere in the workbook or worksheet (for example, to use the same formula in another similar table), copy the cell and paste it in the new location.

Copy with AutoFill

Most often you'll want the relative references to do their job and change the copied formula to suit its new location. For example, when you set up a Quantity column and a Price column and then want to multiply the quantities by the prices for a total price in each row, just write your formula one time at the top of the total column, and click and drag the AutoFill handle down the column to fill the formula cells (see Figure 4.14). If you

Bright Idea

The best way to keep cell references intact and also easily identifiable is to use cell names.

Bright Idea

If you want a formula to calculate one changing cell with one unchanging cell, such as the cells in a Price column and an unchanging TaxRate cell, write the formula quickly with relative references and then change the TaxRate cell reference to absolute. Better yet, name the TaxRate cell.

double-click the Fill handle, the formula or cell entry is filled all the way down the column until there's no entry in the cell to the left.

Formulas copied with AutoFill adjust themselves so that every relative reference refers to the correct cell relative to the formula cell (the relative references do the adjusting).

	A	B	C	D	E	F
1	Coffee Orders for December 2004					
2	Date	Product	Price/lb	Lbs	Total	
3	12/2/04	Santo Domingo	9.50	100	950.00	
4	12/2/04	Antigua	10.50	100	1,050.00	
5	12/4/04	Antigua	10.50	200	2,100.00	
6	12/4/04	Antigua	10.50	150		
7	12/4/04	Antigua	10.50	45		
8	12/4/04	Santo Domingo	9.50	55		
9	12/5/04	Kona	9.25	90		
10	12/5/04	Kona	9.25	80		

Fill handle

Figure 4.14. Click and drag or double-click the Fill handle to copy the formula down the column.

Linking worksheets and workbooks

You can write formulas that reference cells in other worksheets or workbooks; those formulas *link* the worksheets or workbooks.

Formulas that link worksheets

It's a great convenience to be able to write a formula on one worksheet that calculates cells on a different worksheet. For example, I often transcribe client lists of household goods and their replacement values for insurance claims, and the very long list is on one worksheet while the very short summary list is on a second worksheet (which eliminates scrolling to see the totals).

Hack

If you only need to display a value from a different worksheet, start the formula with =, then click the cell on the other worksheet that you want to display and press Enter.

To write a formula that includes a cell on another worksheet, click the sheet tab and click the cell (the sheet name and cell reference are entered in the formula, as shown in Figure 4.15). Click the original sheet tab to return to the original worksheet and continue the formula, or press Enter to finish the formula and return to the original worksheet.

J5	▾		*fx* =SUM(J3,Sheet3!C5)	
	G	H	I	J	K
2					
3				$ 12,000	
4					
5				$ 26,000	
6					

Figure 4.15. This formula references a cell on another worksheet — Sheet3, cell C5.

Formulas that link workbooks

You can also write formulas that calculate cells in other workbooks. For example, if you have workbooks that represent sales from different districts, you can write a formula in another workbook that sums values from the district workbooks.

To write a formula that links workbooks, open all the workbooks in multiple windows, arranged so you have quick access to each of them. Begin the formula with =, write your formula and click the cell in each workbook to include it in the formula, and finish by pressing Enter. Each referenced cell is identified by workbook name, sheet name, and cell address, as shown in Figure 4.16.

J5	▾		*fx* =SUM(J3,'[Quarterly sales.xls]Qtr 1'!$C$71		
	G	H	I	J	K	L
2						
3				$ 12,000		
4						
5				$155,703		
6						
7						

Figure 4.16. This formula references a cell in another workbook — Quarterly Sales.xls, sheet Qtr 1, cell C71.

Inside Scoop

If you open a source workbook while the dependent workbook is open, the linking formula automatically recalculates with the current data in the source workbook. This is faster than waiting for recalculation from a closed workbook.

The workbook with the formula is called a *dependent* workbook, because it depends on input from other workbooks. The input workbooks are called *source* workbooks because they are the data source for the linking formulas.

Each time you open a dependent workbook, you are asked if you want to update it with linked information from the other workbooks. Click Yes to update the linked formulas with current data in the other workbooks; click No to keep the current values or if you don't want to wait for the data to be updated.

If you want to break the link so you can keep the current value and not be prompted with the update question, replace the formula with a static value by copying and pasting values. See Chapter 3 to learn more about pasting values.

Using cell names

Cell names make formulas easier to read because the cells to which they refer are quickly and easily identified (for example, the formula =Subtotal+Tax is easier to understand than =G19+G20). Also, cell names keep cell formulas intact when the formulas reference cell names because cell names are always created with absolute references.

Naming cells

There are a few ways to name cells, the easiest being the Name box and the Create Names dialog box. Each method is most convenient in particular situations.

Bright Idea

Always use some capital letters in a name, because when you type a name in lowercase letters and Excel recognizes the name, the name is switched to its official capitalization. However, if you misspell the name, it won't be capitalized, and that's often a clue to the error you get.

No matter what method you use to name cells, names must follow certain rules:

- Names must start with a letter or an underscore character (_).

- No spaces are allowed. For multiword names, use an underscore or, better yet, use initial capital letters to separate words, as in LastName. Names are not case sensitive, so if you type the name in a formula, you don't have to type the capital letters; however, the initial capitals make the name easier to read.

- Don't use periods. They're allowed, but they may interfere with VBA programming code.

- Keep names shorter than 255 characters (which is too long to be practical, anyway).

- Do not use hyphens or other punctuations marks (if Excel doesn't let you create a name, a punctuation mark may be the problem).

The Name box

The Name box, located on the left end of the Formula bar, is the fastest way to name a range or a single cell.

To name a cell or range with the Name box, select the cell or range you want to name, click in the Name box (see Figure 4.17), type the name, and press Enter.

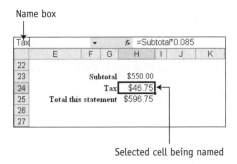

Figure 4.17. Click in the Name box, type a name, and press Enter.

Using the Name box, you can name cells and ranges that have no identifying headings on the worksheet.

No matter what method you use to name cells and ranges, the names appear in the Name box list when you click the arrow next to the Name box. Click the arrow and click a name to select the named range.

The Create Names dialog box

If the names you want to use are already headings in a table or labels for specific cells (such as Total or TaxRate), the fastest way to name the cells to which the labels refer is the Create Names dialog box. The Create Names dialog box not only uses existing names (no typing), but it can also create several names at once (for example, it can name all the columns in a table using the table headings).

To name cells with the Create Names dialog box (shown in Figure 4.18), select the range you want to name (including the headings or labels), then choose Insert ⇨ Name ⇨ Create. Select or deselect the check boxes as needed so that the correct headings or labels are used, and click OK.

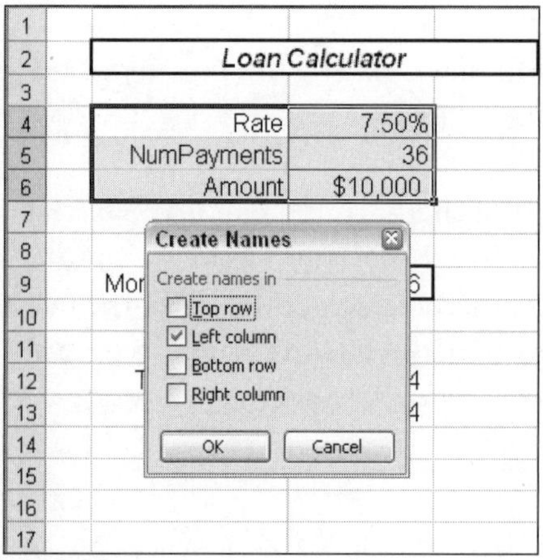

Figure 4.18. The Create Names dialog box

The names are created, and you can select any of the named ranges by clicking its name in the Name box list.

The Define Name dialog box

The Define Name dialog box is not a good choice for naming cells (it's too laborious), but it's the only way you can name constant values and formulas, edit the definition of an existing name, or delete a name.

To define a name for a constant value (for example, a tax rate), choose Insert ⇨ Name ⇨ Define. Type the name (for example, TaxRate) in the Names in workbook box (shown in Figure 4.19); then select and delete everything in the Refers to box (including =), and type =*your value* (for example, =0.75). Click OK (not Close).

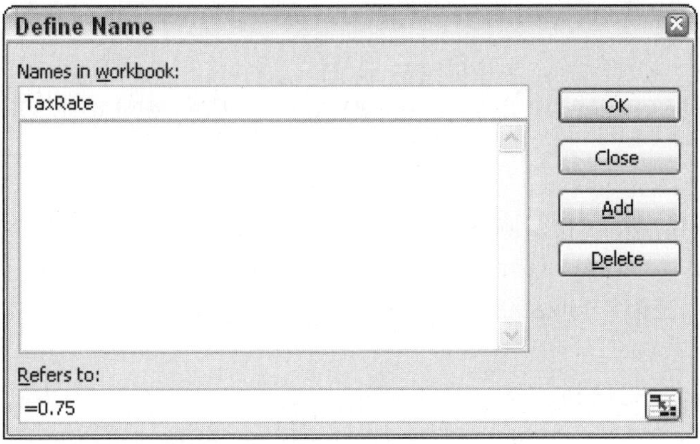

Figure 4.19. The Define Name dialog box

Why would you want to define a tax rate in a named constant value instead of a named cell? Because it doesn't appear in the worksheet, yet it is available to formulas throughout the workbook and all formulas can be updated by editing the named constant value.

To define a name for a formula (for example, a long, complex formula with multiple nested segments), choose Insert ⇨ Name ⇨ Define (shown in Figure 4.20). Type the name (for example, InvoiceNumber) in the Names in workbook box; then select and delete everything in the Refers to box (including =). Type =*your formula* (for example, =LEFT(A3,3)&"-"&RIGHT(H5,4)). Click OK (not Close).

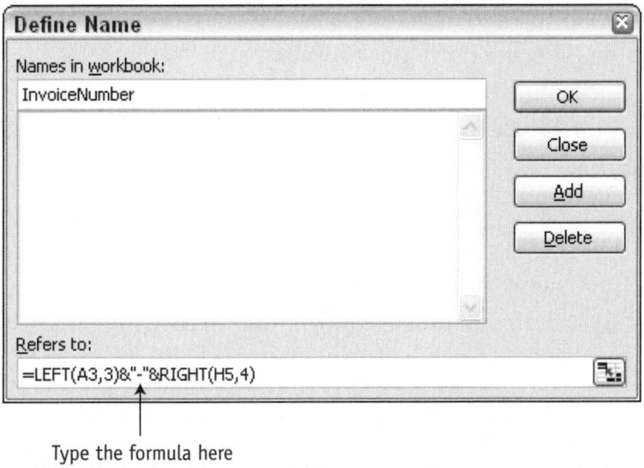

Type the formula here

Figure 4.20. Defining a formula name

Inside Scoop

You won't see formula or constant names in the Name box or the Apply Names dialog box, but you can type them in formulas (so use easily remembered names).

To use a named formula in a cell, type = and the formula name (as shown in Figure 4.21). If the formula is complex and you use it more than once a year, naming it saves a lot of time.

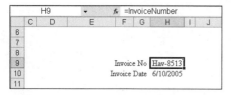

Figure 4.21. Using a named formula in a cell

Edit names

Regardless of the method by which you create a name, you can find it in the Define Name dialog box. Sometimes I want to edit a range name just to add an extra row or column; instead of deleting the existing name and naming the new range, I take the fast route and edit the existing name.

To edit a name, choose Insert ⇨ Name ⇨ Define. In the Define Name dialog box, shown in Figure 4.22, click the name you want to edit in the Names in workbook box, and edit the reference, formula, or constant value in the Refers to box. Press Enter (not Close).

Be careful not to disturb the exclamation point (!), dollar sign ($), or colon (:) marks or you'll break the name and probably have to delete and re-create the name.

Delete names

You must use the Define Name dialog box to delete names, and lest you think this is unnecessary, I dare you to try to figure out what's going on in

Hack

If you want to keep a name definition but change the name, you must add the new name and delete the old. The safest way is to select the old name and type a different name in the Names in workbook box, then click Add, then select the old name and click Delete.

a workbook with lots of formulas and 85 named ranges, many of them duplicates! (I had to do that for a client once, and it was not fun.) Names live on long after the data is deleted.

To delete a name, choose Insert ⇨ Name ⇨ Define. In the Define Name dialog box, click the name you want to delete and click Delete, then click OK or Close (either button works).

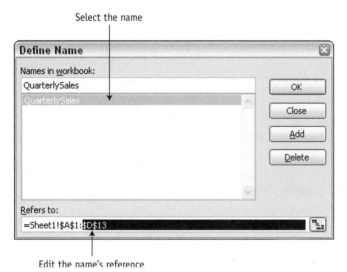

Figure 4.22. Edit a name in the Define Name dialog box.

Using names in formulas

To use a name in a formula, type the name wherever the formula calls for the cell or range reference (see Figure 4.23). If you used at least one capital letter in the name (a very good idea), you can type the name in lowercase letters. When Excel recognizes the name, the letters are switched to their original capitalization. If you misspell the name, Excel won't recognize it. You get an error, and the lack of capitalization tells you that the name is misspelled.

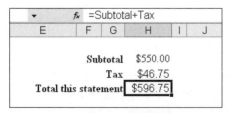

Figure 4.23. Type the name in place of a reference in a formula.

> **Inside Scoop**
>
> If you want to remember what all of your names refer to without slogging through the Define Name dialog box, you can paste a list of all the workbook names and their definitions onto a worksheet. Click a cell, choose Insert ⇨ Name ⇨ Paste, and click the Paste List button.

You can type defined names in formulas as you write them, or in the Function Arguments dialog box (covered in Chapter 5).

Paste names

If you can't remember the name, or it's a long name, you can use the Paste Name dialog box to paste the name into the formula.

To paste names into a formula, start the formula, and place the insertion point where you want to insert the name. Choose Insert ⇨ Name ⇨ Paste, click the name, and then click OK (see Figure 4.24).

If you don't mind memorizing another keystroke, it's faster to click in the reference you want to replace with a name and then press F3 to open the Paste Names dialog box.

Figure 4.24. Paste names instead of typing them.

Apply names

If you've already written formulas using normal cell references instead of named cells, you can quickly change all the named cell references in a worksheet into their names. Select the range of cells that contain formulas (as many cells as you like, including cells that don't contain formulas), and choose Insert ⇨ Name ⇨ Apply. Click every name you want to apply and then click OK (see Figure 4.25).

You can even name cells after you write the formulas and apply those names to the formulas that have cell references.

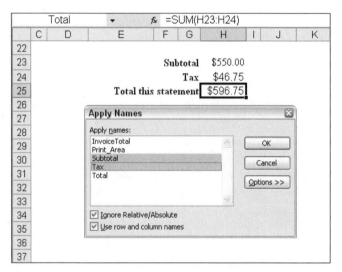

Figure 4.25. Apply names to replace references in formulas.

Named ranges and apply names

When you create names in a table using the table headings as range names, and then AutoFill or otherwise copy a formula that references the cells in those named ranges *and* then apply names to the formulas, what you get is a column of formulas that all look the same.

For example, a Total column has formulas that multiply a Price column by a Quantity column, and the Price and Quantity columns are named ranges. The formulas in the Total column all read =Price*Quantity.

Each formula is using the cells in the named range that are in its own row, so the formulas are correct, even if it's unnerving that they all look the same.

Editing formulas

You can easily change a formula in any way (function, arithmetic operators, referenced cells, or constant values, which pretty much covers everything).

To edit a formula, double-click the cell and select and replace whatever needs changing, as shown in Figure 4.26. Press Enter to finish your edits.

SUMIF	▾ ✕ ✓ ƒ×	=SUM(C2:C6)/B2				
	A	B	C	D	E	F	G
1							
2		10	12				
3			23		=SUM(C2:		
4			55				
5			54		Cell and range references		
6			23		are colored to match		
7					colored borders around the		
8					referenced cells and		
9					ranges in the worksheet		
10							
11							

Figure 4.26. You can edit a formula in the cell or in the Formula bar.

Editing a formula is often easier if you click the cell and do your editing in the Formula bar. Depending on your worksheet font, the formula in the Formula bar is nearly always easier to read and use your mouse in.

Easy ways to change parts of a formula are as follows:

- To replace a referenced cell, double-click the reference to select it, then click the replacement cell in the worksheet.

- To replace a range, double-click and drag over both references (to select the whole range), and then drag to select the replacement range in the worksheet.

- To replace a constant value or arithmetic operator, select the character(s) and type a replacement.

Bright Idea

If you want to replace a cell reference with a different cell reference, don't type the new reference; instead, double-click the old reference and then click the new reference cell on the worksheet.

Watch Out!

Be careful not to click other cells unintentionally while a cell is open for editing, because those unintentional cells are added to your formula. If you inadvertently add other cells to your formula, press Esc to back out of the cell with no changes, and start again.

Tracing a formula

In some worksheets, formulas reference other formulas that reference still other formulas. When you need to dig into a complicated worksheet to understand its architecture, Excel has tools to help you.

The process of tracing formulas is called *auditing*, and there's a toolbar with buttons that do the work. But first, you should understand the terminology of auditing formulas:

- A *precedent* cell is an input cell referenced in the formula you're auditing.

- A dependent cell is a cell that uses the results of the formula you're auditing.

To trace a formula, right-click in the toolbar area and click Formula Auditing to show the Formula Auditing toolbar. Then click the cell with the formula you want to trace (see Figure 4.27). Then:

- To trace precedents, click the Trace Precedents button. The first level back is shown by blue lines that connect the formula cell to all its input cells. Click the Trace Precedents button again to trace the next level back, and continue clicking the Trace Precedents button until no new blue lines appear.

- To trace dependents, click the Trace Dependents button. The first level forward is shown by blue lines that connect the formula cell to all its dependent cells. Click the Trace Dependents button again to trace the next level forward, and continue clicking the Trace Dependents button until no new blue lines appear.

To erase the precedent or dependent lines one generation at a time, click the Remove Precedent Arrows button and the Remove Dependent Arrows button. To remove all the lines so you can trace another cell, click the Remove All Arrows button.

Bright Idea

To see the immediate precedent cells for a formula, double-click the formula cell. The cell references in the open cell are colored; the colors correspond to the colored outlines around the referenced cells and ranges. Press Enter or Esc to close the cell without changing the formula.

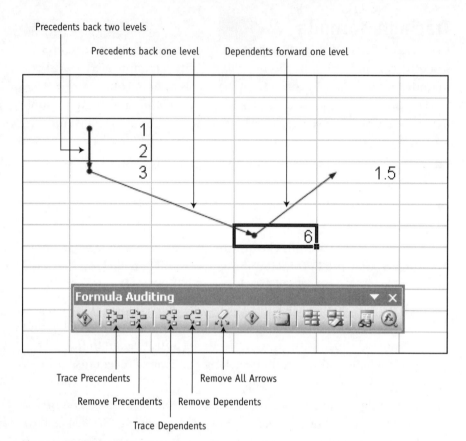

Figure 4.27. Tracing a formula

Locating worksheet errors

Errors and invalid data seem to sneak into even the most scrupulously designed and maintained worksheets. You can find them with the help of a few tools on the Formula Auditing toolbar. If you see an error, refer to Table 4.2, which provides a list of what the errors mean and how to fix them.

To show the Formula Auditing toolbar, right-click in the toolbar area and click Formula Auditing.

Table 4.2. Error values

This error	Usually means this	To fix it, do this
#####	The column isn't wide enough to display the value.	Widen the column.
#VALUE!	Wrong type of argument, value, or cell reference (for example, calculating a cell with the error value #N/A).	Check values, references, and arguments; make sure references are valid.
#DIV/0!	Formula is attempting to divide by zero or by an empty cell.	Change the value or cell reference so the formula doesn't divide by zero.
#NAME?	Formula is referencing an invalid or nonexistent name.	Make sure the name still exists or correct the misspelling.
#N/A	Usually means no value is available or inappropriate arguments were used.	In a lookup formula, make sure the lookup table is sorted correctly.
#REF!	Excel can't locate the referenced cells (for example, if referenced cells are deleted).	Click Undo immediately to restore references, and then change formula references or convert formulas to values.
#NUM!	Incorrect use of a number (such as SQRT(-1), which is not possible), or formula result is a number too large or too small to be displayed.	Make sure that the arguments are correct, and that the result is between $-1*10^{307}$ and $1*10^{307}$.
#NULL!	Reference to intersection of two areas that do not intersect.	Check for typing and reference errors.
Circular reference message	The formula refers to itself, either directly or indirectly.	Click OK in the message; look at the Status bar to see which cell contains the circular reference, and remove references to the formula cell.

Locating errors in formulas

On the Formula Auditing toolbar (shown in Figure 4.28), click the Error Checking button. The tool checks all cells in the worksheet for any sign of an error (and picks up things that aren't errors, such as numbers deliberately preceded by an apostrophe to make them text).

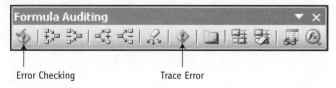

Figure 4.28. The Formula Auditing toolbar

If a perceived error is located, the Error Checking dialog box appears and tells you what it thinks the error is. You can use any of the helpful buttons to understand and fix the error; if you know the error is not an error, click Ignore Error to continue the check.

If you have an error value displayed on the worksheet (see Table 4-2 to see what error values look like), you can open the Formula Auditing toolbar, click in the error cell, and click the Trace Error button. Sometimes the error is not in the cell itself, but is in a precedent cell. The Trace Error button finds what it thinks is the culprit input cell. It might or might not help you, but you still have to fix the error yourself after it's found, using Table 4-2 as a reference.

Then again, you may never need to trace errors, because Excel tries to catch your errors as you enter them. If you enter an alleged error, such as a number with an apostrophe first to make the number text, Excel pops a green triangle into the corner of the cell and when you click the cell you get an error button in the worksheet as well. You can click the error button for a shortcut menu that might or might not help. I think the green triangles are a useless intrusion and turn them off like this: Choose Tools ⇨ Options ⇨ Error Checking, and deselect the Enable background error checking check box.

Finding invalid data in a worksheet

If someone has entered invalid data into a worksheet in which data validation is in effect (see Chapter 3), you can locate the inaccuracies with the Circle Invalid Data button on the Formula Auditing toolbar. (Remember, when you set data validation, if you don't use the Stop style on the Error Alert tab, users can ignore your warnings and enter invalid data; see Chapter 3.)

To locate invalid data, on the Formula Auditing toolbar, click the Circle Invalid Data button. All entries that don't meet validation criteria are circled, as shown in Figure 4.29. You have to fix them yourself.

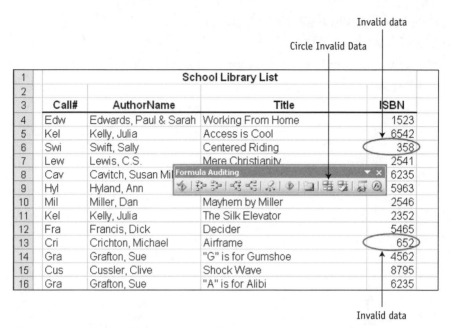

Figure 4.29. Circling invalid data in a data-validation range

If data validation was not set up before the invalid data was entered, you can set up validation after the fact and then run the Circle Invalid Data button to find the bad data.

Just the facts

- Use AutoCalculate for instant, on-the-fly calculations and AutoSum to write fast, simple formulas.

- Relative cell references change when you copy formula cells.

- Absolute cell references never change, even when you move or copy formula cells.

- Change reference types by clicking in the reference and pressing F4 to cycle through the four types.

- Move and copy formula cells with the same methods you use to move and copy nonformula cells, but watch out for reference types.

- Use cell names for easy-to-understand formulas and stable cell references.

- Edit formulas by double-clicking to edit in the cell, or clicking to edit in the Formula bar.

- Locate errors and invalid data with the buttons on the Formula Auditing toolbar.

GET THE SCOOP ON...
Using functions ▪ Common and useful functions ▪
Combining functions for more power

All About Functions

N ot all calculations are simple. Fortunately, Excel can handle tremendously complex calculations for you by using *functions*.

Functions are built-in formulas that perform complex math; in fact, many functions perform math that's not possible by using arithmetic operators alone. Most of the formulas you need on a routine basis depend on functions, and some, such as AVERAGE, can prevent serious miscalculations.

Functions can do a lot more than just math, however. They can look up data in another location, calculate cells only if they meet a specific criteria, combine the contents of two or more cells, tell you what a payment will be for a specific loan, and tell you what the largest and smallest values in a range are (and even format a range to make the largest value stand out in a different color; more about that in Chapter 6). And as useful as functions are when they work alone, they get really powerful when you combine them with other functions.

Using functions

Excel comes with a slew of functions — some you'll use all the time, and some you'll only be interested in if you're an electrical engineer or nuclear physicist.

Functions have specific names, like SUM or AVERAGE or BETADIST, that must be spelled correctly or Excel won't

Inside Scoop

If you create cell names, Excel automatically uses the cell name instead of the reference when you use the cell in a formula.

recognize them; however, Excel provides dialog boxes that do the spelling for you and help you fill in the arguments each function requires.

Each function has a name and a set of parentheses. The parentheses enclose *arguments*, the information the function needs to perform its special calculation. Every opening parenthesis must have a closing parenthesis (which is easy in simple functions, but gets interesting when the formula combines and nests functions, each of which have their own parenthetical sets).

Some functions are so simple that they have an empty set of parentheses, such as the =NOW() function, which returns the current time with no further input from you. Other functions have arguments so arcane that, unless you use the function daily, you probably won't remember them; in those cases, you should use the Function Wizard.

To use the Function Wizard, click the cell for the formula and then click the Insert Function button on the Formula bar (the icon reads *fx*) to open the Insert Function dialog box (see Figure 5.1).

If you know which function you want, select a category in the Or select a category list box; then scroll through the function names in the Select a function list. When you click a function name, a description of the function appears below the list; if you want to know more, click the Help on this function link. When you' decide on a function, select it in the Select a function list and click OK.

A dialog box specific to your function appears (see Figure 5.2), and you get copious help with each argument, as well as displays of argument and function results as you build the function.

Bright Idea

Always type function names in all lowercase letters. If the name is spelled correctly, Excel uppercases it; if it's misspelled, you get an error and the still-lowercase name tells you why.

Inside Scoop

Instead of scrolling through a long list of function names, click in the Select a function list and type the first letter of the function name. The list jumps to the alphabetical point where the letter you typed begins.

Select a function

Get help

Figure 5.1. Use the Insert Function dialog box for help with functions.

Collapse/Expand icons

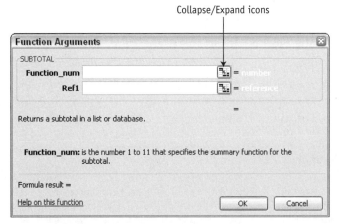

Figure 5.2. The Function Arguments dialog box tells you what to enter in each argument.

Bright Idea

If you know the name of the formula but want help with the arguments, here's a faster way to get it: Type =, the function name, and the opening parenthesis, then click the Insert Function button. The Insert Function dialog box opens directly to your function.

In many arguments, you'll want to select a range of cells. Don't type them; either drag the dialog box out of the way or click the Collapse/Expand icon at the right end of the argument box, and then drag to select your range on the worksheet. To redisplay the dialog box after dragging the range, click the Collapse/Expand icon (at the right end of the argument box) again.

As you add arguments, the cumulative formula result is displayed near the lower-left corner of the dialog box. If you enter an inappropriate argument, the dialog box tells you so next to the argument box. When you're finished, as always, click OK. The current Function Wizard experience is really very efficient and helpful, even to Excel old-timers.

Of course, you don't have to use the Function Wizard. To write a formula using a function you know how to use (such as SUM, which requires only a range of cells entered into its single argument), click the cell where you want the formula, type =, and type the sum name with arguments between parentheses. Again, don't type cell and range references if you don't need to; make sure the insertion point is in place between the parentheses, and drag to select the range on the worksheet. (I talk about SUM functions a little later in this chapter.)

Common and useful functions

In this section, I cover the most common and useful functions, and situations in which they are useful (the situations I present should give you a jumping-off point for adapting them to your own needs). This is by no means an exhaustive list of functions; you can find exhaustive lists in many encyclopedic tomes about Excel.

Bright Idea

When you use a function for the first time, test it to be sure it calculates accurately before using it in real data. Test it with *mock data* (phony numbers) that consists of short text entries and round numbers so you can do the math in your head and know quickly whether you're getting what you want.

AVERAGE

The AVERAGE function is a common and easy-to-write function for which you don't need the Function Wizard.

To write an AVERAGE formula, type =average(*range*), and either drag to select a range reference or type a range name in the function argument. (Remember to type the function name in lowercase.)

The difference between the AVERAGE function and the paper-and-pencil method of summing cells and dividing by the number of cells is displayed in Figure 5.3. If the range of cells you sum and divide by contains any blank cells, the average value is wrong (a blank cell is added as zero), while the AVERAGE function ignores blank cells so you get a true average.

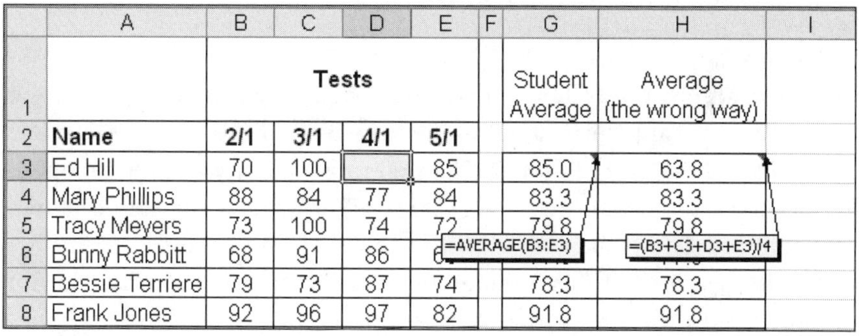

	A	B	C	D	E	F	G	H	I
1			Tests				Student Average	Average (the wrong way)	
2	Name	2/1	3/1	4/1	5/1				
3	Ed Hill	70	100		85		85.0	63.8	
4	Mary Phillips	88	84	77	84		83.3	83.3	
5	Tracy Meyers	73	100	74	72		79.8	79.8	
6	Bunny Rabbitt	68	91	86		=AVERAGE(B3:E3)		=(B3+C3+D3+E3)/4	
7	Bessie Terriere	79	73	87	74		78.3	78.3	
8	Frank Jones	92	96	97	82		91.8	91.8	

Figure 5.3. The AVERAGE function is the safest way to get an accurate average.

In Excel 2003, you don't need to write an AVERAGE function at all unless you want to use it in combination with another function or another Excel feature, because you can use the AVERAGE calculation in the AutoSum button list of functions.

SUM functions

There are three common and useful functions that sum data: SUM, which does simple arithmetic addition; SUMIF, which sums cells according to criteria you set; and SUBTOTAL, which sums only the visible cells in a filtered list. For each function, there are circumstances in which that function is most appropriate.

SUM

The SUM function is universally useful; so much so that Microsoft created several ways to invoke it. But you'll probably have occasion to include it in combined formulas, so you should be familiar with writing your own function and arguments.

To write a SUM formula yourself, type =sum(*range*), as shown in Figure 5.4.

Click and drag cells and ranges to add them to the formula

SUMIF	▾ ✕ ✓ ƒx	=sum(D1:D2)		
	A	B	C	D	E
1				54	
2				35	
3				=sum(D1:D2)	
4					

Figure 5.4. To write your own formula, type it and press Enter.

If the range you select is named, you'll be pleasantly surprised to see the range name appear in the argument instead of the range reference. But instead of dragging to select a named range, after you type the opening parenthesis, choose Insert ⇨ Name ⇨ Paste, click the range name, and then OK. Then type your closing parenthesis and press Enter.

Remember that you can change a reference type by clicking in the reference and pressing F4 to cycle through the types.

As with the AVERAGE function, you don't need to write a SUM function at all unless you want to use it in combination with another function or another Excel feature, because you can use the AutoSum button.

SUMIF

The SUMIF function sums values in a column if they correspond to a criterion in another column. For example, a list of monthly coffee sales of different types appears in Figure 5.5. I want to know how much Kona coffee was sold that month, so I use the SUMIF formula to sum only the Kona sales.

Inside Scoop

Although you can put the SUMIF formula anywhere on the worksheet, it's usually handier near the top of the table.

If you start with the Function Wizard, you'll find the SUMIF function in the Math & Trig and All categories, but save yourself time and start by typing =sumif(and then clicking the Insert Function button.

▾ X √ ƒx	=SUMIF(B3:B56,"Kona",E3:E56)							
B	C	D	E	F	G	H	I
Orders for December 2004							
Product	Price/lb	Lbs	Total				
Santo Domingo	9.50	100	950.00		=SUMIF(B3:B56,"Kona",E3:E56)		
Antigua	10.50	100	1,050.00				
Antigua	10.50	200	2,100.00				
Antigua							
Antigua							
Santo Domingo							
Kona							
Kona							
Santo Domingo							
Santo Domingo							
Coatepec							
Antigua							
Chanchamayo							
Santo Domingo							
Coatepec							
Coatepec							
Santo Domingo							
Santo Domingo	9.50	60	570.00				

Function Arguments ⊠

SUMIF

Range B3:B56 = {"Santo Domingo";"A

Criteria "Kona" = "Kona"

Sum_range E3:E56 = {950;1050;2100;157

= 8186.25

Adds the cells specified by a given condition or criteria.

Sum_range are the actual cells to sum. If omitted, the cells in range are used.

Formula result =   8186.25

Help on this function   [OK]   [Cancel]

Figure 5.5. The SUMIF function sums the sales of a specific coffee in the list.

In the Range argument, drag to select the column that contains the criteria (in this case, the coffee names). If you name the table columns with the Create Names dialog box, you can type or paste the column name here instead.

Bright Idea

A better alternative to typing the criterion name is to enter a cell reference in the Criteria box; then you can enter a criterion name in the referenced cell to change the formula criteria without editing the formula. (You'll have a formula error until you enter a product name in the criteria reference cell.)

Bright Idea

If you used a cell reference instead of a string entry in the Criteria argument, label or format that cell somehow (with a border or color) so you don't lose track of your criteria entry cell.

In the Criteria argument, type the name of the criterion (in this case, the name "Kona") with quotation marks around it to tell Excel it's a string.

In the Sum_range box, drag to select the column with the numbers to be summed, in this case the Total column. Again, if you name the column, you can type or paste the column name here instead.

The Function Arguments dialog box shows you the results of the formula; if it looks right, click OK.

If you entered a cell reference in the Criteria argument, enter the name of an item to be summed in that cell; then enter a different name, and watch the SUMIF function do its magic.

The Conditional Sum Wizard

There is a feature called the Conditional Sum Wizard that is entirely too mysterious and time consuming to use for a single-criteria sum, but it is really the only way to do a multiple-criteria sum, such as summing sales for a particular item and in a specific geographical region.

The Conditional Sum Wizard is an add-in and is not likely to be installed in your computer just yet. To install it, choose Tools ⇨ Add-Ins, select the Conditional Sum Wizard check box, and click OK.

When the Conditional Sum Wizard is installed, choose Tools ⇨ Conditional Sum. Walk through the wizard a few times to get to know it. There's not much in the way of help, because although it was trumpeted as a wonderful new feature in a previous version of Excel, it never really caught on.

SUBTOTAL

Yet another useful member of the SUM family is the SUBTOTAL function. The biggest advantage to using the SUBTOTAL function is that it calculates only the visible cells in a list. Here's the problem: If you filter a list and use the SUM function to sum numbers, the SUM function sums all the numbers in the list, including the hidden numbers. That's rarely what you want (as shown in Figure 5.6). However, the SUBTOTAL function calculates only the numbers displayed by the filter (and it's what Microsoft incorporated in the Total row in its new dynamic lists for this very reason).

	E59	▼		*fx*	=SUBTOTAL(9,E4:E58)			
	A	B	C	D	E	F	G	H
1		Coffee Orders for December 2004						
3	Date▼	Product ▼	Price/l▼	Lb▼	Total ▼	Total ▼		
16	12/8/04	Chanchamayo	11.00	200	2,200.00	2200.00		
22	12/9/04	Chanchamayo	11.00	200	2,200.00	2200.00		
31	12/13/04	Chanchamayo	11.00	200	2,200.00	2200.00		
39	12/19/04	Chanchamayo	11.00	200	2,200.00	2200.00		
44	12/21/04	Chanchamayo	11.00	200	2,200.00	2200.00		
52	12/26/04	Chanchamayo	11.00	200	2,200.00	2200.00		
58								
59					$13,200.00	$67,132.50	Total Sales	
60								
61								
62				=SUBTOTAL(9,E4:E58)		=SUM(F4:F57)		
63				This formula sums only		This formula also		
64				visible cells		sums hidden cells		
65								

Figure 5.6. The SUBTOTAL function ignores cells hidden by a filter.

To write a SUBTOTAL function yourself, type =subtotal(*function number,range*). The *function number* is the number that specifies the calculation function (see Table 5.1); the *range* is the range of values you want to calculate. Use the Function Wizard until the function is familiar.

The SUBTOTAL function can calculate 11 different functions, depending on the arguments you enter. The function arguments are not intuitively numbered — the SUM function is number 9, and I only know that offhand because I've used it for so many years — and while it would be nice if Microsoft would list the function arguments' numbers for us right in the SUBTOTAL dialog box, it never has. You can either click the Help on this function link in the SUBTOTAL dialog box or look up the function number in Table 5.1.

Inside Scoop

The new help file for SUBTOTAL is incorrect. The old arguments, listed in Table 5.1, do indeed ignore hidden values in a filtered list; the new arguments (the old arguments plus 100, such as 109 for SUM) also ignore values hidden by manually hiding columns and rows, which is not as common as filtering.

Inside Scoop

If you use the AutoSum button to write a SUM formula while a list is filtered, you get a SUBTOTAL function instead. More about filtering in Chapter 8.

Table 5.1. SUBTOTAL function arguments

This argument	Performs this calculation
1	AVERAGE
2	COUNT
3	COUNTA
4	MAX
5	MIN
6	PRODUCT
7	STDEV
8	STDEVP
9	SUM
10	VAR
11	VARP

MAX and MIN

The MAX and MIN functions find the maximum and minimum values in a range, respectively. The functions are written =MAX(*range*) and =MIN(*range*).

I'm a big fan of combining Excel's features to get an extraordinary result. A really useful way to use these formulas is in a conditional format, so that within a range of data, perhaps a table of monthly sales commissions for several employees for the year, the single largest and smallest values have colorful formatting that makes them stand out in the sea of numbers, as shown in Figure 5.7. That's much better than a maximum or minimum value sitting in a cell on its own.

I teach you about conditional formatting in Chapter 7.

D14	▼		*ƒx* =MAX(Commissions)					
	A	B	C	D	E	F	G	H	I

	A	B	C	D	E	F	G	H	I
1		Commissions for 2005							
2		Jan	Feb	Mar	Apr	May	Jun		
3	Marcia	4913	3194	3650	2592	1330	3002		
4	Fred	3554	*1006*	4029	2430	1635	4508		
5	Lila	3098	4820	1032	2628	4213	1951		
6	Armelle	1894	4237	3333	3256	2382	2486		
7	Jamie	3423	4609	3707	2441	2896	1327		
8	Tracy	3266	1621	2873	3526	2622	2148		
9	Susannah	2366	2445	4514	4753	4505	*4934*		
10	Tina	4578	2963	2982	1522	2067 ▲	3944		
11	Diane	3217	1248	4004	3449	4563	4542		
12									
13									
14	Highest single month			4934 ◄					
15	Lowest single month			1006					
16						The formula cells and the MAX			
17						and MIN values in the table			
18						share the same formatting			

Figure 5.7. The MAX and MIN formulas, used with conditional formatting

COUNT functions

There are several COUNT functions, but only three are commonly used, and, of course, they are most valuable when used in conjunction with other functions.

COUNT counts the number of cells in a range that contains numbers; to write it, type =count(*range*).

COUNTA counts all the cells in a range that are not empty, regardless of what they contain; to write it, type =counta(*range*).

COUNT and COUNTA are functions I use as arguments in other functions, such as the dynamic OFFSET function described later in this chapter. They can also be used alone, as shown in Figure 5.8.

COUNTIF is similar to the SUMIF function. It counts the number of cells in a range that meet specific criteria. To write it, type =countif(*range,criteria*). The *range* argument can be a range reference or a range name; the *criteria* argument can be a text string enclosed in quotes,

Watch Out!

Even though they have the same names, the count functions are not equivalent in different Excel features. In AutoSum, the Count calculation counts number cells; in AutoCalculate, the Count calculation counts all cells, and the Count Nums calculation counts only number cells.

or a cell reference (you type the criteria in the referenced cell). As an example of COUNTIF in action, Figure 5.9 shows a list of monthly coffee sales of different types. I want to know how many orders of Kona coffee were filled that month, so I use the COUNTIF formula to count only the Kona sales.

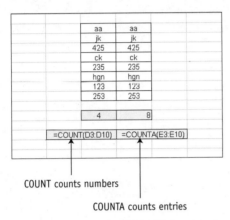

COUNT counts numbers

COUNTA counts entries

Figure 5.8. The COUNT and COUNTA functions in use.

The criteria cell for both formulas

The SUMIF formula

G5	▾	ƒx =COUNTIF(B3:B56,G3)					
	A	B	C	D	E	F	G	H
1	Coffee Orders for December 2004						
2	Date	Product	Price/lb	Lbs	Total		
3	12/2/04	Santo Domingo	9.50	100	950.00		Kona
4	12/2/04	Antigua	10.50	100	1,050.00		8186.25 Sales
5	12/4/04	Antigua	10.50	200	2,100.00		9 Orders
6	12/4/04	Antigua	10.50	150	1,575.00		
7	12/4/04	Antigua	10.50	45	472.50		
8	12/4/04	Santo Domingo	9.50	55	522.50		

The COUNTIF formula

Figure 5.9. COUNTIF counts the cells that meet your criteria.

Bright Idea

Combine the SUMIF and COUNTIF functions to average the sales in a list like in Figure 5.9: SUMIF(*range,criteria,sum_range*)/COUNTIF(*range,criteria*). Use the same *range* reference and *criteria* cell reference in both functions, then type any product name in the *criteria* reference cell.

VLOOKUP

VLOOKUP (and its less-used cousin, HLOOKUP) look up values elsewhere in a worksheet or workbook. For example, in an invoice, you might want Excel to look up the state tax rate for the shipping address; or if you're a teacher keeping grade sheets, you can have Excel look up the letter grades corresponding to your students' test scores.

The only difference between VLOOKUP and HLOOKUP is that VLOOKUP works vertically and HLOOKUP works horizontally in a lookup table (hence the V and H before each name). I'll show you how to use VLOOKUP. In the unlikely event that you ever need to use HLOOKUP, it works just like VLOOKUP, but horizontally instead of vertically (and the help file is very helpful).

To write a VLOOKUP formula, first create a lookup table, such as the scores-and-grades Lookup table in Figure 5.10. The table needs to be set up so that the values you are looking up (in this example, the score/grade cutoff values) are in the leftmost column and sorted in ascending order. The lookup table can have several columns in it, as long as the values the formula looks up are on the left.

Then create the VLOOKUP formula:

=vlookup(*lookup_value,table_array,col_index_num,range_lookup*).

The arguments are

- **lookup_value.** The cell that contains the value you want to look up.

- **table_array.** The lookup table range (drag to select it).

- **col_index_num.** The number of the column in the lookup table where the looked-up values are found (think of the table columns as numbered right to left; in this example, the looked-up grade letter is in column 2).

- **range_lookup.** An optional argument. If you leave it blank, the formula looks down the leftmost column for the closest match (which is why the column is sorted). If you enter FALSE, the formula looks for an exact match. (If, for example, you want to create a lookup table for state tax rates, enter FALSE so the VLOOKUP formula finds an exact match in the leftmost state abbreviations column.)

Bright Idea

If you need to copy the formula down a column in a data table like the actual test scores in the pictured example, use AutoFill.

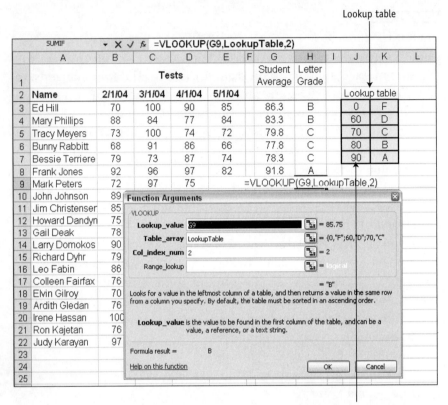

Figure 5.10. A set of test scores and a lookup table for letter grades

IF

The IF function is a way to determine a cell value based on criteria you set, and gives you a result depending on whether or not the criteria is met. The IF function works like this: IF *a statement is true,* THEN *return this first value,* OTHERWISE *return this second value.*

Figure 5.11 shows some examples of the IF function in action.

The IF function is useful for accomplishing specific data management tasks, such as the one explained in the sidebar below, and for controlling data displays in a worksheet. A good example of the IF function in action is in the Checkbook Balance worksheet in Appendix B.

Find duplicates

The IF function is one of several ways to find specific entries in a list. Other ways include sorting, filtering, and Find, but I like the IF function because it's fast and saves me the time it takes to eyeball the entire list. For example, when I need to find duplicate entries in a very long list, I often use the IF function. (This example assumes that the column with the entries begins in A1, and column B is empty—that's where I write my IF function.) First, I sort the entries in column A so duplicates will be sorted together; in cell B2, I write the formula =IF(A2=A1,"xxx","") (there's no space between the quotes). The formula reads "if the cell next to me is the same as the cell above it, display an xxx, otherwise display nothing." Then I AutoFill the formula down column B by double-clicking the Fill handle. If I scroll through the list, duplicates are clearly marked; better yet, I can sort the list by column B, and all the duplicates (the xxx entries) sort to the bottom or top, where the duplicate rows are quick to delete.

Works

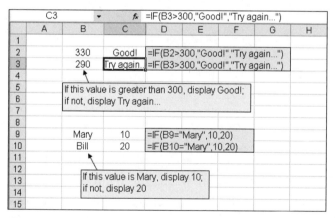

Figure 5.11. The IF function makes decisions about what to display for you.

PMT

If you're shopping for a house, car, boat, or anything else that's expensive enough for a loan, a key piece of information in your decision to buy is probably the size of the monthly payment. The PMT function figures it

Bright Idea

Name the cells in your table so the formula makes more sense.

out quickly for you based on the annual interest rate, number of monthly payments, and initial size of the loan.

You can write just the formula, but it's more helpful to set up a table with all the pertinent information and reference the table cells in the formula (see Figure 5.12).

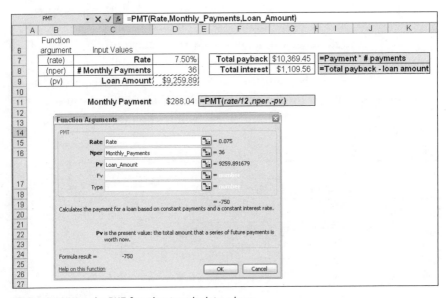

Figure 5.12. Use the PMT function to calculate a loan.

To write a PMT formula, type =pmt(*rate,nper,pv*). The arguments are

▪ **rate.** The rate for the interest period. If you use an annual rate but make monthly payments, enter this argument as *annual rate/*12, so the formula calculates with a monthly rate.

Watch Out!

The most common and often unnoticed source of error in a PMT formula is neglecting to divide the annual interest rate by 12. If you don't divide the rate argument by 12, your payment will be whopping big!

Bright Idea

Set up two or three side-by-side tables with different terms in each. It's a simple way to compare different loan scenarios. If you name the cells in each table, name them rate1, rate2, and so on.

■ **nper.** The total number of payments (for example, if it's a four-year loan with monthly payments, the *nper* argument is 48).

■ **pv.** The amount, or present value, of the loan. Enter this number as negative because it represents money you owe (if you enter it as positive you get a negative payment amount).

To make the loan payment table even more useful, add an extra eye-opening bit of information: total interest paid. Somewhere on the worksheet (as shown in Figure 5.12), write the formulas:

■ **Total loan payback** =*monthly payment* * *number of payments* (click the appropriate cells to add them to the formulas)

■ **Total interest paid** =*total loan payback – loan amount*

NOW and TODAY

The NOW function returns the current date and time; the TODAY function returns the current date. They're handy to have in the corner of a worksheet when you want the time or date to be updated every time the worksheet calculates (which happens every time you make an entry in the workbook or open or print the workbook).

NOW and TODAY have no arguments, and you don't need the Function Wizard. You write them as =NOW() and =TODAY() (don't type anything between the parentheses, and as always, don't add any spaces). Figure 5.13 shows the two functions in use.

Watch Out!

Don't use the NOW or TODAY function in a worksheet that contains historical data, such as an invoice (data that should have an unchanging creation date), because the date or time updates every time you open the worksheet. Instead, use Ctrl+; (semicolon) to enter a current date that won't change.

Bright Idea

If you keep a TODAY formula in the corner of a worksheet, that current date is a permanent part of the printed worksheet. You can always tell how old a printout is by looking at the date.

	D4	▾	*fx*	=TODAY()		
	A	B	C	D	E	F
1						
2						
3						
4	I took this worksheet picture on			10/3/2005	=TODAY()	
5						
6	Right now the time and date are			10/3/2005 20:19	=NOW()	
7						

Figure 5.13. The NOW and TODAY functions in use

Text functions

First, a look at the text case functions: UPPER, LOWER, and PROPER. All three of these functions have the same syntax and take only one argument, *ref,* which is the cell address of the text to change. UPPER(*ref*) changes all the text in the reference cell to uppercase, LOWER(*ref*) changes all the text in the reference cell to lowercase, and PROPER(*ref*) changes every word in the cell to proper case (first letter capitalized). Figure 5.14 shows all three functions in use.

	A	B	C	D	E
1					
2		**Original entries**	**Text formulas**		
3					
4		YEAR END SALES DATA	Year End Sales Data	=PROPER(B4)	
5					
6		YEAR END SALES DATA	year end sales data	=LOWER(B6)	
7					
8		year end sales data	Year End Sales Data	=PROPER(B8)	
9					
10		year end sales data	YEAR END SALES DATA	=UPPER(B10)	
11					

Figure 5.14. The UPPER, LOWER, and PROPER functions in use

You can quickly render a list more professional in appearance by making the letter case match throughout the list. Insert a new column next to the column with the entries you want to change, enter the text formula in the top cell in the new column, then AutoFill the formula down the new column.

Hack

After you use these formulas to create a new column with the correct letter-case entries, copy and paste values in the new column so you won't lose the new entries when you delete the original column of entries.

Other text functions such as LEFT and RIGHT seem rather pointless unless you have a real-life use for them; then they're remarkable.

Each of these functions extracts a specific number of characters from the left and right end of a text string, respectively (as shown in Figure 5.15).

	C18	▾	f_x =RIGHT(B18,4)		
	A	B	C	D	E
13					
14		**Original Entries**	**Text Formulas**		
15					
16		Year End Sales Data	Year	=LEFT(B16,4)	
17					
18		Year End Sales Data	Data	=RIGHT(B18,4)	
19					

Figure 5.15. The LEFT and RIGHT functions in use

To write a LEFT formula, use the Function Wizard until you are comfortable with the function syntax. Type **=left(** and then click the Insert Function button on the Formula bar. In the LEFT dialog box, click in the Text argument, and then click the cell that contains the text string. Click in the Num_chars argument, and type the number of characters you want to extract. The RIGHT function works the same way.

I use these functions and the CONCATENATE function to create unique invoice numbers and change the letter case of entries in a list. I show you how in the "Combining functions for more power" section later in this chapter.

CONCATENATE

The CONCATENATE function joins together the displayed values in two or more cells. It can also join a text string to the value displayed in a cell.

Fortunately for all of us, we don't ever have to type "concatenate" because the shorthand for CONCATENATE is & (ampersand).

To write a CONCATENATE formula, type *=cellref&cellref,* as shown in Figure 5.16.

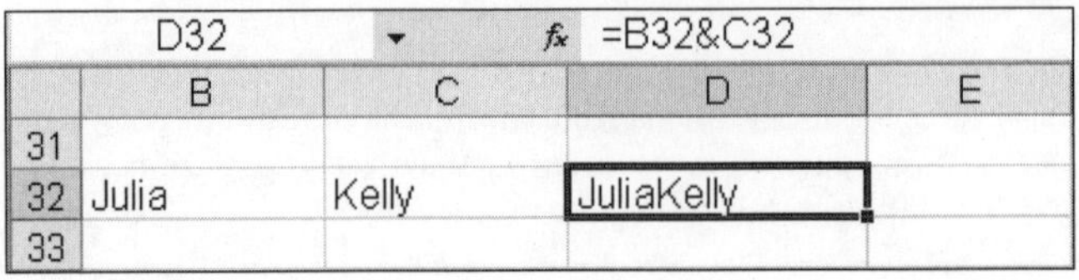

D32	▼	*fx* =B32&C32	
B	**C**	**D**	**E**
31			
32 Julia	Kelly	JuliaKelly	
33			

Figure 5.16. The CONCATENATE function without incorporated spaces

This formula displays the entries from the two referenced cells joined together. As written, the two joined entries are displayed as a single entry with no spaces between them.

You can join spaces, other characters, and other formulas into the formula result. For example, to join two cell entries into a single cell (see Figure 5.17), type =*cellref*&" "&*cellref*, which joins the first cell value to a space character, and then to the second cell value. If you join any text strings (including space characters) into a CONCATENATE formula, you must enclose the text string in quote marks.

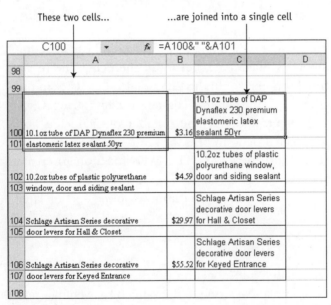

Figure 5.17. My client didn't know how to format wrapped text, so he entered long entries in separate cells; I joined each set of separated entries with the CONCATENATE function.

Watch Out!

If you delete any of the input cells for a CONCATENATION formula, the formula breaks because its input data is gone. To prevent that, after you write the CONCATENATE formula, copy the CONCATENATE formula and then use the Paste button to paste values.

OFFSET

OFFSET is a somewhat elaborate function that I saw no earthly use for until someone showed me how to use it to define *dynamic* ranges, which grow and shrink as data is added to or deleted from a table. What the basic OFFSET function does is define a static range, just as if you dragged to select a range on the worksheet with a specific upper-left cell and a specific number of columns and rows. I explain dynamic ranges in the "Combining functions for more power" section later in this chapter, but before I get to that level, you need to understand how the basic OFFSET function works.

You cannot usefully set up an OFFSET formula in the Function Arguments dialog box, because the OFFSET function defines a range rather than calculating a value. You use an OFFSET function by naming it, as shown in Figure 5.18, and then using the named function in other functions that calculate values.

Function name

Function

Figure 5.18. Naming an OFFSET function

The OFFSET function is
=OFFSET(*reference,rows,cols,height,width*).

The arguments are:

- **reference.** The anchor cell, from which the other arguments measure the defined range.

- **rows.** The number of rows above or below the anchor cell where the range begins. The upper-left cell of the range is this many rows away from the anchor cell (a positive number is rows down; a negative number is rows up).

- **cols.** The number of columns right or left of the anchor cell where the range begins. The upper-left cell of the range is this many columns away from the anchor cell (a positive number is columns right; a negative number is columns left).

- **height.** The number of rows in the range (optional: If you leave it blank, the range is the same height as the *reference* argument range, which is usually 1).

- **width.** The number of columns in the range (optional: If you leave it blank, the range is the same width as the *reference* argument range, which is usually 1).

An OFFSET range, selected by naming the OFFSET formula (see Chapter 4) and then using the Edit ⇨ Go To dialog box, is shown in Figure 5.19.

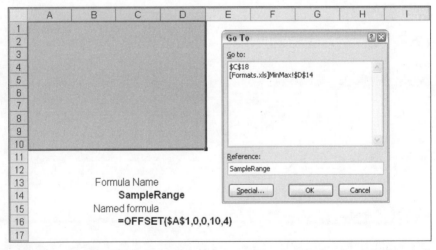

Figure 5.19. A basic OFFSET formula defines this range. The range is named SampleRange, and it can be selected with the Go To dialog box.

The Analysis Toolpak

The Analysis Toolpak is an add-in (an extra program you can add in) that contains *lots* of scientific and engineering functions and several statistical and engineering tools.

Install the Analysis Toolpak

To install the Analysis Toolpak, choose Tools ⇨ Add-Ins. Select the Analysis Toolpak check box and click OK, then wait a minute while Excel installs the small application.

Your Function Wizard just got expanded by a great many functions and a new command — Data Analysis — is added to the Tools menu. You're on your own with the Data Analysis tools — the functions are all well beyond the scope of this book and useful only to high-level engineering, scientific, math, and statistics enterprises — but I really like the CONVERT function, so I keep the Analysis Toolpak installed. (If you want to know more about the Data Analysis tools, look up data analysis in the Help files, or install the Analysis Toolpak and look up help on specific functions just like you would regular functions.)

CONVERT

To convert things like inches to millimeters, grams to ounces, statute miles to nautical miles, yards to meters, liters to cups, degrees Celsius to degrees Fahrenheit, and so on, use the CONVERT function (see Figure 5.20).

Type **=convert(** and then click the Insert Function button to open the CONVERT section of the Function Arguments dialog box. As with any other function, you can type the actual values into the argument boxes, or click cells to enter references in the argument boxes and enter your

Inside Scoop

In the From_unit and To_unit arguments, you must type common abbreviations, not full words. To see what the acceptable abbreviations are, click the Help on this function link in the CONVERT section of the Function Arguments dialog box.

Watch Out!

If you uninstall the Analysis Toolpak, you lose all of the Toolpak's functions.

values in those cells on the worksheet (which makes the worksheet itself a conversion tool).

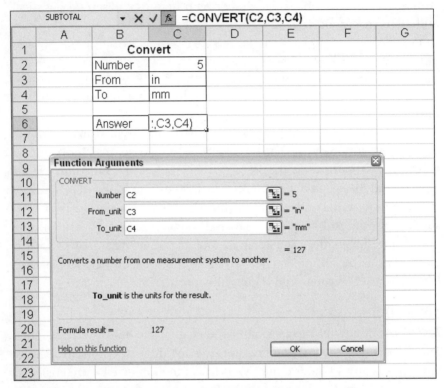

Figure 5.20. The CONVERT function can convert many units to many other units.

Combining functions for more power

Many, if not most, of Excel's functions seem pointless on the face of them because they were never meant to be stand-alone functions. Most functions are designed to be used in concert with other functions, and all functions can be used with other functions to get more elaborate, difficult-to-calculate, and useful results.

Hack

When I need to write a particularly complex formula, I build it without typing = so I can copy and paste bits and pieces in position and see the whole formula take shape while I build it. When the formula looks ready, I type = and press Enter. If it's incorrect, I delete the = and fix it.

In this section, I show you a few examples of combining functions for more computing power.

Dynamic range with OFFSET and COUNTA

In most of my lists, I place a SUM or SUBTOTAL formula at the bottom of the list, and both functions have a *range* argument. Instead of using a static range reference (which both named ranges and dragged ranges are), I use an OFFSET function to define a range that always includes all the cells in the column above, even when the list grows or shrinks.

OFFSET defines a *dynamic* range when it's used in conjunction with the COUNTA function (which counts all the entries in a range).

To create a dynamic range formula, change the *height* and *width* arguments to COUNTA functions.

This formula creates a dynamic range that begins in cell A1 and extends the length of column A and the width of row 1:

=offset($A$1,0,0,counta($A:$A),counta($1:$1))

If your table is in a different location on the worksheet, adjust the first three arguments as necessary.

Test the dynamic range

To see the formula work, name the formula in the Define Name dialog box (see Chapter 4), then choose Edit ⇨ Go To and type the formula name in the Reference box. Add and delete entries to the bottom of column A and the right end of row 1, as shown in Figure 5.21, and watch the named formula select the correct range every time!

Use a dynamic range

How can you use a dynamic range? Well, I use it in expense lists, to sum all the entries in the column above my SUM formula, even as the list

Watch Out!
If you have any empty cells in column A, or any entries in column A outside of the table, your dynamic range will be wrong because the dynamic OFFSET function is counting all entries in that column to create the size of the reference (same goes for row 1).

grows or shrinks. I never need to adjust the range reference being summed because the dynamic OFFSET formula does that for me.

Figure 5.21. Change the number of entries in the table and then go to the named OFFSET formula again.

To do this, I choose a cell at least one row below my column of entries (it can be three or four rows below the column, just not in the row immediately below the column), and put a border around that cell to identify it. For this example I chose cell D11 (the initial cell matters—you may not understand why, but you'll see it work).

Then I enter the formula =OFFSET($D$11,-1,0,) in the Refers to box of the Define Name dialog box (see Figure 5.22), and name it "CellAbove." This formula always selects the cell above cell D11 (1 row up and 0 columns over from the anchor cell). It uses the height and width of the anchor cell (1 high, 1 wide) to determine the size of the range (the optional *height* and *width* arguments are left out, but that last comma is important).

Okay, the named formula is finished. Now, to use it, I enter this formula in cell D11: =SUM($D$2:CellAbove). This formula sums all the entries between D2 (the topmost cell in my column of entries because I have a column header in D1) and the cell above the sum formula cell, as shown in Figure 5.23.

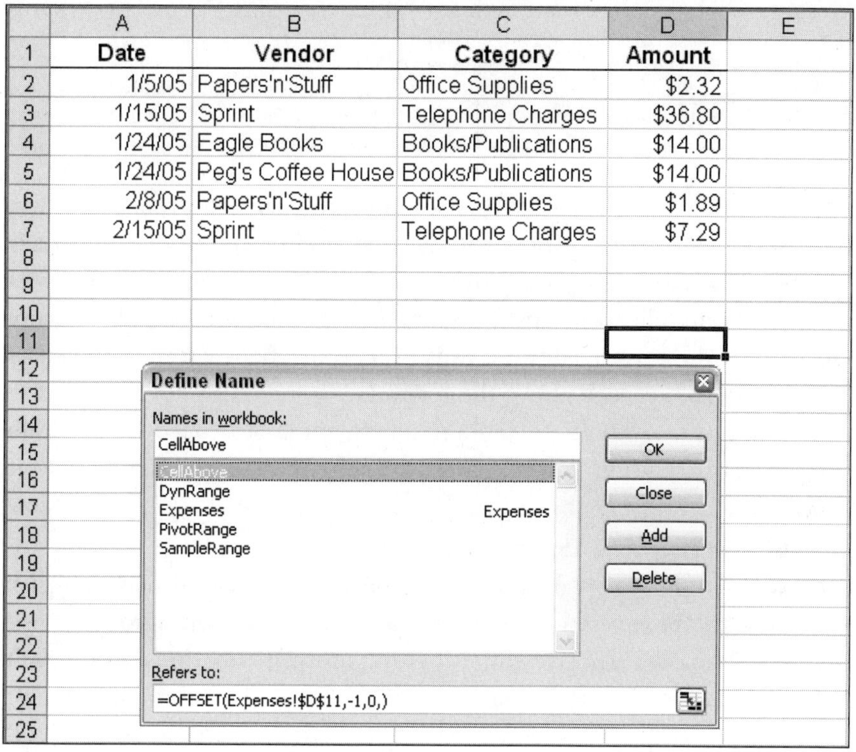

	A	B	C	D	E
1	**Date**	**Vendor**	**Category**	**Amount**	
2	1/5/05	Papers'n'Stuff	Office Supplies	$2.32	
3	1/15/05	Sprint	Telephone Charges	$36.80	
4	1/24/05	Eagle Books	Books/Publications	$14.00	
5	1/24/05	Peg's Coffee House	Books/Publications	$14.00	
6	2/8/05	Papers'n'Stuff	Office Supplies	$1.89	
7	2/15/05	Sprint	Telephone Charges	$7.29	
8					
9					
10					
11					
12					

Define Name

Names in workbook:

CellAbove

CellAbove
DynRange
Expenses   Expenses
PivotRange
SampleRange

OK

Close

Add

Delete

Refers to:

=OFFSET(Expenses!$D$11,-1,0,)

Figure 5.22. Type the OFFSET formula in the Define Name dialog box and name it.

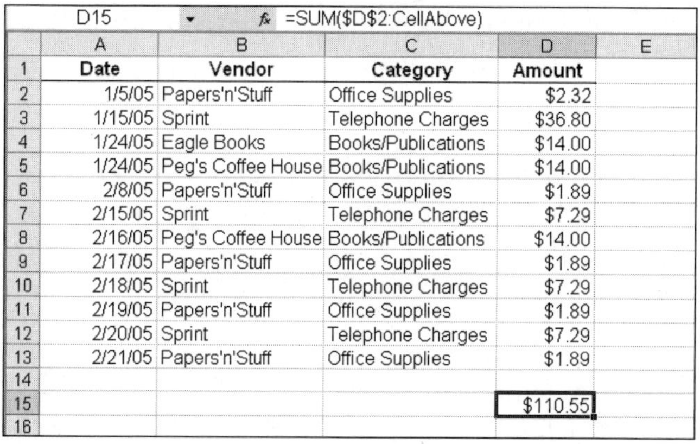

D15   *fx* =SUM($D$2:CellAbove)

	A	B	C	D	E
1	Date	Vendor	Category	Amount	
2	1/5/05	Papers'n'Stuff	Office Supplies	$2.32	
3	1/15/05	Sprint	Telephone Charges	$36.80	
4	1/24/05	Eagle Books	Books/Publications	$14.00	
5	1/24/05	Peg's Coffee House	Books/Publications	$14.00	
6	2/8/05	Papers'n'Stuff	Office Supplies	$1.89	
7	2/15/05	Sprint	Telephone Charges	$7.29	
8	2/16/05	Peg's Coffee House	Books/Publications	$14.00	
9	2/17/05	Papers'n'Stuff	Office Supplies	$1.89	
10	2/18/05	Sprint	Telephone Charges	$7.29	
11	2/19/05	Papers'n'Stuff	Office Supplies	$1.89	
12	2/20/05	Sprint	Telephone Charges	$7.29	
13	2/21/05	Papers'n'Stuff	Office Supplies	$1.89	
14					
15				$110.55	
16					

Figure 5.23. As the formula cell is moved down and data is added to the column, the formula cell continues to sum all the cells above it.

Inside Scoop

If you move the sum cell down to a new location and then open the Define Name dialog box, you see the changed anchor cell reference in the CellAbove formula. (Excel prepends the sheet name to the anchor cell address; just ignore that.)

Here's the dynamic part: When you move the sum formula cell down, the named formula CellAbove changes its anchor cell reference to the cell above the cell where you move it. As I add data to the column, I just move the sum cell down, always at least one row below the column of entries, and the formula always sums every entry between the top cell in the column and the cell above the formula.

You can use a dynamic formula in any formula or procedure in which you want a range argument that adjusts to changing range size.

Nested IF functions

The IF function, which makes a decision for you and displays a result based on criteria you set, can incorporate other functions and be *nested* up to seven levels deep. (Nesting is writing more IF functions inside each other, as shown in Figure 5.24.)

Test Score	Grade	
85	B	=IF(B12>90,"A",IF(B12>80,"B",IF(B12>70,"C",IF(B12>60,"D","F"))))
92	A	=IF(B12>90,"A",IF(B12>80,"B",IF(B12>70,"C",IF(B12>60,"D","F"))))

Figure 5.24. These IF functions are nested.

A three-level-deep nested IF function reads: IF *this first statement is true,* THEN *return this first value,* IF *this second statement is true,* THEN *return this second value,* IF *this third statement is true,* THEN *return this third value,* OTHERWISE (if all previous statements are false) *return this last value.*

Inside Scoop

Some people use nested IF functions in lieu of a VLOOKUP function (for example, to look up letter grades for test scores). I think the VLOOKUP function is more elegant and easier to write, but the nested IF function takes up less worksheet space.

Text functions and CONCATENATION

Here are a couple of ways in which I combine text functions and concatenation: I create unique invoice numbers and change the letter case in long lists without retyping.

Unique invoice numbers

In my invoices, I use a numbering system that automatically creates unique invoices by combining the first three letters of my client name and the last four digits of the current date serial number. I use the LEFT and RIGHT functions to extract the characters, and I join them using the CONCATENATION function (see Figure 5.25).

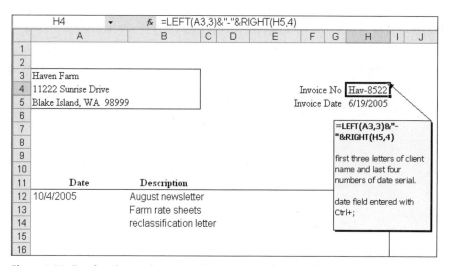

Figure 5.25. Text functions and concatenation create a unique invoice number.

First, this system depends on my client name and the invoice date always being entered in the same cell. Because my invoices are created from a template, the name and date cells and the numbering formula are always in place.

Bright Idea

Automatically pull the highest and lowest figures out of a range of numbers and combine them with an introductory statement: ="The best and worst figures for 2004 were "&MAX(*ref*)&" and "&MIN(*ref*)". Make sure you include appropriate space characters in the text strings.

The formula for the invoice number is

=left(*nameref*,3)&"-"&right(*dateref*,4).

The formula concatenates a hyphen (-) into the result between the name and date characters.

Change letter case

I don't care for lists typed in all uppercase letters or all lowercase letters (it's a personal quirk), so to make imported or received lists look more professional, I change the letter case. I could do it rapidly with the text function PROPER, but that's not quite what I want. I want to change the cell entries such that the first word is proper-cased (that is, initial-capped) and the remaining words are lowercased (for example, I want to change TOASTER OVEN to Toaster oven). To do this, I need to combine a few different functions.

The formula shown in Figure 5.26 proper-cases the first word in the referenced cell and lowercases the rest of the letters in the cell:

=upper(left(*ref*))&right(lower(*ref*),len(*ref*)-1)

		C23	▼	*fx*	=UPPER(LEFT(B23))&RIGHT(LOWER(B23),LEN(B23)-1)		
	A	B		C		D	E	F
21								
22		Original Entry		Text Formula				
23		THIS YEAR'S TOTAL IS		This year's total is				
24								
25				=UPPER(LEFT(B23))&RIGHT(LOWER(B23),LEN(B23)-1)				
26								

Figure 5.26. Combining text functions to make cell entries look professional

The formula is two formulas concatenated together: The first extracts the first letter with the LEFT function and uppercases it with the UPPER function; the second uses the RIGHT function to extract all but the leftmost letter and lowercases them.

Calculating dates and times

Regardless of formatting, Excel sees all dates as serial numbers, beginning with the number 1 on January 1, 1900, and running through December 31, 9999 (at which point Excel 2003 will be obsolete). Because Excel calculates dates as serial numbers, it's easy to ask how many days there are between dates: Type dates in two cells, and in a third cell type *=earliercellref-latercellref*. No functions are involved; just subtract one cell

Hack

If the elapsed time or date result is a negative number, the display is #######.
Make sure you subtracted the correct cell; it's easy to get the two cells switched.

from the other. The same goes for times: To get elapsed time, subtract one time cell from another time cell. You may need to format the result to be something understandable; I show you how in Chapter 6.

The Date and Time functions DAY, WEEK, and MONTH extract the numeric day, week, or month from a date, and are good for combining in other formulas. For example, the formula ="You have" &MONTH(*ref1*)-MONTH(*ref2*)&" months left." (shown in Figure 5.27) calculates the number of months between the cells in *ref1* and *ref2* and concatenates it into a sentence.

	D13	▾		f_x	="You have "&MONTH(C13)-MONTH(C12)&" months l
	A	B	C	D	E	F
11						
12		Start date	1/3/2005			
13		End date	7/14/2005	You have 6 months left.		
14						
15		="You have "&MONTH(ref1)-MONTH(ref2)&" months left."				
16						
17						
18						
19		10/3/2005	10	=MONTH(B19)		
20		10/3/2005	3	=DAY(B20)		
21		10/3/2005	2005	=YEAR(B21)		
22						

Figure 5.27. DAY, WEEK, and MONTH functions in use

Because Excel doesn't see dates any earlier than January 1, 1900, you can't calculate dates earlier than that. You can only enter earlier dates in a cell as text strings.

Just the facts

- Functions perform complex mathematics that you cannot do with arithmetic operators alone.

- Each function has a name and arguments that provide the function with the input data to calculate.

- Use the Function Wizard to write functions you're unfamiliar with; open the Insert Function dialog box by clicking the Insert Function button on the Formula bar.

- Install the Analysis Toolpak for scientific, engineering, and statistical functions and tools.

- Combine functions for more computing power.

Formatting Everything

PART III

GET THE SCOOP ON...

The Formatting toolbar ∎ Formatting font ∎ Formatting borders ∎ Formatting colors ∎ Manipulating text to fit in the cell ∎ Copying formatting with Format Painter ∎ Automatic table formats ∎ Pasting pictures in worksheets

Formatting Cells

Formatting dresses up a worksheet and makes it presentable. But more than that, formatting makes data more meaningful by visually segregating data into groups and highlighting summary information so your audience can grasp your point quickly.

I'll tell you how to create your own cell formatting, including borders, colors, fonts and font sizes, rotating, merging, aligning entries, and fitting entries into cells, rows, and columns, and more. After you do all the creative work to format a single cell or set of cells, I'll show you the fast way to copy that formatting to other cells and to cells in other workbooks. Later in this chapter, I'll show you how to apply Excel's built-in formats to a table (which are quick but uninspired).

This chapter is about formatting cells, the containers that hold your data. Nothing in this chapter changes the display of the values in cells. Chapter 7 covers formatting the values in those cells.

Keep in mind as you read that while it's *fun* to format a worksheet, you shouldn't get too carried away. A worksheet that's too whimsical loses its professional impact.

The Formatting toolbar

The Formatting toolbar, shown in Figure 6.1, holds buttons for the most commonly used formatting choices. Some of the buttons you may use often; some you may never use;

and others that I think ought to be there, aren't. I'll show you how to remove the unnecessary buttons and how to place some really useful buttons on the toolbar instead. In Chapters 19 and 21, I show you how to create a macro and custom toolbar button for your own custom formatting operations, too.

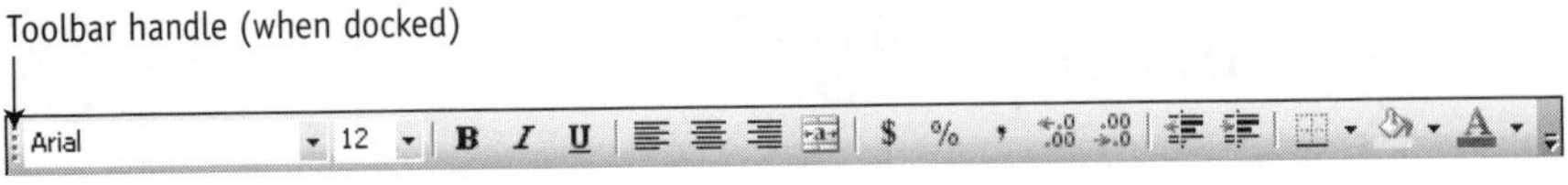

Toolbar handle (when docked)

Figure 6.1. The Formatting toolbar

Display the Formatting toolbar

If your Formatting toolbar isn't displayed, right-click in the toolbar/menu bar area and click Formatting.

Unless the toolbars are displayed separately, you don't have adequate access to all the buttons. If your toolbars are set to display together on a single row, drag the Formatting toolbar by its handle (the vertical row of dots on its left end) to reposition it below the Standard toolbar.

Even when you have your Formatting toolbar on its own row (or floating on the worksheet), there are hidden formatting buttons. To see them (as shown in Figure 6.2), have the toolbar docked in the toolbar area then click the Toolbar Options button (the small triangle) on the right end of the toolbar, click Add or Remove Buttons, and click Formatting. A half-dozen formatting buttons, which you may or may not be interested in, are at the bottom of the list. Buttons with check marks next to them are displayed; buttons without check marks are hidden. Click a button name to hide or show the button.

There are many more-useful Formatting toolbar buttons in the Customize dialog box; why there is easy access to less-useful buttons and more difficult access to more-useful buttons is not for me to say. However, it's worth your time to look through the button offerings in the Customize dialog box (shown in Figure 6.3). Right-click in the toolbar/menu bar area and click Customize. On the Commands tab, click Format in the Categories list and then scroll through the myriad formatting buttons in the Commands list. I have more to say about customizing your toolbars in Chapter 19.

Toolbar Options button

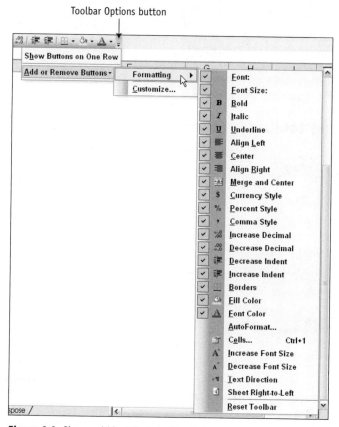

Figure 6.2. Show or hide default toolbar buttons.

Figure 6.3. Add many more buttons from the Customize dialog box.

Bright Idea

Give yourself more worksheet real estate *and* still have access to all the toolbar buttons by dragging the Formatting toolbar down into the worksheet, to "float." Then drag a toolbar border to reshape the toolbar to a more compact rectangle. Drag the floating toolbar by its title bar to reposition it.

Great formatting toolbar buttons

Figure 6.4 shows three tear-away formatting palettes that make borders, cell colors, and font colors much faster to apply.

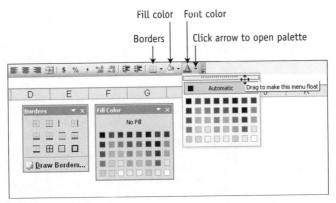

Figure 6.4. Palettes give you fast access to borders and colors.

To open each of these palettes, click the arrow on the toolbar button to open the palette, then drag the palette away from the toolbar using the row of dots across the top of the opened palette. The palette stays open and ready to use while you work in the worksheet. When you want to close it, click its Close (X) button.

Formatting the font

Formatting the font means changing the look of the characters in a cell. Not only can you change the appearance of all the characters in a cell, you can change individual characters within a cell (which is essential when

Bright Idea

Turn off the worksheet gridlines so you can see your formatting better (and see what the printed page will look like, too). Choose Tools ⇨ Options, and on the View tab, deselect the Gridlines check box.

you need superscript or subscript characters to write H_2O or 10^3, for example).

The toolbar buttons don't need detailed explanations; they're fairly intuitive (and if you don't understand one, click a cell and then click the button to see what happens). Buttons apply formatting quickly, and some of them are a great deal more convenient than using the Format Cells dialog box, but you can do a lot more formatting than what the toolbar offers by using the Format Cells dialog box.

Right-click a cell you want to format and click Format Cells. I talk about the Number tab in Chapter 7; in this chapter you look at the Alignment, Font, Border, and Patterns tabs, beginning with the Font tab (see Figure 6.5).

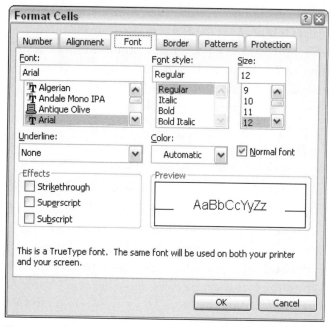

Figure 6.5. The Font tab provides many possibilities for detailed font formatting.

The Font tab settings are mostly self-explanatory, but here are some tips. Every change you make appears in the Preview box. (To format

Inside Scoop

When you use the Font button on the Formatting toolbar, you can jump to the font name you want quickly by opening the list and typing the first one or several letters of the font name. Then click the Font name you want.

specific characters in a cell, open the cell and drag to select those characters before you open the Format Cells dialog box.)

The settings on the Font tab include:

- **Font.** Click a font name and look at the Preview box to see the typeface you clicked. The Font button in the Formatting toolbar button is faster.

- **Font style.** This is just what it says; bold and italic are more quickly applied with the Formatting toolbar buttons or with keystrokes (Ctrl+B for bold, Ctrl+I for italic).

- **Size.** Again, just what it says. Font is measured in points; there are 72 points to the inch.

- **Underline.** Open the drop-down list and click an underline style. Single underline has a button on the Formatting toolbar (and a keystroke, Ctrl+U), and there is a ready-made button for double underlines in the Customize dialog box. Accounting underlines leave a space between characters and the underline, which makes characters more legible because their descending tails aren't hidden by the underline.

- **Color.** Colors the characters (either the whole cell or just selected characters). The Font Color toolbar button is faster.

- **Normal font.** Select this check box to return the font formatting to the workbook's Normal style (see Chapter 7 about Styles).

- **Effects.** Superscript (like ^{this}), subscript (like $_{this}$), and strikethrough (like ~~this~~). Select the specific characters to be formatted (especially for superscript and subscript), then open the Format Cells dialog box and apply the formatting. Oddly, there are ready-made buttons for this in Word, but not in Excel. However, if you use subscript and superscript often, it's worth your while to record a macro and make your own toolbar button (see Chapters 19 and 21).

- **Preview.** Displays your font formatting changes as you make them.

Better borders

I like cell borders that are simple and utilitarian. In most cases for numeric data, simple and nondistracting borders are better for data presentation, but for table headers and highly visual worksheets with charts and worksheet controls, elaborate and colorful borders are terrific. The only borders on a printed worksheet are the ones you create, and they make a big difference in the presentation of any data.

Inside Scoop

Excel doesn't print worksheet gridlines. If you want gridlines printed in addition to your borders, choose File ⇨ Page Setup, and on the Sheet tab in the Print section, select the Gridlines check box.

Simple borders

For simple borders in black, the fastest way to apply them is with the Borders palette (dragged from the Borders button on the Formatting toolbar). Select the cells you want to border, then click buttons to apply individual borders; click the No Border button (in the upper-left corner) to erase all borders in the selected cells. The Borders palette (shown in Figure 6.6) can remain open on your worksheet as long as you need it; it doesn't interfere with working in the worksheet.

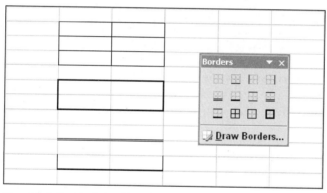

Figure 6.6. The Borders palette

Elaborate borders

If you want to get more colorful, use diagonal lines to make a cell look crossed out, or use double-lined borders, you need the Format Cells dialog box (see Figure 6.7).

Inside Scoop

If you didn't select all the cells to border before you created the borders, you can "paint" (copy) the new borders to other cells quickly with the Format Painter (covered later in this chapter).

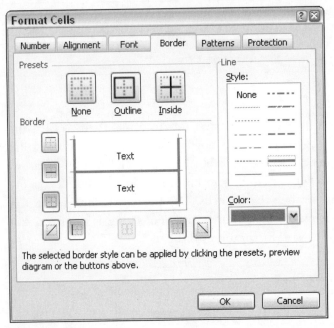

Figure 6.7. Elaborate borders are possible with the Borders tab.

The trick to using the Border tab is to follow a strict and orderly procedure:

1. Click a line style in the Style box.

2. Select a color from the Color drop-down list.

3. Apply the borders by clicking any button on the left in the Border section or by clicking inside the Border box.

When you click OK, the borders you built are applied to the selected cells. To erase all borders, click the None button in either the dialog box Border tab or the Borders palette.

The Borders toolbar

The last borders feature is the Borders toolbar (see Figure 6.8). With it you can draw single rectangular borders in all the same configurations, line styles, and colors as in the Format Cells dialog box, but you cannot apply a border to several selected cells at once. It takes longer to draw borders than to apply them with a click of a toolbar button, but if you draw colored borders, you can see exactly what you're drawing with the Borders toolbar, which you can't do with the Border tab in the Format Cells dialog box.

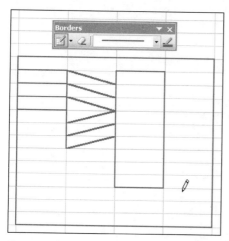

Figure 6.8. The Borders toolbar draws borders one at a time.

To display the Borders toolbar, either right-click in the toolbar area and click Borders, or click the Draw Borders button at the bottom of the Borders palette. To use the Borders toolbar:

■ Choose a color and line style from the Line Color and Line Style buttons.

■ Draw lines from one cell corner to another; draw single borders, rectangular cell borders, and diagonal lines.

■ Erase borders by clicking the Erase Border button and then clicking lines or dragging over bordered cells.

■ Click the Draw Border button at the left end to turn off the pencil and return to working in the worksheet.

Vibrant colors

There are two sources of color in cells: the characters (*font color*) and the cell background (*fill color*). You can apply both font color and fill color from the Format Cells dialog box, but they're much faster to apply from the Font Color and Fill Color palettes. What you cannot apply from the palettes is cell patterns; for patterns, you need the Format Cells dialog box.

Use the color palettes

To display a palette (shown in Figure 6.9), click the arrow on the appropriate toolbar button and then drag the palette away from the toolbar.

Click a cell, and then click a color

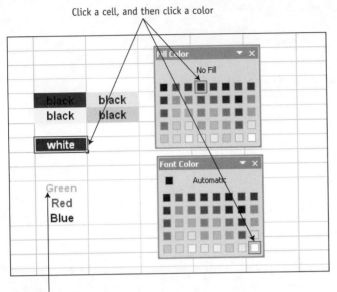

Select characters, and then click a font color.

Figure 6.9. Using the Font color and Fill color palettes

To use the palettes, select cells and click a color on the palette. To color specific characters, double-click the cell, drag to select the characters, and click a color in the Font Color palette.

Use the Format Cells dialog box

There is one thing you must do from within the Format Cells dialog box: Apply patterns to cell backgrounds. Patterns can obscure cell values, but they can also highlight cells gently if you choose a light pattern and a light color, as shown in Figure 6.10.

To apply patterns to selected cells, right-click in the selected cells and click Format Cells. Patterns are on the Patterns tab.

The color palette on the Patterns tab applies a fill color to cells, just like the Fill Color toolbar button.

To apply a pattern, open the Patterns list. The color palette on the patterns list colors the pattern you click. Click a pattern, then click a color (or click a color then click a pattern, it doesn't matter).

Bright Idea

Use colors and/or patterns to create a more pronounced table border. Surround a table with very narrow columns and rows, and apply a color or pattern to the cells in those table-defining rows and columns.

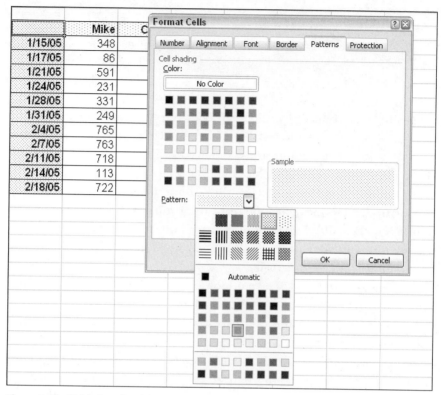

Figure 6.10. Highlight cells with pale patterns and colors.

Create custom colors

You can create custom colors to replace the standard color palette in a workbook. For example, I like my pale yellow, green, blue, and gray shades to be as pale as possible (paler than the default pale shades in the color palette) — you can see the difference in Figure 6.11.

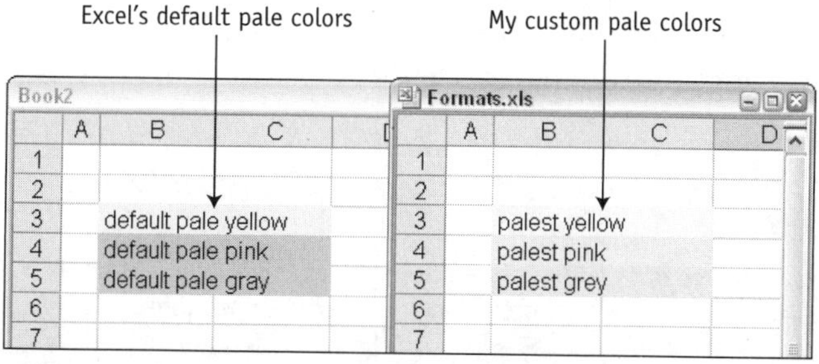

Figure 6.11. One workbook has my custom colors, the other workbook has default colors.

Hack

If you have data in colored cells and you're going to print the worksheet on a black-and-white printer, use the palest colors you can because they'll be gray (often too dark) on the printed page.

To create custom colors, choose Tools ➪ Options, and click the Color tab. In the Standard Colors palette, click the color you want to replace (you only get 40 cell colors and you have to replace one; you can't just add a 41st color). Then click Modify.

In the Colors dialog box, click the Custom tab. Click in the rainbow (use arrow keys to move around, too) until you get the color family you want, then click and drag the slider up and down until you get the color density you want. The new color and the color you are replacing are displayed in the lower-right corner.

As long as you're here, take a look at the Red, Green, and Blue settings. The higher the number, the less dense that particular hue is, and the closer you get to white (and the lower the number, the denser the color and closer to black).

Your custom colors work only in this workbook; to copy them to a different workbook so you don't have to re-create them, keep the custom-color workbook open. Then choose Tools ➪ Options ➪ Color tab in the new workbook and select the custom-color workbook's name in the Copy colors from list box.

To reset all your custom colors to the original built-in colors, choose Tools ➪ Options ➪ Color tab and click Reset.

Fit the text in the cell

Fitting text in the cell is an important way to make your data more readable. You have lots of options, including alignment, merging cells, rotating to a slant or vertical entries, indenting, wrapping text, changing row height and column width, shrinking entries to fit, and transposing a table layout.

Bright Idea

In lists in which you have labels to the left of values, right-align the labels so the reader's eye moves smoothly from each label to its value. Right-aligned labels bleed over to empty adjacent cells on the left, so long labels don't push the labels far from their values.

Alignment

Excel's default alignment is left-aligned for text and right-aligned for numeric entries. You can, however, realign any entry to suit your visual layout (and realignment is usually necessary to make a worksheet look professional).

Alignment possibilities are illustrated in Figure 6.12.

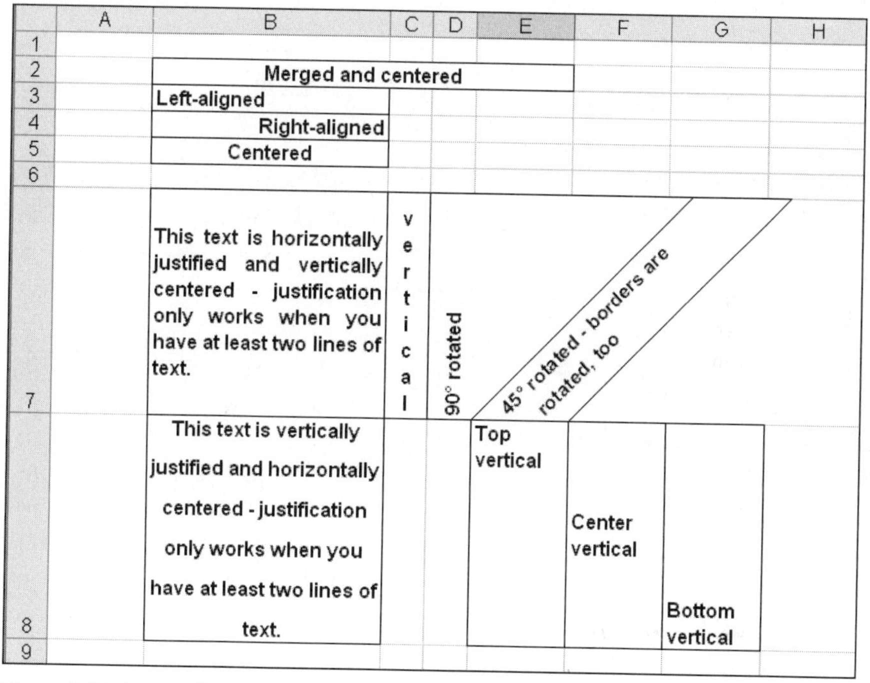

Figure 6.12. Myriad alignment possibilities

The right-aligned, left-aligned, centered, and merged-and-centered alignments are all buttons on the Formatting toolbar. For all the other alignment possibilities, right-click the cell and click Format Cells; you'll find all possible alignment settings on the Alignment tab.

Indent

Indenting entries is a great way to clarify data by making a list look outlined, with major heading labels and indented subheading labels (see Figure 6.13).

	A	B	C	D	E	F	G	H	I	J	K	L	M
1					*Accoutrement & Deshabille, Inc.*								
					Employee Commissions								
2							2005						
3													
4	Dept/Employee	January	February	March	April	May	June	July	August	September	October	November	December
5	Accessories												
6	Marcia	4913	3194	3650	2592	1330	3002	4166	4324	2906	2571	1777	1221
7	Fred	3554	1006	4029	2430	1635	4508	4472	1616	3260	4941	1282	2168
8	Lila	3098	4820	1032	2628	4213	1951	2099	4451	3939	1409	2450	4207
9	Coats												
10	Armelle	1894	4237	3333	3256	2382	2486	1818	1064	3292	2178	3649	4918
11	Jamie	3423	4609	3707	2441	2896	1327	1429	3714	2940	2687	3512	4565
12	Tracy	3266	1621	2873	3526	2622	1327	2094	3449	2420	3600	4588	2776
13	Hats												
14	Susannah	2366	2445	4514	4753	4505	4934	3523	4179	3055	1854	3378	3738
15	Tina	4578	2963	2982	1522	2067	3944	2605	4621	2510	3634	1462	3798
16	Diane	3217	1248	4004	3449	4563	4542	4668	3612	1345	2205	2752	4930
17	Bags												
18	Kurt	1104	2936	2296	1051	2310	3746	2918	3473	3675	1023	3778	2959
19	Jill	1373	1246	2861	3949	1111	3683	1756	1954	1574	3440	1268	2082
20	Elaine	3622	3486	1654	3092	1313	4869	3819	1757	1913	1058	3836	2917
21	Jewelry												
22	Albert	3105	1886	2433	2325	3842	4861	2460	3008	4268	2538	2477	1292
23	Ruby	4855	2797	4422	2312	4336	2969	3630	1064	4850	1559	4723	1792
24	Mariela	4368	2813	1107	3272	3110	3587	4741	1043	3499	1452	4258	3913

H ◀ ▶ H \ **Commissions** / Links / Blank /

Figure 6.13. Clarify groupings of data with indents.

The quickest way to indent is with the Increase Indent and Decrease Indent buttons on the Formatting toolbar. The buttons increase and decrease indentation as you watch (no guessing how much to indent and then closing the dialog box to see the results). As with all formatting, you can select several cells and indent all of them equally at the same time.

Rotate

Rotated labels can keep a table narrow and easy to read (as shown in Figure 6.13). To rotate text, select the cell(s), then right-click the selection, and click Format Cells. On the Alignment tab, click in the Orientation dial to set a rotation angle.

Bright Idea

Give several cells the same rotation angle by setting the angle in one cell and then painting the angle to other cells with the Format Painter; or by selecting all the cells before applying rotation.

Watch Out!

If you see ###### in a text-entry cell, it's because you have too many characters entered; edit the entry to fewer than 255 characters. If you see ###### in a number cell, it's because the number is too big for the column width; make the column wider to display the number.

Change column width and row height

When text entries are longer than the column width, the entry bleeds over into the adjacent cell. When you make an entry in the adjacent cell, the long entry in the first cell is partially hidden. There are a couple of ways to make the entire entry visible, depending on the length of the entry. Usually all you need to do is make the column wider; but if the entry is so long that this isn't practical, you can wrap the text to multiple lines (which makes the row taller but keeps the column width reasonable).

Drag to fit

The fastest way to change column width or row height in a controlled fashion is to click and drag the border of a column letter or row number. To change column width, position the mouse at the right border of the column letter, and click and drag the two-headed arrow to a new width (shown in Figure 6.14). To change row height, position the mouse at the bottom border of the row number, and click and drag the two-headed arrow to a new height.

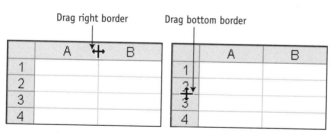

Figure 6.14. Drag a border with the two-headed arrow mouse pointer.

Bright Idea

Separate a table from any worksheet entries above the table with a very narrow row — visually the worksheet looks coherent, but Excel treats the table like the separate table that it is because of the row that separates the table from the entries above it.

If you need to create matching column widths for specific columns (for example, to keep all your number columns the same width), select all the columns first (drag or Ctrl+click column letters to select the columns), then drag the right border of any selected column. All the selected columns are resized to exactly the same width. The same method also works with row heights.

Double-click to fit

An even faster, albeit less controlled, way to change column width or row height is to double-click the border of the column letter or row number. Double-clicking the border "best-fits" the column or row to the biggest entry in the column or row. The hazard in best-fitting a column width is that you may have a very long entry in the column, and unless the long entry is word-wrapped to multiple lines, your best-fitted column might be wider than your visible worksheet.

You can double-click to best-fit multiple columns or rows, and each is sized for its own largest entry (so you won't have identically sized columns or rows).

Wrap text

A useful way to fit a long entry into a narrow column is to wrap text in the cell. As shown in Figure 6.15, wrapped text breaks the entry into multiple short lines that all display within the column; the row height increases to make room.

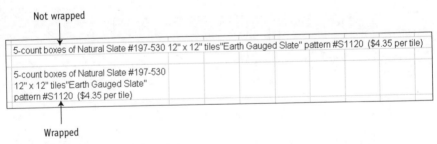

Not wrapped

5-count boxes of Natural Slate #197-530 12" x 12" tiles"Earth Gauged Slate" pattern #S1120 ($4.35 per tile)

5-count boxes of Natural Slate #197-530 12" x 12" tiles"Earth Gauged Slate" pattern #S1120 ($4.35 per tile)

Wrapped

Figure 6.15. Wrapped text keeps columns narrower.

Hack

If you inadvertently best-fit a column that's suddenly too wide, press Ctrl+Z to undo the best fit, then click and drag to widen the cell in a more controlled manner. If the culprit is a wide table title, merge and center the title over the table so it doesn't interfere with best-fitting column widths in the table.

Hack

Double-clicking to AutoFit a wrapped-text row or column entry often doesn't work. When it doesn't work, click and drag to enlarge the column by quite a bit, then double-click the column and then the row to best fit both.

Some procedures, such as justified alignment or inserting a line break, automatically turn on wrapped text. To turn on wrapped text yourself, right-click the cell and click Format Cells. On the Alignment tab, select the Wrap text check box. If you need to turn off wrapped text in a cell, deselect the Wrap text check box.

You'll usually want to resize the column and/or row after applying wrapped text to make the entry look right.

Some wrapped-text entries break at an inconvenient place in the text. To force the entry to break where you want it, click the cell to select it. In the Formula bar, click to place the insertion point where you want the break and then press Alt+Enter.

If you need to remove the forced break, select the cell, and in the Formula bar, click at the end of a broken line and press Delete.

Hide and unhide columns and rows

Often when I work on a long list, I enter data one entire column at a time (depending on the data, it's more efficient), and I want the column I'm entering data in to be right next to a column of labels so I can be sure I'm applying each entry in the correct row. The easiest way to put two spread-out columns together is to hide the columns in between them. (This really is faster and easier to control than splitting or freezing panes.)

To hide columns, select the columns (click and drag or Ctrl+click the column letters), right-click in the selection, and click Hide. You'll know the columns are hidden because the hidden column letters are not visible, as shown in Figure 6.16.

You can hide rows the same way. Select the rows (click and drag or Ctrl+click the row numbers), right-click in the selection, and click Hide.

Bright Idea

Use hidden rows and columns in workbooks you send to others, to hide data the other users don't need to see. For example, you can hide the columns that contain a lookup table for a VLOOKUP formula.

You'll know the rows are hidden because the hidden row numbers are not visible.

To unhide columns or rows, click and drag to select the surrounding column letters or row numbers, then click in the selection and click Unhide.

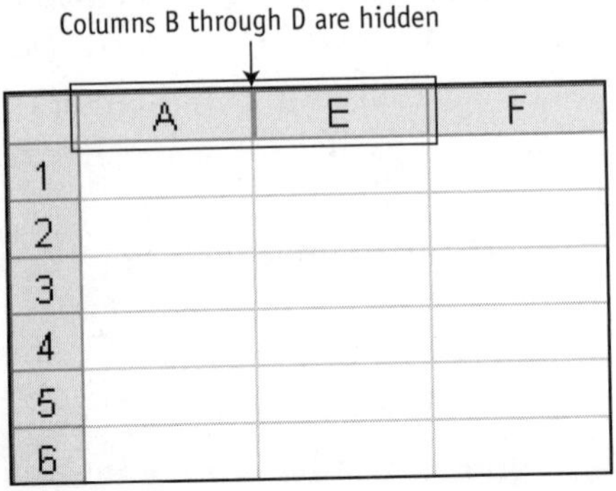

Columns B through D are hidden

Figure 6.16. Hidden columns have hidden letters.

Shrink entries

If you have a cell entry that doesn't quite fit and you don't want to enlarge the column or row to make room for it, you can shrink the entry to fit within the cell. The text shrinks and grows back to normal as necessary when you change the column width (see Figure 6.17).

To shrink an entry, right-click the cell and click Format Cells. On the Alignment tab, select the Shrink to fit check box. To remove the Shrink to fit setting, deselect the check box.

Merge cells

Most tables have a title across the top, and the title is usually too wide for a single cell. In addition, it's difficult to truly center a title over a table if you place it in a single cell. Instead, center the title across the entire table, as shown in Figure 6.18. Select all the cells in a row above the table and click the Merge and Center button on the Formatting toolbar. The selected cell gridlines disappear because you merged them into a single cell. Type your title and it's centered perfectly above the table (and remains centered even when you manipulate column widths in the table). To unmerge a merged cell, select it and click the Merge and Center button again.

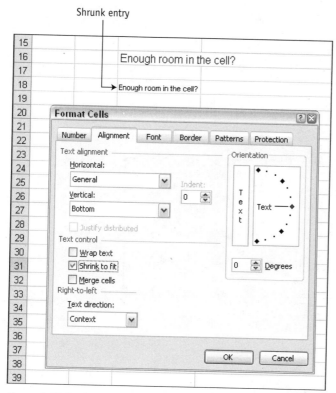

Figure 6.17. Entries shrink or grow to fit the column width.

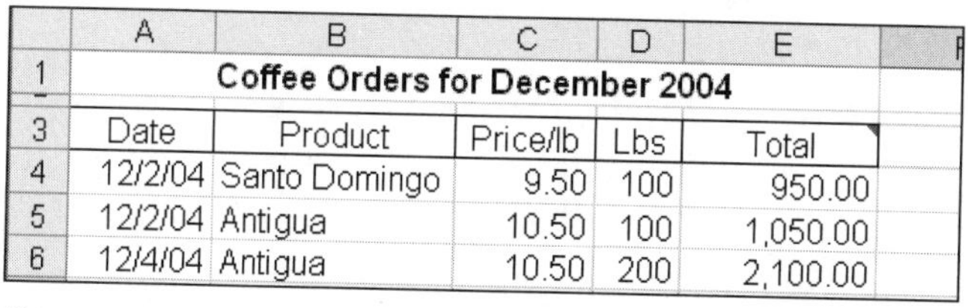

	A	B	C	D	E	
1		Coffee Orders for December 2004				
3	Date	Product	Price/lb	Lbs	Total	
4	12/2/04	Santo Domingo	9.50	100	950.00	
5	12/2/04	Antigua	10.50	100	1,050.00	
6	12/4/04	Antigua	10.50	200	2,100.00	

Figure 6.18. Center titles exactly by merging and centering.

Transpose a table

Sometimes I create a table like the one shown in Figure 6.19 and realize after a fair amount of data entry that my layout is impractical. I want to switch the columns to rows and the rows to columns.

Original wide table

	1/15/05	1/17/05	1/21/05	1/24/05	1/28/05	1/31/05
Mike	348	86	591	231	331	249
Callie	968	161	825	618	354	811
Katie	122	869	261	821	416	987
Mikey	996	111	291	115	608	247
Mary	927	752	699	147	665	746
John	664	183	62	158	133	873

	Mike	Callie	Katie	Mikey	Mary	John
1/15/05	348	968	122	996	927	664
1/17/05	86	161	869	111	752	183
1/21/05	591	825	261	291	699	62
1/24/05	231	618	821	115	147	158
1/28/05	331	354	416	608	665	133
1/31/05	249	811	987	247	746	873
2/4/05	765	885	932	266	341	814
2/7/05	763	851	647	562	15	599
2/11/05	718	867	923	821	794	16
2/14/05	113	426	371	737	45	585
2/18/05	722	993	760	151	456	751

Transposed table

Figure 6.19. A transposed copy of the original is pasted, and the original can be deleted.

To transpose a table, select the table and copy it. Then click a cell away from the table in which to paste the transposed table, click the arrow on the Paste button (on the Standard toolbar), and click Transpose.

Copying formatting with Format Painter

When you format a cell or group of cells and you want to use the same formatting on other cells (even in another workbook), the fastest way to copy the formatting is to use the Format Painter.

The Format Painter is a button on the Standard toolbar (why the Standard and not the Formatting, I don't know) that looks like a paintbrush. Click the formatted cell, click the Format Painter button (shown in Figure 6.20), then click the cell to which you want to copy the formatting.

Bright Idea

Make a table easy to read by coloring the rows with alternating stripes of white and pale green. Color the top row, then select the top colored row and the next white row; then click Format Painter and paint the alternating colors down the table in one continuous mouse drag.

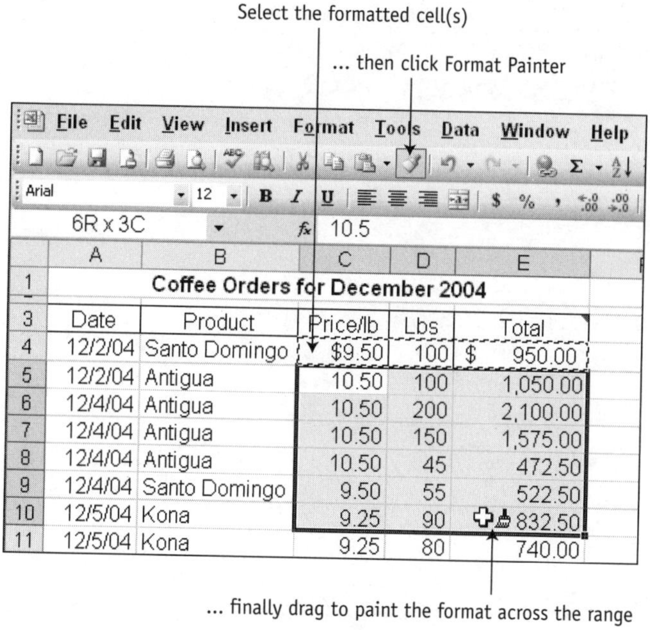

Select the formatted cell(s)

... then click Format Painter

... finally drag to paint the format across the range

Figure 6.20. Painting formatting with the Format Painter

But wait, there's more. If you double-click the Format Painter, it becomes "hot" or switched on; then you can click random cells and ranges anywhere and the format is repeatedly copied until you click the Format Painter again to switch it off.

If you have varied formatting across a row (for example, two white cells, a gray cell, and a blue cell, each with its own special font and number formatting), and want to copy each cell's formatting down its column, do it like this: Select all the formatted cells in one row, click Format Painter, and then paint across all the cells in the next row. Continue to paint to the bottom of the table, all in one continuous drag.

Automatic table formatting

Automatic table formatting, or AutoFormat, is a fast way to apply a format to an entire table, but the formats are limited and uninspired.

Nevertheless, if you're in a hurry or just not feeling creative, this is how you apply an AutoFormat: Click in the table, then choose Format ⇨ AutoFormat. Select a format from the dialog box shown in Figure 6.21, and click OK.

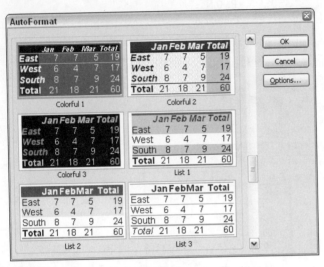

Figure 6.21. AutoFormatting a table

To remove the AutoFormat, press Ctrl+Z right away; to remove an AutoFormat at a later date, click in the table, choose Format ⇨ AutoFormat, scroll to the bottom of the list, and click None.

Just the facts

- Use buttons on the Formatting toolbar for quickest formatting; use the Format Cells dialog box for more elaborate formatting.
- The Fill Color, Font Color, and Borders buttons have tear-away palettes that float on the worksheet while you work.
- Color cell backgrounds and cell text using the Fill Color and Font Color buttons; use the Patterns tab in the Format Cells dialog box to apply patterns to cell backgrounds.
- Fit entries into cells by changing column and row size, wrapping text, and shrinking entries to fit the cell.
- Make data easier to read by aligning and indenting entries. Use the buttons on the Formatting toolbar for the most common alignment settings.
- Center entries across multiple cells by merging them with the Merge and Center button.
- Hide columns and rows for more efficient data entry and to keep worksheet data out of view when necessary.
- Copy formatting fast with the Format Painter button on the Standard toolbar.

Formatting Numbers and Using Styles

I t's not enough to just enter numbers in a worksheet; numbers need to be displayed in a format that's easy to understand (for example, currency, percentages, dates, and times need recognizable formatting to be of any use).

Furthermore, what you see displayed in a cell is not necessarily the value entered in that cell (or calculated by Excel). Occasionally the calculation on the worksheet may appear to be incorrect because in your mind you're calculating the displayed values, while Excel is calculating actual values.

The actual cell value, the number Excel is calculating, is always displayed in the Formula bar.

Number formatting is not only important for data clarity (for example, a date serial number is meaningless to readers), but you can also use formatting to increase a worksheet's effectiveness. For example, a conditional number format can make specific numbers leap off the page visually, and custom formats can display text (such as *8 hrs*) in a cell without affecting the calculable number value in the cell.

Applying number formats to cells

Many number formats can be applied as you type data (such as typing $ or % as you type the numbers). This is efficient

Hack
When you enter a number that's too long for the cell width, the number is displayed in Scientific format (for example, 1.23456E+12). To fix the number format, widen the column and reformat the cell.

if you're only entering data in a single cell or two. But when you need to enter large quantities of numbers—for example, a long list of expenditures in an expenses list—the extra keystroke is tedious. It's faster to enter all the numbers, and then format the cells all at once (or format the cells, and then enter the numbers).

Toolbar buttons for formats

Another fast way to apply the most common formats is to use Formatting toolbar buttons, shown in Figure 7.1:

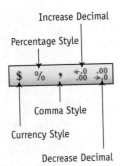

Figure 7.1. Toolbar buttons for formatting

- **Currency Style.** Despite its name, this button applies Accounting Style, *not* Currency style (real Currency style is in the Format Cells dialog box).
- **Percentage Style.** This button applies a percent symbol and tells Excel to calculate the number as a percent, but it only works like you expect if you apply the Percentage style to the cell before you enter the number; if you apply the style after you enter the number, you get a number 100 times larger.

Hack
The Percentage Style button works best if you enter a real percentage, as in .12 for 12%. If you want to simply enter 12% and not figure out the calculable value (.12), forget the button and type %12 or 12%.

- **Comma Style.** This button add a thousands separator (the comma) and two decimal places. If you don't want the added decimal places, click the Decrease Decimal button twice to remove them.

- **Increase Decimal** and **Decrease Decimal.** These buttons add and remove decimal places from the display (they don't change the actual value; they just show more or less precision in the displayed value).

The Format Cells dialog box

The only way to apply exactly the number formats you want (including special and custom formats) is with the Number tab in the Format Cells dialog box (shown in Figure 7.2).

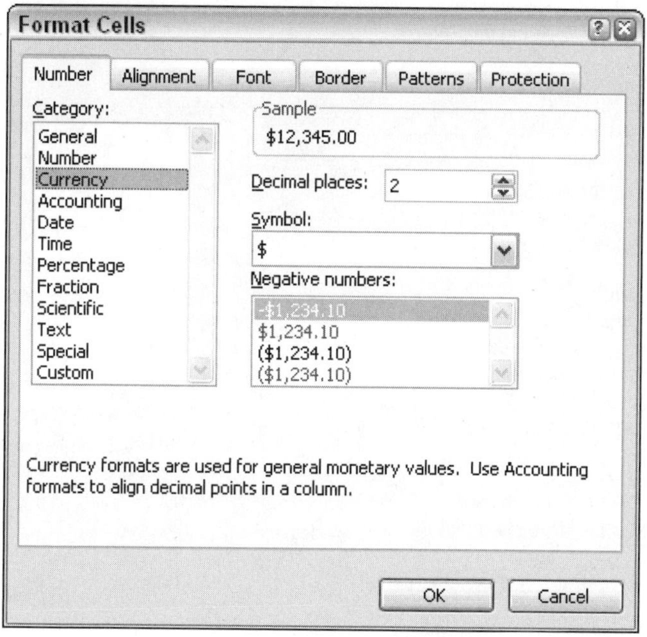

Figure 7.2. All number formatting happens on the Number tab of the Format Cells dialog box.

Right-click a cell that has a number entered, and click Format Cells. On the Number tab, the number in your selected cell is displayed in the selected format in the Sample box, which makes it easy to try different formats until you see the display you want.

Inside Scoop

General is the no-format format; it's the format in empty cells in a new work-sheet. When you clear formats from cells by choosing Edit ➪ Clear ➪ Formats, what's left is General. General format is the best way to see the serial number for a date or time.

Every format category has options specific to that format. Some of the many ways the same number can be displayed using different formats are shown in Table 7.1.

Table 7.1. Number formatting possibilities

This number	In this format	Looks like this
1.2345	Number, zero decimal places	1
	Number, two decimal places	1.23
	Currency	$1.23
	Fraction, up to one digit	1 1/4
	Fraction, up to two digits	1 19/81
12345	Number, two decimals, thousands separator	12,345.00
	Currency	$12,345.00
	Scientific, one decimal place (E indicates that 04 is an exponent)	1.2E+04
	Special, Social Security Number	000-01-2345
.0012345	General	.0012345
	Number, three decimal places	.001
	Percentage, two decimal places	.12%
	Fraction, up to three digits	1/810

Formatting dates and times

Dates and times are formatted, sorted, and calculated as dates and times, even though the date or time you see is actually a serial number that corresponds to that specific date and time.

Bright Idea

When you enter dates, Excel usually enters a four-digit year display, which makes the date entry (and the column in which it's entered) wider than it needs to be. Make the date entries narrower by reformatting the cells to a 2-digit year display.

A serial number that's an integer (no decimals or fractions) indicates the time 12 a.m. (midnight) on the serial number's date; a serial number with a fraction or decimal indicates both a date and a time of day (times are fractions of the 24-hour day).

Occasionally you may enter a number such as 12345 and see it formatted as a date. Excel recognized the number as a date serial number (often because of previous cell formatting). To change the display back to a number, change the cell formatting to General or Number.

The easiest way to format dates and times is to enter them in formats that Excel recognizes.

■ Type **1/7/56** and Excel recognizes the date (you can reformat the entry to any other date display in the Format Cells dialog box's Number tab). Excel recognizes most common date-type entries, such as **jan 7, 56**, and **1-7-56.**

■ Type **1:15** and Excel recognizes the time as 1:15 AM. To specify PM, type **1:15 pm** or **13:15** (the 24-hour clock). The key to entering times is the colon (:), which divides a time entry into hours:minutes:seconds.

Calculating times

Excel calculates times by calculating their serial numbers, which are fractions of a 24-hour day. But if you sum times (as in a weekly timesheet), you get incorrect results when the sum is more than 24 hours.

The key to getting a valid result when the sum is more than 24 hours is to use a custom format. The custom format [h]:mm creates a display that shows the full sum of hours and minutes. A similar custom format, [mm]:ss, shows elapsed time in minutes and seconds for more than 60 minutes.

See the section "Creating custom formats" later in this chapter for more.

Watch Out!
If you subtract one time from another or one date from another and the result is negative, the result is ########. Rewrite your formula to fix it.

If you need a nonstandard date display, such as Jun-05, you must apply it with the Format Cells dialog box's Number tab. Not only are there many ways to format dates and times on the Number tab, but you can create unique formats to better fit your purpose by creating custom formats (see the section "Creating custom formats" later in this chapter).

Formatting text entries

Text entries (such as labels, part numbers, and ZIP codes) might be composed entirely of number characters but are different from number values in that they must retain any leading zeroes and not be included in calculations.

Some entries, such as Social Security numbers, are properly recognized as text when you type the separating dashes, but if you want to type just the numbers and not be bothered with the dash keystrokes, you can format the cells to apply the dashes for you. There are four such formats in the Special category on the Number tab.

Although the Special formats insert punctuation for you and retain leading zeroes, they do not make the formatted entries behave like text; cells with Special formats continue to be calculable numbers.

Creating custom formats

A common use for custom formats is to enter a calculable number but display letter characters alongside the number in the cell. For example, in a timesheet with entries such as 6.5 hrs, the custom format 0.0 "Hrs" displays a one-decimal number with Hrs appended in the cell, but leaves the number calculable (you see just the number in the Formula bar). Custom formats apply to any cells, whether they display entered values or the results of formulas.

To make text characters a part of the cell display, right-click a cell with a number already entered and click Format Cells to open the Format Cells dialog box (shown in Figure 7.3). On the Number tab, click the Custom category. Select any number format in the custom list (look at the Sample box as you select different number formats), and then type

Bright Idea

For an exhaustive list of custom number format codes, type "custom number formats" in the Ask A Question box and press Enter. The help file "Guidelines for custom number formats" has all the information you could want.

your text string, enclosed in quotes, in the appropriate position in the Type box along with the number format characters.

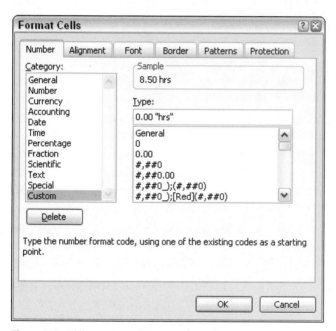

Figure 7.3. Adding a text string to a custom format.

Table 7.2 shows several examples that you can use as starting points for developing your own custom formats.

Table 7.2. Custom formats		
This code	**Gives this result**	**Example (value 01234.333)**
#,##0	Rounds to a whole number; comma separates thousands; no leading zeroes	1,234
# ?/?	Displays decimal portion as a fraction	1234 1/3

continued

Table 7.2. *continued*

This code	Gives this result	Example (value 01234.333)
0.00	Rounds to two decimal places; no thousands separator	1234.33
00000	Displays all digits, including leading zeroes to five places (like ZIP codes)	01234
000-00-0000	Placeholders for all nine digits in a Social Security number; inserts hyphens after you press Enter	123-45-6789
000-0000	Placeholders for seven digits in a telephone number; inserts hyphen after you press Enter	555-1234
(000) 000-0000	Placeholders for an area code and telephone number; inserts parentheses and hyphen after you press Enter	(800) 555-1234
000"."000"."0000	European-style placeholders for digits in a telephone number; inserts periods after you press Enter (quotes distinguish periods from decimal points)	999.555.1234

The fastest way to create the custom format you want is to start with one of the formats already in the list of Custom formats. Click different format codes in the list and watch what happens to your selected cell value in the Sample box. When you have a suitable starting-point format selected, alter the format code in the Type box by adding and removing characters until you have exactly the format you want.

Every custom format you create remains available in the workbook until you delete it; you'll find all your custom formats at the bottom of the list in the Custom category.

Applying conditional number formats

If you have a sea of data and want specific values to stand out, use a conditional number format. A conditional number format is cell formatting that depends on the value in the cell. For example, in a price list, you might format every number greater than $1,000 in a bright red, bold font.

The table in Figure 7.4 is formatted with a conditional number format that uses the MAX and MIN formulas to color the maximum and minimum values in the table. Even when the values change, the conditional number format always highlights the maximum and minimum values. The conditional format is applied to the entire named range and works in addition to any other cell formatting applied to the range.

D14		▾		*fx* =MAX(Commissions)				
	A	B	C	D	E	F	G	H
1				Commissions for 2005				
2		Jan	Feb	Mar	Apr	May	Jun	
3	Marcia	4913	3194	3650	2592	1330	3002	
4	Fred	3554	*1006*	4029	2430	1635	4508	
5	Lila	3098	4820	1032	2628	4213	1951	
6	Armelle	1894	4237	3333	3256	2382	2486	
7	Jamie	3423	4609	3707	2441	2896	1327	
8	Tracy	3266	1621	2873	3526	2622	2148	
9	Susannah	2366	2445	4514	4753	4505	*4934*	
10	Tina	4578	2963	2982	1522	2067	3944	
11	Diane	3217	1248	4004	3449	4563	4542	
12								
13								
14		Highest single month		4934				
15		Lowest single month		1006				
16								

Figure 7.4. This conditional format highlights the minimum and maximum values in the range.

To create a conditional number format, follow these steps:

1. Select the range to which you want to apply the formatting.

2. Choose Format ⇨ Conditional Formatting.

3. In the Conditional Formatting dialog box (see Figure 7.5), set conditions in the Condition 1 boxes, beginning on the left.

4. Click the Format button.

5. In the Format Cells dialog box, set formatting for cells that meet the conditions.

6. To add more conditions and formatting, click Add.

7. Click OK when you're done.

Bright Idea

The Format Painter copies all formatting, both number and cell. If the format you want to apply (including conditional formatting) already exists in any workbook, use the Format Painter to copy it to new cells. Copying a conditionally formatted cell copies the format, not the condition.

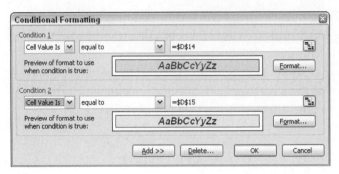

Figure 7.5. The Conditional Formatting dialog box

You can use a formula as part of a condition, as in Cell value is equal to =MAX(*range*), or you can write a formula in a cell outside the table, as I've done, and set the condition Cell value is equal to =*celladdress*.

This is just one example of the good uses to which conditional formatting can be put. Conditional formatting can highlight any values greater or less than your condition, any values between two numbers or not between two numbers, and so on.

Converting actual values to displayed values

If the results of your calculations end up with 11 or 12 decimal places and you want to permanently reduce the values to whole numbers, you can format the values to the number of decimal places you want and then change the calculable value to those simplified values.

For example, if the actual value in a cell is 12.52365987 and you want to lose all but two decimal places, start by formatting the cell to two decimal places. Then choose Tools ➪ Options, and on the Calculation tab, select the Precision as displayed check box, and click OK.

After you change the precision, choose Tools ➪ Options, click the Calculation tab again, and deselect the Precision as displayed check box to turn the behavior off (because you only want to use it once; if you leave it turned on, you lose accuracy every time you reformat a cell).

Watch Out!

This change in calculation accuracy is not reversible; once it's done, it's done, and every cell on every worksheet in the workbook is affected.

Inside Scoop

Excel has 15-digit precision, which means it can use and calculate up to 15 digits, regardless of which side of the decimal point they are on.

Hiding zeroes

On some worksheets, zeroes are important values; they let you know that the value really is zip and not just missing. But on other worksheets, lots of zeroes can be messy, especially when they are the results of formulas. Hiding unnecessary zeroes makes nonzero values more noticeable.

There are three ways to hide zeroes, and each is best in the appropriate circumstances:

- Hide all zeroes on the worksheet, whether they are values or the results of formulas: Choose Tools ⇨ Options, click the View tab, and deselect the Zero values check box. Zero values throughout the workbook are hidden (but you can see them in the Formula bar).

- Hide zeroes only when they are the result of a formula, which limits the hiding to specific cells: Nest the formula in an IF formula, =IF(*formula*=0,"",*formula*), which reads "if the result of the formula is zero, display nothing, otherwise display the result of the formula."

- Create a custom number format to hide zeroes, regardless of the source, in the cells where you apply the format: The custom format #,##0;(#,##0); formats positive numbers as integers with a thousands separator, negative numbers as integers with a thousands separator in parentheses, and no display of zero values. The second semicolon is critical; no format following the second semicolon means zero values have no format and don't appear.

Hack

If you open a worksheet and see no zero values where there should be zeroes, check the three possible causes just discussed. The problem is most likely the Zero values check box when you choose Tools ⇨ Options and click the View tab.

Using styles to streamline formatting

A *style* is a complete package of formats that you can apply all at once. Styles can include font, font size, font and fill color, number formatting, borders, patterns — in short, any formatting you can apply to a cell can be wrapped up in a style. For example, all the formatting shown in Figure 7.6 is applied with one style.

Figure 7.6. Use styles to apply consistent packages of formatting quickly.

Formatting a worksheet with styles is a great timesaver because you can apply all the formatting you need in one step, and every cell to which you apply a specific style is consistently formatted. Here's another time-saver: Occasionally you'll want to change some aspect of a style, such as a color or a font; if you change the style definition, all cells with that style applied are automatically updated with the redefined style formatting.

Get out your Style box

Styles are easiest to use when you put the Style box on one of your toolbars: Right-click in the toolbar area and click Customize; on the Commands tab, in the Categories list, click Format. In the Commands list, drag the Style list box from the dialog box onto a toolbar (see Figure 7.7). Then close the Customize dialog box.

Use the Style box

When you open the Style box list, all the styles in that workbook are displayed (see Figure 7.8); this includes the built-in styles and custom styles. Select a cell or cells, and click a style in the Style list; the style is applied to the selected cell(s).

Bright Idea

Use styles to format table titles and headings for a consistent, professional look and quick application.

Drag the Style box...   ...to a toolbar

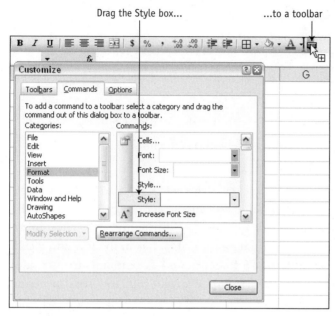

Figure 7.7. Drag the Style box to a toolbar.

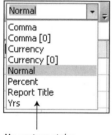

My custom styles

Figure 7.8. The toolbar Style box makes styles much easier to use.

Applying a built-in style

Excel comes with six built-in styles:

- Normal (the default style in every cell in a new workbook)
- Comma (thousands separators with two decimal places)
- Comma [0] (thousands separators with no decimal places)

Inside Scoop

The difference between Currency style and Accounting style is this: In Accounting style the currency symbol ($) is aligned at the left end of the cell, there's a space at the right of the number to leave room for closing parentheses in negative numbers, and the decimal points line up in a column.

- Currency (Accounting style with two decimal places)
- Currency [0] (Accounting style with no decimal places)
- Percent (value*100 with a percent symbol)

Comma, Percent, and Currency styles each have a button on the Formatting toolbar; to apply them to cells, select the cells and click the button. To apply Normal style quickly to a formatted cell, click in an unformatted cell, click the Format Painter, and click in the formatted cell.

A style can incorporate just a few formats — Comma, Currency, and Percent, for example, only have number formatting, and don't override the alignment, font, border, or color settings in the cell — or a style can incorporate every kind of formatting and override any existing formatting in the cell (even though the Normal style appears unformatted, it has every format accounted for).

Changing a style definition

While built-in styles are quick and easy for data entry, they are also uninteresting. If you want a twist to your data display, such as a Currency style that shows negative numbers in red, you can change the definition of a built-in style: Apply the built-in style to a cell and then change the formatting in that cell (formatting changes always override applied styles); then click in the Style box on the toolbar (the style name is highlighted when you click), and press Enter. When asked if you want to redefine the style based on the selection, as shown in Figure 7.9, click Yes. All the cells in the workbook that have that style applied are immediately updated with the new formatting.

Hack

If you changed built-in styles and want to reset them, open a new workbook; in the changed workbook, choose Format ⇨ Style, and click the Merge button. In the Merge styles from list, click the new workbook name. In the Merge Styles that have the same names message, click Yes.

Figure 7.9. Change the definition of a built-in style so the toolbar button gives you a custom format.

Creating a custom style by example

The fastest way to create a custom style is by example. Select a cell and apply all the formatting you want the style to have, then type a name for the style in the Style box on the toolbar, and press Enter. Figure 7.10 shows a custom style created by example. After you create a custom style, you can apply that style just like any built-in style, using the list in the Style box.

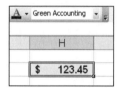

Figure 7.10. Creating a custom style by example

Copying styles from other workbooks

When you spend time creating a great style, it's only available in the workbook in which you created it. But if it's a style that you want to use consistently in all your workbooks, you need an easy way to copy it into other workbooks.

Bright Idea

When you build a long list of styles, scrolling through the Style box list can be tedious. Instead, jump to the style you want quickly by opening the Style box list and typing the first letter of the style.

Hack

Any style can be overridden by applying new formatting to a styled cell, but the Style box will still show the name of the original style. If you decide to return to the style formatting, select the cell, click in the Style box, and press Enter. When asked if you want to redefine the style, click No.

There are two ways to copy styles to another workbook, depending on what you want to do:

- **Copy a single style.** To copy a single style, open the workbook with the style (the first workbook) and the workbook that needs the style (the second workbook). In the first workbook, copy a cell that has the style. In the second workbook, paste the cell. The style is added to the Style list in the second workbook (you can delete the pasted cell).

- **Copy several styles.** To copy several styles to another workbook, open both workbooks. In the workbook that doesn't have the styles, choose Format ⇨ Style. In the Style dialog box, click Merge. In the Merge styles from list, click the name of the workbook that has the styles, and in the Merge Styles that have the same names message, click Yes. All styles in the workbook with the styles are copied into the unstyled workbook, and any styles with the same name are overridden with the new style definition.

Deleting a style

When you have a long list of styles in a workbook (which you will after you experiment with creating styles), you should delete those you no longer need, if only to shorten your Style box list. When you delete a style, all cells with that style applied are returned to Normal style.

To delete a style, choose Format ⇨ Style; in the Style name box (shown in Figure 7.11), select the name you want to delete, click Delete, and then click OK.

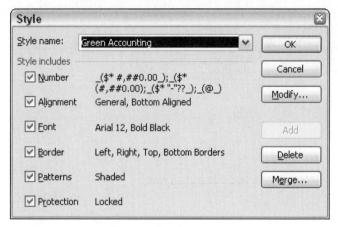

Figure 7.11. Delete a style in the Style dialog box.

Just the facts

- Apply simple formats, such as Currency and Percentage, quickly by typing the punctuation.

- The Formatting toolbar buttons are the next fastest way to apply simple formats to many selected cells at one time.

- For intricate number formatting, right-click the cell(s) and click Format Cells, and then use the Number tab to create the format.

- Format dates and times by entering data in a recognizable date or time format; refine the format, if you need to, in the Format Cells Number tab.

- Format text entries as Text or by typing punctuation as you type the entry; formats in the Special category on the Number tab apply formatting for specific kinds of entries but do not make the entries text.

- Add text strings to number displays by creating Custom formats that incorporate text strings enclosed in quotes.

- Use Conditional Formatting to make numbers that meet specific conditions highly visible.

- Clean up a worksheet and make nonzero values stand out by hiding zeroes, with formulas, custom formatting, or by turning off display of zeroes in the workbook.

- Use styles to apply consistent formatting quickly; put the Style box on a toolbar for quick access to styles.

- Create new styles by example: Format a cell, and then type a style name in the Style box.

Organizing Data

PART IV

Sorting, Filtering, and Querying

Chapter 8

After you enter or import a sea of data into a worksheet, you need to organize the data to render it useful or meaningful. Your first line of defense against a meaningless jumble of data is sorting, while your second line of defense is filtering.

Filtering hides records you don't need to see and displays exactly the records you need to work with; it's the best way I know to display only those records that contain blank cells in a specific field so you can find and fix incomplete data.

Querying is an advanced filtering tool; you can query data from a worksheet table, another workbook or another program, and even from Web pages, pulling out just the data you want to display.

Sorting lists

Sorting lists (I'm talking about any kind of list or table, not just Excel's new dynamic lists) is a basic necessity for organizing data, and some Excel procedures (such as subtotaling a table) require that the data be sorted first.

As always, there are easier ways and there are more cumbersome ways to sort data. I use only the easy ways, so that's what I'm going to show you.

Bright Idea

When you sort a field that has blank cells, the blanks sort to the bottom of the column, so you can use sorts to quickly segregate missing entries in a list. Also, sort a number field in Descending order to locate any alarmingly high numbers that are the result of typographical errors.

When you sort a list, you arrange a specific column, or *field*, in the list in ascending or descending order (see Figure 8.1). The field you sort by is called a *sort key*. When you sort one field, all the attached data — the rest of the list or table — is sorted along with the sort key. Excel expects to find your data in a table, surrounded on four sides by completely blank rows and columns or by the worksheet boundaries, and sorts only the one list; all other data on the worksheet is ignored.

Sort key, sorted ascending   Fields

Region	State	City
Northwest	Idaho	Boise
Northwest	Idaho	Coeur d'Alene
Northwest	Idaho	Sandpoint
Northwest ▲	Washington	Ellensburg
Northwest	Washington	Seattle
Northwest	Washington	Spokane
Southwest	Arizona	Flagstaff
Southwest	Arizona	Phoenix
Southwest	California	Malibu
Southwest	California	Ojai
Southwest	California	Ventura

Click a single cell in the sort key

Figure 8.1. A sorted table

Table or list headings are ignored by Sort procedures as long as the headings are substantially different from the data in the columns; Excel recognizes that the headings are inconsistent with the data and doesn't sort them into the list. If there are no headings in a list, Excel recognizes the consistency of the data and the entire list is sorted.

Watch Out!

When you sort by a field full of numbers that are formatted as text (for example, member numbers in a membership roster), they're sorted in "alpha" order: 1,10,100,2,20,200, and so on. If sorting by that field in numeric order is important, format the entries as numbers, not text.

Sorting hacks

If you get unexpected results when you sort data, knowing a few workarounds can save you time and frustration.

For example, if you ever get the headings sorted into the list because Excel didn't recognize the headings, undo the sort, then choose Data ⇨ Sort to open the Sort dialog box and select the Header row option. Excel recognizes the header row and you can complete the sort.

Another problem you might have with sorting is that when you select an entire column within a table and try to sort it, Excel asks if you want to Expand the selection (sort the whole table) or Continue with the selection (sort just the column). If you sort just the column, your data integrity is lost. If that's not what you intended, choose Expand the selection (better yet, when you want to sort the entire table, select a single cell in the column by which you want to sort the table).

One last problem you may encounter is this: Your column looks like numbers but won't sort correctly. Chances are that somewhere in the column is a badly formatted entry. Instead of wasting time searching for the entry (it could be as simple as a hidden apostrophe at the beginning of the entry), choose Data ⇨ Sort, choose the Header row option (if there is a header row), and click OK. In the Sort Warning dialog box that appears, click the Sort anything that looks like a number, as a number option, and click OK. The Sort Warning dialog box tells you which number is causing the problem; you can locate that number and do whatever is required to reformat the entry as a number.

Sorting a list by a single field

To sort a list by a single field, click a single cell in that column and click either the Sort Ascending or Sort Descending button on the Standard toolbar, shown in Figure 8.2. An ascending sort order is 1–10 or A–Z; a descending sort order is 10–1 or Z–A.

Sort Ascending

Sort Descending

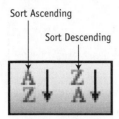

Figure 8.2. The Sort toolbar buttons

Sorting a list by more than one field

There is a Sort dialog box (choose Data ⇨ Sort) that helps if you get confused about the order in which you want to sort fields, but usually sorting is too straightforward to require a whole dialog box. Furthermore, if you need to sort by more than three fields, the Sort dialog box becomes more confusing. It's faster and easier to sort using the Sort buttons.

When you need to sort a list by more than one field, you have *major* and *minor* sort keys. Major keys encompass minor keys. As an example, in a list of regions, states in those regions, and cities in those states, the Region field is the major sort key and the State and City fields are progressively more minor. A logical sort order might be by Region, then by State within Region, then by City within State.

The fast way to perform this sort is to use the Sort buttons on the Standard toolbar: Sort the most minor field first, then the next most minor field, and so on until you sort the major field last. If you set up the table so that your major sort field is on the left and each sort field to the right is progressively more minor (see Figure 8.3), all you do is sort each field from right to left.

Regardless of the number of fields you need to sort by, the Sort buttons on the Standard toolbar will do all the sorting you need.

 Inside Scoop

In a new dynamic list, even though the toolbar that appears with the list has a Sort command on its List button, dynamic lists sort just like normal lists — and the Standard toolbar Sort buttons are faster (one click as opposed to four).

Major key - sort last   Minor key - sort second

    Minor key - sort third   Most minor key - sort first

	Region	Store Type	Store Name	Cap Color	Total Sales
1	Region	Store Type	Store Name	Cap Color	Total Sales
2	North	Affordable	BeeMart	black	$198
3	North	Affordable	BeeMart	red	$124
4	North	Affordable	CostClub	red	$582
5	North	Affordable	CostClub	red	$32
6	North	Affordable	MarkDownTown	black	$67
7	North	Affordable	MarkDownTown	black	$248
8	North	Affordable	WholesaleCity	black	$786
9	North	Affordable	WholesaleCity	red	$494
10	North	High-end	Buttons'n'Bows	black	$768
11	North	High-end	Buttons'n'Bows	red	$177
12	North	High-end	Carriage Notions	black	$52
13	North	High-end	Carriage Notions	black	$67
14	North	High-end	Carriage Notions	red	$36
15	North	High-end	Iron Rose Clothing	black	$65
16	North	High-end	Iron Rose Clothing	black	$389
17	South	Affordable	BeeMart	black	$712
18	South	Affordable	BeeMart	red	$6
19	South	Affordable	CostClub	black	$414
20	South	Affordable	CostClub	black	$249
21	South	Affordable	MarkDownTown	red	$873
22	South	Affordable	MarkDownTown	red	$825
23	South	Affordable	WholesaleCity	black	$583
24	South	Affordable	WholesaleCity	red	$463
25	South	High-end	Buttons'n'Bows	black	$561
26	South	High-end	Buttons'n'Bows	red	$427
27	South	High-end	Carriage Notions	black	$733

Figure 8.3. Sort from right to left, minor to major.

Sorting according to a custom order

You can sort any field in an ascending or descending order, but what if you want to sort a list in an order that's neither ascending nor descending? For example, you might want to sort a list of day or month names or people's names. In this case, you need to use the Sort dialog box.

First, create a custom list of the entries with the sort order you want (see Chapter 3). Day and month names already exist as custom lists.

Inside Scoop

If you need to sort a table by its headings from left to right, open the Sort dialog box, click Options, select the Sort left to right option, and click OK twice. The fields are rearranged in sort order from left to right.

Next, choose Data ⇨ Sort, and click Options in the Sort dialog box. In the First key sort order box (see Figure 8.4), select the sort order for your field, and then click OK. Back in the Sort dialog box, select the Ascending or Descending option next to the Sort by box, and click OK.

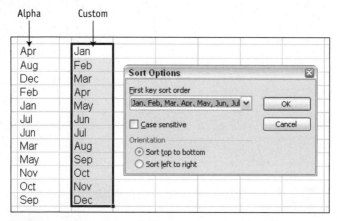

Figure 8.4. Sort in a custom list order rather than alphabetically.

Undoing a sort

Sometimes you need to sort a list temporarily but don't want to keep that sort order. There are two ways to undo a sort:

- To undo a sort and return the list to its former arrangement, press Ctrl+Z (or click the Undo button on the Standard toolbar) before you do anything else in the worksheet.

- To be able to return to a presort arrangement after lots of worksheet manipulation, insert a column of consecutive numbers sorted in ascending order down the right or left side of the table, as shown in Figure 8.5. (Insert a column, type the numbers 1 and 2 at the top, and double-click the fill handle to fill the column.) Then ignore the new column and work with your data. When it's time to return to the initial sort order, sort the column of numbers you inserted.

Bright Idea

If you need to sort a list randomly, add a column filled with the =RAND() function. Every time you sort on the RAND field, the list is randomly sorted again. Delete the RAND field when the list is randomly sorted to your satisfaction.

Region	Store Type	Store Name	Cap Color	Total Sales	re-sort
North	Affordable	BeeMart	black	$198	1
North	Affordable	BeeMart	red	$124	2
North	Affordable	CostClub	red	$582	3
North	Affordable	CostClub	red	$32	4
North	Affordable	MarkDownTown	black	$67	5
North	Affordable	MarkDownTown	black	$248	6
North	Affordable	WholesaleCity	black	$786	7
North	Affordable	WholesaleCity	red	$494	8
North	High-end	Buttons'n'Bows	black	$768	9
North	High-end	Buttons'n'Bows	red	$177	10
North	High-end	Carriage Notions	black	$52	11

Figure 8.5. The easy way to return a table to its original sort order: Add a re-sort column.

Filtering records

When you need to focus on particular *records*, or rows, in a large table, you can *filter* the table to show only the records you need to work with and hide all the data you don't need to see.

The fastest way to filter a list is with AutoFilter. Using AutoFilter, you can look for records that have a specific entry in one field or records that have specific entries in two or more fields (as shown in Figure 8.6), and you can run custom filters that find, for example, entries greater than $100 or entries that contain the text string "lamp." You can also filter for blank cells or nonblank cells.

Date ▾	Vendor ▾	Purpose ▾	Category ▾	Amount ▾
5/11/05	Spokane Times	newspaper	Office Supplies	$32.50
5/28/05	Papers'n'Stuff	pens, ink jet paper	Office Supplies	$3.39
5/30/05	Papers'n'Stuff	copies	Office Supplies	$1.56
			Subtotal	$37.45

Figure 8.6. AutoFilter quickly filters the records you need. This table is filtered in two fields — Date and Category.

Records are filtered based on criteria. A criterion is an entry or partial entry that several records have in common. You designate the criterion, and AutoFilter displays all the records that share that criterion (and hides all records that don't).

To turn on the AutoFilter, click a cell in the table you want to filter, and choose Data ⇨ Filter ⇨ AutoFilter. Gray filter arrows appear on each column heading.

Inside Scoop
The AutoFilter you turn on is exactly the same AutoFilter that is automatically applied to a dynamic list. All of these procedures apply to AutoFilters whether they are in a dynamic list or a normal list.

When you're done filtering, turn AutoFilter off by choosing Data ⇨ Filter ⇨ AutoFilter again.

Filter with a single criterion

To filter a list by a single criterion (a specific entry) in one field, click the filter arrow on that field's column header. A list of all the entries in the field, in alphabetical order, opens (see Figure 8.7). Click the entry for which you want to display records.

▼ Category	▼ Amount ▼
Sort Ascending	$2.32
Sort Descending	$14.87
(All)	$14.87
(Top 10...)	$59.46
(Custom...)	
Books/Publications	$36.80
Equipment Rental	$14.00
License	
Office Equipment	$1.89
Office Supplies	
On-Line charges	$32.50
Tax preparation	$55.56
Telephone Charges	
Travel	$14.87

Figure 8.7. Choose the filter criterion from the AutoFilter list.

Records that contain the criterion you select are displayed and all other records are hidden. The filter arrow on the filtered field is blue.

To show the hidden records again, click the filter arrow and click All (at the top of the list).

Bright Idea
You can preserve the filtered results by copying the filtered range and pasting it elsewhere.

Filter with multiple criteria

Quite often you'll need to filter for multiple or complex criteria such as these:

■ You can filter on two different fields (for example, in an expenses list I want to see all records for Office Supplies from a specific Vendor).

■ You can filter on two criteria in the same field (for example, in an expenses list I want to see all records of expenses at two different stores in the Vendor field).

■ You can filter on a criteria range (for example, I want to see all the records for my office expenses in January).

■ You can filter for specific text strings (in Figure 8.8, I filter for all the records in which the Purpose field contains the word "paper").

Date	Vendor	Purpose	Category	Amount
1/15/05	Office Depot	printer paper	Office Supplies	$59.46
2/10/05	Spokane Times	newspaper	Office Supplies	$32.50
4/27/05	Papers'n'Stuff	envelopes, paper clips	Office Supplies	$2.61
5/11/05	Spokane Times	newspaper	Office Supplies	$32.50
5/28/05	Papers'n'Stuff	pens, ink jet paper	Office Supplies	$3.39
7/15/05	Office Depot	printer paper	Office Supplies	$1.26
8/11/05	Spokane Times	newspaper	Office Supplies	$32.50
			Subtotal	$164.22

Figure 8.8. AutoFilter can find specific text strings, such as the text string "paper" in the Purpose field.

AND Filter or an OR Filter

When you filter for two or more criteria, you run either an AND filter or an OR filter. An OR filter displays records that meet either of the criteria; it reads "show me any entries that are X OR Y." An AND filter displays records that meet both (or all) the criteria; it reads "show me each entry that's both X AND Y." If you create an AND filter and get no results, you probably want an OR filter instead.

Filter with two different fields

A filter on two different fields (such as the filter in Figure 8.6) is an AND filter. It reads "show me records that have a criterion in this field AND a criterion in that field." You can filter on as many fields as you need.

To run a multiple-field filter, click the filter arrow in one field and set your criterion, then click the filter arrow in another field and set your criterion.

Both filtered fields have blue filter arrows to help you remember where you set the filter criteria.

Filter with two criteria in the same field

A two-criteria filter in the same field might be an OR filter or an AND filter. An OR filter shows records that have one criteria OR another in the same field (such as one store OR another in a Vendor field); an AND filter shows records that meet one criteria AND another in the same field (such as records that have dates greater than or equal to January 1, 2005, AND less than or equal to January 31, 2005, in the Date field).

To set up a two-criteria filter in the same field, click the Filter button and click Custom. In the Custom AutoFilter dialog box (see Figure 8.9), set the first criterion in the top row, then select the And or the Or option, and set the second criterion in the bottom row.

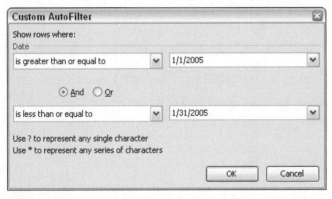

Figure 8.9. This AND filter shows all the records with dates in January 2005.

Filter for a text string

Suppose you don't have a specific entry for a criterion, but want to see all the records that have a specific word or text string in the filter field. You can filter for entries that begin with, end with, or contain specific text strings, and for entries that do not begin with, end with, or contain specific text strings.

Inside Scoop

The Top 10 command on the Filter button list can filter either the top several values in the field or the top percentage of values that you set. The top percentage filter is worthwhile, but the top values are quicker to see with a descending sort.

To filter on a text string, click the Filter button and click Custom. In the Custom AutoFilter dialog box, shown in Figure 8.10, in the upper-left box, scroll to the bottom of the list and select a qualifier; then type the text string in the upper-right box. Just type the characters — there's no need to put them in quotes.

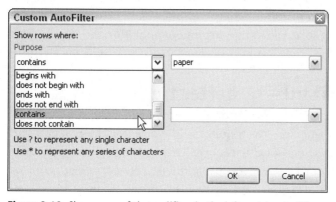

Figure 8.10. Choose one of the qualifiers in the leftmost box to filter on a text string.

Calculating filtered records

Viewing a filtered list is a good beginning, but without calculations it's just a list of numbers. Usually you want to sum a subset of records in a filtered list, but you need the right formula to get an accurate sum when the list is filtered.

The SUBTOTAL function gives you the right formula. SUBTOTAL calculates only the visible cells in a filtered list, whereas the SUM function calculates the entire list, including the hidden cells. (If your list is a dynamic list, the SUBTOTAL formula is already written for you as part of the list structure.)

The fastest way to write a SUBTOTAL formula for a filtered list is to filter the list (filter it for anything, as long as it's filtered), and use the

Inside Scoop

The AutoSum button gives you a choice of functions when you open its list, but those choices don't translate into different SUBTOTAL calculations. To use a different SUBTOTAL calculation (such as AVERAGE), let AutoSum write the SUBTOTAL formula and then change the calculation argument.

AutoSum button on the Standard toolbar to write the formula. (If you use the AutoSum button when the list is not filtered — even if AutoFilter is turned on — you get a SUM function instead of a SUBTOTAL function.)

It matters where you write the formula on the worksheet, because if you put the formula alongside the list, it will be hidden whenever a filter hides that row. Put the formula at the bottom of the list below the calculated column so it isn't hidden when you filter the list, or put it in the header row but be sure the range argument includes the whole field range.

The Query Wizard — A better filter

If you use Access or any other relational database program, you probably already know what queries are. A query is like a better filter. When you use a filter, you can select specific records (rows), but you get every field (column) in the record. When you use a query, you can select not only specific records but also specific fields within those records. For example, in an expenses list with Date, Vendor, Category, and Amount fields, I can extract specific records and include only the Date and Amount fields, as shown in Figure 8.11.

Furthermore, when you run a filter, you are filtering a table in an open Excel workbook. Queries are the only way to extract data from a source that's too large to be imported into a worksheet, or from a source that is closed (that's right — you can extract data into a worksheet from a closed file). And you can run the same query for updated data repeatedly every day, every month — whatever schedule you need — without having to re-create the query.

The Query Wizard in Excel helps you to pinpoint exactly the data you want to extract; you can use the wizard to extract data from Excel lists, Access database table and queries, and other database program files. The procedures for querying all these file types is similar; once you know how to query an Excel list, you are able to query other database files just as easily. And you can also query Web pages, which is covered later in this chapter.

Queried data is not formatted

Date	Vendor	Purpose	Category	Amount	Date	Amount
1/5/05	Papers'n'	tax receipts enve	Office Supplies	$2.32	5/11/05	32.5
1/15/05	US West	business phone	Telephone Cha	$14.87	5/28/05	110
2/15/05	US West	business phone	Telephone Cha	$14.87	5/28/05	3.39
1/15/05	Office De	printer paper	Office Supplies	$59.46	5/30/05	1.56
1/15/05	Sprint	long distance cha	Telephone Cha	$36.80		
1/24/05	Sparrow I	Tea book (resea	Books/Publicati	$14.00		
2/8/05	Papers'n'	copies	Office Supplies	$1.89		
2/10/05	Spokane	newspaper	Office Supplies	$32.50		
2/13/05	B&N	Access & VB bo	Books/Publicati	$55.56		
3/15/05	US West	business phone	Telephone Cha	$14.87		
4/15/05	US West	business phone	Telephone Cha	$16.01		
3/7/05	Papers'n'	copies	Office Supplies	$1.82		
3/9/05	Sparrow I	Access book	Books/Publicati	$43.23		
3/12/05	Papers'n'	copies	Office Supplies	$2.72		
6/24/05	US West	business phone	Telephone Cha	$16.47		

Figure 8.11. This query pulls out only the data I want from the large table.

Prepare to run a query

Before you run a query on an Excel table, name the range of data you're querying so that the wizard can find the data more easily. Then save and close the workbook that has the data.

The first time you run a query, it's a two-part process. First, you define a data source (tell Query Wizard where to look for the data), and then you run the Query Wizard and indicate exactly what data to extract from the data source.

After you define the data source, the Query Wizard remembers the data source, and you don't need to redefine it the next time you want to extract information from that data source. All you do is run the Query Wizard each time you want to pull data from that source.

Define the data source

The procedure for defining a data source is similar whether the data source is an Excel workbook, an Access database, or another type of database file.

1. Open the workbook in which you want to place the queried data.

2. Choose Data ⇨ Import External Data ⇨ New Database Query.
   If you're asked to install Microsoft Query, click Yes and wait a few

minutes while the components are installed (if you have a problem starting Query after installing it, restart Windows).

3. In the Choose Data Source dialog box (shown in Figure 8.12), on the Databases tab, double-click <New Data Source>.

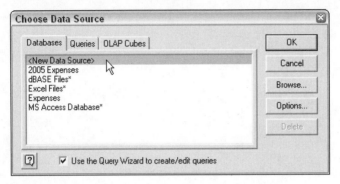

Figure 8.12. To create a new query, set up a new data source.

4. In the Create New Data Source dialog box (shown in Figure 8.13), in box 1, type a name for your data source (something you'll recognize later; for example, March Vendors). In box 2, click the arrow and select Microsoft Excel Driver, then click Connect.

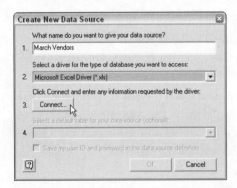

Figure 8.13. Name the data source and choose the Excel driver.

5. In the ODBC Microsoft Excel Setup dialog box (shown in Figure 8.14), choose Excel 97-2000 (Query hasn't been updated since Excel 2000) and click Select Workbook.

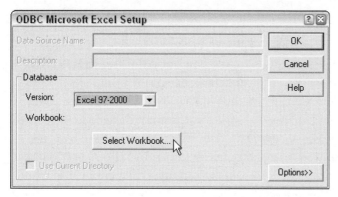

Figure 8.14. Choose the Excel version and click Select Workbook.

6. In the Select Workbook dialog box (shown in Figure 8.15), navigate
to the workbook that contains your data source and double-click the
workbook filename. The ODBC Microsoft Excel Setup dialog box
from Step 5 reappears and the workbook name and path appear in
the Workbook line.

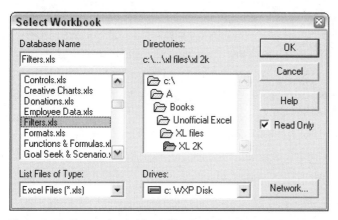

Figure 8.15. Choose the workbook file where the source data resides.

7. Click OK in the ODBC Microsoft Excel Setup dialog box, and again
in the Create New Data Source dialog box. The Choose Data Source
dialog box reappears with your new data source name in the list.

Inside Scoop

After you define a database, the name you type in Step 4 appears in the
Databases tab list in the Choose Data Source dialog box. When you come back
later to query this data source, select its name in the Databases tab in the
Choose Data Source dialog box.

Querying other programs

Microsoft Query can query most types of databases. If you have Access or any other Microsoft database programs installed on your system, you'll find entries for those programs in the Choose Data Source dialog box. If, for example, you want to query an Access database, select MS Access Database on the Databases tab in the Choose Data Source dialog box, navigate to find the Access database (on your computer or on a network), and then create and run your query just like in Excel.

Your new data source is set up and ready to use any time you want to query it. At this point, you can either click OK to close the Choose Data Source dialog box and come back to perform queries later, or you can continue setting up the query in the Query Wizard in the next section.

Run the Query Wizard

After you define a data source, you can set up the actual query.

If you've just finished defining the data source, the Choose Data Source dialog box is still open and you can start at Step 2. If you defined the data source some time ago and want to set up a new query using that data source, begin with Step 1.

1. Choose Data ⇨ Import External Data ⇨ New Database Query.

2. In the Choose Data Source dialog box (shown in Figure 8.16), double-click your named data source.

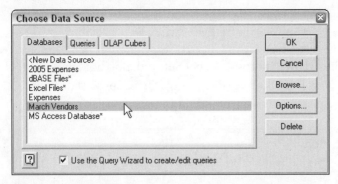

Figure 8.16. Double-click your named data source to set up the query.

3. When the Query Wizard – Choose Columns dialog box appears (shown in Figure 8.17), named ranges in the data source (including the range you named before you defined the data source) are listed. Each named range has a small plus symbol (+) next to it; click the plus symbol to display the list of column headings in that range. The plus symbol changes to a minus symbol (-) once it has been clicked.

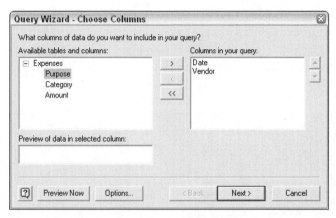

Figure 8.17. Click the plus symbol to display the list of columns in that range.

4. Double-click each column you want to include in the query, and then click Next. Double-clicked columns move to the Columns in your query field.

5. In the Query Wizard – Filter Data dialog box (shown in Figure 8.18), click a column name in the Column to filter list, then set your filter criteria in the Only include rows where section. Setting filter criteria here is the same as setting filter criteria for AutoFilter. (If you want all of the data from just a few columns, don't set any criteria — just click Next.)

6. In the Query Wizard – Sort Order dialog box (shown in Figure 8.19), you can choose a sort order for the extracted data, but you don't have to. Click Next.

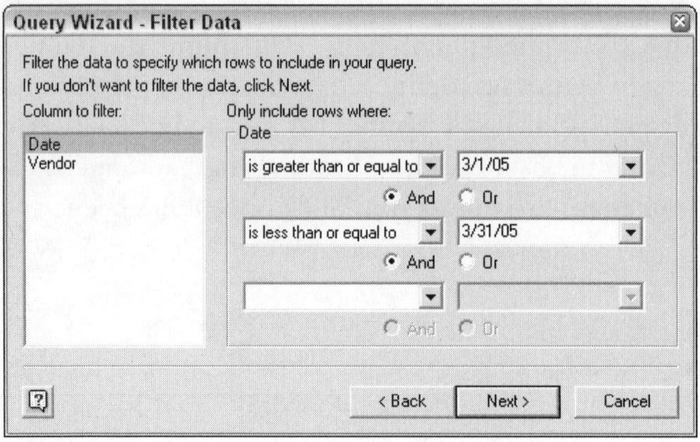

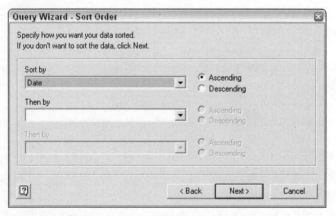

Figure 8.18. Set filter criteria for each column.

Figure 8.19. Choosing a sort order makes the extracted data easier to understand.

7. In the Query Wizard – Finish dialog box (shown in Figure 8.20), you're extracting data into an Excel worksheet, so leave the default option (Return Data to Microsoft Office Excel) selected and click Finish.

To save the query, click Save Query and give the query a recognizable name in the Save As dialog box. Don't change the folder in the Save in box; save the query in the default Queries folder, which is deeply nested in your computer files, so that Microsoft Query can find the saved query easily when you want to reuse it.

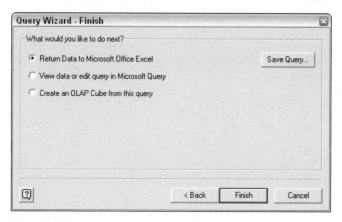

Figure 8.20. Choose an option and click Finish; click Save Query first if you want to save and reuse the query in another workbook.

8. After Query spins its wheels for a few seconds, an Import Data dialog box appears (shown in Figure 8.21) asking where to paste the data. Click the cell where you want to paste the upper-left corner of the extracted data (or click New worksheet to create a new worksheet for the extracted data) and click OK. The data you filtered from the data source is pasted in the worksheet.

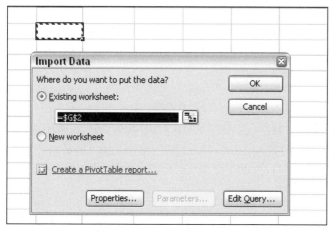

Figure 8.21. Choose a location for the extracted data.

When extracted data is pasted into a worksheet (shown in Figure 8.22), you get a new toolbar along with the data. The External Data toolbar buttons are active when you click in the extracted range.

Bright Idea

If you're planning on making a PivotTable with the extracted data, click the Create a PivotTable report link instead of OK. The PivotTable Wizard Step 3 of 3 appears, and you're almost finished with the PivotTable. I cover PivotTables in Chapter 10.

Refresh Data

Refresh All

Figure 8.22. A query result and the External Data toolbar

The Refresh Data button refreshes the data in the selected query; the Refresh All button refreshes all the queries in the workbook.

When data in the data source changes, all you need to do to update your extracted data is click in the extract range and click the Refresh button. For example, if you query the company database for information about your department employees once a month, all you need to do is refresh the data in the existing query.

Reuse a query

If you want to periodically refresh the data in your query, use the Refresh button. But what if you want to run the same query in another workbook? If you saved the query, you can run the saved query without having to redefine the source data.

To reuse a saved query, click a blank cell in the worksheet, then choose Data ⇨ Import External Data ⇨ New Database Query. In the Choose Data Source dialog box, click the Queries tab (shown in Figure 8.23). Click the name of the saved query you want to run, and click Open.

The Query Wizard starts and you have the opportunity to refine your query fields and criteria; if you don't want to make any changes, click Next all the way through the wizard steps and then click Finish in the last step.

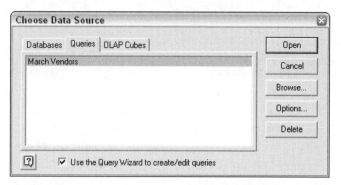

Figure 8.23. Saved queries are listed on the Queries tab.

If you want to use this query in another computer or back it up, you can send a copy of the saved query file to wherever is convenient. Saved queries are files with the extension .dqy (in your Queries folder if you didn't save the query in a different folder). Search your file system for the Queries folder or files named *.dqy to find the query file.

Delete a query

Queries last forever. A query is really just a definition, a paragraph of instructions to Microsoft Query to "go to this data source and extract this data." A query doesn't take up enough computer memory to blink at; nevertheless, you might want to delete a query one day (perhaps you queried sensitive information and don't want anyone else to have access to it).

Deleting all the data in an extracted range doesn't delete the query; when you click an empty cell that was a part of the extract range, the External Data toolbar buttons are active and you can bring all that queried data back again (and current) by clicking the Refresh button.

Deleting all the rows or columns in which the query resides deletes the query in that worksheet; but if you save the query, it can be run again in any workbook.

To delete a saved query, choose Data ⇨ Import External Data ⇨ New Database query. In the Choose Data Source dialog box, click the Queries tab. Click the name of the saved query and click Delete.

Query a Web page

The Web is chock full of information that is a great deal more useful once you get it into an Excel or Word file so you can analyze it.

Watch Out!

Your Web query will work the first time you set it up, but if the Web page address changes, the page structure changes, or the page requires you to log on, the query will break the next time you use it. There's nothing you can do but re-create the query.

If all you want to do is save the information on a Web page one time, you don't need to query it; on the Web page, drag to select just the information you want to extract and press Ctrl+C to copy it, then click in an Excel or Word file and press Ctrl+V to paste.

When you want to repeatedly pull data from a specific Web page, perhaps to update a stock portfolio, a Web query is quick and reusable (mostly).

To create a Web query, get the address of the Web page. Excel won't help you find the address, so open your browser, go to the Web page, and copy the entire URL out of the browser's Address bar (paste it somewhere handy—I use Outlook Notes, but you can paste it in a worksheet, a Word document, or anywhere convenient).

Then open the worksheet where you want to place the queried data and choose Data ⇨ Import External Data ⇨ New Web Query. The New Web Query dialog box opens to your browser's home page (shown in Figure 8.24). Copy the URL you pasted somewhere handy and paste it in the Address box at the top of the New Web Query dialog box, then click Go (or press Enter).

Figure 8.24. The New Web Query dialog box opens to your browser's home page.

After the New Web Query dialog box opens to your chosen Web page (see Figure 8.25), select the table you want to extract from the Web page. Web pages are laid out in tables (some more efficiently than others), and each table has a yellow arrow box at the upper-left corner. Click the arrow box for any table you want to extract (you can click as many as you like), and the yellow arrow box becomes a green check mark. (If you change your mind about a selection, click the green check mark to deselect the table.)

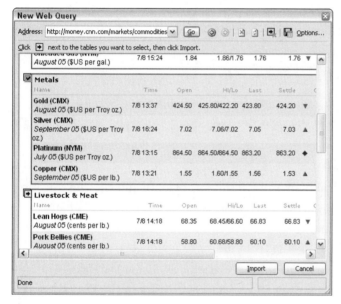

Figure 8.25. Click the arrow boxes for tables you want to extract.

When you've selected all the tables you want, click Import. Just like in a normal query, the Import Data dialog box asks you where to place the query results. Click a cell in the worksheet and click OK. Wait a few seconds and the queried data appears in the worksheet (shown in Figure 8.26).

Bright Idea

Some Web information can be looked up quickly in the new Excel Research task pane (choose View ⇨ Task Pane, then click the arrow in the task pane title bar and select Research). Type something you want to look up in the Search for box and select a research site in the second box.

	A	B	C	D	E	F	G
1	URL: http://money.cnn.com/markets/commodities/						
2							
3							
4	Metals	Price	Change	High	Low	Settle	Last Update †
5	Gold (CMX)	477.7	2.7	479.1	469.9	477.7	10/7 1:51pm
6	December 05 ($US per Troy oz.)						
7	Silver (CMX)	7.77	0.18	7.79	7.64	7.77	10/7 1:37pm
8	December 05 ($US per Troy oz.)						
9	Platinum (NYM)	939.1	8.4	939.5	935	939.1	10/7 1:14pm
10	January 06 ($US per Troy oz.)						
11	Copper (CMX)	1.81	0.03	1.81	1.79	1.81	10/7 1:26pm
12	December 05 ($US per lb.)						
13							
14							
15							

Figure 8.26. The results of a Web query

Don't spend too much time formatting this data, because much of your formatting is lost the next time you query the Web page.

Just the facts

- Sort a list by clicking in a cell in the sort column and clicking the Sort Ascending or Sort Descending button on the Standard toolbar.

- Sort a list by multiple sort keys with the Sort buttons on the Standard toolbar, sorting from minor to major sort keys.

- Sort according to a custom sort order by choosing Data ⇨ Sort; click the Options button and select a sort order in the First key sort order box.

- Filter records with AutoFilter (choose Data ⇨ Filter ⇨ AutoFilter to turn AutoFilter on or off).

- Calculate filtered records with the SUBTOTAL function.

- Create reusable queries to extract data from closed workbooks, large files, or other programs.

- Create reusable queries to extract current data from a Web page without opening the Web page.

Finding and Comparing Answers

Chapter 9

When you have a long list of data, such as a checkbook register or a list of products sold, sorting, filtering, and calculating the list is an important starting point, but you need to summarize the details to make the data useful. One rapid way to summarize a long list of data is to *consolidate* it into categories. Another is to *subtotal* it, which consolidates data into categories but retains the details that can be hidden or displayed. (PivotTables are the next rung up on the big-data-picture ladder, but are complex enough to deserve their own chapters. I address them in Chapters 10 and 11.)

One of a computer's most important functions is to help us make better decisions. The capability to calculate and summarize large quantities of data is sometimes not enough, and there are a few more tools with which Excel can help you make better decisions.

If you have several different possible situations or scenarios, you should compare the results of different courses of action before moving ahead with one of them. Excel's Scenario Manager can help you to compare those different scenarios.

If you're working on a problem and you know what result or solution you want, Excel can help you figure out what you need to do to get there. The Goal Seek and Solver tools work problems "backward" to find input values that give the results you want.

Consolidating a table

Consolidation has been an Excel tool for a long time, and it's as useful now as it was in Excel 5 (which is to say, very useful — I use it every year to get my tax numbers ready for my accountant). Consolidation is quick and easy and the results are a simple list of the data categories alongside the calculated data for each category.

I've seen some folks create their own consolidation-type tables by writing a list of SUMIF formulas (summing data that matches each category), but a consolidation table gives the same result much more quickly, reliably, and reusably.

To create a consolidation table:

1. Select a *destination area* where the consolidated list will be pasted. The destination area can be on the same worksheet, a different worksheet, or in a different workbook.

2. At the top of the destination area, enter (better yet, copy and paste) the headings of the category and number columns that you want to consolidate; then select the destination area headings (but only the headings).

3. Choose Data ⇨ Consolidate. The Consolidate dialog box opens.

4. Select a function in the Function box (usually Sum), then click in the Reference box and drag to select the range you want to consolidate (shown in Figure 9.1). After selecting the range, click Add to add the range to the All references box.

   To consolidate similar data from several different ranges, worksheets, and workbooks, add multiple references to the All references box. You can also type or paste range names, and you can include multiple number columns, as long as the column headings are identical.

5. Select the Top row and Left column check boxes, then click OK.

Inside Scoop

There's no need to sort a table before consolidating it. Consolidation works like a mass SUMIF function; it finds and calculates all the data related to each category label, regardless of sort order.

Labels in leftmost column of consolidation range   Destination area

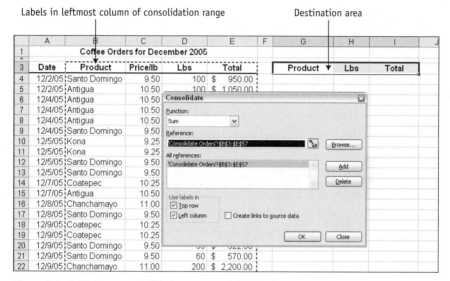

Figure 9.1. Setting up a consolidation range and destination area

Figure 9.2 shows the finished consolidation table for this orders list example.

	A	B	C	D	E	F	G	H	I	J
1		Coffee Orders for December 2005								
3	Date	Product	Price/lb	Lbs	Total		Product	Lbs	Total	
4	12/2/05	Santo Domingo	9.50	100	$ 950.00		Santo Domingo	1305	$ 12,397.50	
5	12/2/05	Antigua	10.50	100	$ 1,050.00		Antigua	1785	$ 18,742.50	
6	12/4/05	Antigua	10.50	200	$ 2,100.00		Kona	885	$ 8,186.25	
7	12/4/05	Antigua	10.50	150	$ 1,575.00		Coatepec	1425	$ 14,606.25	
8	12/4/05	Antigua	10.50	45	$ 472.50		Chanchamayo	1200	$ 13,200.00	
9	12/4/05	Santo Domingo	9.50	55	$ 522.50					
10	12/5/05	Kona	9.25	90	$ 832.50					
11	12/5/05	Kona	9.25	80	$ 740.00					

Figure 9.2. Consolidation summarizes the categories in a long list.

Watch Out!

The reference range must have the category labels in the leftmost column and the column labels in the top row. Other data in the range doesn't matter, but Excel looks for category labels in the left column and numbers in the columns whose headings match the consolidation table headings.

Watch Out!

If the reference range changes, be sure you select the previous range in the All references list and delete it, and add the new reference range. If you don't delete the previous reference range, the table consolidates twice.

Consolidation tables do not automatically update. When data changes in the raw-data table, select the consolidation table headings (just the headings), choose Data ⇨ Consolidate, make sure the reference range is correct, and click OK to reconsolidate.

If any reference ranges are in closed workbooks, leave the workbooks closed (unless you need to check reference range validity). You don't need to open the workbooks to rerun the consolidation.

Subtotaling a table

Subtotaling goes a step beyond consolidation, providing collapsible levels of detail along with category subtotals. Subtotaling can include several levels of category-label columns as well as number columns. Subtotaling happens within the data table rather than outside the table as in consolidation and PivotTables.

Figure 9.3 shows the same orders list that I consolidated in the previous section, but this time the table was subtotaled. On the left side of the worksheet are outline buttons: The 1, 2, and 3 buttons at the top expand and collapse entire detail levels of the table, and the plus/minus buttons along the side expand and collapse individual categories.

	A	B	C	D	E
1	Coffee Orders for December 2005				
3	Date	Product	Price/lb	Lbs	Total
19		Antigua Total			$ 18,742.50
20	12/8/05	Chanchamayo	11.00	200	$ 2,200.00
21	12/9/05	Chanchamayo	11.00	200	$ 2,200.00
22	12/13/05	Chanchamayo	11.00	200	$ 2,200.00
23	12/19/05	Chanchamayo	11.00	200	$ 2,200.00
24	12/21/05	Chanchamayo	11.00	200	$ 2,200.00
25	12/26/05	Chanchamayo	11.00	200	$ 2,200.00
26		Chanchamayo Total			$ 13,200.00
36		Coatepec Total			$ 14,606.25
46		Kona Total			$ 8,186.25
62		Santo Domingo Total			$ 12,397.50
63		Grand Total			$ 67,132.50
64					

Figure 9.3. Subtotaling preserves details within the subtotaled outline.

Bright Idea

If there are columns of data in the table that don't need to be included in the subtotal results, hide those columns. They won't be visible, but the data won't be lost, either.

To subtotal a table:

1. Arrange the table so the columns are logically organized, and sort the columns in order from minor to major sort keys (from right to left).

2. Click a cell in the table, and click Data ⇨ Subtotals.

3. In the Subtotal dialog box (see Figure 9.4), in the At each change in box, select the major category to which you want to apply subtotals; select a function in the Use function box; in the Add subtotal to box, select check boxes for the number columns you want to subtotal (and deselect all other check boxes); then click OK.

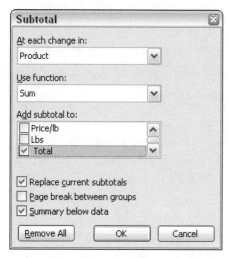

Figure 9.4. The Subtotal dialog box for the subtotaled table shown in the previous figure

Bright Idea

The subtotal category labels are bold, but (inexplicably) the subtotaled sums are not bold and blend into the detail numbers. To bold the subtotaled sums: Collapse the outline to labels and sums; select the sum cells; choose Edit ⇨ Go To; click Special, Visible Cells Only, and OK; then format Bold.

Outlining without subtotals

Subtotaling creates a collapsible/expandable outline that is useful even without the calculated data; in fact, you can outline a table that has no calculable data at all. For example, you might have a table that lists company departments and the names and personal information of employees in each department. By outlining the table, you can expand and collapse individual departments. Or you can outline just part of a table rather than the entire table.

To outline a table, select adjacent rows that you want to combine into a collapsible/expandable level, then choose Data ⇨ Group and Outline ⇨ Group. Continue selecting and grouping each set of rows that you want to outline.

To remove manual outlining, expand and select a single group of rows from which you want to remove outlining, then choose Data ⇨ Group and Outline ⇨ Clear Outline.

If you have only one level of categories to subtotal, stop here; you're done.

To apply more levels of subtotals, repeat Steps 1 through 3, but be sure you deselect the Replace current subtotals check box before you click OK.

If you get confused and need to start over, or if you just want to remove the subtotals and have your normal table back again, click in the table, and choose Data ⇨ Subtotals, and click Remove All.

Scenarios

Scenarios are a tool for setting up the same formulas with different input values so you can compare the results before making decisions. For example, scenarios are a good way to compare different loan possibilities. In a scenario, you can have as many different changing input values as you like (such as different rates, terms, and amounts for the same loan); the key to having organized scenarios to compare is to name them well so you can identify them easily.

When you create scenarios, you create several different sets of values and results, but only one set appears on the worksheet at a time; you use the Scenario Manager dialog box to switch between the scenarios displayed on the worksheet. While this in itself is neither efficient nor useful, the feature that makes scenarios worthwhile is the Scenario Summary report, which is a separate worksheet that shows all your scenarios side by side.

Create scenarios

To use scenarios to compare answers, follow these steps:

1. Set up your first scenario on a worksheet. I'll use the loan calculator, which uses the PMT function, as a simple example.

2. Choose Tools ⇨ Scenarios. In the Scenario Manager dialog box, click Add.

3. In the Add Scenario dialog box, type an easy-to-understand name for the scenario, then delete any cell references in the Changing cells box and leave the Changing cells open with the cursor blinking in it, as shown in Figure 9.5.

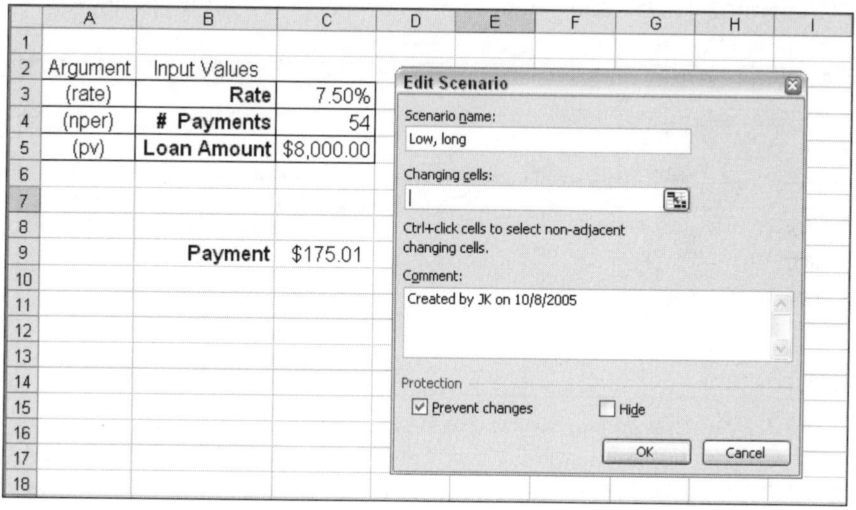

Figure 9.5. Setting up the first scenario

4. On the worksheet, click, drag, or Ctrl+click to select all the cells in which you want to change values in different scenarios. For example, in the loan calculator (see Figure 9.6), I want to change the rate and the number of payments in these scenarios, so I click and drag to select both input cells. Then click OK.

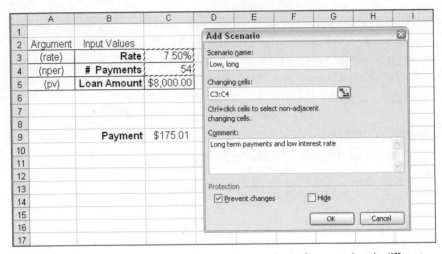

Figure 9.6. Select all the cells whose values you want to change for comparison in different scenarios.

5. In the Scenario Values dialog box (shown in Figure 9.7), enter a value for each changing cell in this scenario. You can change just one value or all values, depending on what you want to compare.

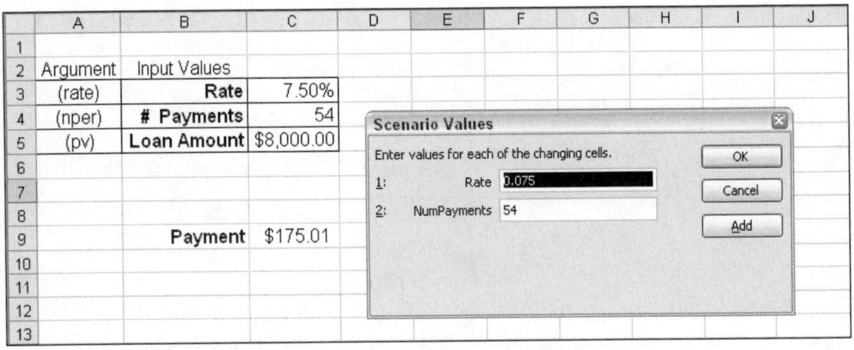

Figure 9.7. Enter values for the changing cells in this scenario.

6. Click OK, and follow Steps 2 through 5 to set up more scenarios.

Each scenario name appears in the Scenarios list in the Scenario Manager dialog box (shown in Figure 9.8). To display a particular scenario on the worksheet, click that name and click Show. If you're done creating/viewing scenarios, click Close. When you choose Tools ⇨ Scenarios again, all the scenarios on this worksheet are available.

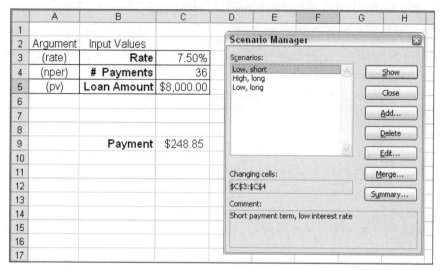

Figure 9.8. Click Summary to create a summary of all scenarios.

Create a scenario summary

Scenarios aren't at all useful for comparison when you can only display one at a time, but when you create a summary, you can compare all the scenarios side by side.

If the Scenario Manager dialog box is not open, choose Tools ⇨ Scenarios.

To create a scenario summary, click Summary in the Scenario Manager dialog box (refer to Figure 9.8).

In the Scenario Summary dialog box (shown in Figure 9.9), leave the Scenario summary option button selected, and delete any cell reference in the Result cells dialog box. With the insertion point in the Result cells box, click the cell that contains the formula (in the loan calculator example, it would be the Payment formula cell). Then click OK.

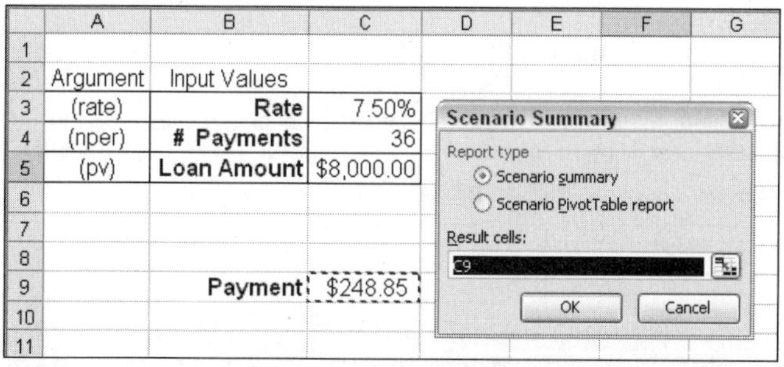

Figure 9.9. Put the formula cell reference in the Result cells box.

A new Scenario Summary worksheet like the one in Figure 9.10 appears in the workbook.

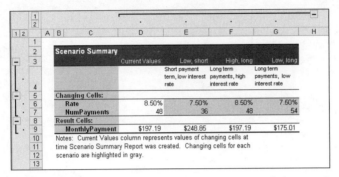

Figure 9.10. A scenario summary allows you to compare all the scenarios you create.

Compare answers with data tables

A data table is another useful way to compare answers by laying out formula results for many different values in one or two formula input cells.

There are two kinds of data tables: A *one-input* data table returns results for many formulas but can only calculate those results for one changing input value. A *two-input* data table returns results for only one formula but can use changing input values in two of the formula's input values.

One-input data table

A typical use for a one-input data table is a loan table that compares payments for different interest rates (see Figure 9.11). In this example, the data table calculates the same formulas as a loan calculator using the PMT function, but the loan calculator calculates just one result while the data table calculates several results for comparison. (You find the PMT function used in a loan calculator in Chapter 5.)

Inside Scoop

Data tables are more limited than Scenario Manager, which can calculate and compare scenarios with many changing input values, but data tables take less time to set up, and display results more concisely.

Inside Scoop

You can have as many formulas in the leftmost column as you like, as long as they all depend, directly or indirectly, on the same changing input value.

	A	B	C	D	E	F	G	H	I
1	Argument	Input Values							
2	(rate)	Rate	7.50%						
3	(nper)	# Payments	36						
4	(pv)	Amount	$ 5,000.00						
5									
6				7.00%	7.20%	7.40%	7.60%	7.80%	8.00%
7		Payment	$ 155.53	$ 154.39	$ 154.84	$ 155.30	$ 155.76	$ 156.22	$ 156.68
8		Total payback	$ 5,599.12	$ 5,557.88	$ 5,574.35	$ 5,590.86	$ 5,607.39	$ 5,623.95	$ 5,640.55
9		Total interest	$ 599.12	$ 557.88	$ 574.35	$ 590.86	$ 607.39	$ 623.95	$ 640.55
10									

Figure 9.11. This data table calculates results for three different formulas based on one changing input value, the interest rate.

To build a table like the one shown in Figure 9.11, follow these steps:

1. Enter starting argument values in input cells for the formula, as shown in Figure 9.12. A data-table formula needs cell references for argument values.

2. In the leftmost column of the one-input data table, enter the formulas that return the results. This data table uses the formulas already set up in a PMT-function loan calculator (the PMT function is covered in Chapter 5), and those formulas reference the cells with starting argument values from Step 1.

3. Enter the changing input values in the row along the top of the data table.

4. Select the entire table range to include all the column formulas and all the row input values (but not the row labels).

5. Choose Data ⇨ Table. In the Table dialog box, click in the Row input cell box and then click the single input cell (the Rate cell on which the formulas depend).

6. Click OK. The table calculates formula results for all the changing input values.

Watch Out!

A Data Table writes a set of array formulas that are, in reality, all one formula shared by several cells. You cannot change or delete part of an array formula (including deleting cells), but you can delete the entire table.

Starting argument value

Input cell reference

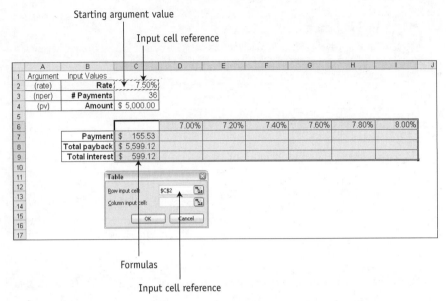

Formulas

Input cell reference

Figure 9.12. Building the one-input data table in Figure 9.11, Steps 1 through 5

Two-input data table

A two-input data table calculates formula results for each set of two changing input values. A typical example of a two-input data table is a loan table (see Figure 9.13) that compares payments for different interest rates and for different loan amounts at each of those interest rates.

This example table uses the PMT function, the same as a loan calculator. (You find the PMT function used in a loan calculator in Chapter 5.)

To build a two-input data table:

1. Enter starting argument values in input cells for the formula.

2. In the cell that will be the upper-left corner of the data table, enter the formula; reference the input cells from Step 1 for arguments.

Bright Idea

A useful twist on this two-input data table would compare total interest paid for varying interest rates and terms (number of payments) for the same loan amount.

3. Enter one set of changing values in the row next to the formula (in this example, the changing rates).

4. Enter the other set of changing values in the column below the formula (in this example, the changing loan amounts).

5. Select the entire table region, including the formula cell and the changing values cells, then choose Data ⇨ Table.

6. In the Table dialog box, click in the Row input cell box and then click the input cell that the formula references (in this example, the Rate cell from Step 1).

7. In the Table dialog box, click in the Column input cell and then click the input cell that the formula references (in this example, the Amount cell from Step 1).

8. Click OK. The data table is created.

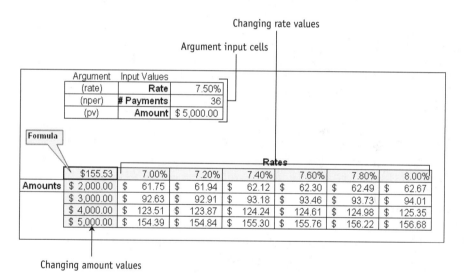

Figure 9.13. This two-input data table calculates results for one payment formula with two changing input values: the interest rate and the loan amount.

Hack

The result cells are formatted General until you reformat them. If the results are currency, select the result cells and use the Currency Style button to format them quickly.

Goal seeking for simple answers

The Goal Seek tool works problems "backward" to find a specific value that gives you the answer you want. For example, the PMT function gives you a payment for a specific loan amount; you know what payment you can afford but need to know how big a loan you can get for that payment.

Goal Seek is an *iterative* tool — it uses iterations, repeated trials of potential input values, getting closer and closer to the input value that produces the result you want. You could do the same thing manually, but Goal Seek does it at lightning speed.

Goal Seek a simple problem

I'll demonstrate Goal Seek with the PMT function. First, enter your formula (in this example, a PMT formula) and its input arguments in a worksheet, as shown in Figure 9.14.

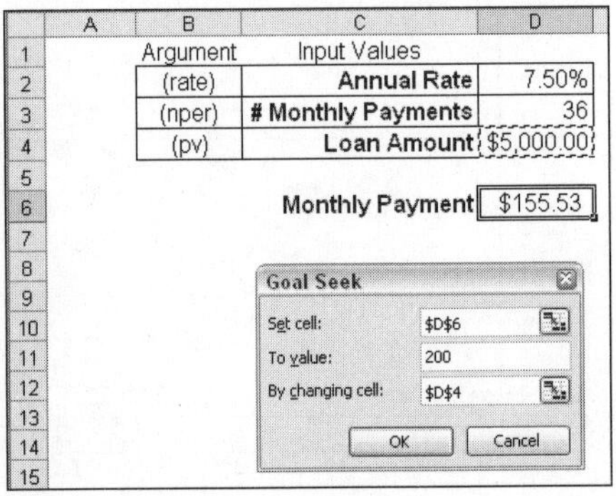

Figure 9.14. Goal Seek finds the input values that give the result you want.

Fill in the input values that won't change (in this example, the annual rate and number of monthly payments). Then choose Tools ⇨ Goal Seek.

In the Goal Seek dialog box, set the formula result equal to a specific value by changing an input cell. For this example, delete the value in the Set cell box and then click the cell that contains the formula (in this example, the Monthly Payment cell). In the To value box, type the value you want for a formula result. Click in the By changing cell box, and then click the input cell that will change to give you the formula result you want (in this example, the Loan Amount cell). Then click OK and wait a fraction of a second.

The result is displayed in the worksheet cells and in a Goal Seek Status message, shown in Figure 9.15. To keep the new values in the worksheet, click OK in the message. If you want to run Goal Seek again with different numbers, click Cancel and start over.

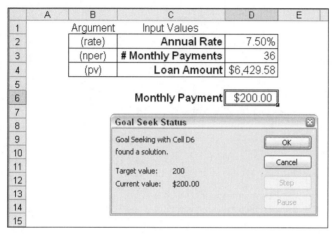

Figure 9.15. A Goal Seek result

Goal Seek something more difficult

Goal Seek can solve very difficult problems as long as there's only one variable to change. For example, Goal Seek can help with that bane of high school algebra, the quadratic equation (not to mention science and engineering problems). As an example, the quadratic equation $Y = X^3 + 7X + 25$ is tough when you know what Y should be but need to find the value of X that gives you that Y result.

To solve this particular equation with Goal Seek, decide on an X cell (the input value cell) and a Y cell (the result cell in which you write the formula). To illustrate this example, make cell A1 the X cell and cell A2 the Y cell. In the Y cell (A2), write the equation =A1^3 + 7*A1 + 25. In the Goal Seek dialog box, set cell A2 (the Y cell), To value *your desired value*, By changing cell A1 (the X cell), as shown in Figure 9.16.

When you first write the formula in the Y cell, you see an erroneous result based on the blank input in the X cell; after you run Goal Seek, you have logical and correct numbers in both cells, as shown in Figure 9.17.

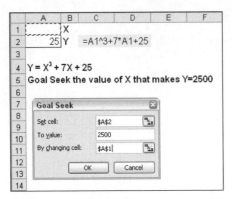

Figure 9.16. Goal seeking an answer to a complex problem

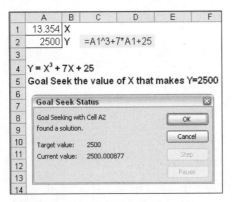

Figure 9.17. The quadratic solution

Answering complex questions with Solver

Like most Excel authors, I know how to use Solver; unlike most Excel authors, I admit that I never use it. I never have any reason to use it; most Excel users don't. But some of you do have complex questions that Solver can help with, so I'll give you an overview in using Solver.

Like Goal Seek, Solver is an iterative tool — it uses iterations, repeated trials of potential input values, getting closer and closer to the input values

Inside Scoop

Solver is not a Microsoft product; it's a third-party program created by Frontline Systems, which also sells higher-level versions of the Solver tool. You can find these tools as well as sample worksheets that use Solver for more complex problems at www.solver.com.

that produce the results you want. Unlike Goal Seek, Solver can work with multiple changing cells and with rules and relationships between those cells.

Solver finds solutions to more complex problems, such as how to allocate limited raw materials for maximum factory production or balance an optimal investment portfolio.

Solver is an add-in, which means it's an accessory program that you have to install.

Install the Solver add-in

If you don't see the Solver command on the Tools menu, you need to install it. To install the Solver add-in, choose Tools ⇨ Add-Ins. Select the Solver Add-In check box, and click OK. Wait a bit while Excel installs it.

Solver terminology

Before you use Solver, you need to understand a few terms:

- **Target cell.** The target cell contains the value for which you want to find input solutions. It doesn't have to be a specific number; it can also be as large or small a number as possible within the rules you set up for the Solver.

- **Changing cells.** Changing cells contain the input values that solver adjusts to find the target value within your rules. You can have multiple changing cells.

- **Unchanging cells.** These cells contain values that affect the solution but never change; they must depend in some way on the changing cell values or the target cell. You can set constraints on them just like changing cells.

- **Constraints.** Constraints are rules that govern the possible solutions Solver can find, such as a maximum and minimum value for each changing cell.

A Solver example

Solver must be taught by example; it's too complex for a simple set of general steps. The example I use here is a very simple one: optimizing workshop production to maximize total profits.

In this example, a workshop produces three products: nuts, bolts, and screws in case units, and it can produce a maximum of 300 units per day of any combination of products. Figure 9.18 shows a worksheet set up to show the profit potential for each item at maximum production for that item.

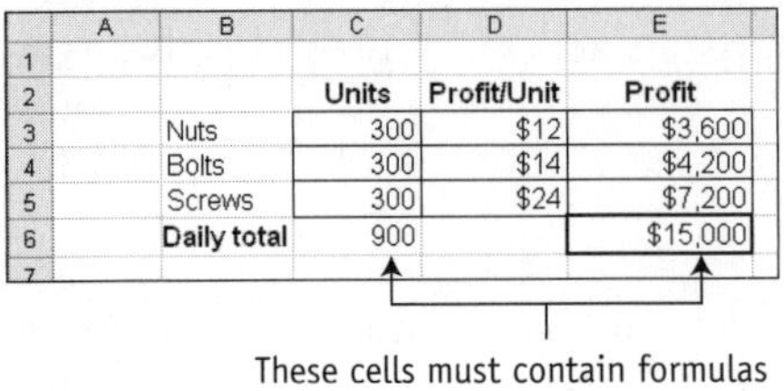

	A	B	C	D	E
1					
2			Units	Profit/Unit	Profit
3		Nuts	300	$12	$3,600
4		Bolts	300	$14	$4,200
5		Screws	300	$24	$7,200
6		Daily total	900		$15,000
7					

These cells must contain formulas

Figure 9.18. Profit potential for each item at maximum production for that item

Because screws have the greatest return, the workshop could produce nothing but screws for maximum profit. But there are constraints on production:

- The workshop can only produce 300 units per day of anything.
- There is an existing order of 70 units of nuts to be filled.
- There is an upcoming order for 30 units of bolts.
- The screws are a specialty item and the market is limited; market demand limits production to no more than 50 units.

The problem becomes how to allocate production capacity to the three products to meet the existing market and still maximize profits.

The quick how-to on Solver is this: Set up a worksheet with values and formulas and logical formatting; choose Tools ⇨ Solver; set the target cell; set the changing cells; add the constraints on the changing cells; and let Solver go to work.

To follow this example:

1. Set up a worksheet as shown in Figure 9.18, and choose Tools ⇨ Solver. The Solver Parameters dialog box opens.
2. With the Set Target Cell box highlighted, click the target cell—in this example, cell E6, the Total Profit cell. In the Equal To options, select Max (to maximize the Total Profit value).
3. Click in the By Changing Cells box and drag (or Ctrl+click) the changing cells (the Units cells).

4. Set constraints for the problem, which are the production limit and the market limits for each product. In this example, the constraints are Total Production (the sum of all three products) = 300, Nuts >= 70, Bolts >= 30, and Screws <= 50, as shown in the Subject to the Constraints list in Figure 9.19. I've also given each product a maximum of 300 because the workshop cannot produce more than 300 units per day of anything.

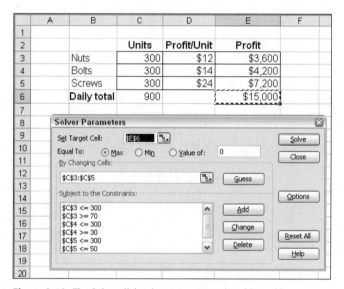

Figure 9.19. The Solver dialog box set up to solve this problem

To set a constraint, click Add; in the Cell Reference box, click a changing cell, then set the constraints for that cell value, as shown in Figure 9.20.

5. When you've added all your constraints, click OK to return to the Solver Parameters dialog box.

6. Click Solve. Solver finds a solution to the problem (shown in Figure 9.21) and asks if you want to keep the solution or return to the original values. To store the Solver solution as a scenario, click Save Scenario in the Solver Results dialog box. The solution is stored in the worksheet just like any other scenario.

	A	B	C	D	E	
1						
2			**Units**	**Profit/Unit**	**Profit**	
3		Nuts	300	$12	$3,600	
4		Bolts	300	$14	$4,200	
5		Screws	300	$24	$7,200	
6		**Daily total**	900		$15,000	
7						
8						

Add Constraint

Cell Reference:　　　　　　　　　　Constraint:

$C$6　　　　　　　<=　　300

OK　　　Cancel　　　Add　　　Help

Figure 9.20. Adding a constraint to a changing cell

	A	B	C	D	E	F
1						
2			**Units**	**Profit/Unit**	**Profit**	
3		Nuts	70	$12	$840	
4		Bolts	180	$14	$2,520	
5		Screws	50	$24	$1,200	
6		**Daily total**	300		$4,560	
7						

Solver Results

Solver found a solution. All constraints and optimality
conditions are satisfied.

Reports

Answer
Sensitivity
Limits

◉ Keep Solver Solution
○ Restore Original Values

OK　　　Cancel　　　Save Scenario...　　　Help

Figure 9.21. Solver's solution

If Solver leaves a mess in the worksheet instead of a usable solution, select the Restore Original Values option. Try setting different constraints on the problem, and check your initial table formulas for accuracy.

There are many more options in Solver that can help you find a better solution, especially with more complex problems. To work with Solver's

Hack

If you click Add after you set your last constraint, Solver expects another constraint and tells you that you're not done. If you've already clicked Add, click Cancel to close the Add Constraint dialog box.

options, click Options in the Solver Solutions dialog box. Explaining the options in the Solver Options dialog box is beyond the scope of this book; if you want to delve more deeply into Solver, check out the recommended books in Appendix A and the Frontline Systems Web site at www.solver.com.

Because Solver is so complex, you cannot always trust it to arrive at the best solution in just one try. Be sure you understand Solver very well before making any major decisions based on Solver solutions.

Just the facts

- For fast subtotaling of data by category, use data consolidation.

- To create a collapsible outline with subtotals by category, use subtotaling.

- To compare different inputs and results for a problem, use scenarios and create a scenario summary for side-by-side comparison.

- To create a comparison table for formula results in which a single argument or input value changes, use a one-input data table.

- To create a comparison table for formula results in which two arguments or input values change, use a two-input data table.

- To work a question backward and find the input value that produces the answer you want, use Goal Seek.

- For complex problems with many changeable input values, try Solver.

Summarizing Data Dynamically with PivotTables

Chapter 10

PivotTables are an interactive and flexible presentation of data. They allow you to *pivot* your data to analyze it from different angles, move categories around, change calculation functions easily, and show or hide details on the fly. In a PivotTable, you can change the data layout merely by clicking and dragging items with your mouse, even during a video presentation to a room full of people.

In this chapter, I'll use a long expenses list to demonstrate creating and working with a PivotTable.

Using PivotTables

When you summarize data with a PivotTable, you can:

■ Summarize data from several sources such as Excel lists, external databases, multiple worksheets, and other PivotTables.

■ Pivot the table to change its orientation.

■ Group items in a field (for example, group dates into months or quarters).

■ Change the calculation for a field.

Inside Scoop

PivotTables are very maneuverable but also take a little more time to create. If all I need is a static list of summaries by category (for example, summarizing my business expenses for my accountant), I take the easy route and do a consolidation instead of a PivotTable (see Chapter 9).

- Show the details underlying a single summarized item.
- Format the PivotTable for a professional and reader-friendly presentation.

PivotTable terms

PivotTables use some new terms that are summarized in Figure 10.1 and Table 10.1.

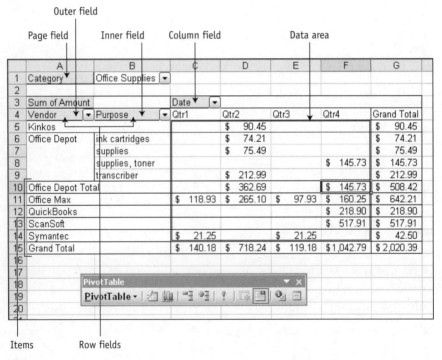

Figure 10.1. PivotTable terminology

Table 10.1. PivotTable terms

Term	Definition
Page field	A field that displays one item at a time.
Page field item	The item displayed by the page field.
Row field	A field with data displayed in rows.
Column field	A field with data displayed in columns.
Item	A specific row or column heading in a field.
Data area	The part of the PivotTable where data and calculations are displayed.
Field label	The label that identifies a row or column field; also called *field heading* and *field button*.
Outer field	When more than one field is displayed in the row or column area, the outermost field is the outer field; each outer-field item encompasses one or more inner-field items.
Inner field	When more than one field is displayed in the row or column area, the innermost field is the inner field; each inner field is grouped within an outer-field item.
Source data	The data from which the PivotTable is created.
Refresh data	To update the PivotTable with changed source data.

Creating a PivotTable

The PivotTable Wizard guides you through the process of creation and through the process of editing a PivotTable when you want to make changes.

First, decide what your source data is. If you want to create a PivotTable from external data such as an Access or other database, from multiple worksheets, or from another PivotTable, you can make that selection in the first step of the PivotTable Wizard and follow the initially

Bright Idea

For a list of sample data to use while you get familiar with PivotTables, type **sample data** in the Ask A Question box (in the upper-right corner of the program window) and search Microsoft Office Online. Download one of the Excel sample files (some come with PivotTable worksheets already set up).

Inside Scoop

If you have an existing PivotTable and need to create another PivotTable from the same data source, it's more memory efficient to create the second PivotTable from the first PivotTable; better yet, when you refresh the data in either PivotTable, both PivotTables are refreshed.

different wizard steps. Here, I give you the quick how-to for creating a PivotTable from a single worksheet list.

To create a PivotTable from worksheet data, follow these steps:

1. Click in the worksheet table (the source data) from which you want to create a PivotTable, and choose Data ⇨ PivotTable and PivotChart Report.

2. In Step 1 of the PivotTable Wizard, shown in Figure 10.2, leave the Microsoft Office Excel list or database option selected, and then click Next.

	A	B	C	D	E	F
1			Business Expenses			
3	Date	Vendor	Purpose	Category	Amount	
4	1/3/04	Amazon Books	books	Books	$89.78	
5	2/9/04	Amazon Books	books	Books	$36.44	
6	4/29/				$81.10	
7	5/22/				$55.65	
8	4/8/				$22.30	
9	6/18/				$63.84	
10	6/18/				$7.44	
11	7/16/				$28.74	
12	7/22/				$26.57	
13	12/6/				$55.83	
14	9/13/				$114.99	
15	6/16/				$9.82	
16	12/31/				$214.00	
17	5/14/				$90.45	
18	9/2/				$11.05	
19	12/17/				$16.07	
20	4/16/				$212.99	
21	4/20/				$37.51	
22	4/20/04	Office Depot	ink cartridges	Office Supplies	$74.21	
23	6/1/04	Office Depot	supplies	Office Supplies	$25.23	
24	6/15/04	Office Depot	supplies	Office Supplies	$12.75	
25	10/16/04	Office Depot	supplies, toner	Office Supplies	$145.73	
26	3/5/04	Office Max	Quicken 2004 Premiere	Office Supplies	$95.35	
27	3/15/04	Office Max	supplies	Office Supplies	$2.43	
28	3/23/04	Office Max	supplies	Office Supplies	$21.15	

PivotTable and PivotChart Wizard - Step 1 of 3

Where is the data that you want to analyze?
- ⊙ Microsoft Office Excel list or database
- ○ External data source
- ○ Multiple consolidation ranges
- ○ Another PivotTable report or PivotChart report

What kind of report do you want to create?
- ⊙ PivotTable
- ○ PivotChart report (with PivotTable report)

Cancel   < Back   Next >   Finish

Figure 10.2. Step 1 of the PivotTable Wizard

Bright Idea

Name your data source range and type the range name in the Step 2 of the wizard, in which you identify the data source range.

3. In Step 2 of the wizard, shown in Figure 10.3, check that your source data range is correct, and click Next. (It's probably correct—PivotTable is one of those features that detects the table around the active cell.)

	A	B	C	D	E	F
3	Date	Vendor	Purpose	Category	Amount	
4	1/3/04	Amazon Books	books	Books	$89.78	
5	2/9/04	Amazon Books	books	Books	$36.44	
6	4/29/04	Amazon Books	books	Books	$81.10	
7	5/22/04	Amazon Books	books	Books	$55.65	
8	4/8/04	Borders	books	Books	$22.30	
9	6/18/04	Borders	books	Books	$63.84	
10	6/18/04	Borders	books	Books	$7.44	
11	7/16/04	Borders	books	Books	$28.74	
12	7/22/04	Borders	books	Books	$26.57	
13	12/6/04	Bc			$55.83	
14	9/13/04	Cc		ipment	$114.99	
15	6/16/04	Ha			$9.82	
16	12/31/04	Ice		vice	$214.00	
17	5/14/04	Ki		plies	$90.45	
18	9/2/04	Mail Boxes, Etc.	shipping	Postage	$11.05	
19	12/17/04	Mail Boxes, Etc.	shipping	Postage	$16.07	
20	4/16/04	Office Depot	transcriber	Office Supplies	$212.99	
21	4/20/04	Office Depot	supplies	Office Supplies	$37.51	

PivotTable and PivotChart Wizard - Step 2 of 3

Where is the data that you want to use?

Range: $A$3:$E$55   Browse...

Cancel   < Back   Next >   Finish

Figure 10.3. Step 2 of the PivotTable Wizard

4. In Step 3 of the wizard, shown in Figure 10.4, choose the location of the PivotTable. You can choose a new worksheet that the wizard creates, or an existing worksheet that you select — in this example I'm creating the PivotTable on a new worksheet.

PivotTable and PivotChart Wizard - Step 3 of 3

Where do you want to put the PivotTable report?

◉ New worksheet
○ Existing worksheet

Click Finish to create your PivotTable report.

Layout...   Options...   Cancel   < Back   Next >   Finish

Figure 10.4. Step 3 of the PivotTable Wizard

5. Click Layout to finish the wizard. This is the "old-fashioned" way to lay out a PivotTable; Microsoft's new way is confusing (the PivotTable layout lines on the worksheet shrink up as soon as you place the first field in position).

6. In the PivotTable and PivotChart Wizard – Layout dialog box (shown in Figure 10.5), click and drag field names from the PivotTable Field List and drop them into areas in the PivotTable. If you change your mind about where you dropped a field, drag its gray field button to a different area.

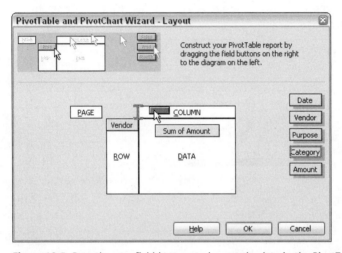

Figure 10.5. Drag the gray field buttons to lay out the data in the PivotTable.

7. When you finish laying out the fields, click OK. The Step 3 wizard reappears — click Finish to see your finished PivotTable. Close the PivotTable Field List.

If the data is unusable, such as a Date field that lists hundreds of individual dates, you can fix that later by grouping those dates. In fact, your new PivotTable might look quite messy (as shown in Figure 10.6); in the next several sections, I show you how to clean it up and change the layout, the calculations, and a number of other aspects.

Inside Scoop

Fields in the Data area must be calculable fields for summarizing, although they don't have to be numbers. If you drop a non-numeric field in the Data area, the PivotTable automatically counts the data instead of summing it.

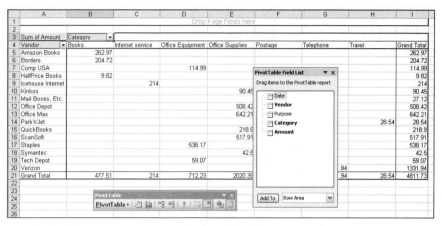

Figure 10.6. The initial finished PivotTable probably needs adjustment.

When you finish laying out the PivotTable, you can close the PivotTable Field List; you can easily open the list again from the PivotTable toolbar when you need to rearrange the PivotTable.

When you create a PivotTable, the PivotTable toolbar automatically appears, and appears again every time you click in your finished PivotTable. If you close the toolbar, you can open it again by right-clicking the toolbar area and clicking PivotTable. I discuss the PivotTable toolbar a little later in this chapter.

Change the data source range

When more rows or columns of data are added to the data source, the PivotTable doesn't automatically update to include them.

To change a data source range when data is added or deleted, right-click a cell in the PivotTable and click PivotTable Wizard. In Step 3 of 3 of the wizard, click Back; in the Step 2 of 3 of the wizard, click and drag to select the new data source range, then click Finish.

Refresh data

Refresh is the PivotTable term for updating a PivotTable with current data. When data in the source data range changes, you must refresh the PivotTable to update.

Inside Scoop

If you make your data source into a new Excel dynamic list, the source range automatically expands and contracts.

Create a dynamic source range

You can use Excel's new dynamic list to create a dynamic source range, or you can create your own dynamic source range using a named OFFSET/COUNTA formula, which is covered in Chapter 5. With a dynamic source range, the PivotTable data source automatically expands and contracts as you add or delete rows of data in the data source, so that when you refresh the PivotTable, you get all the data in the source range regardless of how it may have changed size. Follow the procedure in Chapter 5 to create a named OFFSET/ COUNTA formula for your range, and then type that formula name (with no equal sign) in the Range box in Step 2 of 3 of the PivotTable Wizard. In fact, if your data source range begins in cell A1 (and you have no entries outside of the table in column A or row 1), the formula =OFFSET($A$1,0,0,COUNTA($A:$A), COUNTA ($1:$1)) will work for you.

Defining a dynamic range with a named OFFSET/COUNTA formula works well for charts and print areas, too, as does using a new dynamic list as a data source.

To refresh a PivotTable, on the PivotTable toolbar, click the Refresh Data button (shown in Figure 10.7). All PivotTables and PivotCharts created from that data source are refreshed at the same time.

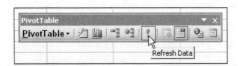

Figure 10.7. Click Refresh Data to update the data in the PivotTable.

Delete a PivotTable

If you want to delete a PivotTable and start again, click and drag to select the entire PivotTable, and choose Edit ➪ Clear ➪ All.

The PivotTable toolbar

Table 10.2 explains the PivotTable toolbar buttons. All of the functional and useful toolbar buttons are also commands available on the shortcut menu when you right-click any cell in the PivotTable. Those buttons that

Hack

The techniques for some procedures, such as hiding and showing details in the PivotTable, are part of the PivotTable structure (where they actually work, unlike the buttons on the toolbar that don't work).

don't appear on the shortcut menu or in Table 10.2 are either pointless or nonfunctional.

Table 10.2. PivotTable toolbar buttons

Icon	Name	Purpose
PivotTable ▾	PivotTable	Menu of some PivotTable commands
	Format Report	Opens AutoFormat dialog box
	Chart Wizard	Creates PivotChart from PivotTable
	Hide Detail	Hides inner field details
	Show Detail	Shows inner field details
	Refresh Data	Updates PivotTable with current source data
	Field Settings	Opens PivotTable Field dialog box
	Show Field List	Displays the PivotTable Field List

Changing PivotTable arrangement

As I mentioned, PivotTables can be very messy when you first create them, but they're also very fixable. I'll show you how to easily make the most common fixes in disorganized PivotTables in the following sections.

Pivot the table

You pivot a PivotTable by dragging gray field buttons to new locations, as shown in Figure 10.8. If you drag a field button and don't like the results,

Hack

If dragging fields in the worksheet PivotTable gets too confusing, it's easier to use the old layout dialog box. Right-click in the PivotTable and click PivotTable Wizard. In the wizard, click Layout. In the Layout dialog box, drag field buttons to the appropriate areas, then click OK and Finish.

press Ctrl+Z to undo the move. If you inadvertently drag a field button out of the table and lose it, see the next section to add it back.

Drag a field button from one part of a table to another

	A	B	C	D
1				
2				
3	Sum of Amount	Vendor		
4	Category	Amazon Books	Borders	Comp USA
5	Books	262.97	204.72	
6	Internet service			
7	Office Equipment			114.99
8	Office Supplies			
9	Postage			
10	Telephone			
11	Travel			
12	Grand Total	262.97	204.72	114.99
13				

Figure 10.8. Pivot the layout by dragging field buttons.

Add fields

To add a field to the PivotTable, right-click in the PivotTable and click Show Field List. Drag field names from the PivotTable Field List dialog box to the PivotTable and drop them in the appropriate areas, as shown in Figure 10.9. Close the PivotTable Field List dialog box when you're done.

If you add another field to an area that already contains a field, you create an inner and outer field in that area. You can have several inner fields in a single area. In Figure 10.10, the Date field has an outer field

Hack

Remember, if your PivotTable layout gets out of control and you get frustrated trying to fix it, right-click in the PivotTable, click PivotTable Wizard, click Layout, and rearrange the layout in the PivotTable and PivotChart Wizard – Layout dialog box.

(quarters) and an inner field (months) because the Date field was grouped by both quarters and months (I show you how to group items later). The Category field is an inner field because I dragged the Category field button into a Row orientation along with the Date field.

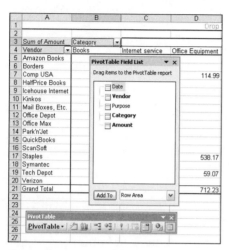

Figure 10.9. Adding a field to the PivotTable

	A	B	C	D
1				
2				
3	Sum of Amount			
4	Quarters ▼	▼ Date ▼	Category ▼	Total
5	Qtr1	Jan	Books	89.78
6			Telephone	103.74
7		Jan Total		193.52
8		Feb		168.28
9		Mar		219.07
10	Qtr2			1366.17
11	Qtr3			693.77
12	Qtr4			2170.92
13	Grand Total			4811.73
14				
15				
16				

Outer field   Inner fields

Figure 10.10. In this PivotTable, the Date field is grouped into quarters and months (months is an inner field), and the Category field is another inner field in the Row area.

If you want to swap the positions of an inner field and an outer field, all you need to do is drag one field button to the opposite side of the other field button (see Figure 10.11).

Drag from here...

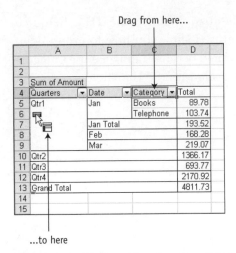

...to here

Figure 10.11. Switch positions from inner field to outer field.

Remove fields

To remove a field from a PivotTable, drag its gray field button out of the PivotTable and drop it on the worksheet (as shown in Figure 10.12).

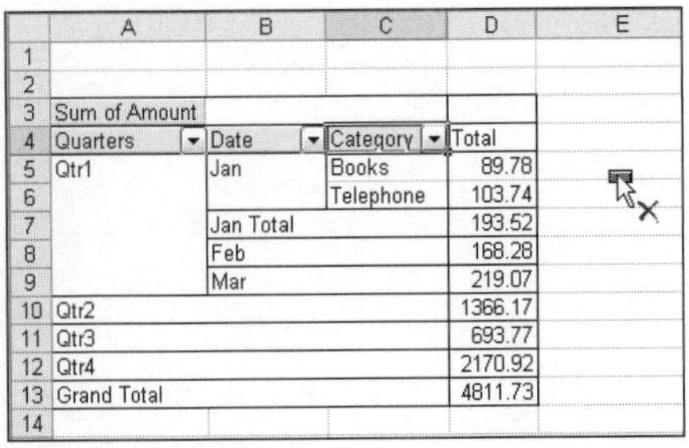

Figure 10.12. Remove a field by dropping its button outside of the PivotTable.

Show and hide inner-field details

The big advantage of an inner field is that you can show or hide inner-field details for a specific outer-field item. For example, in Figure 10.13, the Category details are displayed just for January.

To show inner-field details for a specific outer-field item, double-click the outer-field item (in Figure 10.13, I double-clicked Qtr 1 and January). To hide the details again, double-click the outer-field item again.

	A	B	C	D	
1					
2					
3	Sum of Amount				
4	Quarters ▼	Date ▼	Category ▼	Total	
5	Qtr1	Jan	Books	89.78	
6			Telephone	103.74	
7		Jan Total		193.52	
8		Feb		168.28	
9		Mar		219.07	
10	Qtr2			1366.17	
11	Qtr3			693.77	
12	Qtr4			2170.92	
13	Grand Total			4811.73	
14					
15					

Figure 10.13. Show and hide inner-field items.

To hide or show all inner-field details for an outer field, click the outer-field button, and then click the Hide Detail or Show Detail button on the PivotTable toolbar (see Figure 10.14).

Hide Detail

Show Detail

	A	B	C	D	E
1					
2					
3	Sum of Amount				
4	Quarters ▼	Date ▼	Category ▼	Total	
5	Qtr1	Jan	Books	89.78	
6			Telephone	103.74	
7		Jan Total		193.52	
8		Feb		168.28	
9		Mar		219.07	
10	Qtr2	Apr	Books	103.4	
11			Office Supplies	376.83	
12			Telephone	123.6	
13		Apr Total		603.83	
14	PivotTable				
15	PivotTable ▼				
16					
17		May Total	Show Detail	470.2	
18		Jun	Books	81.1	
19			Office Equipment	31.74	
20			Office Supplies	37.98	
21			Telephone	112.78	
22			Travel	28.54	
23		Jun Total		292.14	
24	Qtr3	Jul	Books	55.31	
25			Office Supplies	21.25	
26			Telephone	111.23	
27		Jul Total		187.79	
28		Aug	Office Equipment	59.07	
29			Office Supplies	97.93	
30			Telephone	111.23	
31		Aug Total		268.23	
32		Sep	Office Equipment	114.99	

Figure 10.14. Show or hide all inner-field details.

Hack

If you open the list and don't make any changes, you must click Cancel to close the list.

Show and hide specific details

To hide a specific detail in a field (such as the Telephone item in Figure 10.15), click the arrow on the right side of the field button to open a list of the field items. On the list of field items that appears, deselect the check boxes for any items you want to hide, or select the check boxes for any hidden items you want to show, then click OK. Hidden details are not included in the PivotTable totals.

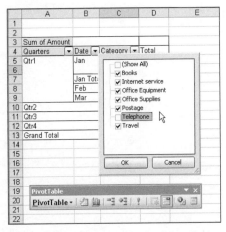

Figure 10.15. Hide a specific detail in a field.

Group items in a field

When you include a date field in a PivotTable, you'll probably get a listing of every individual date in the data source, which is not at all useful. To make the date data useful, group it into months, quarters, or years. Not every field can be grouped; if the data in a field cannot be grouped, a message to that effect appears.

Right-click any cell in the field that you want to group, or right-click the gray field button (see Figure 10.16). On the shortcut menu, point to Group and Show Detail, and click Group. If you are grouping details in

Hack

When you select a grouping, deselect any other groupings or you get additional layers of groupings for the same field (although you might find it useful to have data grouped by quarter and by month within a quarter, which you can have by selecting both Month and Quarter).

a Date field, Excel offers several likely date groupings. Select one and click OK.

To ungroup items in a field, right-click a grouped item or the field button, point to Group and Show Detail, and click Ungroup.

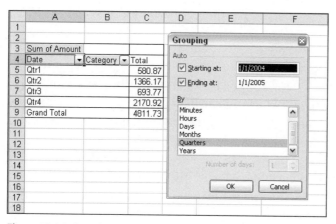

Figure 10.16. Grouping dates — the shortcut menu and the results

Create page fields

Another way to make a PivotTable more useful is to put a field in the Page area. The Page area makes the PivotTable show data for just one item in the Page area field at a time. For example, if I have a field of Vendors in an expenses list and the Vendors field is in the Page area, I can show PivotTable data for just one Vendor at a time.

To create a Page field, drag a field button into the Page area (see Figure 10.17). If you drag the field button above the PivotTable, a rectangular hatched border appears around the Page area; drop the field when you see the hatched rectangle.

Initially, the Page field displays all field items; to limit the data displayed in the PivotTable to just one Page field item, click the arrow in the cell next to the Page field button and click the item you want to display.

Page area

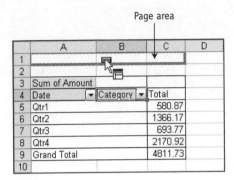

Figure 10.17. Drag a field button into the Page area.

Create separate pages

When you have a Page field in a PivotTable, you can separate the PivotTable data into separate pages, or worksheets, for each item in the Page field. For example, if I have a Page field for Vendors in an expenses list, I can create a separate PivotTable for each vendor in the source data, and each PivotTable is on its own worksheet.

To create separate pages, on the PivotTable toolbar, click the PivotTable button, and click Show Pages. In the Show Pages dialog box, click OK. Figure 10.18 shows one of several pages created from the Vendors field in the PivotTable.

Changing PivotTable calculations

Although SUM is the most common PivotTable calculation, you can change the data calculation in the Data area to any of several other functions, including AVERAGE, MIN, MAX, and COUNT.

To change the calculation function for a field, right-click a data cell for which you want to change the function, and click Field Settings. The PivotTable Field dialog box appears. In the Summarize by list, shown in Figure 10.19, double-click the new function with which you want to calculate.

Watch Out!

In the PivotTable Field dialog box, you can change the field button name in the Name box; but be careful—changing the field name isn't a problem, but if you delete the field name or change the function name, the function name won't update if you change the function again.

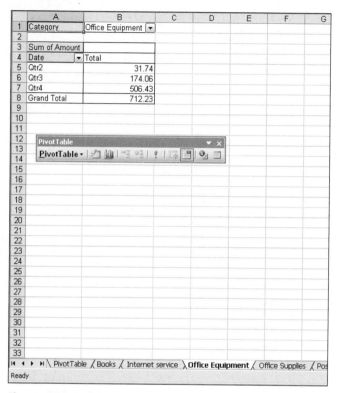

Figure 10.18. Pages from the Vendors field

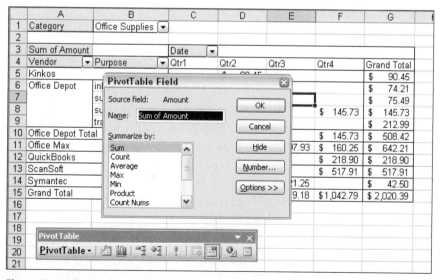

Figure 10.19. Change the calculation function for a field.

Get a better view

For a better view of the PivotTable and the calculated fields in the Data area, right-click in the PivotTable and click PivotTable Wizard. In the wizard, click Layout. The Layout dialog box is the original (and often easier, I think) way to lay out a PivotTable and change calculations in Data area fields.

To pivot a PivotTable in the Layout dialog box, click and drag the field buttons from one area into another, drag them out of the PivotTable layout, or drag new fields from the right side of the dialog box into the layout. Dragging a data field into the Data area multiple times for different calculations is easier to see in the Layout view.

To change calculations in a data field, double-click the field button in the Data area and make your changes in the PivotTable Field dialog box. This is the same PivotTable Field dialog box you've seen before. To format the numbers for the data field, click Number.

The name of the field button, which was probably Sum of *field*, changes to the calculation and the field name. The numbers aren't formatted, however; see the section "Formatting a PivotTable" later in this chapter to learn more about formatting the numbers.

You can add a second calculation to the Data area by adding the same field to the Data area a second time and changing the calculation. For example, you can show a Sum of data and an Average of data, side by side or one on top of the other (see Figure 10.20).

	A	B	C
1	Category	Office Supplies ▼	
2			
3	Date ▼	Data ▼	Total
4	Qtr1	Sum of Amount	$ 140.18
5		Average of Amount	35.045
6	Qtr2	Sum of Amount	$ 718.24
7		Average of Amount	79.80444444
8	Qtr3	Sum of Amount	$ 119.18
9		Average of Amount	59.59
10	Qtr4	Sum of Amount	$ 1,042.79
11		Average of Amount	208.558
12	Total Sum of Amount		$ 2,020.39
13	Total Average of Amount		101.0195
14			
15			

Figure 10.20. A PivotTable can show multiple calculations of the same data.

To display multiple calculations, drag the data field you want to calculate into the Data area a second time, and change the calculation for the second field.

To change the orientation of the calculations from side by side to one over the other, click and drag the Data field button down and to the left into the innermost inner field. To switch the calculations back to side by side, click and drag the Data field button slightly to the right.

The best way to see what you're doing is to watch the mouse pointer (see Figure 10.21). The small pointer has a blue bar that shows you whether your dragged field will be a row layout (side by side) or a column layout (one over the other).

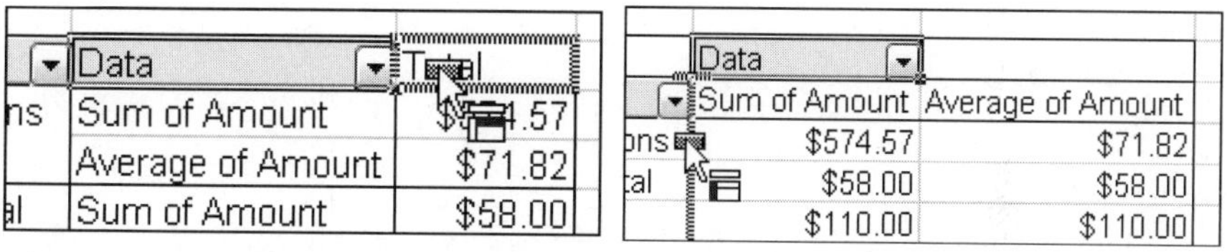

Figure 10.21. The mouse pointer shows you what will happen to the field you drag.

Showing underlying details

You can display the raw data underlying any PivotTable data detail by *drilling down* for the source data.

To drill down for source data, double-click a calculated data cell. A new worksheet is created that shows the raw data underlying the cell you double-clicked, as shown in Figure 10.22.

	A	B	C	D	E
1	Date	Vendor	Purpose	Category	Amount
2	5/29/2004	Office Max	Microsoft FrontPage 2003	Office Supplies	212.98
3	4/30/2004	Office Max	supplies	Office Supplies	6.38
4	4/26/2004	Office Max	supplies	Office Supplies	45.74
5	6/15/2004	Office Depot	supplies	Office Supplies	12.75
6	6/1/2004	Office Depot	supplies	Office Supplies	25.23
7	4/20/2004	Office Depot	ink cartridges	Office Supplies	74.21
8	4/20/2004	Office Depot	supplies	Office Supplies	37.51
9	4/16/2004	Office Depot	transcriber	Office Supplies	212.99
10	5/14/2004	Kinkos	business cards	Office Supplies	90.45
11					

Figure 10.22. Drilled-down source data for a data cell in the PivotTable

Hack

If you can't drill down for details, someone has been messing with your PivotTable options. To reenable drilldown, right-click in the PivotTable and click Table Options to open the PivotTable Options dialog box. In the Data options section, select the Enable drill to details check box and click OK.

Formatting a PivotTable

PivotTables need formatting just like any other data table. You need to format both numbers and the whole table layout (well, you don't need to format the table layout, and I usually don't, but you do need to format the numbers). Figure 10.23 shows a PivotTable with numbers formatted as Accounting.

	A	B	C	D	E	F
1						
2						
3	Sum of Amount	Date				
4	Category	Qtr1	Qtr2	Qtr3	Qtr4	Grand Total
5	Books	$ 126.22	$ 240.15	$ 55.31	$ 55.83	$ 477.51
6	Internet service				$ 214.00	$ 214.00
7	Office Equipment		$ 31.74	$ 174.06	$ 506.43	$ 712.23
8	Office Supplies	$ 140.18	$ 718.24	$ 119.18	$1,042.79	$2,020.39
9	Postage			$ 11.05	$ 16.07	$ 27.12
10	Telephone	$ 314.47	$ 347.50	$ 334.17	$ 335.80	$1,331.94
11	Travel		$ 28.54			$ 28.54
12	Grand Total	$ 580.87	$1,366.17	$ 693.77	$2,170.92	$4,811.73
13						

Figure 10.23. Number-formatted data in a PivotTable

Format numbers

To format the numbers in a single field, right-click a number cell and click Field Settings. In the PivotTable Field dialog box, click Number. In the Format Cells dialog box, set a number format for that field (formatting field numbers is exactly like formatting number values in cells — see Chapter 7).

You can also select specific cells (or all the cells in a field or in the table) and format them using the buttons on the Formatting toolbar. For

Bright Idea

To preserve PivotTable results permanently, freeze the table so the layout and values can't be altered. Copy the entire PivotTable and paste values to another worksheet.

example, if you want to add or remove decimal places to a set of currency numbers, it's fastest to select the number cells and click Increase Decimal or Decrease Decimal. When you format a cell, it retains that format even when you pivot the table.

Format the table

When you want to format a PivotTable to dress it up a bit, it's best to use the Table AutoFormat tool because cell formatting you apply manually can get lost when you pivot the table. Even then, the AutoFormat tool usually rearranges your PivotTable (not good) and none of the AutoFormats looks very good. (AutoFormats in earlier versions of Excel were good-looking and well behaved; for no apparent reason they've been changed for the worse.)

If you really want to apply a table AutoFormat, click in the PivotTable. On the PivotTable toolbar, click the PivotTable button. Click Format Report, select a format in the AutoFormat dialog box, and click OK.

Wait until you finish pivoting the table to apply an AutoFormat, because once an AutoFormat is applied, it becomes more difficult to pivot. If you want to get rid of the ugly AutoFormat, select the PivotTable Classic format at the bottom of the list to return the PivotTable to its original formatting.

Just the facts

- To create a PivotTable, click in a data source table and then choose Data ⇨ PivotTable and PivotChart Report. Follow the wizard steps to create the initial PivotTable.
- To change the data source, right-click in the PivotTable, click PivotTable Wizard, click Back, click and drag to select a new data source for the Range box, and click Finish.
- Refresh PivotTable data by clicking the Refresh button on the PivotTable toolbar.
- Pivot the PivotTable by dragging field buttons to new locations.
- Add fields by dragging them from the Show Field List dialog box onto the PivotTable.
- Remove fields by dragging field buttons away from the PivotTable.

- To group items in a field, right-click a cell in the field, point to Group and Show Detail, click Group, and select a group type.

- Create Page fields by dragging a field button into the Page area.

- To change the calculation function for a field, right-click a data cell and click Field Settings, then double-click the new function.

- Format numbers by right-clicking a data cell and clicking Field Settings; in the PivotTable Field dialog box, click Number, and format the numbers.

GET THE SCOOP ON...
PivotCharts versus normal charts ▪ Create a PivotChart
from a PivotTable ▪ Create a PivotChart from source data
▪ Create a normal chart from PivotTable data ▪ Rearrange
PivotCharts ▪ Format PivotCharts ▪ Embed a PivotChart
on a worksheet

Displaying PivotTables Graphically with PivotCharts

P ivotCharts are just like PivotTables and are a lot simpler if you create the PivotChart from an existing PivotTable.

PivotCharts are a graphical representation of the data in a PivotTable, whether or not you create a PivotTable first.

You have a couple of options when working with PivotCharts: You can create a PivotChart directly from the underlying data without first creating a PivotTable (both are created at the same time), or you can create a PivotChart from a PivotTable you've already created. You can also create a normal chart from PivotTable data, but not directly (I'll tell you how).

If you create a PivotChart from an existing PivotTable (which is what most folks do), the PivotChart mirrors the PivotTable; any changes you make in the PivotTable (such as sorting, adding/deleting fields, changing calculations, and so on) are automatically updated to the PivotChart, and some changes you make in a PivotChart (such as removing a field) are automatically updated to the PivotTable.

For illustrations in this chapter, I use the data I used in the PivotTables in Chapter 10.

PivotCharts versus normal charts

PivotCharts and normal charts are similar in many ways but different in little ways that can be annoying if you don't expect them. For example, some things you can do in normal charts that you can't do in PivotCharts are:

- Move and resize chart titles.
- Move and resize the plot area by dragging.
- Change values by resizing a data marker.
- Reposition the legend by dragging.
- Move the PivotChart to a different workbook from the workbook of the linked PivotTable (the chart becomes a static picture chart, unlinked to source data).

PivotCharts use the same terminology that you find in PivotTables: Row, Column, Page, and Data fields. They also use standard chart terminology: Value and category axes, data markers, legends, and so on. PivotCharts are a combination of a PivotTable and a normal chart, and are quite useful if you don't have your heart set on resizing or repositioning chart elements.

Creating PivotCharts

PivotCharts are quick to create from a PivotTable and just a little more work to create directly from source data. You can also create a normal chart from PivotTable data, which is usually a better idea than creating it directly from detailed source data.

Create a PivotChart from a PivotTable

Creating a PivotChart from a PivotTable couldn't be more simple: Click in the PivotTable, and on the PivotTable toolbar (or on the Standard toolbar), click the Chart Wizard button. A new chart sheet appears in the workbook (see Figure 11.1) with your PivotTable data charted and some PivotTable-type buttons and fields.

You must hide the PivotChart field buttons to make the chart look normal (see the section "Formatting PivotCharts").

The PivotChart has the same data layout as the PivotTable from which it was created, so make your PivotTable layout as simple as possible — like the one in Figure 11.2 — to create the best possible chart.

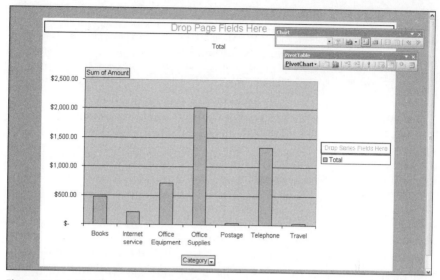

Figure 11.1. A PivotChart corresponds exactly to the PivotTable from which you create it; this PivotChart was created from the PivotTable in Figure 11.2.

	A	B	C	D
1				
2				
3		Sum of Amount		
4		Category	Total	
5		Books	$ 477.51	
6		Internet service	$ 214.00	
7		Office Equipment	$ 712.23	
8		Office Supplies	$2,020.39	
9		Postage	$ 27.12	
10		Telephone	$1,331.94	
11		Travel	$ 28.54	
12		Grand Total	$4,811.73	
13				
14		PivotTable		
15		PivotTable ▾		
16				
17				

Figure 11.2. This is the PivotTable from which the PivotChart in Figure 11.1 was created.

Create a PivotChart from source data

Creating a PivotChart directly from source data, without first creating the PivotTable, is exactly like creating a PivotTable:

1. Click in the source data table.

2. Choose Data ⇨ PivotTable and PivotChart Report.

3. In Step 1 of the PivotTable Wizard, select the type of source data, then select the PivotChart Report (and PivotTable Report) option, and click Next.

> **Hack**
>
> Don't include more than one row or column field and one data field in the PivotTable for a PivotChart; although it's easy to visually follow a combination of row and column fields (and inner and outer fields) in a PivotTable, too many fields make a very confusing and unreadable chart.

4. In Step 2 of the wizard, select the source data range, then click Next.

5. In Step 3 of the wizard, select the location of the new PivotTable and PivotChart, and click Finish.

You get a new worksheet and a new chart sheet, both containing empty Pivot layouts. Whether you add fields to the PivotChart or to the PivotTable, both respond to your changes identically.

Don't set up the data in the PivotChart (it's difficult to set up what you want). Switch to the PivotTable sheet and set up your data there (arrange fields, group, sort, set calculation functions, format data fields, and so on). Then look at the PivotChart.

Create a normal chart from PivotTable data

You can always create a normal chart from a data source range, but in the usual detailed list you have hundreds of rows of data and hundreds of corresponding entries in the chart, which is completely unusable.

If I create a normal chart (which I like better than PivotCharts because they're more formattable) from a long list of data, I don't often bother with a PivotTable; I consolidate the detailed list first (see Chapter 9) and chart the consolidated list. That way, only the summarized data I want to chart is in the chart's source data range.

But if I want more maneuverability in the data source than I can get with a consolidation, I create a PivotTable first and pivot the data into the arrangement I want to chart. Then I copy the entire PivotTable and paste values (either in place or in another location), click in the new static table, and click the Chart Wizard button on the Standard toolbar to create a normal chart (see Chapter 12). Figure 11.3 shows a PivotTable (on the left) and a static table (on the right) created by copying and pasting values — the static table is the one from which I created a normal chart.

	A	B	C	D	E	F
1						
2						
3		Sum of Amount			Sum of Amount	
4		Category ▼	Total		Category	Total
5		Books	$ 477.51		Books	$ 477.51
6		Internet service	$ 214.00		Internet service	$ 214.00
7		Office Equipment	$ 712.23		Office Equipment	$ 712.23
8		Office Supplies	$2,020.39		Office Supplies	$ 2,020.39
9		Postage	$ 27.12		Postage	$ 27.12
10		Telephone	$1,331.94		Telephone	$ 1,331.94
11		Travel	$ 28.54		Travel	$ 28.54
12		Grand Total	$4,811.73		Grand Total	$ 4,811.73
13						

Figure 11.3. Making a normal chart from a PivotTable

Rearranging PivotCharts

Because a PivotChart is a graphical representation of a PivotTable, the layout looks somewhat familiar — it's a hybrid of PivotTable and chart.

Here are a few things you can do to rearrange a PivotChart:

- **Change a calculation function.** Double-click the data field button and change the calculation in the PivotTable Field dialog box.

- **Hide or show items on the Category axis.** Click the arrow on the axis field button and select or deselect check boxes to show or hide items.

- **Remove a field.** Drag the field button out of the chart.

- **Add a field.** Click Show Field List on the PivotTable toolbar and drag the field button to the appropriate area on the PivotChart.

- **Sort the chart data** (for example, sort the values from highest to lowest). Switch to the PivotTable and sort the column in the PivotTable — the data is sorted in the PivotChart to match the PivotTable.

- **Limit the data to just one item in a specific field.** Drag that field button to the Page area (at the top of the chart), then click the arrow in the field button and click the item for which you want to limit the chart display.

Watch Out!

Don't start dragging field buttons around at random; a PivotChart is not as maneuverable as a PivotTable, and if you break it you'll need to rebuild the linked PivotTable. It's easier just to rearrange fields in the PivotTable than to pivot the PivotChart.

Formatting PivotCharts

Formatting PivotCharts is just like formatting regular charts; see Chapters 12 and 13 to learn about changing the chart type, formatting chart elements, colors and lines, and so on.

Most important in formatting a PivotChart is hiding the PivotChart buttons. When you hide the PivotChart buttons, you hide the field buttons and the empty PivotChart areas, and the PivotChart looks like a normal chart (see Figure 11.4). The PivotChart is not pivotable when the field buttons are hidden, but it still responds to all changes you make in its source PivotTable.

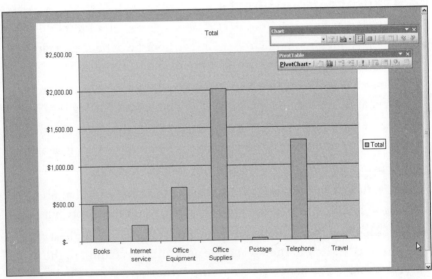

Figure 11.4. Hide the field buttons to make the PivotChart look like a normal chart.

To hide the PivotChart buttons and elements, click the PivotChart, then click the PivotChart button on the PivotTable toolbar and click Hide PivotChart Field Buttons (as shown in Figure 11.5). If you need to maneuver the PivotChart, click the PivotChart, then click the PivotChart button on the PivotTable toolbar and click Hide PivotChart Field Buttons again.

Bright Idea

Use normal chart techniques to add identifying axis titles to the chart after hiding field buttons (see Chapter 13).

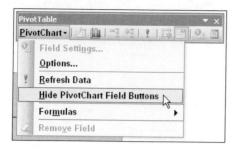

Figure 11.5. Hiding the field buttons

Embedding a PivotChart on a worksheet

It's very convenient to have a chart on the same worksheet as the source table, and you can put a PivotChart on a worksheet just like you can put a normal chart on a worksheet (see Figure 11.6). The only difference is you have to move the PivotChart to the worksheet after you create it, instead of creating it on the worksheet to begin with like you can with a normal chart.

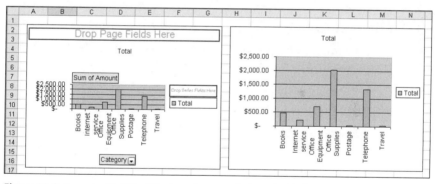

Figure 11.6. An embedded PivotChart, and a copy of the embedded PivotChart with field buttons hidden

To embed a PivotChart (make it a floating object) on a worksheet, right-click anywhere in the PivotChart and click Location on the shortcut menu. In the Chart Location dialog box, shown in Figure 11.7, click the As object in option button, and select the worksheet name in the associated list box. The PivotChart object pops into the selected worksheet (and you lose the PivotChart chart sheet).

Figure 11.7. Embed a PivotChart on a worksheet by changing its location.

An embedded PivotChart works just like a full-sheet PivotChart, but it also works like a normal embedded chart, in that you can move it by dragging it, and resize it by dragging border handles.

An embedded PivotChart is so much smaller than a full-sheet PivotChart that you'll want to hide the field buttons and the legend. Click in the PivotChart, then click the PivotChart button on the PivotTable toolbar and click Hide PivotChart Field Buttons. In the Chart toolbar, click Legend.

Just the facts

- Create a PivotChart by creating a PivotTable and then clicking the Chart Wizard button on the PivotTable toolbar.

- Create a PivotChart by using the PivotTable Wizard and selecting PivotChart (and PivotTable) in Step 1.

- Change calculation function and hide/show item details using the same techniques as in PivotTables.

- Make most PivotChart changes more easily by making the changes in the linked PivotTable.

- Hide the buttons and areas in a PivotChart by clicking Hide PivotChart Field Buttons (on the PivotChart button menu on the PivotTable toolbar).

- Embed a PivotChart on a worksheet by right-clicking the PivotChart, clicking Location, and selecting As object in and a worksheet name.

Creating Charts
and Graphics

GET THE SCOOP ON...
Creating a chart ▪ The Chart toolbar ▪ Types of charts ▪
Changing the chart type ▪ Changing chart data ▪
Changing chart orientation ▪ Moving and resizing an
embedded chart ▪ Changing the chart location

Presenting Data Visually with Charts

C harts present data visually, which makes the trends in data much easier to grasp. When you want your audience to quickly understand what the numbers are telling them, present the numbers with a chart; when you want to find the trends in your own data quickly and clearly, chart the data.

This chapter is about normal charts, not PivotCharts. Normal charts are more formattable and easier to work with than PivotCharts (you can create a normal chart from a PivotTable summary of data by freezing the PivotTable to create a static table before you chart it — see Chapter 11).

Charts exist as either *chart sheets,* separate sheets in a workbook that contain nothing but the chart, and *embedded charts,* charts that float on top of a worksheet and can be moved, resized, and displayed alongside the data. A chart can be initially created as either a chart sheet or an embedded chart, and can be relocated to switch between chart sheet and embedded chart after creation.

Creating a chart

Charts are easy to create. You can create them instantly (and then make changes to them after they're finished), or you can use the Chart Wizard to make the changes you need as you create the chart.

Inside Scoop

Dragging to select the data for a chart is the only way to be sure that only chartable data is included in the chart, but you can also separate your data table (headers and data) from a chart title by inserting a very narrow row between the table and the chart title.

Create an instant chart

An instant chart is a default chart that Excel creates based on a logical interpretation of the data in your table. It's great for charting data on the fly, when you need a fast, temporary picture of trends or you're rushing out to a meeting and don't have time to create a more polished chart.

You have two options for creating an instant chart:

- Click in the data table (or click and drag to select the chartable data), and press F11. Excel creates an instant chart sheet with a column chart type.

- Click in the data table (or click and drag to select the chartable data), and select a chart type from the Chart Type button palette on the Chart toolbar. Excel creates an instant embedded chart of the type you selected in the Chart Type palette.

You can create and save a custom chart type, with all your own formatting, and set that chart as the default chart type. When you create an instant chart, the new chart will be your default custom chart type. See Chapter 13 for custom chart types.

Use the Chart Wizard

Like all the Excel wizards, the Chart Wizard asks you questions in a series of steps and builds the chart in response to your answers.

At any point during the Chart Wizard steps, you can click Finish to complete the chart with the selections you've made up to that point.

To use the Chart Wizard:

1. Click and drag to select the data to chart.

   - Select a rectangular range of data, including any row and column headers that you want to appear in the chart.

   - Ctrl+drag to select nonadjacent rows or columns for inclusion in the chart.

- Don't include grand totals in the data — they throw the scale out of balance and make the chart very difficult to read.

- Instead of selecting the data to chart, you can use a range name or a named OFFSET/COUNTA formula (see Chapter 5); type the range or formula name in the Data Range box in Step 2 of the Chart Wizard.

2. On the Standard toolbar, click the Chart Wizard button. In the wizards Step 1 of 4 (shown in Figure 12.1), click a chart type in the Chart type list, and click a subtype in the Chart sub-type section. As you look at the chart types, click the Custom Types tab and look through the custom types — they're mostly new and highly formatted, and your data is displayed in the Sample box with custom type applied. Click Next.

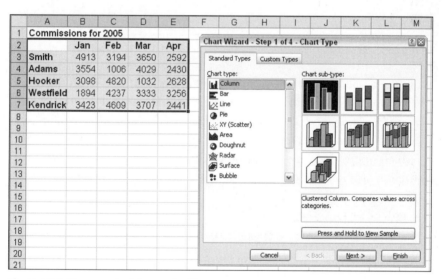

Figure 12.1. Choose a chart type and subtype.

3. In the wizard's Step 2 of 4 (shown in Figure 12.2), choose a data orientation. Click both of the Series in option buttons until the sample picture looks the way you want it, and then click Next.

Bright Idea

On the Standard Types tab of the dialog box, use the Press and Hold to View Sample button to see your data in the chart type and subtype you selected.

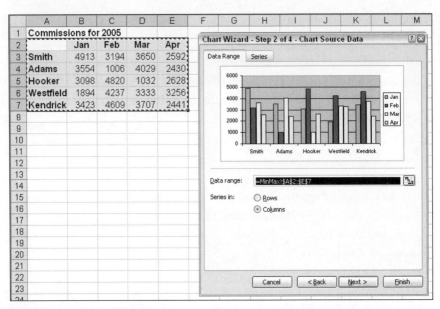

Figure 12.2. Set the data orientation.

4. In the wizard's Step 3 of 4 (shown in Figure 12.3), set up all the extra features for your chart. You can select options from the Titles, Axes, Gridlines, Lengend, Data Labels, and Data Table tabs. (Everything here can be added or changed later by choosing Chart ⇨ Chart Options, which opens the same dialog box.) Changes appear in the chart preview as you make them. Click Next when you finish adding features.

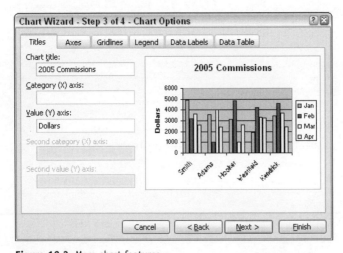

Figure 12.3. More chart features

Inside Scoop

Like everything else in the chart, the titles can be changed, reformatted (font, color, font size, placement), or deleted after the chart is finished.

5. Lastly, choose a location for the chart — on a chart sheet or embedded as an object in the worksheet of your choice (see Figure 12.4). Click Finish.

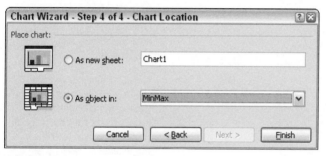

Figure 12.4. Choose a chart location.

The chart is created. Now comes the fun part: changing and formatting to make the chart really informational and professional, or to conform to a company standard. Changing the features is covered in the rest of this chapter; formatting the elements is covered in Chapter 13.

The Chart toolbar

Usually the Chart toolbar appears automatically whenever a chart object is active (that is, when you click a chart object or select a chart sheet). If you've ever closed a Chart toolbar to get it out of your way, it doesn't reappear automatically; you must select a chart object and then right-click the toolbar area and click Chart for it to become automatic again.

The buttons on the Chart toolbar help you to make common changes quickly. Table 12.1 explains the buttons.

Icon	Name	Purpose
Chart Area ▾	Chart Objects	A list of all chart elements. Select a specific element by dropping the list and clicking the name.
	Format Selected Object	Opens a Formatting dialog box for the selected element.
	Chart Type	Opens a palette of chart types; to float the palette, drag its title bar away from the toolbar.
	Legend	Click to remove or replace the legend; when you remove the legend, the plot area resizes to fill the chart (unless you move or resize the legend).
	Data Table	Click to add or remove a data table at the bottom of the chart.
	By Row	Changes orientation to put rows along the X-axis.
	By Column	Changes orientation to put columns along the X-axis.
	Angle Clockwise	Angles labels on selected axis clockwise.
	Angle Counterclockwise	Angles labels on selected axis counterclockwise.

Table 12.1. The Chart toolbar buttons

Types of charts

There are several types of charts, each of which is better suited for displaying a particular kind of data. For example, a Column or Bar chart is good for displaying several series in relation to each other; a Pie chart is good for displaying proportions in a single series; and a Line chart is good for displaying changes over time. Most important in selecting a

Bright Idea

For some data, a combination chart — combining different kinds of markers (such as line and column) — is helpful. To create a combination chart, right-click a marker in the series you want to change, click Chart Type, click the type, and then click OK. If you don't like the change, press Ctrl+Z to undo it.

chart type is that you and your audience can easily read and understand what that chart type displays.

The key ideas to keep in mind when choosing a chart type are:

▪ What king of data are you charting? Consider whether you are showing, for example, discrete comparisons between categories of data, changes over time, percentages of a whole, correlations between two numeric values, or three sets of values, which are most easily displayed in a three-dimensional format.

▪ What kinds of charts are your audience accustomed to seeing and interpreting? If you choose a chart type with which your audience isn't familiar, the audience is less likely to understand the data you're presenting.

Line and Area charts (shown in Figure 12.5) are good for showing changes over time. Area charts are best used for a single series, because in a two-series Area chart, one series partially hides the other.

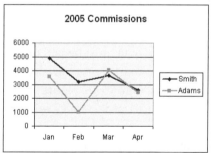 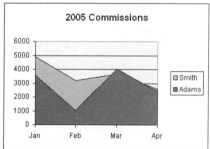

Figure 12.5. Line and Area charts for the same data

Column, Bar, Cylinder, Cone, and Pyramid charts (shown in Figure 12.6) are all good for comparing discrete categories of data at a specific point in time (such as total sales in each department for the month of January).

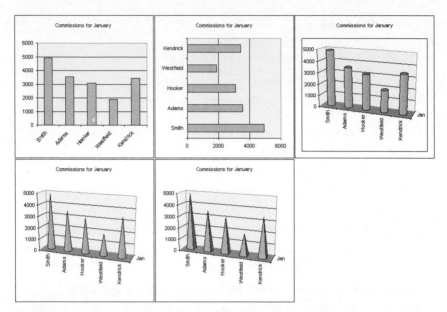

Figure 12.6. Column, Bar, Cylinder, Cone, and Pyramid charts for the same data

When you want to show how data breaks down into percentages of a total amount, the Pie and Doughnut charts and the 100% Stacked-Column chart do the job effectively (see Figure 12.7). The caveats are that the Pie chart can show only a single series, and all of these charts have more impact if you limit each series to a half-dozen data points.

For keeping track of investment performance, there are several versions of the Stock charts you see in financial reports. The important thing to remember about Stock charts is that the data must be laid out in the table in the same order as the name of the chart. For example, the data for a Volume-Open-High-Low-Close chart (shown in Figure 12.8) must be presented in the data source table in this order: date, volume, open, high, low, close.

Charts such as the Radar, Bubble, and Surface charts (shown in Figure 12.9) are used in scientific applications but not much seen (or understood) by other audiences.

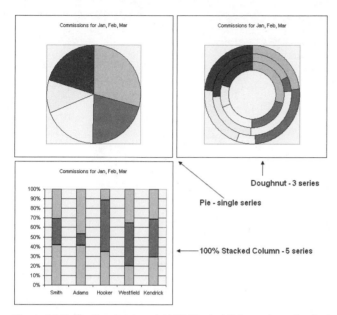

Figure 12.7. Pie, Doughnut, and 100% Stacked-Column charts for the same data. Pie and Doughnut charts need data labels to identify the data points.

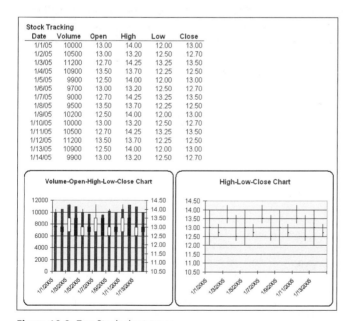

Figure 12.8. Two Stock chart types

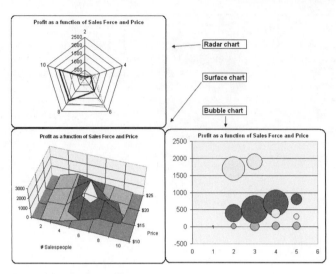

Figure 12.9. Radar, Bubble, and Surface charts

XY Scatter charts (shown in Figure 12.10) are common in scientific applications in which two values are correlated, such as the heights and weights of individuals in a test population, and they are the appropriate chart type for trendlines, which are discussed in Chapter 13.

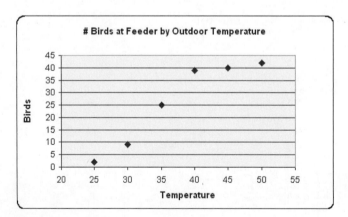

Figure 12.10. An XY Scatter chart

Changing the chart type

While you can make a quick change in chart type by clicking the Chart Type button on the Chart toolbar, the choices on the Chart Type button palette, shown in Figure 12.11, are limited.

Hack

If you apply a custom type and then change your mind and try to reapply a standard type, the chart retains the custom formatting. To get the original standard formatting back, choose Chart ⇨ Chart Type, and on the Standard Types tab, select the Default formatting check box.

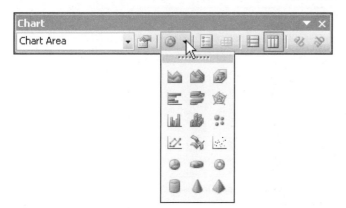

Figure 12.11. Instant chart type changes from the Chart Type toolbar button palette

For a better selection of chart type choices, click the chart to select it (a Chart menu appears on the menu bar in place of the Data menu), then choose Chart ⇨ Chart Type, and you get the same Chart Type dialog box as in the Chart Wizard Step 1. Click the type and subtype you want (don't forget about the Custom types tab), and click OK.

Changing chart data

Charts are linked to their data source ranges and update automatically when the source data changes. But when you add or delete rows or columns of data to the source range, the chart doesn't update automatically (unless you use a new dynamic list or a named OFFSET/COUNTA formula as the data source range).

Add data to an embedded chart

When you click an embedded chart, colored borders and handles appear around the source data range (as shown in Figure 12.12). Click and drag the handles to change the size of the source data range.

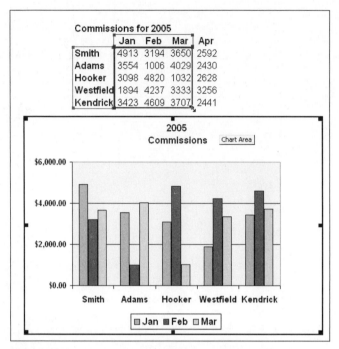

Figure 12.12. New rows aren't automatically added to the chart.

Add data to a chart sheet

Choose Chart ⇨ Source Data. Excel switches to the worksheet where the data range is located, puts a moving marquee around the data, and displays the Source Data dialog box. On the worksheet, click and drag to select the entire new data range, then click OK in the dialog box.

Change the source range

To change the data range completely (in a chart sheet or an embedded chart), click the chart to select it, then choose Chart ⇨ Source Data. Click and drag the new range, then click OK in the Source Data dialog box (shown in Figure 12.13).

Bright Idea

If you've created a terrific chart and want to reuse it with other data, you can copy the chart (drag to move it and press Ctrl when you drop it), then click the new copy, choose Chart ⇨ Source Data, and drag the new data range.

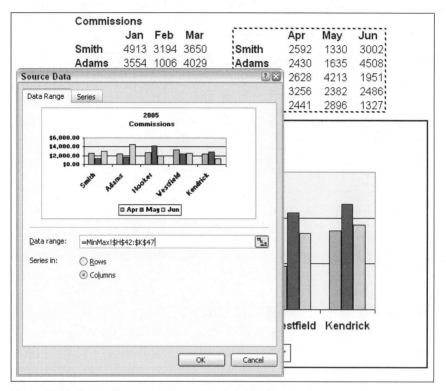

Figure 12.13. Change the source data completely by dragging a new source range.

Add a data table

A data table places the charted numbers in a table attached to the bottom of the chart (see Figure 12.14). To add or remove a data table, click the Data Table button on the Chart toolbar.

While it's true that displaying the actual values of each data marker on the chart can be illuminating, a data table is not the best way to do it—a data table shrinks the chart to make room for the table below the chart, and data tables are not terribly attractive (although you can format them somewhat). I find that a better (and quite formattable) way to display values along with the data markers is to add data labels to the series (see Chapter 13).

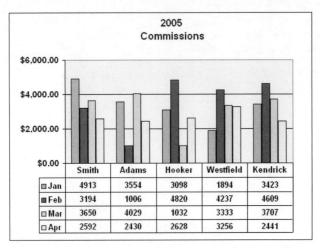

Figure 12.14. A data table displays actual values below the chart.

Changing chart orientation

If you didn't choose the most usable chart orientation (row labels or column labels along the category axis—the horizontal axis in a column chart), you can change it at any time.

When you click a chart or open a chart sheet to select the chart, the buttons on the Chart toolbar show you the current orientation (see Figure 12.15). One of the orientation buttons, either the By Row button or the By Column button, is highlighted to show you which orientation is applied.

To change the orientation, click the other orientation button.

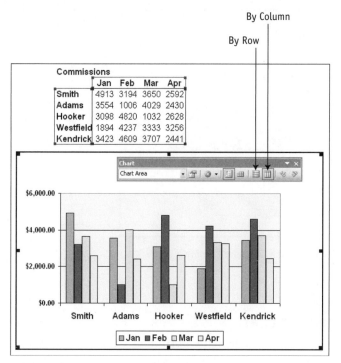

Figure 12.15. Change the chart orientation quickly.

Moving and resizing an embedded chart

A newly created embedded chart is unlikely to be the right size or in the right position on the worksheet, but resizing and moving is a snap.

Move an embedded chart

To move a chart, click the chart near its perimeter so the chart area is selected (handles appear around the chart border, as shown in Figure 12.16), and drag the chart to a new location.

Bright Idea

Make more room for the plot area by moving the legend to a horizontal display across the bottom of the chart: Double-click the legend, and on the Placement tab, click the Bottom option.

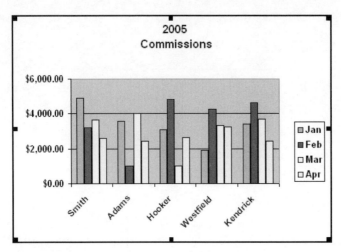

Figure 12.16. Click and drag near the perimeter to move a chart; drag a handle to resize a chart.

Resize an embedded chart

To resize a chart, click the chart near its perimeter so the chart area is selected (handles appear around the chart border), then click and drag a handle to resize the chart.

- Press and hold Shift while you drag a corner handle to retain the chart's proportions while you resize it.
- Press and hold Ctrl while you drag to resize a chart symmetrically (both sides or top-and-bottom move in or out equal distances).
- Press and hold Alt while you drag any handle to "snap" the corner or border to worksheet gridlines.

Changing the chart location

When you want to print a chart along with its source data, you want the chart—at least temporarily—on the worksheet with the data. When you want a large chart in which you can display lots of details, you want the chart on its own full-page chart sheet.

To move a chart from being embedded on a worksheet to a chart sheet, or from a chart sheet to embedded on a worksheet, right-click the chart and click Location from the menu that appears. Select the As new sheet option (as shown in Figure 12.17) or the As object in option, and click OK.

Figure 12.17. Relocating an embedded chart to a chart sheet.

If you're relocating a chart onto a chart sheet, the default chart sheet name, Chartnumber, is in the Location dialog box. While the chart sheet name is highlighted, type a more intuitive name for the new chart sheet.

Just the facts

- Create an instant chart by pressing F11 or clicking the Chart Type button on the Chart toolbar.

- Set chart features as part of the chart creation process by using the Chart Wizard (click in the data, then click the Chart Wizard button on the Standard toolbar).

- Choose a chart type that's appropriate for both the data you want to display and the audience to which you present it.

- Change a chart type quickly with the Chart Type button on the Chart toolbar, or for a wider selection of available chart types, click the chart, and choose Chart ⇨ Chart Type.

- Change a chart's source data range by choosing Chart ⇨ Source Data, and dragging to select the new source data range.

- Click the Data Table button on the Chart toolbar to add or remove a data table.

- Click the By row or By column button on the Chart toolbar to change the chart orientation.

- Relocate a chart to a chart sheet or to a worksheet by right-clicking the chart and clicking Location, then select the new location.

GET THE SCOOP ON...
Formatting chart elements ▪ Changing axis scale ▪
Reordering the series ▪ Resizing and exploding a pie
chart ▪ Changing 3-D perspective ▪ Adding a trendline ▪
Adding a secondary axis ▪ Working with data labels ▪
Creating picture markers ▪ Saving and reusing your
custom chart format

Formatting Charts

L ike worksheets, charts can present data in a utilitarian manner, or you can format them to make them look professional, graphically striking, or silly, depending on your audience.

Chart formatting possibilities

When you create a chart, you get Excel's default colors, fonts, and so on, and your chart looks like every other chart ever created in Excel; but after you create a chart, your options for changing the look of your chart are endless (see Figure 13.1).

There are also many ways to make your data more meaningful, including changing the axis scale to focus on the range of values, adding a secondary axis to present series with very different ranges of values, adding data labels to place the actual values of each marker directly on the markers, adding trendlines to display the validity of data correlation, and more.

Bright Idea

After spending a lot of time formatting a chart, you can save and reuse the entire formatting package on any new (or old) chart by saving the formatting as a custom format — see the section at the end of this chapter.

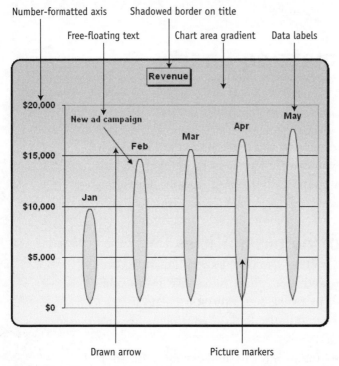

Figure 13.1. These are just a few of your formatting opportunities in Excel charts.

Formatting chart elements

To keep your audience's attention during a presentation, make your charts visually attractive with color, line, and font formatting. To make a presentation involving several charts consistent and professional, give all the charts a uniform look by using the same formatting for all of them.

Select a chart element to format

To select any chart element, such as a data series, an axis, the plot area, gridlines, the legend, or an individual legend entry (called a key), click the element.

When the mouse is positioned over any element, the name of the element appears near the mouse pointer in a ScreenTip.

If clicking the element is difficult because it's too small to grab with the mouse, use the Chart Objects list box on the Chart toolbar (shown in Figure 13.2) to select the element.

Figure 13.2. The Chart Objects list box shows the name of the selected element.

Another way to select a difficult-to-grab chart element is to click any chart element and then use the arrow keys to move from element to element until the element you want is selected. The name of each selected element is displayed in the Chart Objects list box on the Chart toolbar.

Format an element

For quick fill color, font color, or font/font size changes for a selected element, use the buttons on the Formatting toolbar.

For more formatting choices for a selected element, double-click the element and make your changes in the Format dialog box (see Figure 13.3).

Different elements have different formatting options; investigate all the tabs in a Format dialog box to see what the options for that element are.

Interpolate missing data points

In a Line chart, missing data points are shown as breaks in the line (as shown in Figure 13.4). To show a continuous line through missing data points (*interpolating* the missing values), click the chart to select it, then choose Tools ⇨ Options, click the Chart tab, and select Interpolated. (This only works in a Line chart, not in a Line series in a combination chart.)

Hack

If you want to interpolate a Line series in a combination chart, such as a combination Line/Column chart, first change the entire chart to a Line chart; then interpolate the chart; then switch the Column series back to Column type.

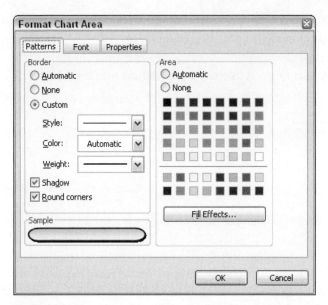

Figure 13.3. Use a chart element's Format dialog box for maximum formatting choices.

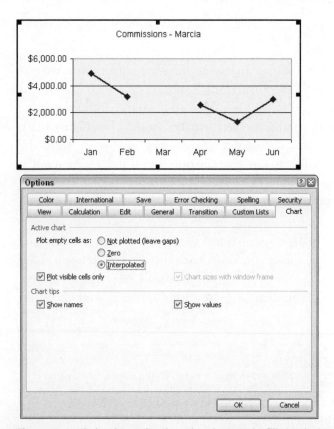

Figure 13.4. Missing data points in a Line chart can be filled in by interpolating the data.

Add free-floating titles

The fastest way to add titles and extra labels to a chart is to just type them. Click any element in the chart and type your title or label, then press Enter. When you press Enter, a text box with your label appears in the middle of the chart, as shown in Figure 13.5. (While you type, your characters appear in the Formula bar; when you press Enter, the characters disappear from the Formula bar and appear in a free-floating label in the chart.)

The text box is fully formattable, movable, and resizable. See Chapter 14 for more about text boxes and other graphical objects.

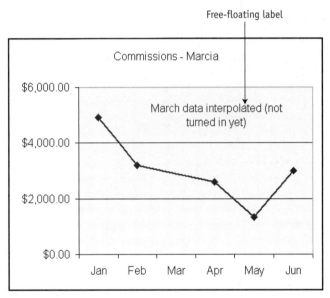

Figure 13.5. To add a free-floating label, click anywhere in the chart, type the label, and press Enter.

Delete a chart element

To delete a chart element, select the element and press Delete. If you change your mind after deleting the element, press Ctrl+Z to undo the deletion.

Changing axis scale

Changing the axis scale, the range of data displayed on an axis, can persuade an audience to your point of view. Changing axis scale doesn't alter the values at all, but it can magnify the differences between values.

Inside Scoop

You can dramatically display values that fail to meet a minimum by setting the Category (X) axis Crosses at value to that minimum value. All values that fall below the value you set appear to be negative values. Their actual values are difficult to determine, but you can display their actual values with data labels.

In Figure 13.6, the number of trees was counted in four different quadrants of land. Both charts use the same source data, but I changed the value axis scale in the chart on the right so it would persuade the audience that there is a large difference between Quad2 and the other quadrants.

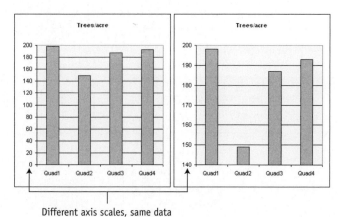

Different axis scales, same data

Figure 13.6. The chart with the narrower range on its value axis makes the value differences much more prominent.

To change the scale of the value axis, double-click the value axis (the axis with the number values). In the Format Axis dialog box (shown in Figure 13.7), click the Scale tab. In the Minimum and Maximum boxes, type the bottom and top values you want on the axis. The Major and Minor units set the gridline crossing points on the axis.

Reordering the series

When you create a chart, the data series are plotted in the order in which Excel finds them in the source data, but you're not limited to that series order. You might want to rearrange the series order, especially if you create a 3-D chart in which a tall series in front can hide shorter markers behind it (as shown in Figure 13.8).

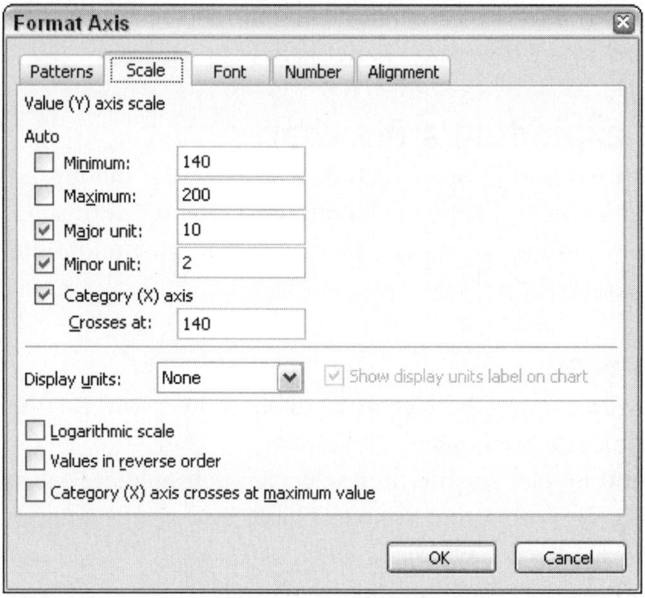

Format Axis   ⊠

| Patterns | Scale | Font | Number | Alignment |

Value (Y) axis scale

Auto
- ☐ Mi_n_imum: 140
- ☐ Ma_x_imum: 200
- ☑ M_a_jor unit: 10
- ☑ M_i_nor unit: 2
- ☑ Category (X) axis
     _C_rosses at: 140

Display _u_nits: None   ▾   ☑ Show display units label on chart

☐ _L_ogarithmic scale
☐ Values in _r_everse order
☐ Category (X) axis crosses at _m_aximum value

[OK]   [Cancel]

Figure 13.7. Changing the scale of the value axis

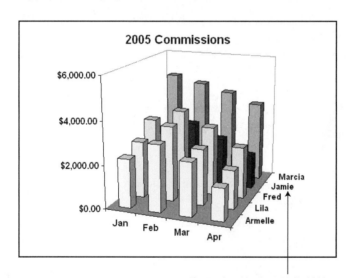

The Jamie series is partially hidden

Figure 13.8. Some of the data series in this 3-D chart hide other series.

To reorder the series in a chart, double-click any series in the chart. In the Format Data Series dialog box, click the Series Order tab, and rearrange the series order by clicking a series name and clicking the

Move Up or Move Down button to reposition it. (Watch the sample picture in the dialog box to see how your changes affect the chart.)

Resizing and exploding a Pie chart

Pie charts are great for showing how much of the total "pie" belongs to each data point, and if you make the pie larger and "explode" it by separating the slices (or by pulling out a single slice), you can call attention to individual items in your data.

Make the pie bigger

To make the pie bigger, resize the legend to make more room for the pie, and then drag the plot area to make it larger.

Click in the legend to select it, and then select a much smaller font in the Font Size box on the Formatting toolbar. The legend resizes smaller to accommodate the smaller font.

Next, select the Plot area (click just outside the pie, or use the Chart Objects list box on the Chart toolbar) and drag a corner handle to make it larger. Move the resized plot to give it more room by dragging just inside the plot border.

Figure 13.9 illustrates all these changes.

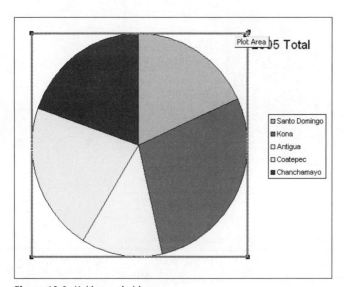

Figure 13.9. Making a pie bigger

Bright Idea

Make even more room for the pie by removing the legend completely, and identify the slices by adding data labels to them. Remember, you can change the dimensions of the chart area, too, to make more room for a larger pie. See the section "Working with data labels" later in this chapter.

Explode the pie

To call attention to a specific data point in a Pie chart, click and drag that slice out of the pie. You can also explode the entire pie by dragging all the slices away from the center.

To drag a single slice away, click in the pie so the entire pie (the whole set of slices) is selected, then click the slice you want to drag away so that only the one slice has handles, and finally click and drag the slice away from the pie (see Figure 13.10).

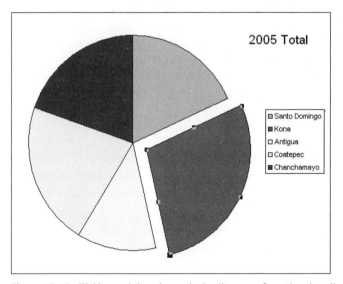

Figure 13.10. Clicking and dragging a single slice away from the pie calls attention to that data point.

To return the slice to the pie, click and drag the slice back into the center of the pie.

To explode the entire pie, click in the pie so the entire pie (the whole set of slices) is selected, and click and drag any of the slices away from the center of the pie (shown in Figure 13.11). All the slices separate.

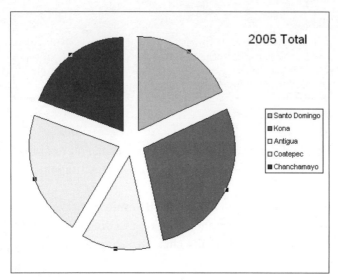

Figure 13.11. Click a slice one time to select the whole set, then drag one slice to move them all away or back together.

To rejoin the slices, click any of the slices to select the whole set, and drag any of the selected slices back into the center of the pie (unless you click a second time to select a single slice, all the slices move at the same time).

Changing 3-D perspective

A 3-D chart can be an effective way to get your point across (although usually 3-D charts are used just because they look fancy), but it can be difficult to see all the markers because they hide behind one another.

To bring hidden markers into view, you can rotate a 3-D chart on all three axes. You can rotate it quickly (sometimes with uncontrollable and dreadful results) by clicking and dragging a corner of the plot area; or more carefully by opening a dialog box that gives you precise control of the rotation.

Hack

If you rotate a 3-D chart by clicking and dragging a corner of the plot area (a wall or floor corner point) and create a mess, the quickest way out is to right-click a wall or the floor, click 3-D View, click Default, and click OK.

Rotate by dragging

To rotate a 3-D chart by clicking and dragging, click a wall or the floor (handles appear on the corner points). Drag a handle carefully (as shown in Figure 13.12) and watch the skeleton view of the chart as you drag. If the rotation gets out of hand, press Ctrl+Z to undo the rotation and start over.

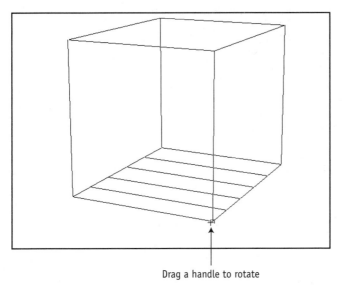

Drag a handle to rotate

Figure 13.12. Rotating a 3-D chart by dragging a handle

Rotate with precision

To prevent your chart from quickly ending up upside down and inside out, use the 3-D View dialog box to rotate the chart more slowly and precisely.

To rotate with the dialog box, right-click a wall or the floor of the chart and click 3-D View. In the 3-D View dialog box (see Figure 13.13), click the various axis buttons and watch what happens to the sample skeleton chart.

Hack

If you double-click a rotation button, the chart begins to rotate nonstop. To stop the rotation, click the button again. If the rotation gets out of hand and you end up with a mess that takes a long time to fix, click Default to start over.

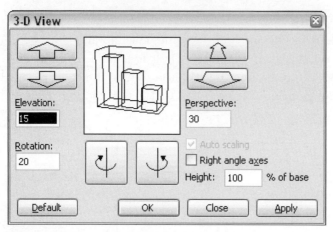

Figure 13.13. The 3-D View dialog box lets you rotate the chart slowly but with precision.

Adding a trendline

Trendlines are of real value and are commonly used in the scientific and statistical arenas to demonstrate the validity of data. They are essential in appropriate circumstances, but also widely misunderstood and misused outside of the scientific arena.

The purpose of a trendline is to prove mathematically whether there is a true correlation — a trend — among a set of data points. For example, if you have data that compares miles per gallon used by a vehicle and miles per hour driven in that vehicle, a trendline can show whether there is truly a correlation between speed and gasoline consumption. Moreover, a valid trendline is predictive — if a trendline in this example is valid, you can predict gasoline consumption at any given speed by using the trendline calculation.

The two charts in Figure 13.14 show similar data and trendlines. The upper chart has a valid trendline, which means the data points fit the line closely and the trendline can be used to predict gas consumption from speed. The lower chart has an invalid trendline, meaning the data points are too widely scattered to be correlated, and this data cannot be used to reliably predict gas consumption from speed. The R^2 (R-squared) value tells you whether the data is correlated enough to be meaningful and useful — the closer the R-squared value is to 1, the more valid the data is.

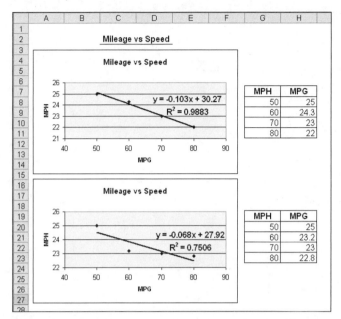

Figure 13.14. Two charts with trendlines. The top chart is valid and the bottom chart is invalid.

The best, and really the only appropriate, type of chart for a trendline is an XY Scatter chart like those in Figure 13.14. The data normally charted in a Scatter chart—two sets of numeric values—are the sort that a trendline is designed to analyze. A trendline is a visual representation of a regression analysis of the data points; a regression analysis is a mathematical measurement of how closely data points fit a perfect line or curve, and therefore how useful the data is in predicting unmeasured data. The R-squared value is the numerical result of the regression analysis equation (for this example, a linear regression).

Add a trendline to a chart

To add a trendline to a series, right-click one of the data points and click Add Trendline. In the Add Trendline dialog box, click the Type tab, as shown in Figure 13.15. Click the type of trendline that's appropriate for your data (Linear, Logarithmic, Polynomial, Power, Exponential, or Moving Average), and on the Options tab, select the Display equation on chart check box and the Display R-squared value on chart check box.

Right-click a data point

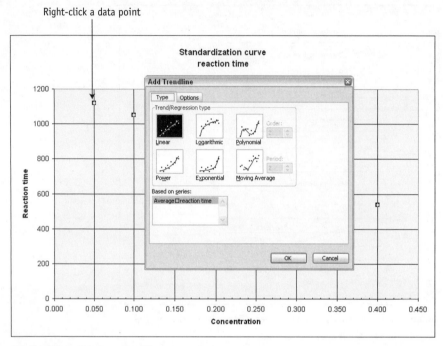

Figure 13.15. Creating a trendline

Click OK, and the trendline and a text box with the equation and R-squared value appear on the chart (see Figure 13.16).

If you present this data to others, it's imperative that you include the equation and the R-squared value on the chart, because without them the trendline is meaningless. The equation measures the slope of the trendline (and shows your audience that you used the correct trendline type), and the R-squared value measures the closeness with which the set of data points adheres to the line.

An R-squared value of 1.0000 is a perfect correlation of the data. In most cases, an R-squared value must be at least 0.98 to be valid; each laboratory and procedure has its own strict limits for validity.

Inside Scoop

For explanations of the actual mathematical equations used by each type of trendline, search Excel's online help files. Type **trendline types** in the Ask A Question box and press Enter, then select the help topic About trendline types.

The truth about trendlines

Too many books about Excel are written by authors who, although are experts in Excel and in areas such as finance, really don't understand what trendlines are for (and they write that you can use them to extrapolate sales or profits into the future, which is a foolish and dangerous way to make business decisions).

I come from a hard-sciences background, and I've used trendlines quite a lot (not just in Excel, but in the laboratory environment), and I can tell you exactly what trendlines are designed for. They are the visual representation of specific mathematical equations that, with or without the graphical trendline, prove or disprove the correlation of data points. In appropriate circumstances — such as rate of radioactive decay or level of mineral concentrations in drinking water — they are appropriately used to extrapolate data into the future or outside of the range of standardized calibration tests.

For example, when water is tested for the concentration of a chemical, the testing equipment is first calibrated by testing standardized samples of chemical concentrations, and then charting the test results against the known standardized concentrations. The two sets of data — the test results and the known concentrations — are charted as an XY Scatter chart, and a linear trendline and its R-squared value are calculated. The R-squared value tells me whether the data points are adequately correlated (whether the equipment is functioning properly and the standardization tests were run with precision) and whether the trendline is valid enough to determine the concentrations of the tested chemical in unknown water samples. Then the unknown samples are tested, and the trendline is used as a measuring stick to determine the chemical concentrations — in essence, you mark the test results on one axis of the XY chart, draw a line across the chart to the trendline, then take a right turn at the trendline and draw a line to the other chart axis to find the concentration that corresponds to the test result. (In reality, the concentrations are determined mathematically in a computer program such as Excel, not with a printed chart and a pencil, but you get the idea.)

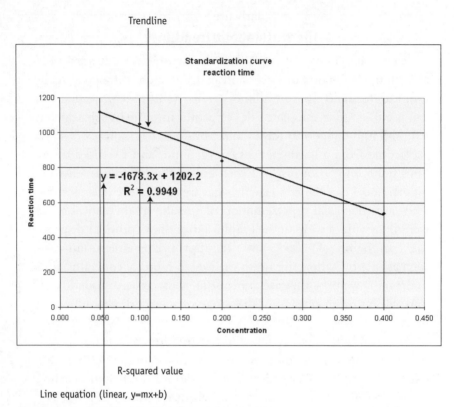

Figure 13.16. A trendline, line equation, and R-squared value are displayed on the chart.

Format the trendline and text box

The trendline is formattable: Right-click the trendline and click Format Trendline, then change the line weight, style, or color on the Patterns tab.

The text box with the equation and R-squared value is also formattable, as well as movable. Click in the text and drag the text box border to move it. The fastest way to format the text box is with the buttons on the Formatting toolbar.

Delete a trendline or text box

To delete the trendline or text box, click the line or text box and press Delete.

Use a moving average in business data

The one type of trendline that's useful in business (nonscientific) data is the moving average, which smoothes out fluctuations over time to give you a better overall picture of performance.

Moving averages are particularly useful for tracking short-term trends in data such as stocks and futures prices, factory output, workplace-accident rates, and seasonal sales of specific items. A moving average can highlight regular, periodic increases or decreases in value so you can plan for the next increase or decrease.

Like a trendline, a moving average can only be applied to a single data series. In a High-Low-Close chart of stock prices, for example, you must select the data series (the high, low, or close price series) for the moving average.

To add a moving average to a series, right-click a data point in the series and click Add Trendline; on the Type tab, click Moving Average. In the Period box, type the number of data points to average together for the data point on the moving average line (the higher the number of periods, the smoother the line). Then click OK. Figure 13.17 shows a Stock chart with a moving average.

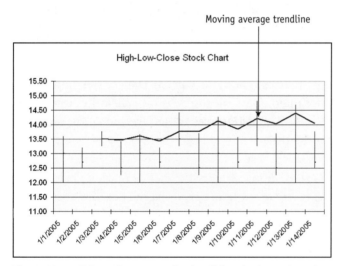

Figure 13.17. This moving average for the High series has a three-day period.

Inside Scoop

The moving average line doesn't begin at the first data point; because it's an average of a number of periods, it begins at the first point where there are that many periods (data points) to average. So if the periods value is 5, the moving average line begins at the fifth data point.

Adding a secondary axis

A secondary axis is ideal for comparing data that's related but is on two different scales. For example, suppose you're in charge of a department store sales staff and your burning questions are: How are total sales related to the number of salespeople on the staff? Does adding salespeople result in more sales revenue? At what point does a larger sales staff result in only marginally larger sales revenues?

You might find your answers by charting total revenue versus the number of salespeople for several months. But if total revenue is in excess of $10,000 and salespeople number between 10 and 20, how can you put both sets of numbers on the same chart? The sales force values are so much smaller than the revenue values that they're off the scale and not visible in the chart. You need a secondary axis to show both sets of values.

To add a secondary axis to a chart, you need to select the data series with values so small they're hidden. Select the chart, then in the Chart Objects list box on the Chart toolbar, select the hidden data series. Handles appear on the hidden data series (along the bottom axis in a column chart).

Next, on the Chart toolbar, click the Format Data Series button. In the Format Data Series dialog box, on the Axis tab, click the Secondary Axis option and click OK. The two sets of values are shown on separate value axes (see Figure 13.18).

For a secondary axis, it's best to use a combination chart, such as a Line and Column chart, so it's obvious which set of markers belongs to which axis. To change the series chart type, right-click the secondary series and then select the new chart type from the Chart Type button on the Chart toolbar.

Working with data labels

Data labels add value to a chart by positioning data labels or values right next to their markers in a chart and can sometimes make a legend unnecessary. In Figure 13.19, the labels are formatted as pale yellow so they can be seen easily.

Data labels show text or values from the source data range, so if you make changes in the source data, the changes automatically appear in the data labels. You can add data labels to any chart type; they're particularly useful in Pie charts.

Secondary series changed to Line type

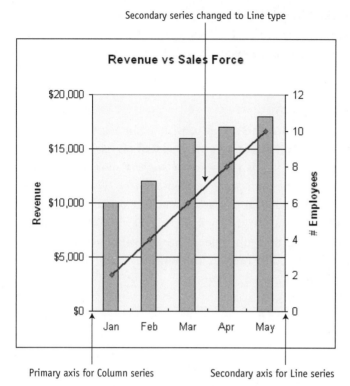

Primary axis for Column series   Secondary axis for Line series

Figure 13.18. A secondary axis makes both sets of values visible and easy to compare.

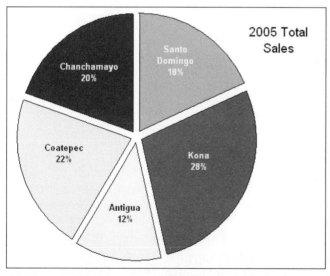

Figure 13.19. Without a legend, this Pie chart has more room for display; these data labels are individually formatted for better visibility against the pie slice colors.

Data labels can be moved, formatted, and deleted both individually and as a group. They are so formattable and maneuverable that I find them much more useful than a data table, which takes up too much room at the bottom of the chart.

Add data labels

To add data labels, right-click the series to which you want to add data labels, and click Format Data Series. On the Data Labels tab, select check boxes for the types of data labels you want (Category name is the data point labels, and Value is the data point values).

To add a data label to a single marker, click again on that single marker to select it alone, then right-click the marker and click Format Data Point; on the Data Labels tab, select check boxes for the types of data labels you want for that data marker. In Figure 13.20, a label with the data marker value has been added.

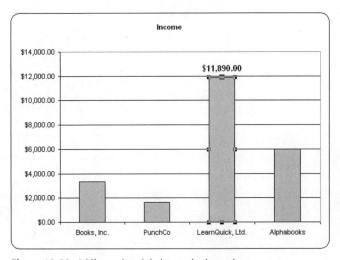

Figure 13.20. Adding a data label to a single marker

Format data labels

To format the entire set of data labels, double-click a single data label to select the whole set and display the Format Data Labels dialog box.

For simple, quick formatting, select the data labels you want to format and use the buttons on the Formatting toolbar. If you want borders, however, you need to use the Format Data Labels dialog box.

Hack

If you format label text white to show up on a dark data marker, you may get a black background in the label that you can't remove. Instead, format the text a pale color, such as yellow or blue; the pale text is easily readable against the dark series marker, but without the black label background.

To format individual data labels, click a data label to select the set, then click the single data label you want to format. Right-click the selected label and click Format Data Labels to display the Format Data Labels dialog box.

Delete data labels

To delete the entire set of data labels, click a single data label to select the set, and press Delete.

To delete a single data label, click a single data label to select the set, then click the label you want to delete, and press Delete.

Creating picture markers

Picture markers can wake up a drowsy audience by adding a touch of whimsy to a chart. A good way to use picture markers is to call attention to a particular data point by turning that single data point into a picture marker.

You can use any picture you want as a data marker: clip art, objects you've drawn in graphics programs such as Windows Paint, or even a company logo graphic (as shown in Figure 13.21). Remember that simpler is better as the picture will be pulled out of proportion by the varying values.

The fastest way to create and use a simple picture marker is to draw the marker picture in the worksheet, then copy the drawn object, select the series (or a single marker in the series), and press Ctrl+V to paste the picture in place of the marker. (See Chapter 14 for more about drawing objects in Excel.)

Bright Idea

Even if you delete the graphical object from the worksheet, you can copy a graphical object picture marker from one data marker to another. Select the picture marker, press Ctrl+C, select the marker to which you want to copy the picture, and press Ctrl+V.

The fastest way to use graphics files such as clip art as picture markers is to use the Clip Art task pane to find a suitable figure and insert the symbol in your worksheet. Then copy the clip art picture, select the series (or a single marker in the series), and press Ctrl+V to paste the picture in place of the marker.

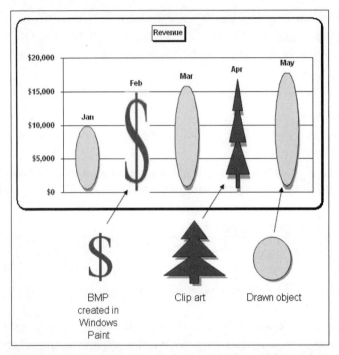

Figure 13.21. You can create a simple picture in the worksheet and use that picture as a data marker.

You don't need to keep the original picture in your worksheet after you create your picture marker(s). When you delete the original graphic image for your worksheet, the chart is unaffected.

To use a graphics file such as a picture you draw in Windows Paint, you can insert it in your worksheet and follow the procedures already

Bright Idea

To use a picture as the background for a chart area or the plot area, double-click the chart or plot area, click the Patterns tab, and click Fill Effects. On the Picture tab, click Select Picture. Navigate to the picture file, click Insert, and click OK twice.

outlined for copying and pasting it onto a marker, or you can open the Format Data Series or Format Data Point dialog box, click the Patterns tab, and click Fill Effects. On the Picture tab (shown in Figure 13.22), click Select Picture. Navigate to the picture file, click Insert, and click OK twice. Neither way seems to be faster.

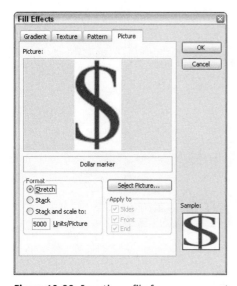

Figure 13.22. Inserting a file from your computer into a data marker.

Saving and reusing your custom chart format

When you put a lot of time into formatting all the elements of a chart (or if someone sends you a workbook containing a beautifully formatted chart that you want to use), you can save all that formatting work as a custom chart format; then you can apply all that painstaking formatting to new charts with just a couple of clicks.

Save a custom chart format

To save chart formatting as a custom chart type, right-click the formatted chart and click Chart Type. In the Custom Types tab of the Chart Type dialog box, select the User-defined option and click Add. In the Add Custom Chart Type dialog box (shown in Figure 13.23), type a name for the chart and type a memorable description for the chart format. Then click OK twice.

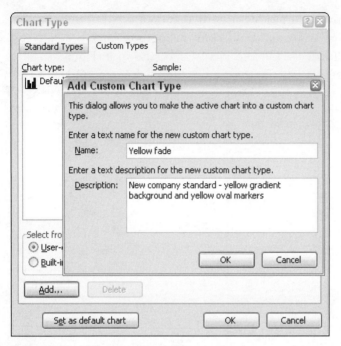

Figure 13.23. Adding a custom chart type

Apply a custom chart format

To apply a custom chart format to a new chart as you build it, start the Chart Wizard, and in Step 1, click the Custom Types tab, click User-defined, and then click the custom chart name in the Chart type list. Then continue with the Chart Wizard.

To apply a custom chart type to an existing chart, right-click the chart area and click Chart Type; click the Custom Types tab, click User-defined, and click the custom chart name in the Chart type list (shown in Figure 13.24). Click OK.

If the custom chart type is one you want to use all the time, click the Set as default chart button on the Custom Types tab and type a name for the chart.

To reset the default chart to Excel's original, in the Chart Type dialog box, click Column on the Standard Types tab and click Set as default chart.

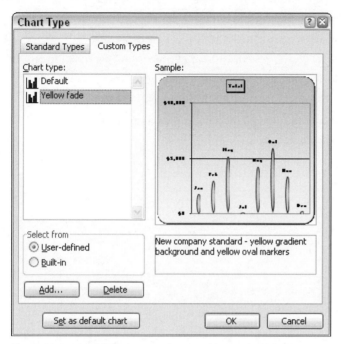

Figure 13.24. Applying a custom chart type to an existing chart

Just the facts

- Format chart elements quickly by selecting an element and using the buttons on the Formatting toolbar.

- Create more elaborate formats by double-clicking an element and setting formatting in the Format dialog box.

- Add free-floating titles, labels, and text by clicking in the chart, typing the text, and then repositioning the new text box.

- Explode a pie chart by clicking in the pie to select all the slices, and then dragging a slice away from the center.

- Drag a single slice away from a pie chart by selecting the series, then click the single slice and drag that slice away from the pie.

- Add a trendline or a moving average by right-clicking the series to which you want to add the trendline and clicking Add Trendline.

- Add a secondary axis by double-clicking the second-axis series and clicking Secondary axis on the Axis tab.

- Add data labels to a series by double-clicking the series to open the Format Data Series dialog box and then selecting the check boxes for the labels you want on the Data Labels tab.

- Save chart formatting to reuse by saving it as a custom chart format in the Chart Type dialog box.

GET THE SCOOP ON...
Using the Drawing toolbar ▪ Drawing basic shapes ▪
Formatting for all graphic objects ▪ Creating AutoShapes ▪
Drawing text boxes ▪ 3-D and shadows ▪ Creating WordArt ▪
Inserting pictures and clip art ▪ Creating diagrams and
organization charts ▪ Pasting pictures of cells

Adding Pictures and Graphic Objects

E xcel isn't about art, but all worksheets look the same until you customize yours with graphics and formatting. Like other Office 2003 programs, Excel has extensive tools for drawing graphic objects. What's more, graphic objects can be functional: You can assign a macro to a graphic object and run the macro by clicking the object.

You can draw and insert objects in worksheets and in embedded charts and chart sheets, but be sure you click an embedded chart to select it before you draw or paste graphics in it. If you don't, your graphics are drawn in a layer on top of the worksheet rather than in the chart, and won't move or copy or resize with the chart.

Using the Drawing toolbar

The Drawing toolbar has all the buttons you need for creating graphic objects in a worksheet or chart. You can show it or hide it by clicking the Drawing button on the Standard toolbar.

Table 14.1 explains the buttons on the Drawing toolbar.

Table 14.1. Buttons on the Drawing toolbar

Icon	Name	Purpose
Draw ▾	Draw	Menu of drawing commands.
	Select Objects	Enables the mouse pointer to select objects; click to deactivate when you want to select a cell.
AutoShapes ▾	AutoShapes	Menu of AutoShape categories.
	Line	Draws a straight line.
	Arrow	Draws an arrow.
	Rectangle	Draws a rectangle or square.
	Oval	Draws an oval or circle.
	Text Box	Draws a box that holds text.
	Insert WordArt	Starts the WordArt applet.
	Insert Diagram or Organization Chart	Creates a diagram or organization chart.
	Insert Clip Art	Opens the Clip Art task pane.
	Insert Picture from File	Opens the Insert Picture dialog box.
	Fill Color	Palette of fill colors.
	Line Color	Palette of line colors.
	Font Color	Palette of font colors.
	Line Style	Palette of line weights (thicknesses) for lines, arrows, and borders.

Icon	Name	Purpose
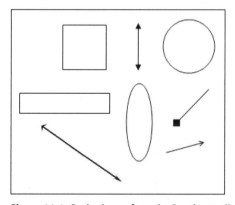	Dash Style	Palette of line dash styles for lines, arrows, and borders.
	Arrow Style	Palette of arrow styles for lines and arrows.
	Shadow	Palette of object shadows.
	3D	Palette of 3-D styles.

Drawing basic shapes

Basic shapes are lines, arrows, ovals, and rectangles. They are often more effective than fancy AutoShapes (which I discuss later in the chapter, in "Creating AutoShapes") because they're not as distracting and you can layer them on top of each other for unique graphic objects.

To draw a basic shape, click the object button and either click on the worksheet (for default objects that you can move, resize, and rotate) or drag to draw the object in the worksheet (which you can also move, resize, and rotate). Figure 14.1 shows a variety of shapes you can draw.

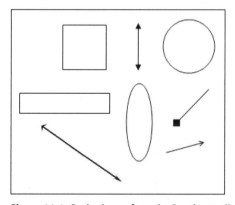

Figure 14.1. Basic shapes from the Drawing toolbar

Inside Scoop

To delete all the objects in a worksheet, choose Edit ➪ Go To, click Special, and then Objects to select them all, then press Delete.

Here are some tips for drawing and formatting basic shapes:

- To draw a perfectly vertical or horizontal line (or arrow), press and hold Shift while you draw the line (Shift forces the line into 15-degree angles).

- To draw any object from the center out, press and hold Ctrl while you draw.

- To draw a perfect square or circle, press and hold Shift while you draw a rectangle or oval. A perfect circle created using this method is in the upper right of Figure 14.1.

- Arrows are just lines with arrowheads; to convert an arrow to a line or a line to an arrow, select the line or arrow and choose a different style from the Arrow Style button.

- To change line or border weight (thickness), select the object, then click a line weight from the Line Style button.

- To move an object, click it and drag it with the four-arrow move pointer.

- To resize or reshape an object, click it and drag a handle.

- To draw several lines, arrows, ovals, or rectangles, double-click the shape button and draw lots of objects. Click the shape button again to turn it off.

- To rotate an object, drag the green handle. If you don't see a green handle, the object cannot be rotated. (To rotate a line or arrow, drag an end handle.)

- To copy a shape, press Ctrl while you drag and drop the object.

- To assign a macro to an object, right-click the object, click Assign Macro, click the Macro name, and click OK.

- To select a group of objects (to group them, format them identically, or move them together), click the Select Objects button and then draw a rectangular "lasso" around the group of objects you want to select.

Inside Scoop

If you want to select some objects but not other nearby objects, press and hold Shift while you click the specific objects you want to select.

Formatting for all graphic objects

For the best display of any graphics in a worksheet, turn off the worksheet gridlines. To turn off gridlines, choose Tools ⇨ Options, and on the View tab, deselect the Gridlines check box. Even when the gridlines are turned off, objects can be "snapped" to the gridlines by pressing and holding Alt while you move or resize an object.

Formatting objects

All objects can be formatted quickly and simply with the formatting buttons on the Drawing toolbar, and for some formatting (such as making text in an AutoShape bold) you can use buttons on the Formatting toolbar. Like the buttons on the Formatting toolbar, some of the Drawing toolbar buttons — Fill Color, Line Color, and Font Color — have tearaway palettes that you can float on the worksheet for easy access while you format objects.

But for access to all the formatting possibilities for a specific type of object, double-click the object and make your changes in the object's Format dialog box. Most of the Format dialog box tabs are self-explanatory, but here are some explanations of the less intuitive options in the Properties, Colors and Lines, and Protection tabs.

Properties tab

The Properties tab (see Figure 14.2) is where you can choose to print a worksheet without printing a specific graphic (for example, if you don't want to print a company logo on the worksheet you're sending to a particular customer). Graphic objects, including embedded charts, are printed with the worksheet by default, but you can set an object to not print by deselecting the Print object check box.

The Object positioning options control the object's behavior relative to the cells around it. For example, the Move and size with cells option allows an object to move or resize if the columns or rows beneath it are resized; the Move but don't size with cells option allows the object to

Bright Idea

Turning off (and on) gridlines is much faster with the Toggle Grid button. See Chapter 19 about personalizing your toolbars. Toggle Grid is in the Forms category, in the Customize dialog box, Commands tab.

Hack

If you can't select cells or an embedded chart, look at the Select Objects button on the Drawing toolbar. If the button is highlighted (turned on) you can select only objects; click the button to turn it off and return to data mode.

move if columns beneath it are inserted, deleted, or resized, but the object won't change size; and the Don't move or size with cells option (usually the most useful option) keeps an object permanently anchored on the worksheet no matter what happens to the cells beneath it.

Figure 14.2. The Properties tab

Colors and Lines tab

These options are self-explanatory, but the one worth pointing out is the Transparency option (see Figure 14.3). If you set an object's Fill color to a Transparency level, anything under the object (cells, other objects) shows through the somewhat transparent object.

Inside Scoop

So how can you select a cell beneath a transparent object? Select a cell outside of the object and use arrow keys to tunnel into the cell beneath the object.

Format AutoShape

| Colors and Lines | Size | Protection | Properties | Web |

Fill

Color: [▼]

Transparency: [◄]————[ ]————[►] [67 %] [⇕]

Line

Color: [████████ ▼]   Style: [————————— ▼]

Dashed: [————————— ▼]   Weight: [0.75 pt] [⇕]

Connector: [▼]

Arrows

Begin style: [▼]   End style: [▼]

Begin size: [▼]   End size: [▼]

[OK] [Cancel]

Figure 14.3. The Colors and Lines tab

If you're looking for more interesting Fill color effects, open the Color list box in the Fill area and click Fill Effects; you can fill the object with color gradations, textures, patterns, or a picture.

Protection tab

The only option on the protection tab is for locking (or unlocking) an object to control whether changes can be made to that object. Locking also applies to cells, and it has no effect until you protect the worksheet. You can learn more about locking and worksheet protection in Chapter 17.

Change the stack order

The stack order is the order in which objects overlap. The objects on top of a stack of overlapping objects are said to be in front, and those underneath other objects are said to be behind. In Figure 14.4, the white center circle is in front; it is the top object in the stack.

As you draw objects, each object you draw is drawn on top of any objects it overlaps. To change the stack order, select a single object, then from the Drawing toolbar, choose Draw ⇨ Order, and click an order command. Bring to Front and Send to Back place an object on the top or bottom of a stack of objects, respectively. Bring Forward and Send Backward move an object by one position within a stack of multiple objects.

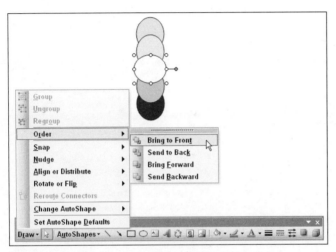

Figure 14.4. Objects stacked, or layered, on top of each other

Align and distribute objects

When you've got multiple identical objects that need perfect alignment or spacing, allow Excel to do the perfect alignment or spacing for you. Click the Select Objects button on the Drawing toolbar, and then drag to lasso all the objects. Then from the Drawing toolbar, chose Draw ⇨ Align and Distribute, and click an alignment or distribution command.

Inside Scoop

When you create worksheet and form controls (see Chapter 20), it's especially important to align and distribute controls well for proper function and ease of use. All the graphic object procedures in this chapter also apply to worksheet and form controls.

Bright Idea

Move one object into the exact position for the alignment, then drag all the other objects away from the alignment position (for example, to align left, drag all the objects a bit to the right of the object in the alignment position). Then lasso all the objects and align them — they'll align to the leftmost object.

The Alignment commands align all the selected objects with the one selected object that is already furthest in that direction (for example, Align Left aligns all the objects with the leftmost of the selected objects, as shown in Figure 14.5).

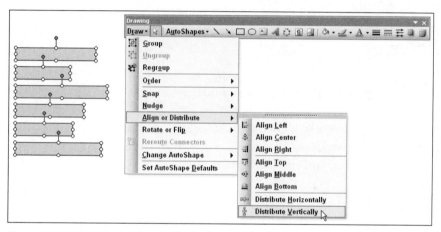

Figure 14.5. Left-aligned and vertically distributed objects

The Distribute commands space the objects perfectly equidistant from one another.

Group objects

When you carefully draw, layer, align, distribute, and stack several objects, it is very unpleasant to have your perfect arrangement inadvertently disturbed. To maintain the arrangement of several objects, click the Select Objects button and drag the mouse to draw a lasso around the entire group of objects, and then choose Draw ⇨ Group on the Drawing toolbar.

The lasso must encompass every object completely; any object that's only partially included in the lasso won't be selected. If you can't lasso an object you want without including objects you don't want, select the objects you want by Ctrl+clicking the remaining objects.

When a set of objects is grouped, the group moves, copies, and formats as a single object (see Figure 14.6).

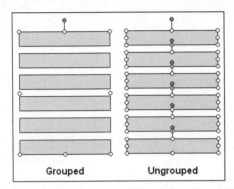

Figure 14.6. The left group is grouped and selected; the right group is ungrouped and all the separate objects were selected by lassoing.

If you need to make a change to any of the grouped objects, click the group and choose Draw ⇨ Ungroup. Click away from the group to deselect all the objects, and you can work on individual objects.

Creating AutoShapes

AutoShapes are prebuilt complex shapes such as banners and block arrows that you can select from a menu. After creating an AutoShape, you can move, resize, reshape, and format it just like any other object.

To create an AutoShape, click the AutoShapes button, point to a category, and click an AutoShape. There are two things you can do with AutoShapes (see Figure 14.7) that you can't do with basic shapes:

■ Manipulate the shape of many AutoShapes by dragging the yellow diamond handle.

■ Add text to an AutoShape by right-clicking the object and clicking Add Text. The text in an AutoShape behaves like text in a text box that's attached to the AutoShape. To edit or delete text, right-click the AutoShape and click Edit Text. However, text in an AutoShape is not as easy to manipulate as text in a text box — I almost always put text in a text box on top of an AutoShape instead of in the AutoShape.

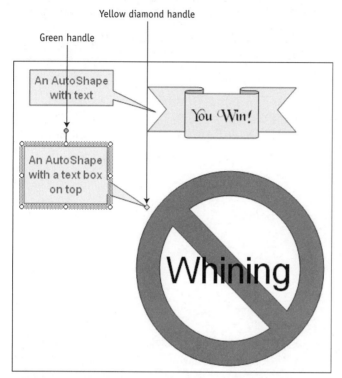

Figure 14.7. Most AutoShapes have a yellow diamond handle for reshaping and can carry text like a text box.

To put text in a basic shape such as a rectangle or oval, create a text box on top of the basic shape. Rotate the text box using a green handle that appears. Remove the text box border and fill color, color the text to be visible against the color of the basic shape object, and group the text box and basic shape so they are a single unit.

Drawing text boxes

Text boxes are free-floating text labels that you can use to add information to a worksheet or chart. They are fully formattable (colors, borders, fonts) and movable/resizable just like other graphic objects.

To draw a text box, click the Text Box button, then either click in the worksheet and start typing (the text box expands to accommodate what you type) or drag to draw a box in the worksheet and then type your text.

To format a text box, double-click the text box.

Hack

If you double-click inside a text box, the text is selected for editing. To open the Format Text Box dialog box, double-click the text box border.

3-D and shadows

All objects can be shadowed or made 3-D (see Figure 14.8), but not both (these settings are mutually exclusive).

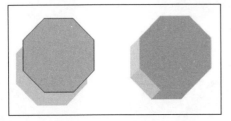

Figure 14.8. The object on the left is shadowed; the object on the right is 3-D.

To add either a shadow or a 3-D rendering, select the object, click the Shadow or 3-D button, and then click a shadow or 3-D shape.

After you apply a shadow, fine-tune the shadow by clicking Shadow Settings on the Shadow button menu. The Shadow Settings toolbar appears; you can nudge the shadow in different directions and change the shadow color and transparency.

After you apply a 3-D rendering, fine-tune the 3-D by clicking 3-D Settings on the 3-D button to make the 3-D Settings toolbar appear. You can spin the 3-D object on all three axes, change the surface texture of the object and the color of the 3-D portion, change the perspective, and change the lighting angle. In fact, you can waste quite a lot of time fine-tuning a 3-D object!

Bright Idea

If there is more than one 3-D object in the same worksheet, it looks more professional if they all have the same perspective, lighting angle, and so forth. Fine-tune one object, then click it and use the Format Painter on the Standard toolbar to paste the formatting to the other objects.

Creating WordArt

WordArt is a powerful, memory-intensive graphic mini-program that creates shapes from your text. It creates arresting graphics like the one shown in Figure 14.9, but a word of caution is in order: It eats up printer memory. Don't plan on printing WordArt graphics on an older printer that's low on memory.

Figure 14.9. WordArt creates arresting graphic images.

To create a WordArt graphic, follow these steps:

1. Click the Insert WordArt button.

2. In the WordArt Gallery dialog box, click a graphic and click OK.

3. In the Edit WordArt Text dialog box (shown in Figure 14.10), type your text. Select a font and a size (and bold or italic, if you want them). Then click OK.

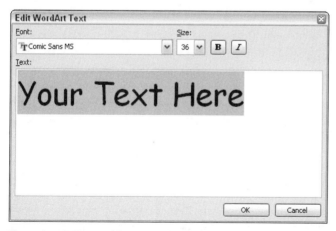

Figure 14.10. Type and format the WordArt text.

The finished WordArt graphic and WordArt toolbar appear in your worksheet. Move, resize, and rotate the object as you would any other graphic object.

Unlike other graphic objects, when you double-click a WordArt graphic, the Edit WordArt Text dialog box appears. Any formatting changes are most easily made using the buttons in the WordArt toolbar.

Inserting pictures and clip art

Logos and graphic images like those shown in Figure 14.11 can make a worksheet more visually interesting. For example, you can place a logo in a workbook template to tie the company's image together — every workbook created from the template has the logo in place — or place pictures of products in invoice worksheets.

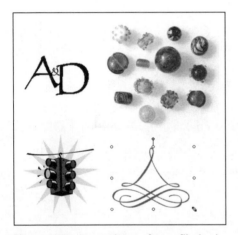

Figure 14.11. Insert pictures from a file (top) or clip art (bottom) to enliven a worksheet.

To paste a picture on a worksheet, click the cell where you want to paste the upper-left corner of the picture (make sure you make room for the picture by adding more rows and/or columns, as it will lie on top of worksheet cells). Then choose Insert ⇨ Picture, and choose Clip Art (for clip art) or From File (for your own picture or logo graphic).

If you select Clip Art, the Clip Art task pane opens. Search for the clip art you want, and double-click it.

Bright Idea

When you open the Clip Art task pane to search for clip art, make your search faster and more convenient by widening the task pane (point to the left border of the task pane and drag the two-headed pointer arrow).

To organize clip art images that you use often so you can find them quickly, select an image, then click the arrow that appears in the image; click Copy to Collection, and click OK in the Copy to Collection dialog box. The image is copied into the default My Collections dialog box. To find images, select My Collections in the Search In list in the Clip Art task pane.

If you select From File, the Insert Picture dialog box appears. Search for the file you want and double-click it.

When you click an inserted picture to select it, the Pictures toolbar appears (if the toolbar doesn't appear, right-click in the toolbar area and click Picture). The Picture toolbar buttons are listed in Table 14.2.

Table 14.2. Picture toolbar buttons

Button	Button name	Button function
	Insert Picture From File	Opens the Insert Picture dialog box so you can insert another picture.
	Color	Select from Automatic (original colors), Gray Scale (converts to shades of gray), Black and White (converts to black and white), or Watermark (converts to a bright, low-contrast watermark).
	More Contrast	Increases the intensity of the colors.
	Less Contrast	Reduces the intensity of the colors.
	More Brightness	Adds white to lighten colors.
	Less Brightness	Adds black to darken colors.
	Crop	Trims the image when you drag a handle.
	Rotate Left 90°	Rotates the image in quarter-turns.
	Line Style	Adds a border.

continued

Table 14.2. *continued*

Button	Button name	Button function
	Compress Pictures	Compresses selected picture or all pictures for better resolution in print or on a Web page.
	Format Picture	Opens the Format Picture dialog box.
	Set Transparent	Makes a color transparent so you can see the cell contents or other pictures beneath it (click the button, then click the color you want to set transparent in the image).
	Reset Picture	Undoes image manipulation.

You'll probably need to manipulate pictures in the worksheet after inserting them:

■ To resize a picture, click and drag a handle — drag corner handles to resize and keep proportions; drag a side, top, or bottom handle to resize and change proportions.

■ To resize a large picture quickly, double-click the picture; on the Size tab, under Scale, type a smaller number (for example, 25) in either the Height or the Width box. When you click OK, the picture is reduced to a manageable size.

■ To move a picture, click and drag it.

■ To place pictures on top of one another, set or change the order of appearance by right-clicking the picture and pointing to Order; click an order for the selected picture.

To import a picture from a scanner or digital camera, connect the hardware so your computer has access to the picture file. Then choose Insert ⇨ Picture ⇨ From Scanner or Camera and follow the steps in the dialog box.

Bright Idea

You can make a picture into a worksheet background, behind the cells. Choose Format ⇨ Sheet ⇨ Background, and double-click the picture file. The picture is repeated to cover the whole worksheet. The background is only on-screen. It doesn't print.

If your digital camera or memory card is connected through a USB port (the best and fastest way to get digital photos into your computer), the computer sees your camera or memory card as another storage device in the My Computer folder. Click either the Insert Picture From File button on the Drawing toolbar or choose Insert ⇨ Picture ⇨ From File, navigate to the picture, and insert it directly into the worksheet or chart.

Creating diagrams and organization charts

Even though workbooks are primarily for number crunching, they are also quite useful for sharing information of other kinds, such as the relationships or hierarchies of people, things, or procedures. For example, along with the production numbers for a factory, you can show a diagram of the processes involved in production or a hierarchy of the personnel in the department. Diagrams and organization charts are ideal for this kind of information, and these are the same diagrams and charts that you find in the other Office programs, such as Word and PowerPoint. They are the same as, but a lot easier than, drawing ovals, text boxes, and connecting lines and arrows.

To create a diagram or organization chart, click the Insert Diagram or Organization Chart button on the Drawing toolbar. In the Diagram Gallery dialog box, double-click the type of diagram you want (if you're not sure, click each type and read the description that appears). A large diagram with a dotted border is created in the worksheet (see Figure 14.12), and the Diagram (or the Organization Chart) toolbar appears.

When the diagram is in place, type text in the text boxes provided.

Like a chart, every element in a diagram or organization chart is separately formattable; double-click an element to open its Format dialog box. Here are a few more tips:

- To add another element to an organization chart, click an element in the chart and then select an option in the Insert Shape button's list.

- To add another element in any of the diagrams, click the Insert Shape button.

- Diagrams can be converted to different diagrams by choosing a different diagram in the Change To button's list.

- To reposition a text label in a diagram, click the label to select it, and then click one of the Move buttons in the Diagram toolbar.

Watch Out!
Don't hide the Diagram or Organization Chart toolbar — it's the only place to find the buttons and tools for customizing your diagrams and organization charts. If you inadvertently hide the toolbar, right-click the diagram or organization chart and click Show Diagram (or Organization Chart) Toolbar.

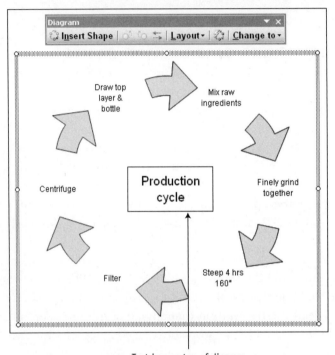

Text box on top of diagram

Figure 14.12. A diagram of a process

Pasting pictures of cells

Pasting pictures of cells is an old and useful feature I've used for years. For example, in a long list of data with a total at the bottom, I paste a picture of the total cell at the top of the list so I can see the total without scrolling down to find it (see Figure 14.13).

To take a picture of a cell (or a range or a chart) that you can paste elsewhere on a worksheet or in another worksheet, you need to use the Camera button. Chapter 19 covers toolbars and buttons in more detail, but here I'll show you quickly how to get the Camera tool onto a toolbar and use it to take a picture.

	A	B	C	D	E	F	G
1		Coffee Orders for December 2004				$67,132.50	
2	Date	Product	Price/lb	Lbs	Total		
3	12/2/04	Santo Domingo	9.50	100	950.00		
4	12/2/04	Antigua	10.50	100	1,050.00		
5	12/4/04	Antigua	10.50	200	2,100.00		
6	12/4/04	Antigua	10.50	150	1,575.00		
7	12/4/04	Antigua	10.50	45	472.50		
8	12/4/04	Santo Domingo	9.50	55	522.50		
9	12/5/04	Kona	9.25	90	832.50		
10	12/5/04	Kona	9.25	80	740.00		
11	12/5/04	Santo Domingo	9.50	60	570.00		
12	12/5/04	Santo Domingo	9.50	95	902.50		
13	12/7/04	Coatepec	10.25	150	1,537.50		
14	12/7/04	Antigua	10.50	100	1,050.00		
15	12/8/04	Chanchamayo	11.00	200	2,200.00		
16	12/8/04	Santo Domingo	9.50	125	1,187.50		
17	12/9/04	Coatepec	10.25	250	2,562.50		
18	12/9/04	Coatepec	10.25	75	768.75		

Figure 14.13. The pasted picture at the upper right of the total cell keeps the total conveniently visible.

Put the Camera button on a toolbar

To put the Camera button on a toolbar, follow these steps:

1. Right-click in the toolbar area and click Customize.

2. In the Customize dialog box, in the Commands tab, in the Categories list, select Tools.

3. In the Commands list, scroll down to Camera (see Figure 14.14).

4. Drag the Camera icon from the Customize dialog box onto a toolbar.

5. Close the Customize dialog box.

Take a picture

To take a picture of a cell (or cells), select the cell(s), then click the Camera button. Next, click where you want to paste the picture.

A linked picture of the cell(s) is pasted, and any changes in the source cell(s) are automatically updated in the picture. The picture is a graphic object; it's movable, resizable, and can be rotated. Unlike an object, however, when you double-click a picture, the source range is selected.

To take an updatable (linked) picture of a chart, you must take a picture of the cells behind the chart. Anything in or on the selected cells will be in the picture, and any changes you make in or on those pictured cells will be automatically reflected in the picture.

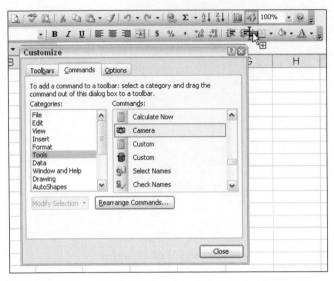

Figure 14.14. Drag the Camera icon from the dialog box to a toolbar.

To paste a picture of an unlinked chart, click the chart, then press Shift and choose Edit ⇨ Copy Picture; right-click where you want to paste the unlinked picture and click Paste. The pasted chart is truly just a picture object, unlinked to data, and formattable with a double-click.

Just the facts

- The Drawing toolbar is the source of all graphic objects in Excel.
- Show the Drawing toolbar by clicking the Drawing button on the Standard toolbar.
- Use the buttons on the Drawing toolbar for simple formatting of fill color, font color, and line color.
- Double-click an object for more formatting options for that particular type of object.
- Use the Draw menu on the Drawing toolbar to change stack order, alignment, and distribution of multiple objects, and to group or ungroup objects.
- Use Drawing toolbar buttons to create AutoShapes, text boxes, and WordArt.
- Enhance objects with 3-D or shadow effects.

■ Insert pictures and clip art using the buttons on the Drawing toolbar; import pictures directly from a scanner or camera using the Insert ⇨ Picture ⇨ From Scanner or Camera menu command.

■ Use Drawing toolbar buttons to create diagrams and organization charts.

■ Put the Camera button on a toolbar and use it to take linked pictures of cells that you can paste elsewhere in the worksheet or workbook.

Printing

GET THE SCOOP ON...
Previewing printed pages ▪ Printing a quick copy of a
worksheet ▪ Printing part of a worksheet ▪ Printing
a chart ▪ Printing several worksheets

PART VI

Printing Just What You Need

Even though lots of companies would like to run paperless offices, we all know that's a pipe dream. We still need printed data to mail out, pass around at company meetings, and file as a backup to often-fragile electronic data storage. Also, paper is more quickly accessible and easier to read (errors you don't notice on-screen often seem to jump right out on paper).

The question is not whether you need to print your Excel data, but how to print exactly what you need, quickly and easily, without wasting a lot of paper trying to get it right.

In this chapter, I talk about how to print specifically what you want; in the next chapter, I cover the details and finer points of formatting your printed pages.

Previewing printed pages

Always, always, always preview your pages before you print them. It takes just a moment and can save you not just paper but time reprinting a report.

To preview printed pages, click the Print Preview button on the Standard toolbar. The printed pages appear just as they will look when you send them to a printer (see Figure 15.1).

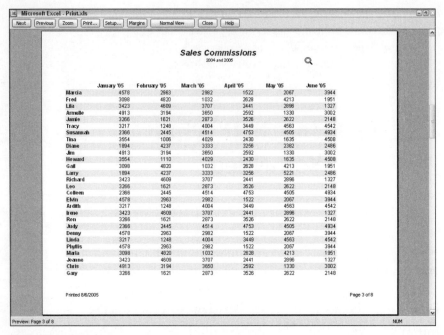

Figure 15.1. Print Preview is the only way to be sure you print what you intend.

In Print Preview mode, the mouse becomes a magnifying glass on the page. Click anywhere on the page to zoom in for a closer view of that area; click again to zoom back out.

If the printout is multiple pages, click the Next and Previous buttons in the toolbar to flip through the pages. If your mouse has a scroll wheel, you can probably flip through the pages in Print Preview by using the scroll wheel instead of clicking the Next and Previous buttons.

If the preview looks good, click the Print button on the toolbar to print the worksheet.

If the worksheet needs more work, click the Close button on the toolbar to return to normal view and edit the worksheet.

I discuss the Setup and Margins buttons in the next chapter.

Bright Idea

To quickly see how many pages will be printed, look at the lower-left corner of the screen. If the number seems high, it's especially important to flip through the pages and see if you have extra pages that are printing; for example, just one column that should be fit onto the main pages.

Inside Scoop

When you point the mouse at the Print button, a ScreenTip tells you which printer the job will be sent to. If that's not the printer you want to use, choose File ➪ Print and use the Print dialog box to choose a different printer.

Printing a quick copy of a worksheet

To quickly print a single copy of everything on a worksheet, click the Print button on the Standard toolbar. You don't get to Print Preview first when you use the Print button, but if you already know how the printed page is going to appear, you probably don't need to preview the page(s).

When you use the Print button, Excel prints the worksheet on as many pages as the worksheet data requires, using whatever print settings you've been using during the current Excel session (or using Excel's default print settings if you haven't made any changes to the print settings).

Printing part of a worksheet

You won't always want to print your entire worksheet. Your options for selective printing are to set a print area or print a selected range.

Set a print area

If you know you'll always be printing the same range in a particular worksheet, set that area as a print area and you can quickly print the worksheet in the future.

To set a print area, select the range of cells you want to print, then choose File ➪ Print Area ➪ Set Print Area.

Change the print area

To change the print area, just set a new print area (it replaces the old print area).

Bright Idea

If you send the worksheet to others and you want to be sure they print the worksheet correctly, set the print area in the worksheet before you send it. That way all they have to do is open the worksheet and click Print for a complete, correct printout.

Hack

To set the order in which multiple selected areas print, Ctrl+select the print areas in the order in which you want the pages printed (the first area you select is page 1, the second area you Ctrl+select will be page 2, and so on).

Set multiple print areas

To set multiple print areas, select the first area, then press and hold Ctrl while you select other areas. When you choose File ⇨ Print Area ⇨ Set Print Area, all the Ctrl+selected areas are set as print areas, and they print on separate pages.

Here are a couple of ways to print several nonadjacent areas on the same page:

■ Hide the rows and columns between the nonadjacent areas on the same worksheet, and set a single print area to contain all the areas you want to print.

■ Use the Camera button to take pictures of different areas and paste them side by side on another worksheet, then set a single print area (select all the cells behind the pasted pictures to set the print area). This method also works for printing ranges from different worksheets on the same page. You must add the Camera button to a toolbar — it's in the Tools category in the Customize dialog box.

Remove a print area

To delete a print area, choose File ⇨ Print Area ⇨ Clear Print Area. All print areas in the worksheet are removed.

Print a selected range

When you need to print a selected range on the fly, don't bother with setting a semipermanent print area; all you need to do is select the range you want to print, and then choose File ⇨ Print. In the Print dialog box

Inside Scoop

A print area is really a range named Print_Area, which you can see in the Define Name dialog box and in the Name box. You can create a self-adjusting, dynamic print area by defining the name Print_Area with the OFFSET/COUNTA formula (see Chapter 5).

(see Figure 15.2), in the Print what area, select the Selection option, and click OK.

If you want to preview the printed page before you print it (which I urge you to always do), click Preview; from the Print Preview window, click the Print button on the toolbar to print the page(s), or click the Close button on the toolbar to return to the worksheet.

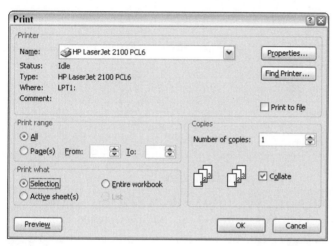

Figure 15.2. Select the Selection option to print just your selected range.

Print specific pages

Sometimes I catch an error such as a misspelling after I print a worksheet that's several pages long. I have to change and reprint the pages with the corrections, but it's a waste of time and paper to print the entire worksheet again.

Instead, print just the changed pages. Open the report in Print Preview and make a note of which pages need reprinting; close Print Preview and choose File ⇨ Print. In the Print dialog box, shown in Figure 15.3, in the Print range area, type the page numbers to reprint in the From and To boxes, and click OK to print.

Hack

Unlike Word, you cannot tell Excel to print nonadjacent pages in a single operation. If, for example, you need to print pages 2 and 5, you must print Pages From:2 To:2 in one operation, and Pages From:5 To:5 in a second operation.

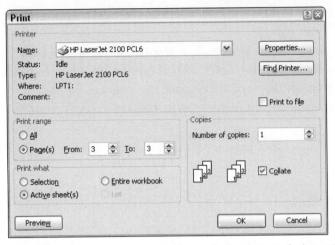

Figure 15.3. This Print dialog box is set to print just page 3 of a long printout.

Print a custom view

When you print a worksheet that contains data that you don't want to print (for example, sensitive company or employee data, or masses of detailed data), you can hide the rows and columns that contain that data, and set the print area so that only the data that should be presented gets printed.

If you routinely need to print a worksheet like this, save yourself the time of hiding the data and resetting the print area every time by creating a custom named view that sets all those items for you.

To create a custom named view, set up the worksheet the way you want it printed (hidden data, print area(s), specific print settings for the worksheet or chart, and so on). Then choose View ⇨ Custom Views, click Add, and type a name for the view. Select both check boxes, and click OK.

To print the worksheet with all your settings, choose View ⇨ Custom Views, select the view name, and click Show. Then print the worksheet.

Note that you cannot create a custom view when any worksheet in the workbook contains a new Excel dynamic list. (I don't know why you can't, but you can't.)

Hack

Excel knows whether your printer is black-and-white or color, and shows you the appropriate print preview. If you have two printers connected, black-and-white and color, and the chart print preview is in shades of gray, open the Print dialog box and switch to the color printer. The print preview switches to color.

Printing a chart

A chart can exist as an embedded chart object in a worksheet, or it can stand alone as a separate chart sheet. Right now I'm going to tell you how to print each type of chart, and in the next chapter I'll walk you through the finer points of formatting charts before you print them.

Print a chart sheet

If the chart is a chart sheet, it is always printed alone. Printing a chart sheet is just like printing a worksheet: Display the chart sheet; then either click the Print button on the Standard toolbar, or click the Print Preview button on the Standard toolbar; check the chart; and click the Print button on the Print Preview toolbar to open the Print dialog box.

Print an embedded chart

If the chart is an object on a worksheet, you have three print choices:

- **Print the chart alone.** Click in the chart (anywhere — it doesn't matter which element is selected), check the Print Preview, and click the Print button on the Standard toolbar.

- **Print the worksheet without the chart.** To print the underlying worksheet without printing the chart, you must make a minor change in the chart's properties so that the chart won't print. Right-click in the Chart area, and click Format Chart Area; in the Format Chart Area dialog box (shown in Figure 15.4), deselect the Print object check box, and click OK. Check the worksheet in print preview — the chart's not there.

- **Print the worksheet and the chart.** Click in the worksheet and click the Print button on the Standard toolbar. The worksheet and all objects (including charts) are printed.

Watch Out!

If you've set a print area in the worksheet, the chart must be wholly inside the print area to be printed with the worksheet. If the chart is only partially within the print area, it will only be partially printed.

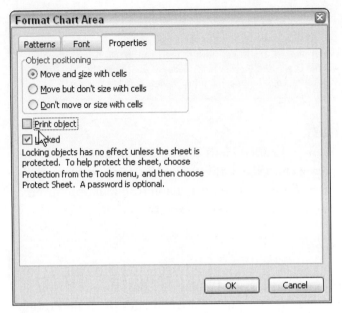

Figure 15.4. Use the Format Chart Area dialog box to set chart object properties, including printing with the worksheet.

Printing several worksheets

Most folks print worksheets one at a time because they get used to plodding through the same steps — but you can save yourself time by printing as many worksheets as you want, all at once. As an added incentive, if you print several copies of separate worksheets that need to be collated for handing out or mailing, the printer prints the worksheets in collated order (as long as the Collate check box is selected in the Print dialog box). You can select the sheets you want to print, or you can print the whole workbook.

First, be sure every worksheet is printed appropriately by setting the print area and orientation for each one, and be sure you check the whole set in print preview before you print. (Page orientation is covered in the next chapter.)

Bright Idea

If you're printing several copies of multiple worksheets, arrange the worksheets in the workbook in the order in which you want them collated (sheet tabs left to right) so they'll be printed in that order. Then all you have to do is staple them.

To print multiple worksheets (but not the whole workbook), select the worksheets you want to print by Ctrl-clicking their tabs. In Figure 15.5, worksheets Invoice Jan-05, Invoice Mar-05, and Invoice Apr-05 have been selected. Use any method you like to print them — by default, Excel prints all active sheets (worksheets and chart sheets).

Figure 15.5. All the active (selected) worksheets are printed in one print operation.

To print the entire workbook, choose File ⇨ Print, and in the Print dialog box (see Figure 15.6), in the Print what section, select the option for Entire workbook. If you want the sheets printed in a specific order, arrange the sheet tabs in that order, from left to right.

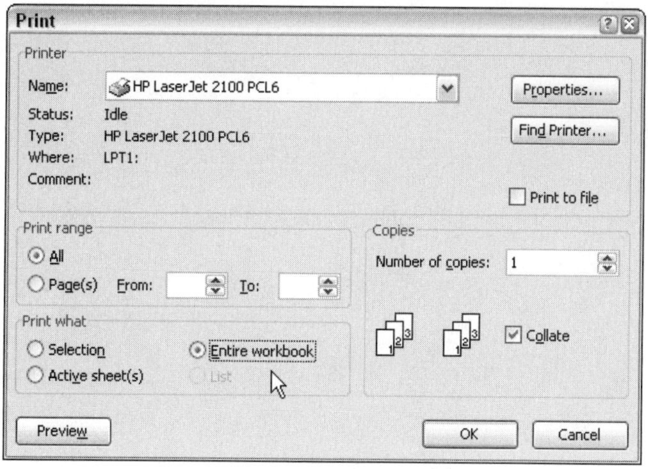

Figure 15.6. Print all the sheets in the workbook.

Just the facts

- Choose File ⇨ Print Preview, or click Preview in the Print dialog box to preview your pages before printing.
- Print a quick copy of a worksheet with the Print button on the Standard toolbar.
- Control which part of a worksheet is printed by setting a print area, or just print a selected range by selecting the range in the worksheet and then selecting the Selection option in the Print dialog box.

- Print specific pages of a multipage printout by typing the page numbers in the From and To boxes in the Print dialog box.

- Print an embedded chart alone by clicking the chart to select it before printing.

- Print a worksheet without its embedded chart by formatting the Chart area. Deselect the Print object check box in the Format Chart Area dialog box.

- Print several sheets at once by Ctrl+clicking the sheets you want to print before printing.

- Print an entire workbook by selecting the Entire workbook option in the Print dialog box.

GET THE SCOOP ON...
Setting page breaks ▪ Changing the page layout ▪
Printing a specific number of pages ▪ Printing row/
column labels on every page ▪ Creating a header
or footer ▪ Printing worksheet gridlines ▪ Printing in
black and white ▪ Formatting printed charts

Formatting the Printed Page

C hapter 15 probably left you with some questions about fine-tuning what you print. My goal in this chapter is to answer those questions.

Now that you know how to print, there are many more details you can adjust to change the look and presentation of your printed pages. And it's those details that make the difference between a professional presentation and a quick print.

For example, what if the pages break badly and leave just one column on a second page? And how do you set up page headers for a report title on every page, or page footers for page numbers? And what if you want to print worksheet gridlines or the row numbers and column letters? In this chapter, I tell you how to do these things and much more.

Setting page breaks

Excel automatically sets page breaks at the page margins, but the automatic page breaks often break information at inappropriate places in a table. You can change the page breaks so that tables are broken where you choose. There are two ways to set your own page breaks: in the worksheet and in Page Break Preview. The best and fastest way is in Page Break Preview.

Inside Scoop

Page Break Preview is just an altered view of the worksheet; the worksheet functions normally in Page Break Preview, and anything you can do in Normal view, you can do in Page Break Preview (including zooming in for a better view of cell contents).

To set page breaks in the worksheet (the old way, before Page Break Preview was invented), select a column, row, or single cell where you want to insert a page break, and choose Insert ⇨ Page Break. To remove page breaks, select the column to the right or the row beneath the break, and choose Insert ⇨ Remove Page Break.

Page Break Preview (see Figure 16.1) is the best way to handle page breaks.

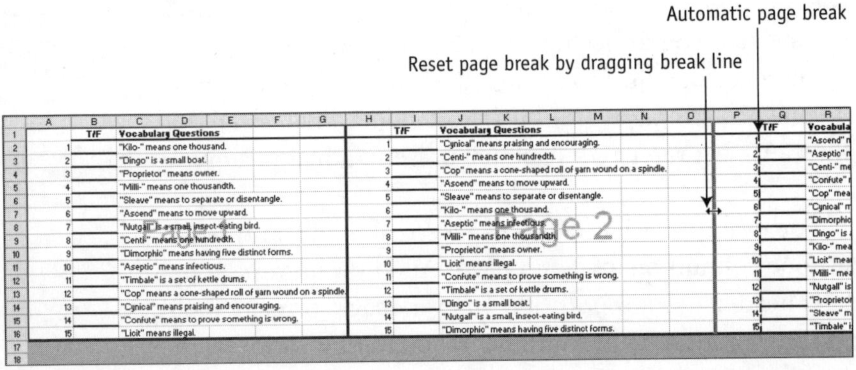

Automatic page break

Reset page break by dragging break line

Figure 16.1. Page Break Preview is an aerial view of the worksheet that shows page breaks and page numbers for printing.

To open a worksheet in Page Break Preview, choose View ⇨ Page Break Preview (and to return to normal view, choose View ⇨ Normal).

Page Break Preview displays the worksheet print area (the white area within solid blue lines) and page break lines (the broken and solid blue lines that transect the white print area), with each page number displayed in printing order.

Here are some guidelines for setting and moving page breaks while in Page Break Preview:

- To change page breaks, drag a break line to a new break position.
- To change the print area, drag the blue borders around the white print area to new positions.

> **Watch Out!**
>
> If you set page breaks larger than the printable page, Excel often accommodates the change by printing everything smaller to fit it all on one page. To avoid reducing the size of the printed text, choose File ⇨ Page Setup, click the Page tab, and make sure Adjust to is set to 100%.

- To insert a new page break, select the column to the right or row below the new break, and choose Insert ⇨ Page Break.
- To remove a page break, drag it to the next page break or to a print area border.

If you drag a line to make a page larger and a new broken line appears, the broken line shows you where the page must break given the current margins and page settings.

Changing the page layout

Several aspects of the page layout usually need your attention:

- Orientation, either *landscape* (wide) or *portrait* (tall)
- Paging order, either over, then down or down, then over
- Centering the information on the page
- Changing page margins

All of these items, and others, are set in the Page Setup dialog box. To open the Page Setup dialog box, choose File ⇨ Page Setup.

Change page orientation

Some worksheets and charts need to be printed in landscape orientation as shown in Figure 16.2, whereas others are better presented in a portrait orientation, as you can see in Figure 16.3.

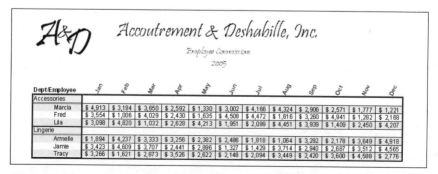

Figure 16.2. Landscape orientation works best for wide worksheets.

Inside Scoop

If you're working in Print Preview and you notice a page setup issue that needs to be changed, click the Setup button on the Print Preview toolbar.

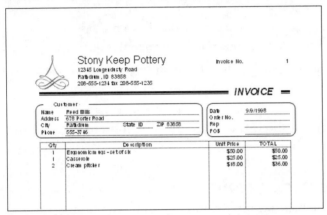

Figure 16.3. Portrait orientation works best for tall worksheets.

To change page orientation, choose File ⇨ Page Setup, and click the Page tab (see Figure 16.4); under Orientation, select the Portrait or Landscape option. Click OK to close the dialog box, or click Print Preview to see the results of the change.

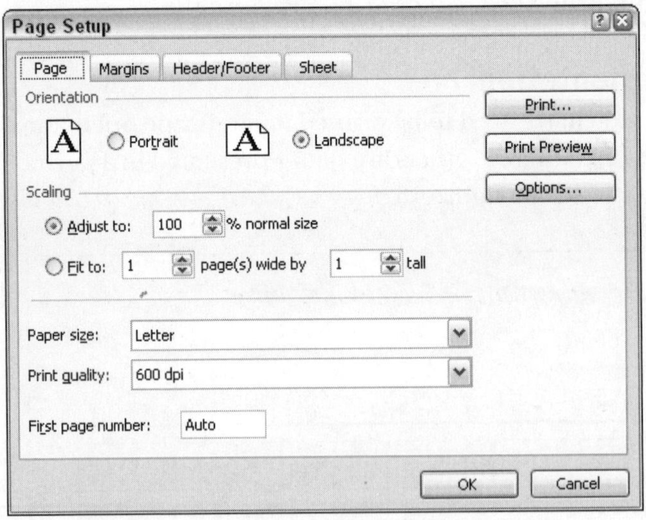

Figure 16.4. The Page tab in the Page Setup dialog box

Change paging order

Paging order is the order in which the pages in the worksheet are printed. If you have a worksheet that's several pages wide and several pages long, you can choose whether to have pages printed across the width of the worksheet or down the length. Choosing a paging order saves you time you would otherwise spend sorting and collating the printed pages. In Figure 16.5, the order is Over, then down.

	January '04	February '04	March '04	April '04	May '04	June '04	July '04	August '04	September '04	October '04	November '04	December '04	January '05
Marcia	4913	3194	3650	2592	1330	3002	4166	4324	2906	2571	1777	1221	4578
Fred	3554	1110	4029	2430	1635	4508	4472	1616	3260	4941	1282	2768	3098
Lila	3098	4820	1032	2628	4213	1951	2099	4451	3939	1409	2450	4207	3423
Armelle	1894	4237	3333	3256	5221	2486	1818	1064	3292	2178	3649	4918	4913
Jamie	3423	4609	3707	2441	2896	1327	1429	3714	2940	2687	3512	4565	3266
Tracy	3266	1621	2873	3526	2622	2148	2094	3449	2420	3600	4588	2776	3217
Susann	2366	2445	4514	4753	4505	4934	3523	4179	3055	1854	3378	3738	2366
Tina	4578	2963	2982	1522	2067	3944	2605	4621	2510	3634	1462	3798	3554
Diane	3217	1248	4004	3449	4563	4542	4668	3612	1345	2205	2752	4930	4579
Jim	4913	3194	3650	2592	1330	3002	4166	4324	2906	2571	1777	1221	1894
Howard	3554	1110	4029	2430	1635	4508	4472	1616	3260	4941	1282	2768	3554
Gail	3098	4820	1032	2628	4213	1951	2099	4451	3939	1409	2450	4207	3098
Larry	1894	4237	3333	3256	5221	2486	1818	1064	3939	1409	2450	4207	3894
Richard	3423	4609	3707	2441	2896	1327	1429	3714	2940	2687	3649	4918	3423
Leo	3266	1621	2873	3526	2622	2148	2094	3449	2420	2687	3512	4565	3423
Colleen	2366	2445	4514	4753	4505	4934	3523	4179	3055	1854	4588	2776	3266
Elvin	4578	2963	2982	1522	2067	3944	2605	4621	2510	3634	3378	3738	2366
Ardith	3217	1248	4004	3449	4563	4542	4668	3612	1345	2205	1462	3798	4579
Irene	3423	4609	3707	2441	2896	1327	1429	3714	2940	2687	2752	4930	3217
Ron	3266	1621	2873	3526	2622	2148	2094	3449	2420	2687	3512	4565	3423
Judy	2366	2445	4514	4753	4505	4934	3523	4179	3055	3600	4588	2776	3266
Denny	4578	2963	2982	1522	2067	3944	2605	4621	2510	3634	1462	3798	2366
Linda	3217	1248	4004	3449	4563	4542	4668	3612	1345	2205	2752	4930	4578
Phyllis	4913	3194	3650	2592	1330	3002	4166	4324	2906	2571	1777	1221	3217
Marla	3554	1110	4029	2430	1635	4508	4472	1616	3260	4941	1282	2768	4578
Jeanne	3098	4820	1032	2628	4213	1951	2099	4451	3939	1409	2450	4207	3098
Chris	1894	4237	3333	3256	5221	2486	1818	1064	3292	2178	3649	4918	3423
Gary	3423	4609	3707	2441	2896	1327	1429	3714	2940	2687	3649	4565	4913
Lisa	3266	1621	2873	3526	2622	2148	2094	3449	2420	2687	3512	4565	3266
Steve	2366	2445	4514	4753	4505	4934	3523	4179	3055	1854	3378	3738	3217
Brian	4578	2963	2982	1522	2067	3944	2605	4621	2510	3634	1462	3798	2366
Glenda	3217	1248	4004	3449	4563	4542	4668	3612	1345	2205	2752	4930	3554
Mark	4913	3194	3650	2592	1330	3002	4166	4324	2906	2571	1777	1221	1894
David	3554	1110	4029	2430	1635	4508	4472	1616	3260	4941	1282	2768	4913
Collette	3098	4820	1032	2628	4213	1951	2099	4451	3939	1409	2450	4207	3554
Jack	1894	4237	3333	3256	5221	2486	1818	1064	3292	2178	3649	4918	3098
John	3423	4609	3707	2441	2896	1327	1429	3714	2940	2687	3512	4565	1894
Elaine	3266	1621	2873	3526	2622	2148	2094	3449	2420	3600	4588	2776	3423
Leanda	2366	2445	4514	4753	4505	4934	3523	4179	3055	1854	4588	2776	3266
Tia	4578	2963	2982	1522	2067	3944	2605	4621	2510	3634	3378	3738	2366
Mollie	3217	1248	4004	3449	4563	4542	4668	3612	1345	2205	1462	4930	4578
Maddie	3423	4609	3707	2441	2896	1327	1429	3714	2940	2687	3512	4565	3423
Heather	3266	1621	2873	3526	2622	2148	2094	3449	2420	3600	4588	2776	3266

Figure 16.5. In Page Break Preview the page numbers show in the background.

To change paging order, choose File ⇨ Page Setup, and click the Sheet tab (see Figure 16.6); in the Page order section, select an order option. The small preview to the right shows what each option does.

Change page centering

By default, the data on printed pages is aligned against the top and left margins of the page, as shown in Figure 16.7. Often your data looks better if it's centered horizontally (and sometimes vertically).

Page Setup

Page | Margins | Header/Footer | **Sheet**

Print area: A1:N21

Print titles

Rows to repeat at top:

Columns to repeat at left:

Print

☐ Gridlines   ☐ Row and column headings

☐ Black and white   Comments: (None)

☐ Draft quality   Cell errors as: displayed

Page order

○ Down, then over

◉ Over, then down

Print...

Print Preview

Options...

OK   Cancel

Figure 16.6. The Sheet tab of the Page Setup dialog box

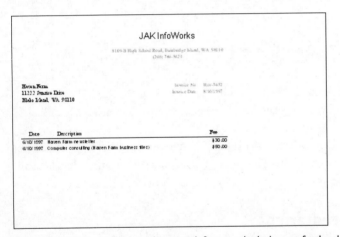

Figure 16.7. Data pushed into the upper-left corner looks less professional.

To center data in the page, choose File ⇨ Page Setup, and click the Margins tab (see Figure 16.8). In the Center on page section, select the check boxes for the centering you want.

Change page margins

Two common situations might prompt you to change the margins on your printed pages: to reduce the number of pages by fitting more rows or columns onto each page, and to change the size of a printed chart.

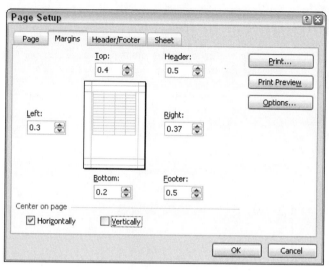

Figure 16.8. Centering data on the page

You can change margins precisely and identically by setting numerical margins in the Page Setup dialog box, or you can change them quickly and visually by dragging the margin lines in Print Preview.

Set margins precisely

To set margins with precision and perfect balance, choose File ⇨ Page Setup (if you're in Print Preview, click the Setup button on the toolbar), and click the Margins tab; type margin measurements in the Top, Bottom, Left, and Right boxes. When you click in a box to change the setting, a line appears on the small preview (see Figure 16.9) that shows you exactly which margin you're setting.

Set margins visually

Quite often you don't need precise margin measurements but want to change margins quickly (and see the results while you change them).

Inside Scoop

Printers have margin limits, and if you set very narrow margins, you may be warned that the margins are too narrow for the selected printer. If you print anyway, you may or may not get the whole page; the only way to know if your margins are really too narrow is to try it.

Watch Out!

Header and footer spaces should always be *less* than top and bottom margins, or you'll get bleed-over of the header/footer text into the worksheet data. On the other hand, if you have no text in a header or footer, you can ignore them. Header/footer text should fit between the two margin lines.

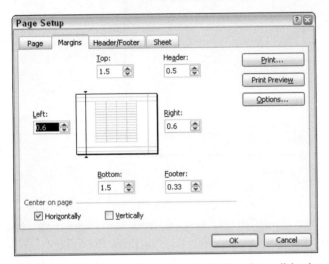

Figure 16.9. Set margins with precision in the Page Setup dialog box.

To change margins visually, switch to Print Preview. On the Print Preview toolbar, click the Margins button. Point to a margin line; when the mouse pointer is a two-headed arrow (see Figure 16.10), drag to reposition the margin.

Printing a specific number of pages

Suppose you have a table of data that's just a few rows too long for three pages, but you don't want to print a fourth page just for those few extra rows. Instead of spending time messing with the margins and page layout to make the data fit on three pages, you can have Excel shrink the data to fit precisely on three pages.

To shrink data to fit a number of pages, choose File ⇨ Page Setup, and click the Page tab; in the Scaling section, select the Fit to option (see Figure 16.11), then type numbers in the page(s) wide by and tall fields.

Bright Idea

While you have margins displayed, if you notice that a column is too narrow or too wide, drag its column border marker to resize it.

Top margin

Header margin

Column border markers

Drag margin lines

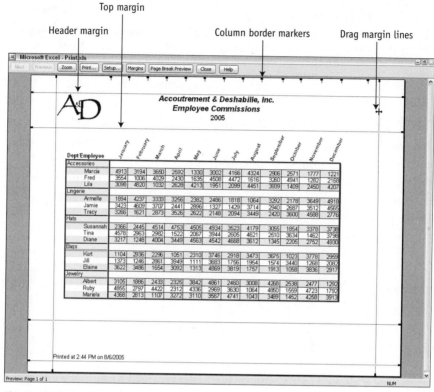

Figure 16.10. Setting margins visually gives you a better feel for the results.

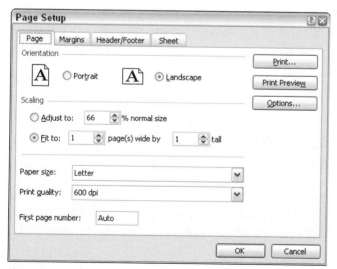

Figure 16.11. Shrink the text to fit the report onto a specific number of pages.

Bright Idea

If you know the table will grow in length but the number of columns won't change, set the Pages wide by box to 1, and set the tall box to 50. Excel prints as many pages as needed for the length of the list, and the large number (50) gives the list plenty of room to grow without changing the setup.

Printing row/column labels on every page

This concept is easier to see than to explain. When you print a table that's several pages long and wide, the identifying column and row labels appear only on the first page, in the top row and left column, which leaves the data in the middle pages (see Figure 16.12) unidentified and meaningless.

Microsoft Excel - Print.xls						

| Next | Previous | Zoom | Print... | Setup... | Margins | Normal View | Close | Help |

Sales Commissions

2094	3449	2420	3600	4588	2776	3217
3523	4179	3055	1854	3378	3738	2366
2605	4621	2510	3634	1462	3798	3554
4668	3612	1345	2205	2752	4930	1894
4166	4324	2906	2571	1777	1221	4913
4472	1616	3260	4941	1282	2168	3554
2099	4451	3939	1409	2450	4207	3098
1818	1064	3292	2178	3649	4918	1894
1429	3714	2940	2687	3512	4565	3423
2094	3449	2420	3600	4588	2776	3266
3523	4179	3055	1854	3378	3738	2366
2605	4621	2510	3634	1462	3798	4578
4668	3612	1345	2205	2752	4930	3217
1429	3714	2940	2687	3512	4565	3423
2094	3449	2420	3600	4588	2776	3266
3523	4179	3055	1854	3378	3738	2366
2605	4621	2510	3634	1462	3798	4578
4668	3612	1345	2205	2752	4930	3217

Printed 10/13/2005

Page 6 of 8

Preview: Page 6 of 8   NUM

Figure 16.12. What data is this? The columns and rows need labels on every page.

In Figure 16.13, the same page has columns and rows identified, even though this data set is in the middle of a very large data table. Adding the appropriate row and column labels to every page makes the data clear and understandable.

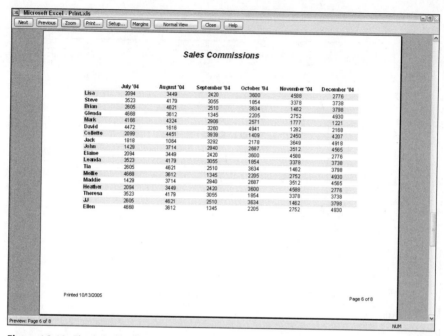

Figure 16.13. That's better. Now you know exactly what the data is on every page.

I know people who actually insert the column and row labels into each page at the page breaks, which is not the best way to solve the problem (it's too much work and it limits the printed page maneuverability). The best solution is to let Excel add the column and row labels on each page for you, by setting print titles — row and column labels that are printed on every page to identify the data.

Print titles are not the same as page headers. Page headers print identical information at the top of every page and are completely separate from the worksheet data; print titles print the appropriate column and row labels for the data on every page.

To set print titles, follow these steps:

1. Display the worksheet in Normal view or Page Break Preview, and choose File ⇨ Page Setup.

2. On the Sheet tab (see Figure 16.14), under Print titles, click in the Rows to repeat at top box.

This row contains the column labels.

	A	B	C	D	E	F	G	H
1		January '04	February '04	March '04	April '04	May '04	June '04	July '04
2	Marcia	4913	3194	3650	2592	1330	3002	4166
3	Fred	3554	1110	4029	2430	1635	4508	4472
4	Lila							
5	Armelle							
6	Jamie							
7	Tracy							
8	Susanna							
9	Tina							
10	Diane							
11	Jim							
12	Howard							
13	Gail							
14	Larry							
15	Richard							
16	Leo							
17	Colleen							
18	Elvin							
19	Ardith							
20	Irene							
21	Ron							
22	Judy							
23	Denny							
24	Linda							
25	Phyllis							
26	Marla							
27	Jeanne							
28	Chris							
29	Gary							
30	Lisa							
31	Steve							
32	Brian							
33	Glenda	5211	1240	4664	3445	4505	4542	1000
34	Mark	4913	3194	3650	2592	1330	3002	4166
35	David	3554	1110	4029	2430	1635	4508	4472

Page Setup   [?] [X]

Page | Margins | Header/Footer | **Sheet**

Print area: [   ] [🔲]   [Print...]

Print titles

Rows to repeat at top: [$1:$1|] [🔲]   [Print Preview]

Columns to repeat at left: [$A:$A] [🔲]   [Options...]

Print

☐ Gridlines   ☐ Row and column headings

☐ Black and white   Comments: [(None) ▾]

☐ Draft quality   Cell errors as: [displayed ▾]

Page order

◯ Down, then over

⦿ Over, then down

[OK]   [Cancel]

Figure 16.14. Set Print Titles so that the data on every page is labeled with row and column headers.

3. In the worksheet, click or drag the row selectors for the rows that contain the column labels. The row references are entered in the Rows to repeat at top box; these rows of column labels are repeated across the top of the data table on each printed page.

4. Click in the Columns to repeat at left box, then click or drag the column letters in the worksheet that contain the row labels. The column references are entered in the Columns to repeat at left box, and these columns of row labels are repeated down the left side of the data table on each printed page.

5. Click OK to close the dialog box, or Print Preview to see the changed pages.

Watch Out!

If you set print titles, *don't* include those rows or columns in the print area or they'll be printed twice.

Creating a header or footer

Headers and footers are an important part of the printed page; they are displayed on every page and show information that's not a part of the worksheet but that identifies the report and pulls the multiple pages together as a unit. Useful information in headers and footers usually includes a report title, page numbers, and the date and time the report was printed (some of which Excel will calculate for you).

Figure 16.15 shows a page with a custom header and footer. It has a company logo on the left and a centered title with a formatted font, and a footer with custom text.

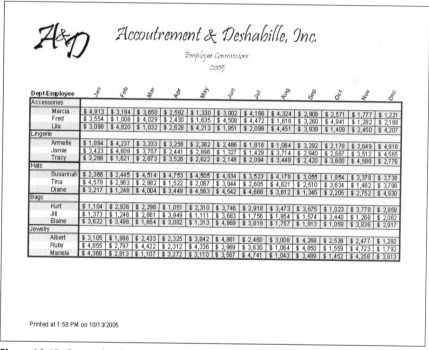

Figure 16.15. Custom headers and footers make a printed page look professional.

Headers and footers are created the same way; the only difference is that a header displays at the top of each page and a footer displays at the bottom of each page.

To create any header or footer, choose File ⇨ Page Setup, and click the Header/Footer tab (see Figure 16.16).

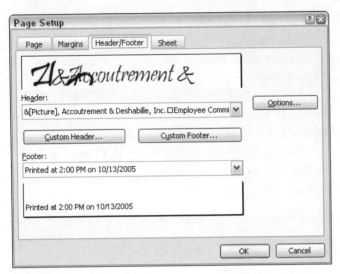

Figure 16.16. The preview windows give you a general idea what your header and footer look like on the page.

Use a prebuilt header or footer

To use a prebuilt header or footer, click in the Header or Footer list box and select a ready-made header or footer (Excel creates these from combinations of the filename, sheet name, username, page numbers, and so on).

Create a custom header or footer

To create a custom header or footer, click Custom Header or Custom Footer.

In the Header (see Figure 16.17) or Footer dialog box, click in the section of the box where you want your header/footer to appear. The sections align your entries on the page (left, center, or right).

Type any text you want for the header or footer, and click buttons to insert automatic field entries (filename, sheet name, date, and so on). To insert a line break in a multiline header or footer, press Enter.

The Header and Footer buttons have never been labeled, but in earlier versions of Excel, you could at least get quick help to identify them. Not any more. If the button icons are not intuitive enough, your fastest way to identify them is to click one and read the inserted field (or you can look them up in Table 16.1).

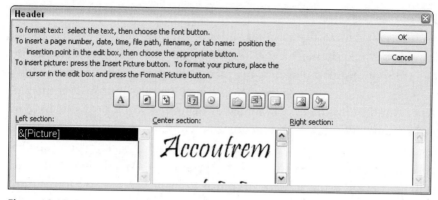

Figure 16.17. Custom headers and footers can have any text you want, be highly formatted, and contain graphics.

Table 16.1. Custom Header/Footer buttons

Button	Title
A	Font
#️	Page number
⊞	Number of pages
📅	Current date
🕐	Current time
📁	Path and filename
📄	Filename
▭	Sheet name
🖼	Insert picture
🎨	Format picture

Insert a picture

To insert a picture (for example, a logo) in a header or footer, click in the section box, then click the Insert Picture button and navigate to the picture you want. Double-click the picture filename to insert it.

After you insert a picture, the Format Picture button is available. When you insert a picture in a header or footer, you'll probably have to make it smaller. Click in the section that contains the picture, then click the Format Picture button; on the Size tab, under Scale, type a smaller percentage, then press Tab (both Height and Width are scaled to match). Click OK three times to return to Print Preview and look at the header/footer you created.

Edit and customize your headers/footers

You can edit headers and footers just like any text. Even if you used a pre-built header or footer, you can edit it by clicking Custom Header or Custom Footer.

Of course, you'll want to edit headers and footers if you find a misspelling, but you can also make your headers and footers more professional by adding and rearranging text.

Here are a couple of tips for editing header and footer text:

- To create a useful footer that reads "Page 1 of 4," type **Page**, then a space, click the Page number button, type another space, type **of**, another space, and click the Number of pages button.

- The ampersand (&) is part of field coding in headers and footers — so how do you include & as part of a header or footer? By typing it twice — && — to force the ampersand to be a text character.

To format text in a header or footer, open the header or footer in the custom Header or Footer dialog box, select the text you want to format, click the Font button, and set any font formatting you want (font, size, bold, and so on).

 Inside Scoop

Just as with charts, if Excel is currently set up with a black-and-white printer, you see header/footer graphics in shades of gray in Print Preview; if your current printer is color, you see header/footer graphics in color. If you use multiple printers, open the Print dialog box to switch printers.

Printing worksheet gridlines

Gridlines are not printed unless you specifically set them to print. But sometimes that's exactly what you want (for example, to print a worksheet form that people can fill out in pencil).

To print gridlines, choose File ⇨ Page Setup, and on the Sheet tab, select the Gridlines check box.

Printing in black and white

I like to use cell colors in my worksheets to highlight important cells, but I don't want the cell colors (or shades of gray) printed. Instead of removing cell colors from the worksheet, printing, and then replacing the cell colors, I tell Excel to print the worksheet in black and white, which hides all colors and shades of gray.

To print in black and white, choose File ⇨ Page Setup, and on the Sheet tab, select the Black and white check box. Click OK to finish or click Print Preview to see the changed pages.

Formatting printed charts

You might want to make two changes to your charts before printing:

- Change the size or proportions of the printed chart.
- Switch the colors of the data markers to black-and-white patterns for clear differentiation on a black-and-white printer.

Resize a printed chart

When you're about to print a chart without a worksheet (whether it's a chart sheet or a chart object), take a look at the chart in Print Preview before you click the Print button — what you see might need some tweaking.

A printed chart is automatically stretched to fit within the margins of the printed page, which can stretch a tall or wide chart completely out of proportion.

 Inside Scoop

A solitary chart always looks better when it's centered, so unless you have a reason for pinning the chart into a corner of the printed page, click Setup in Print Preview and use the Margins tab to center the chart both horizontally and vertically.

There are two ways to change the size or proportions of a printed chart:

■ Change the page margins to resize and reposition the chart on the page.

■ Select one of the three options in the Chart tab of the Page Setup dialog box.

Use the page margins

To resize and reposition a chart using page margins, display the chart in Print Preview; click the Margins button on the toolbar, and drag margin lines (see Figure 16.18) — the chart remains within the margins in accordance with the size/scale options set in the Page Setup dialog box.

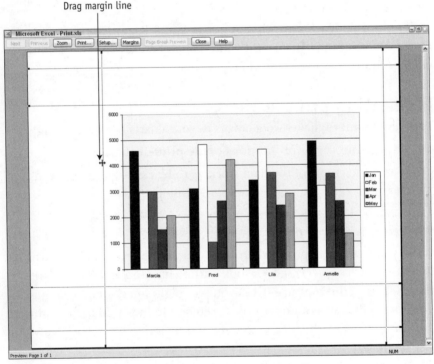

Figure 16.18. Resize and move the chart by dragging the margin lines.

If you drag a margin line and nothing happens to the chart, you probably dragged a header or footer margin line. To see which margin line you're dragging, click on the line and look at the left end of the Excel Status bar — you see both the name and size of the margin.

Use the Page Setup dialog box

To set the size/scale options you want, whether or not you've dragged the margin lines, display the chart, then choose File ➪ Page Setup and click the Chart tab (see Figure 16.19).

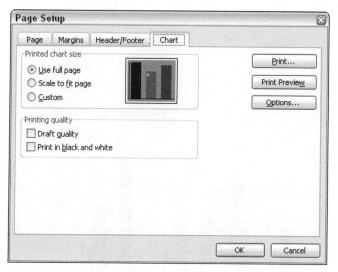

Figure 16.19. Set printed chart size and scale options on the Chart tab.

Click one of the options under Printed chart size. The options are explained in Table 16.2.

Table 16.2. Printed chart size/scale options	
This option	**Does this**
Use full page	Stretches the chart to fill all the space within the margin lines
Scale to fit page	Resizes the chart to fit within the margin lines without changing the chart's original height/width proportions
Custom	Makes the printed chart the same size and shape as the chart area in the embedded chart or chart sheet

Inside Scoop

Don't like the boxy shape of the chart on a chart sheet? To reshape a chart on a chart sheet, choose File ➪ Page Setup, click the Chart tab, and then Custom. Now the chart area is bordered; click the border to select it, then drag border handles to reshape the chart. When you print, it retains its shape.

Print data markers in black and white

If you print to a black-and-white printer, you'll be disappointed at what happens to your beautifully colored chart; sometimes the markers are difficult to differentiate and identify because they're all in shades of gray.

The solution to this problem is to have Excel print your data markers and corresponding legend keys in black-and-white patterns, as shown in Figure 16.20.

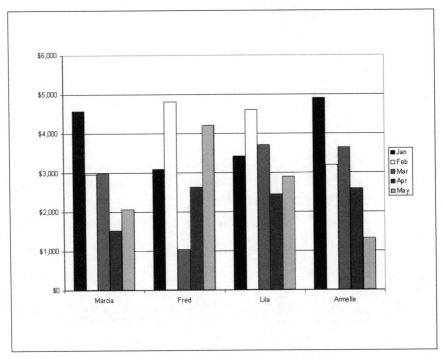

Figure 16.20. This chart is formatted to print on a black-and-white printer.

To print data markers in black-and-white patterns, choose File ⇨ Page Setup, click the Chart tab, and select the Print in black and white check box. You won't see any change in the chart; you see the change in Print Preview.

You won't notice the patterns unless you have more than two data series (the first two will be solid black and solid white). The plot area will still be a shade of gray, so for black-and-white printing, it's a good idea to color the plot area a light color.

Just the facts

- Set page breaks and change the print area easily by switching to Page Break Preview (choose View ⇨ Page Break Preview). Choose View ⇨ Normal to switch back to normal view.

- Change page orientation on the Page tab in the Page Setup dialog box.

- Change paging order on the Sheet tab in the Page Setup dialog box.

- Center data in the page on the Margins tab in the Page Setup dialog box, and change page margins on the Margins tab or by dragging margin lines in Print Preview (click the Margins button on the Print Preview toolbar to display margin lines).

- Shrink data to fit a specific number of pages on the Page tab in the Page Setup dialog box under Scaling.

- Set print titles (appropriate row and column labels on every page) on the Sheet tab in the Page Setup dialog box.

- Create headers and footers on the Header/Footer tab in the Page Setup dialog box.

- To format printed charts, select the chart, then use the Chart tab on the Page Setup dialog box.

Sharing Data with Other Users and Other Programs

PART VII

Sharing a Workbook with Other Users

You may never need to share a workbook with another user, but you might very well want to send a workbook to someone, or route a workbook to others and have it find its way back to you when they are finished with it. And if you send a workbook to someone else to review, it's not a bad idea to protect it so that the other user(s) can't make unacceptable (or inadvertent) changes in it. The opposite end of the spectrum is not sharing at all — locking up your workbook file so that no one can open it without a password. You learn how to do all these things in this chapter.

Usually if someone else has a workbook open when you try to open it, you see a message that allows you to choose between opening the workbook as read-only (so you can read it but not make changes) or being notified by an on-screen message when the workbook is closed and available.

If, however, you *share* a workbook with other users on a network, two or more people can use the workbook simultaneously. When a workbook is shared, no one has to wait for a turn to open and make changes in a workbook. (Shared workbooks were Microsoft's first foray into the "team" concept of corporate work.)

Bright Idea

Use a shared workbook as a communications device: If your officemates must take turns with a resource that can't be shared (such as seats on a Go To My PC Web site), use a shared workbook on a network drive to sign in, sign out, and monitor the use of those shared resources.

Sharing a workbook

Before you can use a workbook simultaneously with another user (or use copies of a workbook you want to merge later), you must open the workbook and set its "shared" setting.

To share a workbook, choose Tools ⇨ Share Workbook. On the Editing tab, shown in Figure 17.1, select the Allow changes by more than one user at the same time check box, and then click OK.

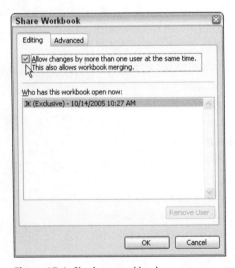

Figure 17.1. Sharing a workbook

When you work in a shared workbook, you find yourself unable to perform some tasks, such as:

- Delete worksheets
- Insert or delete ranges (although you can insert/delete entire rows and columns)
- Merge cells
- Create conditional formats
- Create or change data validation settings

- Create or change charts, pictures, objects, or hyperlinks
- Draw graphical objects
- Create, change, or view scenarios
- Create automatic subtotals
- Group or outline data
- Create or change PivotTables
- Take pictures with the Camera button
- Do anything involving macros in the shared workbook's modules (although macros in personal.xls are operable)

To test and practice sharing workbooks, it's a good idea to get some-one on another computer to open a shared workbook with you; or, if you have a second computer at hand, test shared workbooks with yourself on the second computer (but it must be running at least Excel 97 to share workbooks).

Who's using a shared workbook?

When you open a shared workbook, the word [Shared] in the title bar tells you it's available to others, but you can't tell from the title bar whether someone else is currently using the workbook (or who the other users are).

To see who's using the workbook (if anyone), choose Tools ⇨ Share Workbook. On the Editing tab, shown in Figure 17.2, all current users are listed in the Who has this workbook open now list. (The names come from the users' Tools ⇨ Options, General tab, User Name boxes.)

Saving a shared workbook

If more than one user has made saved entries in a shared workbook, you see the new entries when you save the workbook.

To save a shared workbook, click Save on the Standard toolbar. If you make changes that others need to see, you must save the workbook for the changes to appear in the other copies.

If you save your copy of a shared workbook and see a message that other users have made changes, read the message and click OK to close it.

Inside Scoop

Any user can remove any other user by selecting his or her name and clicking Remove User. This might be necessary when users finish using the shared work-book but leave it open on their computers, for example.

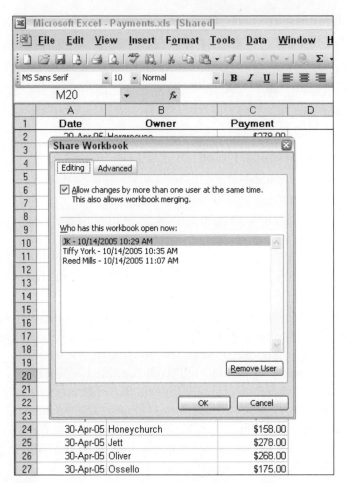

Figure 17.2. These people have the workbook open right now.

Changed cells have a colored border and a colored triangle in the upper-left corner (as shown in Figure 17.3); the color identifies who made the change. The colored borders and triangles disappear after the changes are accepted or rejected (which is covered in the next few sections).

When you point to a changed cell, a comment tells you who made the change and what the change was.

Reviewing changes in a shared workbook

If two or more people have made changes to the same cell, a conflict arises when the workbook is saved: Which changes should Excel keep?

	A	B	C	D	E	F	G	H
1	**Date**	**Owner**	**Payment**					
2	20-Apr-05	Hargreaves	$278.00					
3	23-Apr-05	Brown	$358.00					
4	23-Apr-05	Klobuchar	$248.00					
5	23-Apr-05	Klobuchar	$263.00					
6	27-Apr-05	Carter	$376.00					
7	28-Apr-05	Collins	$300.00					
8	28-Apr-05	Crosby	$308.00					
9	28-Apr-05	Kelly	$248.00					
10	29-Apr-05	Donner	$188.00					
11	29-Apr-05	Gardner	$233.00					
12	29-Apr-05	Geller	$225.00					

Reed Mills, 10/14/2005 11:10 AM:
Changed cell C7 from '$283.00 ' to '$300.00 '.

Figure 17.3. The bordered cells' values were changed by other users (different colored borders) indicate different users).

Excel keeps track of all changes made in a shared workbook; you can review all the changes and decide individually which changes to keep, either when you save the workbook or later when you want to see what's been happening in the workbook while you were away.

Resolving change conflicts

When you save a workbook that contains conflicting changes to the same cells, you see the Resolve Conflicts dialog box (see Figure 17.4).

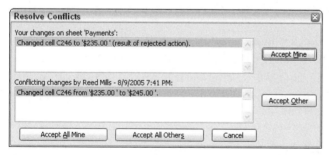

Figure 17.4. When there are two or more saved changes to the same cell, the Resolve Conflicts dialog box appears.

Your choices are pretty simple: Select one change at a time and click Accept Mine or Accept Other, or click Accept All Mine or Accept All Others to deal with all the conflicts at once. (Or click Cancel to deal with the changes later.)

Bright Idea

Resolve conflicts in advance by setting up the workbook so that whoever saves the workbook gets the changes saved (no conflicts). Choose Tools ⇨ Share Workbook. On the Advanced tab, under Conflicting changes between users, select The changes being saved win.

Tracking changes in a shared workbook

If you just opened a shared workbook and you want to see what changes were made in your absence, you can tell Excel to highlight every changed cell and then accept or reject the changes.

To highlight changes, choose Tools ⇨ Track Changes ⇨ Highlight Changes. In the Highlight Changes dialog box (see Figure 17.5), narrow the changes you want to see by selecting the check boxes and selecting alternatives from the list boxes. Make sure the Highlight changes on screen check box is selected.

Figure 17.5. Choose the range of changes you want to see.

You can turn off both change tracking and workbook sharing from within the Highlight Changes dialog box. If you deselect the Track changes while editing check box, change tracking is turned off, every change in the workbook is replaced with the last saved entry, and the workbook is unshared.

Accepting and rejecting tracked changes

After you highlight changed cells, you can accept or reject them. Choose Tools ⇨ Track Changes ⇨ Accept or Reject Changes. You might or might not see a message that the workbook will be saved (click OK to continue). Then you might or might not see the Resolve Conflicts dialog box (depending on whether there have been any conflicting changes made); you must accept or reject the conflicting changes to satisfy the dialog box.

Hack

To check the entire worksheet for changes, leave the Where check box and range box empty.

Finally, the Select Changes to Accept or Reject dialog box appears. Use the When, Who, and Where check boxes and list boxes to limit the changes you want to see, then click OK. If there are changes made within the When, Who, and Where parameters you set, you can accept or reject them one by one or all at once.

Printing a history of changes

By default, Excel keeps track of changes made to a shared workbook for 30 days. You can print a change history—a separate worksheet that lists all the changes made to cells in a specific worksheet—as long as the workbook is still shared. (Once you unshare a workbook, the history of changes is irretrievably gone.)

To create a change history, choose Tools ⇨ Track Changes ⇨ Highlight Changes. In the Highlight Changes dialog box (see Figure 17.6), deselect the When, Who, and Where check boxes, and select the List changes on a new sheet check box. Click OK.

Figure 17.6. Deselect all the check boxes to list all the changes in the current history, and select the List changes on a new sheet check box.

A new worksheet named History is created with a table of cell addresses, changes, time, date, and username, and AutoFilter buttons so you can filter the list (see Figure 17.7).

You can change the number of days of tracked history or turn off the change history without unsharing the workbook on the Advanced tab of the Share Workbook dialog box (see Figure 17.8).

Bright Idea
If there are lots of changes to the same cells, print the history to show other users who has been wrangling over which data.

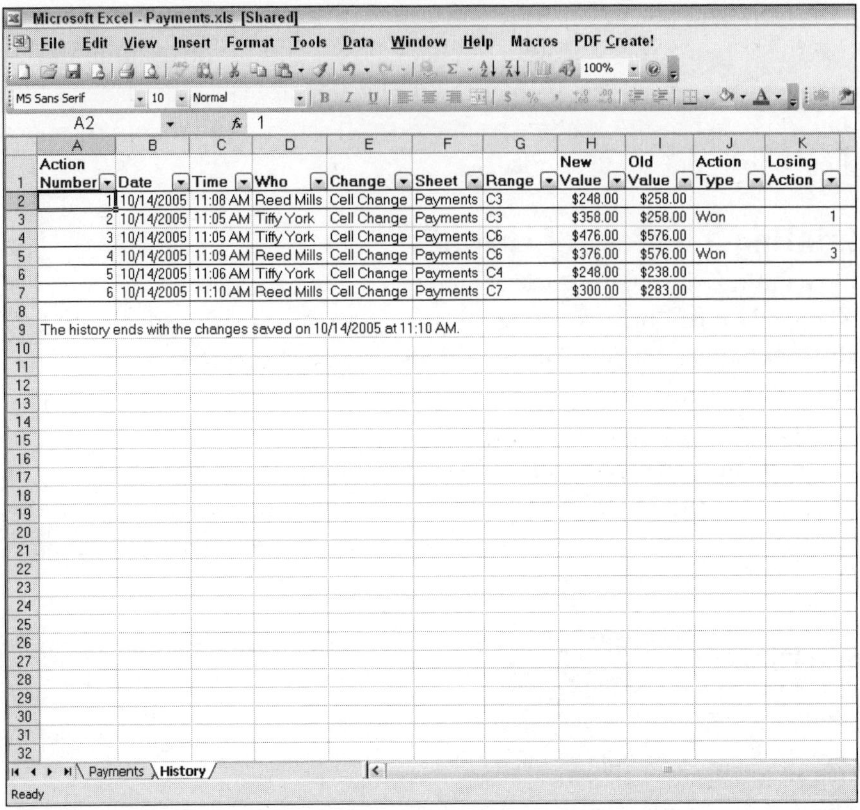

Figure 17.7. These changes have been made since the workbook was shared.

Figure 17.8. Change the History settings.

Watch Out!

If you want to keep a copy of the History sheet, print it before you unshare or save the workbook; when the workbook is unshared or saved, the History sheet is deleted.

Protect change tracking in a shared workbook

The whole point of tracking changes in a shared file is to see a history of who did what in that file.

To share a workbook but make sure all changes by others are inescapably tracked, choose Tools ⇨ Protection ⇨ Protect and Share Workbook, and select the Sharing with track changes check box. The workbook is both shared and protected in one step.

Removing both protection and sharing from a workbook are two separate steps that must be performed on the same machine (but anyone with the shared workbook open can do this):

1. Choose Tools ⇨ Protection ⇨ Unprotect Shared Workbook.

2. Choose Tools ⇨ Share Workbook, and deselect the Allow changes check box.

Unsharing a workbook

The time will come when you need to be proprietary about a workbook — for example, you want to create PivotTables or a chart, neither of which you can do in a shared workbook.

In theory, unsharing a workbook is simple: Any user can choose Tools ⇨ Share Workbook and deselect the Allow changes check box.

In practice, it's sometimes a little more complicated. When one user unshares the workbook, other users are locked out of the workbook, even though it's still open on their machines (and when the first user reshares the workbook, the locked-out workbooks are not reshared). Locked-out users must close the workbook without saving, or save a copy of the workbook with another name (and they can't merge a copy with unsaved changes because the copy was made after the workbook was unshared).

Hack

If the Allow changes check box in the Share Workbook dialog box is grayed out, someone protected the shared workbook. Choose Tools ⇨ Protection ⇨ Unprotect Shared Workbook, and then choose Tools ⇨ Share Workbook and deselect the Allow changes check box.

In fact, if any user other than the original user (the one who shared the workbook) makes changes to the shared and protection settings, a host of problems ensue for the other users. My advice is: Leave the sharing and protection settings alone unless you are the owner of the workbook, and warn other users when you're about to unshare the workbook.

Merging shared workbooks

You're going on the road (or working at home) and you need to take a certain workbook with you; but other people might be using that same workbook in the office, and all will be making changes to it. How are you going to reconcile all sets of changes?

You share the workbook, set a generous number of days to track change history, and then make a copy of it to take with you by choosing File ⇨ Save As (the copy will have a different filename). When you're back in the office, merge the copies of the workbook to reconcile all changes in all copies. You can make (and merge) as many copies of a shared workbook as you like.

To merge copies of a shared workbook, open the copy that will become the main shared workbook. Choose Tools ⇨ Merge Workbook; in the Select Files to Merge Into Current Workbook dialog box, navigate to and double-click the name of a copy to merge. Repeat these steps for each copy you want to merge.

The main shared workbook shows all the changes and conflicts — and you handle them just like any other tracked changes in a shared workbook.

Sending and routing workbooks

You don't have to share a workbook to send it to someone else; in fact, chances are good that you'll often send workbooks such as invoices or estimates to other people and never need to share them.

You can send a workbook directly to someone else in an e-mail message, or you can use e-mail to route a workbook to others and bring it back to you after it's made its rounds.

Watch Out!
Note that you cannot merge similar workbooks, or even copies of workbooks. You can only merge copies of a workbook that are created after the workbook is shared, and in which changes are being tracked.

Watch Out!

Don't unshare any shared workbook or copy that you're going to use for merging; once you unshare a workbook or shared copy, its tracked changes are lost and you cannot merge it with any other workbooks.

Send a workbook

There are two ways to send a workbook to someone else: Choose File ⇨ Send to in the open workbook, or open an e-mail message and attach the file.

To send a file from the open workbook, choose File ⇨ Send to ⇨ Mail Recipient.

- Mail Recipient (for Review) asks you to make a shared copy of the workbook to send for review. When your recipient opens the file, the file has the name *workbookname*1.xls. When you get the file back, you can merge it with the original.

- Mail Recipient (as Attachment) opens an e-mail message and attaches a copy of the file.

Both Mail Recipient commands send a copy of the workbook in its last saved status (changes made since saving and before sending won't be sent).

Personally, I think the Send to commands are overkill. I always send my files the time-honored way: Open a message and insert the file, or drag the filename from a folder window into the message. Either way, the file is attached to the message.

Even better, you can send a specific table of data in a message by copying the table in Excel and pasting the copied table in the body of the message. When you send data this way, the message is much smaller and is sent and received more quickly.

Along the same lines, if you use Outlook 2003, you can send a worksheet as an e-mail message from within Excel. If you have Outlook 2003 installed in your computer, you have an E-mail button on the Standard toolbar; when you click the E-mail button, a message header opens across the top of your workbook window. Fill in the message header information just like a

Inside Scoop

You might have different commands in a computer that doesn't use Outlook for a mail program.

normal message and click Send this sheet to send the message to your Outlook Outbox (you must send the message from Outlook with the rest of your outgoing mail). The entire active worksheet goes out as an HTML-formatted e-mail message, but it's only for viewing. If you need to send an actual Excel file (a binary file that can be opened and worked in), send the workbook as an attachment.

Route a workbook

If you work on a team, you can route a workbook to other people for review, updates, and so forth, and make it easy to send the workbook back to you after everyone else has seen it. Nobody needs to enter any e-mail addresses for further routing because you enter all the routing e-mail addresses before you send the workbook.

To route a workbook, choose File ⇨ Send to ⇨ Routing Recipient. Fill in the Routing Slip dialog box (see Figure 17.9); the file is attached to an e-mail message that has instructions for the user for sending the file on its way.

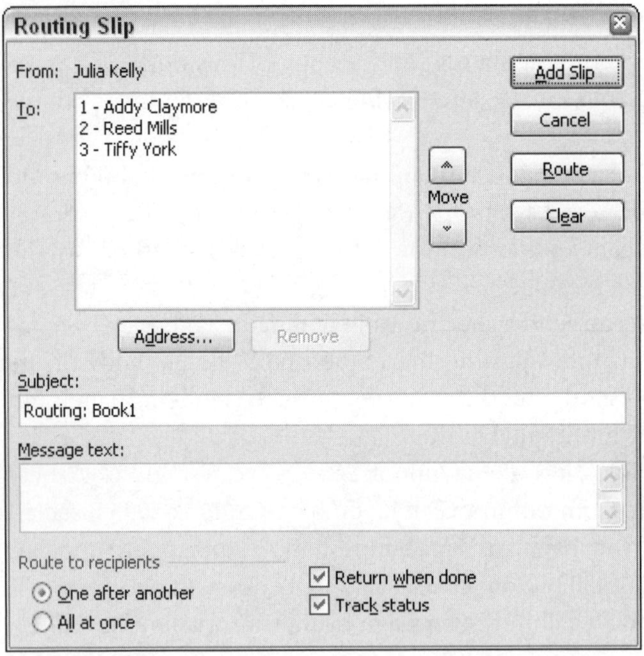

Figure 17.9. Route the workbook to all concerned parties and then back to you.

When you send a workbook into a routing cycle, the Mail Recipient (as Attachment) command disappears until the workbook finishes its route and is returned to you.

Watch Out!

Unless you shared the workbook before routing it, an unmergeable copy of the workbook is routed. If you want to track changes made in the workbook, share it before you route it.

Here are some pointers on the routing options:

- The One after another option sends the same copy around to each recipient in turn. Each person sends it to the next routing recipient, and the last person on the list sends it back to you.

- The All at once option sends copies out to everyone in the routing recipients list; each of them sends it directly back to you. If all you want are comments, and quickly, this option gets the job done fast.

- Selecting the Return when done check box brings it back to you. If you don't select this check box, routing is the same as sending an attachment.

- Selecting the Track status check box does nothing — ignore it.

- The Add Slip button attaches a routing slip to the file without sending it; when you're ready to send the file, choose File ⇨ Send to ⇨ Next Routing Recipient, and send your outgoing e-mail.

Protecting workbooks and worksheets

When you go to great effort to create a complex worksheet or workbook full of intricately constructed formulas, complex graphical objects, or important charts, you don't want other people to inadvertently change or delete any of those formulas, objects, or charts.

Excel has a few locks and keys to help you protect your work: You can protect an entire workbook or individual sheets within a workbook. The method you choose depends on what you want to protect or prevent.

You should protect a workbook when you want to prevent:

- Deleting or inserting worksheets
- Renaming worksheets
- Copying or moving worksheets
- Hiding or unhiding worksheets
- Changing the size or shape of workbook windows
- Splitting or unsplitting panes
- Freezing or unfreezing panes

Inside Scoop

The Permission button on the Standard toolbar only works on networks with Windows Server 2003 installed and running Windows Rights Management Services, and then only after you download the Window Rights Management client. To learn more, click the button, then click the Learn more link.

You should protect a worksheet when you want to prevent changes to:

■ Cell contents

■ Charts

■ Graphical objects

■ Scenario definitions

You should protect a workbook file when you want to prevent it being opened at all without a password, or allow it to be opened but prevent any changes whatsoever without a password.

Protect and unprotect a workbook

To protect an unshared workbook, choose Tools ⇨ Protection ⇨ Protect Workbook. In the Protect Workbook dialog box (see Figure 17.10), select either or both check boxes; type a password if you want one, and click OK.

Figure 17.10. Without a password, anyone can unprotect the workbook.

Bright Idea

If you don't do a lot of file sharing but want occasional password protection, always use the same simple password (such as "zzz"). That way you won't forget it.

To unprotect an unshared workbook, choose Tools ⇨ Protection ⇨ Unprotect Workbook. If you protect the workbook with a password, you must type the password and click OK.

When you protect a shared workbook, your only protection option is to protect the change history so that it can't be removed.

Protect a worksheet

To protect the active worksheet, chose Tools ⇨ Protection ⇨ Protect Sheet. In the Protect Sheet dialog box (see Figure 17.11), select check boxes to allow users to make specific changes in the sheet, and click OK.

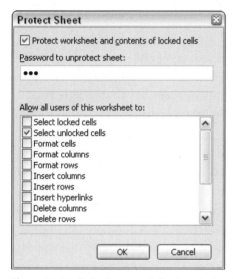

Figure 17.11. Protect your worksheet contents with the Protect Sheet dialog box.

To unprotect a worksheet, choose Tools ⇨ Protection ⇨ Unprotect Sheet.

By default, all cells on worksheets are locked, so all cells are protected when you protect a worksheet. If you want to protect formulas but allow users to enter values for those formulas to calculate, you need to unlock the cells where values can be entered (which is explained in the next section), and then protect the worksheet.

Bright Idea

To hide the intricate behind-the-scenes machinery in a shared workbook, put your not-to-be-seen formulas and tables in a separate worksheet and hide the worksheet. Choose Format ⇨ Sheet ⇨ Hide to hide it; choose Format ⇨ Sheet ⇨ Unhide to display it again.

Protect yourself

When I e-mail invoices, I send them as a single-worksheet workbook (because Excel makes it so easy to calculate fees), but I always protect it completely — by password-protecting everything in the worksheet — so that no one can change anything in it.

Here's something many people are unaware of: You can also protect Word documents and Outlook e-mails so that recipients cannot edit them. (Even though this is a book about Excel, I can't help but pass along these nuggets of information.)

To protect a Word document, choose Tools ⇨ Protect Document, and choose the protection you want.

To protect an Outlook e-mail from being edited, click the Options button in the new message, and under Message settings, in the Sensitivity box, select Private. The other settings are advisory only, but the Private setting makes the message uneditable after you send it (the Edit ⇨ Edit Message command is grayed out).

Unlock cells before protecting a worksheet

To unlock cells so they can be changed after the worksheet is protected, select the specific cells and choose Format ⇨ Cells; on the Protection tab (shown in Figure 17.12), deselect the Locked check box.

When you protect the worksheet, be sure you mark the Select unlocked cells check box (shown in Figure 17.13) to allow users to make changes in the unlocked cells.

Protect a workbook file

When you protect workbooks and worksheets, others can still open and read the workbook files regardless of the level of workbook and worksheet protection. There is another level of protection: You can password-protect the file from opening.

Bright Idea

The Protection tab has a Hidden check box — it hides the formula in a cell. If you create an intricate formula that you don't want to share, hide and lock the cell and then protect the worksheet so that nobody can "borrow" your formula.

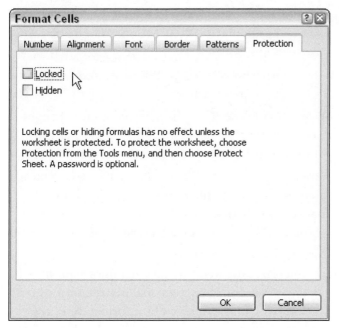

Figure 17.12. Unlock specific cells so you can enter data in them after you protect the worksheet.

Figure 17.13. You also need to make the unlocked cells selectable in the protected worksheet so you can enter data in them.

To protect the workbook file, choose Tools ⇨ Options. On the Security tab, type passwords to open or modify the file. The options in the Security tab are:

- **Password to open.** The workbook is completely protected; it cannot be opened at all without the password.

- **Password to modify.** The workbook can be opened but no changes can be saved without entering the password (although a user can still make a copy of the workbook with the Save As command).

- **Read-only recommended.** When the file is opened, users see a message suggesting that they open the file as read-only so as not to make and save inadvertent changes. It's only a reminder — it offers no protection for the workbook because all a reader must do is click No and the workbook opens normally.

- **Privacy options.** If you select the Remove personal information from file properties on save check box, personal information (the Author, Manager, Company, and Last saved by information in the File ⇨ Properties dialog box) is erased when the workbook is saved. Also removed are any names associated with comments and tracked changes (the names are changed to Author). And because this option prevents names from being tracked in tracked changes, you cannot share a workbook that has the Privacy option selected.

To change or remove file protection, open the workbook, choose Tools ⇨ Options, and change the settings on the Security tab.

Just the facts

- Share a workbook if more than one person needs to work on it at the same time.

- To share a workbook, choose Tools ⇨ Share Workbook and select the Allow changes check box.

- Review changes and print a change history in a shared workbook by choosing Tools ⇨ Track Changes ⇨ Highlight Changes.

- Take a copy of a shared workbook away to work in it, then reconcile changes by merging the copy with the original.

- Prevent changes to workbook structure by choosing Tools ⇨ Protection ⇨ Protect Workbook.

- Protect a worksheet's contents by choosing Tools ⇨ Protection ⇨ Protect Sheet.

- Unlock cells before you protect a worksheet by selecting the cells and choosing Format ⇨ Cells; deselect the Locked check box on the Protection tab.

- Keep a workbook file from being opened without a password by setting a Password to open in the Tools ⇨ Options dialog box, Security tab.

GET THE SCOOP ON...
Shared-data terminology ▪ Sending data between Excel
and Word ▪ Sending data between Excel and Access ▪
Pasting Excel data into PowerPoint ▪ Dragging a hyperlink into Excel ▪ Saving a worksheet as a Web page

Sharing a Workbook Between Programs

A big advantage in having Microsoft's entire suite of Office programs on your computer is that they can cooperate and share data with one another. By sharing data between programs, you can create reports that combine data from Word documents and Excel worksheets on the same page.

A table of data or a chart can be copied to a Word document as simple data or a picture, an embedded object that can be changed with Excel tools (without opening Excel), or a linked object that's always current.

Most commonly, data is shared between Excel and Word, so this chapter focuses on Excel-Word data sharing. Fewer people use Access, but I also cover Excel-Access data sharing.

Lots of other (non-Microsoft) programs also share data. The only way to know whether and how they share data is to test them. You can almost always copy and paste Excel data into other programs.

Shared-data terminology

This chapter uses several terms — *object, paste, embed,* and *link* — that you need to understand as I explain how to share data between programs. These terms are defined in Table 18.1.

Table 18.1. Shared-data definitions

Term	Definition	Double-click results	Editing results
Object	A "container" of information that's inserted in another file	Depends on whether the object is linked or embedded	
Paste	Data that is inserted as text; it becomes part of the file into which it's inserted	No special results; pasted data is not connected to its source	
Embed	An object that is connected to the program in which it was created, but not to its source file.	Source program opens so you can change the object with its own editing and formatting tools.	Editing changes only the embedded object, not the source file. A file containing an embedded object is larger because it contains all the object's data and formatting.
Link	An object that is connected directly to its source file.	Source file and program open so you can change the source file.	Editing changes a linked object's source file; all linked copies reflect the changes. A file containing a linked object is smaller because it contains only the link.

Sending data between Excel and Word

Sending data from Excel to Word is not as easy as it should be.

You can drag and drop data between an Excel program window and a Word program window and you get an embedded object, but the embedded object is the entire Excel workbook, even if you only dragged and dropped part of a table. Unless you have a reason to open the Excel environment and edit/format the data, it's entirely too much trouble to work with (and it makes the document much larger because all the Excel data and formatting in the workbook are included).

If you link an object, you get a picture of the Excel data that's really an updatable live link to the workbook; but the source workbook must be in a shared folder or drive on the same network for the link to function.

A linked object looks just like an embedded object (see Figure 18.1) — the difference becomes noticeable only when you double-click the object.

Linked

Competitor	Payment
Kelly	$255.00
Mills	$150.00
York	$155.00
Burns	$100.00

Embedded

Competitor	Payment
Kelly	$255.00
Mills	$150.00
York	$155.00
Burns	$100.00

Pasted

Competitor	Payment
Kelly	$255.00
Mills	$150.00
York	$155.00
Burns	$100.00

Pasted and converted to text

Competitor	Payment
Kelly	$255.00
Mills	$150.00
York	$155.00
Burns	$100.00

Figure 18.1. Linked and embedded objects look identical; pasted objects can be turned into Word text easily.

The easiest way to get Excel data into Word, whether it's data, a chart, or a PivotTable, is to use simple copy and paste commands to paste your selection.

You can remove the table format from pasted cells by selecting the table and choosing Table ⇨ Convert ⇨ Table to Text in the Word document.

Paste data

For most users, usually all that's needed is to get the data, a PivotTable, or a chart into a Word document (without any fancy features such as linking for updating or embedding so the data can be edited or formatted). The best way to do that is a simple copy and paste.

To copy simple data, select the cells (or PivotTable or chart area), right-click the selection, and click Copy. (If it's a PivotTable, you must choose Edit ⇨ Copy.)

To paste the copied data, right-click in the document and click Paste.

Cells and PivotTables become Word tables, as you can see in Figure 18.2, and you edit and format them using Word commands. Charts become graphic objects in Word, and are minimally formattable but fully resizable, just like other graphic objects.

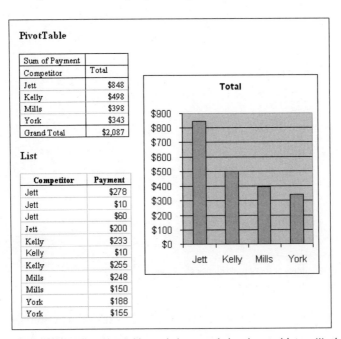

Figure 18.2. A list, PivotTable, and chart, copied and pasted into a Word document

Link data

A linked object is a small piece of the original source file (such as a chart or table of data) that is dynamic; a link is just a short set of directions to the location of the source file, and a linked object displays the current data in the source file.

When would a linked Excel object in Word be useful? If you routinely generate reports or letters that contain current data that's maintained in Excel (such as prices or a chart of performance), a linked object in the Word document saves you the trouble of looking up the data because the linked object data is always current.

To create a linked object, follow these steps:

1. In Excel, copy the data or chart you want to link.

2. In Word, choose Edit ⇨ Paste Special.

3. In the Paste Special dialog box (see Figure 18.3), select the Paste link option.

4. In the As list, select Microsoft Office Excel Worksheet Object (or Microsoft Office Excel Chart Object if you're linking a chart), and click OK.

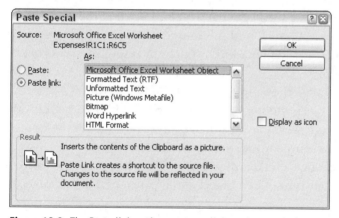

Figure 18.3. The Paste link option creates a link to the source data.

Bright Idea

Linked data is useful if you need to make several copies of the same data, because if you need to change the data, all you have to do is change the source file; all linked copies are updated with the change automatically (as long as they're in network contact with the source file).

Hack

If you can only see part of a linked object, its text-wrapping properties need to be changed. Open the Picture toolbar (right-click the toolbar area and click Picture), and click the object to select it. Click the Text Wrapping button, and choose different layouts until you get one that works for you.

Linked objects in an open Word document usually update automatically when the workbook source data changes, but sometimes they need to be updated manually.

To make sure a linked object is current, right-click the object and click Update Link.

When you open a document that contains a linked object, you are asked if you want to update the document with data from linked files — click Yes. (Clicking No retains the existing data in the linked object.)

When you double-click a linked object, the source file opens in its own program; make your changes and save and close the source file.

Change a link's source

The Office programs have become really good at tracking the movements of linked source data. I tried and tried to break a link by moving and renaming the source workbook, and when I opened the document with the linked object, Word found the source data every time — so you probably won't need to change a link's source in response to a broken link.

If you want to change the source for a linked object, editing a link (by right-clicking the object and choosing Link Worksheet Object ⇨ Links) generally doesn't work — when you switch source files you get the entire first page of the new source workbook as your linked object.

If you want to change a linked object to a different source, the easiest way is to delete the current linked object and create a new linked object.

Freeze linked data

When you want to keep the data as a picture but not be bothered with update questions when you open a document, you can freeze the data.

To freeze linked data as a picture, right-click the linked object; choose Link Worksheet Object ⇨ Links; click the Break Link button and click Yes when asked if you're sure.

Delete a linked object

A linked object is like any other graphic object—to delete it, click the object to select it and press Delete.

Embed data

This is the fastest way to create an embedded Excel object in Word: Resize both the Word window and the Excel window so you can see them both side by side on your screen (see Figure 18.4), then select the data in Excel and drag its border into the Word document (press Ctrl when you drop the data to drop a copy).

As a reliable alternative, you can right-click and drag the data and click Copy Here when you drop it.

When you drag and drop, you get the entire workbook (which makes the Word document much larger than a pasted range or a linked range), as seen in Figure 18.5.

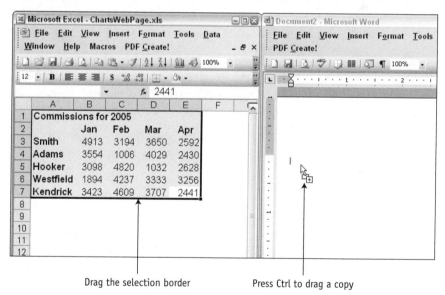

Drag the selection border   Press Ctrl to drag a copy

Figure 18.4. Put the Excel and Word windows side by side.

Hack

If you forget to Ctrl+drop the data in Word (and you lose the data in the worksheet), click the worksheet and press Ctrl+Z right away to restore the data. If you forget to press Ctrl+Z right away, close the worksheet without saving; when you reopen it, the data is restored.

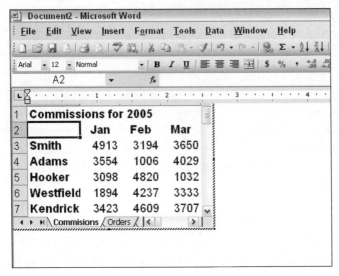

Figure 18.5. This object was created by dragging and dropping a handful of cells — it's open in the Excel environment in a Word document.

Here are a few pointers for working with an embedded Excel object in Word:

- Double-click the object to open an Excel environment. Many of the toolbar buttons and menu commands are functional Excel commands, but some may not be and you won't know which until you try.

- An embedded object is not linked; when you open the table in the Excel environment, you can change data and formatting without affecting the original worksheet.

- In the Excel environment, you can display any part of the worksheet (or other worksheets in the workbook) by dragging the hatched borders to make the display larger or smaller, and by dragging the scroll bars to display different parts of a worksheet in the object window. Whatever is displayed in the Excel environment is displayed in the object when you close the Excel environment.

Hack

If you drag and drop data from Excel to Word, you may find some entries truncated. For example, if the column of data is center-aligned in Excel, its entries may not be completely visible in the embedded object. You must left-align the column in Excel and then drag and drop it again.

Bright Idea

I often send data from Word to Excel (more often than the other way around) — for example, when I transcribe a handwritten list of items, I use voice-recognition software to get it easily into Word, and then copy and paste the Word list into Excel.

To close the Excel environment, click in the document.

To delete an embedded Excel object, click in the document to deselect the object, then click in the object once to select it without activating Excel, and press Delete.

Send data from Word to Excel

Sending data from Word to Excel is exactly like sending data from Excel to Word — pasting, embedding, and linking all work the same way (and when you embed a Word object, you embed the whole document).

If for some reason you want to paste text that's not a list (such as a letter) into a worksheet, paste it as a linked or embedded object so that it doesn't get parsed into cells. Most often, however, Word data that you want to use in Excel is in lists and is suitable for parsing into cells.

To copy a list from Word into Excel, copy the list in Word (select the list, right-click the selection, and click Copy), and paste it in Excel (right-click a cell and click Paste). The pasted data is parsed neatly into cells.

Figure 18.6 shows a Word list that's been pasted into a worksheet.

Sending data between Excel and Access

Sending data from Excel to Access was much easier in previous versions of Excel. There was a time when you could select a table, right-click the selection, and send it to Access. But in the interest of making all their programs easier for the computer illiterati, Microsoft eliminated this option altogether and hasn't replaced it with anything equally useful.

Inside Scoop

If the list is multicolumn and the columns are separated with Tab characters, the list is parsed into multiple columns in Excel; but if the columns are separated with space characters, all the text and spaces in a line are pasted into a single cell.

Inside Scoop

Microsoft Access is not part of the Standard Microsoft Office suite. To use Access — which is well suited to relational data — you must either have the Professional version of Microsoft Office or purchase Access separately.

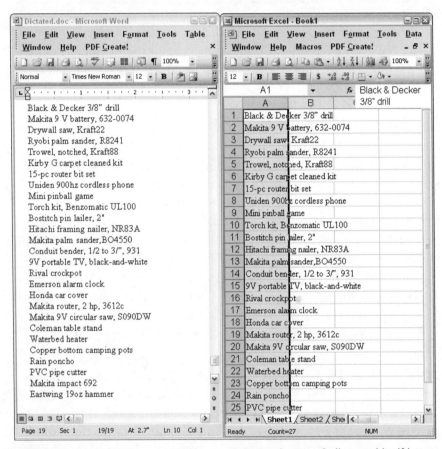

Figure 18.6. This Word list was pasted into a worksheet and automatically parsed itself into the cells in a column.

In Excel 2003, the fastest way to send an Excel table straight to Access 2003 is:

1. Open a database in Access, and open the worksheet with the data table in Excel.

2. Resize both the Access and Excel program windows so that you can see both the Excel data and the database window on your screen (see Figure 18.7).

3. Select the Excel table (including headings), and drag it into the database in the Access window. Press Ctrl when you drop the data in Access so that you drop a copy rather than moving the data out of the worksheet.

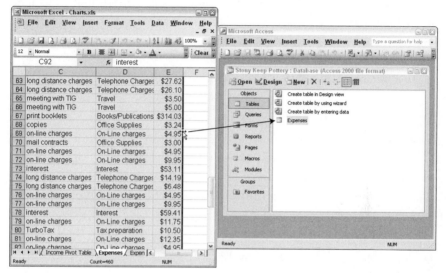

Figure 18.7. Resize the windows so you can drag data from Excel into the database.

A new table, named with the worksheet name, is created in the Access database.

Moving data from Access into Excel is a little simpler. Open the database table you want to copy to a worksheet, and choose Tools ⇨ Office Links ⇨ Analyze it with Excel.

Whether or not Excel is open, a new, saved workbook is created, named with the name of the database table, and saved in the current folder (the folder you last had open in Excel).

Because it isn't obvious where the new workbook is saved, choose File ⇨ Properties in the new workbook and look at the General tab; the Location line tells you the path to the file.

Hack

If you forget to press Ctrl when you drop the data (and the data disappears from the worksheet), click the worksheet to select it and then press Ctrl+Z to bring the data back. It won't affect the data in Access, but the data is replaced in Excel.

Pasting Excel data into PowerPoint

The charting feature in PowerPoint is the same as in Word and Access; you're much better off creating a chart in Excel and pasting it into a PowerPoint slide for a presentation.

To paste a chart into a PowerPoint slide, display the slide into which you want to paste the chart. Switch to Excel and copy the chart, then switch back to PowerPoint, click in the slide where you want to paste the chart, and choose Edit ⇨ Paste.

The chart isn't linked in any way to Excel or the source file.

Dragging a hyperlink into Excel

When you create a hyperlink, you create a colored, underlined, active link to another file; when the link is clicked, the other file opens in its own program. Using the Insert Hyperlink dialog box is covered in Chapter 1; here I give you the quick way to insert a link to an open document or workbook.

To insert a hyperlink to an open Word Document, follow these steps:

1. Open the Word document and Excel workbook side by side so you can see them both (see Figure 18.8).

2. Select a word or phrase in the Word document that you want displayed when the file opens (the file opens at your selected text).

3. Right-click and drag it into the worksheet where you want to create the hyperlink. In Figure 18.8, there are two hyperlinks already created and you can see a third being added.

4. Release the mouse button and click Create Hyperlink Here.

You'll want to edit the hyperlink, if only to change the name and ScreenTip.

To edit a link, right-click the link and click Edit Hyperlink; change the text in the Text to display box, and click the ScreenTip button to enter a user-friendly ScreenTip.

To remove a link, right-click the link and click Remove Hyperlink, then delete the unlinked text in the cell.

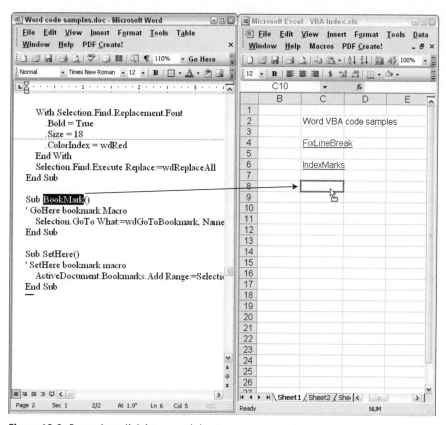

Figure 18.8. Drag a hyperlink into a worksheet.

Saving a worksheet as a Web page

If you have a Web site and want to add a page that's data from an Excel worksheet, open the worksheet and choose File ⇨ Save as Web Page.

Bright Idea

To preview what the Web page will look like before you create and save it, choose File ⇨ Web Page Preview. You might see changes you want to make in the workbook before you save it.

Watch Out!

A published page is not interactive on a machine that's not running Microsoft Office with the Office Web Components installed. It's useful on a corporate intranet, but not on a public Web site.

In the Save As dialog box (see Figure 18.9):

- Select the Entire Workbook option (to publish the whole workbook, with sheet tabs) or the Selection: Sheet option (to publish just the active worksheet).

- Select the Add interactivity check box to allow readers to enter data, change formulas and formatting, and pivot PivotTables. If you want an interactive page, you can only publish a single worksheet.

- Click Change Title to create a title for the top of your Web page.

- Type a File name so you can identify the file later when you want to open it on your browser or delete it from a Web site.

- Click Publish to set up the page for publication.

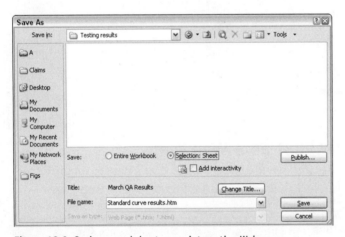

Figure 18.9. Saving a worksheet as an interactive Web page

In the Publish as Web Page dialog box (see Figure 18.10):

- Select the portion of data you want to publish in the Choose list box (click the drop-down arrow and make a selection — the options available change with each selection).

- If you publish a single sheet, you can add interactivity by selecting the Add interactivity with check box, and then selecting Spreadsheet functionality or PivotTable functionality (you can't have both); if you want the data to be noninteractive, deselect the check box.

- Click Change if you want to change the title.

- Select the Open published web page in browser check box so you can see the finished page when you're done.

- Take note of the filename and path, so you can double-click the filename in the folder window to open the page in your browser.

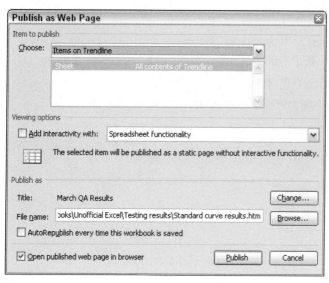

Figure 18.10. Finishing the Web page publishing process

Just the facts

- The easiest way to get Excel data into another program such as Word (and vice versa) is a simple copy and paste.

- Create an embedded object by selecting, dragging, and dropping data from one program into the other; an embedded object can be edited using its native program and is not linked to the source data at all.

- Create a linked object by copying the data in one program and choosing Edit ➪ Paste Special in the other program; select the Paste link option to paste an object that's linked to its source and shows current data.

- Send data from Excel to Access by dragging the data table (including headers) from the workbook window into a database window.

- Send data from Access to Excel by opening the table and then choosing Tools ➪ Office Links ➪ Analyze it with Excel.

- Send data to PowerPoint by copying the data and pasting it in a slide.

- Create a hyperlink to another file by right-clicking and dragging data from the other file into a worksheet cell and clicking Create Hyperlink Here. Right-click the link and click Edit Hyperlink to change the displayed text and the ScreenTip.

- Save a worksheet or workbook as a Web page by choosing File ➪ Save as Web Page.

Customizing and Automating

PART VIII

Customizing Your Workspace

Chapter 19

A person's computer is a unique and personal electronic environment. I always find it disconcerting to work at someone else's machine because we all like to set up our machines in our own way. Setting up your machine to suit you makes your work more pleasant and helps you work more efficiently.

One way to make your computer more efficient and comfortable is to set your view of Excel so that you can see as much of the worksheet as possible without squinting at tiny print. You can do that with a few different screen display settings.

Another aspect of your workspace you'll want to personalize is your toolbar display (and to a much lesser extent, perhaps, your menu display). You work much more efficiently when your toolbars display all the buttons you want and none of the buttons you never use (you can add and remove commands on your menus, too, but that's generally not as useful).

Changing your screen display

Because the default screen display for workbooks is functional and useful as it is, there usually isn't a compelling reason to change it. A few years ago, monitors were small and didn't provide much on-screen real estate, and there

431

were tricks such as full-screen view to make the most of what little screen area you had. Now, however, most people have larger monitors with higher screen resolution capability and can see as much of the workbook as they need with no changes. But if you find yourself working on an older monitor or a laptop with a small screen, you may want to resort to full-screen view and zooming the view.

Fill the screen

If you have a small monitor and want to see more of the worksheet area, you can switch to full-screen view by choosing View ⇨ Full Screen.

As you can see in Figure 19.1, you get just the active worksheet, maximized and bordered by the menu bar, row numbers, column letters, and the vertical scroll bar. The title bar, toolbars, and sheet tabs are hidden (unless you set the taskbar to AutoHide — when the taskbar is hidden, the sheet tabs and horizontal scroll bar are in view). You also get a toolbar with one button — Close Full Screen — with which you can switch back to the normal workbook view.

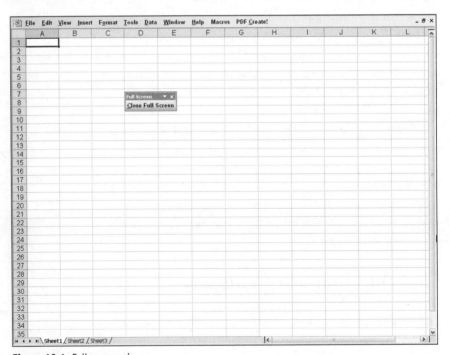

Figure 19.1. Full-screen view.

Hack

If you close the Full Screen toolbar, you can return to normal view by choosing View ⇨ Full Screen, but you lose the Full Screen toolbar. To get the Full Screen toolbar to open automatically again, right-click the menu bar, click Customize, and on the Toolbars tab, select Full Screen (and click Close).

Zoom the view

A more useful way to change your on-screen real estate (especially if you have a larger monitor) is to zoom in or out of the worksheet. Zooming changes the screen display by magnifying or reducing the cells in the worksheet.

The fastest way to zoom in or out is to use the Zoom button on the Standard toolbar. Click the arrow on the button and select a standard zoom level. You'll probably find that none of the levels is perfect; in that case, don't bother with the list of zoom levels — click in the Zoom button, type a custom zoom level, and press Enter.

If you work at very high resolution (that is, gaming resolution) or you can't find your glasses, select the range you want to focus on and click the arrow on the Zoom button; click Selection to zoom in to view just your selected range (see Figure 19.2).

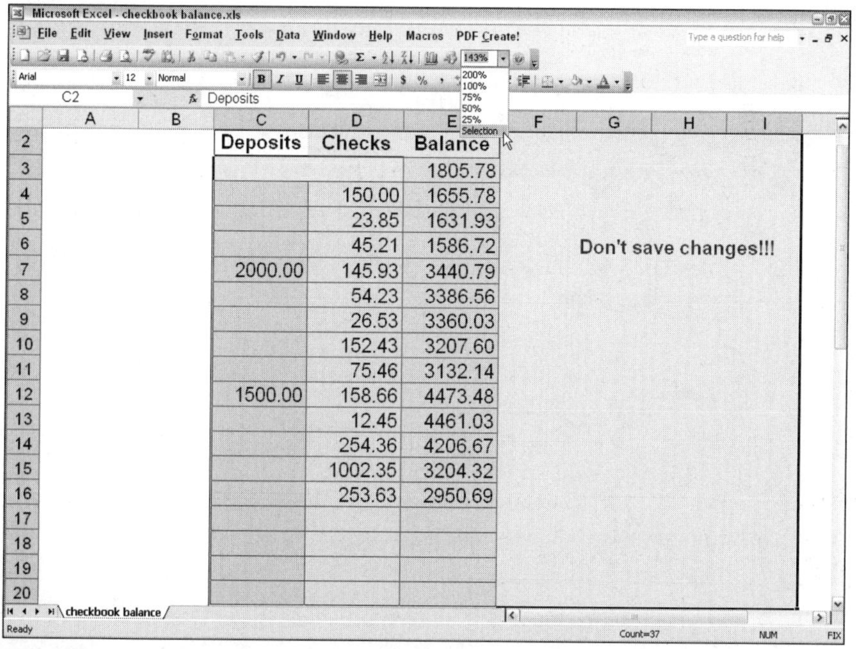

	Deposits	Checks	Balance
2			
3			1805.78
4		150.00	1655.78
5		23.85	1631.93
6		45.21	1586.72
7	2000.00	145.93	3440.79
8		54.23	3386.56
9		26.53	3360.03
10		152.43	3207.60
11		75.46	3132.14
12	1500.00	158.66	4473.48
13		12.45	4461.03
14		254.36	4206.67
15		1002.35	3204.32
16		253.63	2950.69

Don't save changes!!!

Figure 19.2. This view is zoomed to fit the selection.

Personalizing your toolbars

Customization is essential with toolbars. The standard one-size-fits-all toolbars are a good beginning, but there are bound to be buttons you never use and buttons you use frequently that are not on the built-in toolbars (not to mention custom buttons to run your own macros). In addition to displaying the Standard and Formatting toolbars (with some additions and deletions), I always keep one custom toolbar displayed with just my custom and hard-to-find buttons.

First, I want to discuss moving, hiding, and showing toolbars; then I'll discuss the buttons (changing and customizing them).

Move toolbars

The usual position for a toolbar is *docked*, which means it is stuck to a border of the program window. But floating the toolbar (allowing it to hover freely anywhere you choose on the worksheet) on the worksheet is often more convenient.

- To move a docked toolbar, drag its handle (the four dots at the end of the toolbar, shown in Figure 19.3); drag the toolbar against another border of the program window to dock it, or drag it into the worksheet to float it.

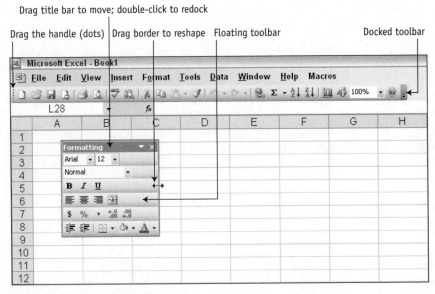

Figure 19.3. Maneuvering toolbars

Hack

If you knock your menu bar out of position while maneuvering toolbars, it's not a problem. The menu bar is just another toolbar (technically, they are all *command bars*), and you can reposition it by dragging its handle (the four dots on the left end).

- To move a floating toolbar, drag it by its title bar.
- To reshape a floating toolbar, drag any toolbar border in or out.
- To re-dock a floating toolbar, double-click its title bar.
- To position toolbars on the same row or separate them into their own rows, drag them where you want them by their handles.

Hide and show toolbars

You probably already know how to hide and show the most common toolbars: Right-click the toolbar area and click the toolbar name.

There are many more toolbars than what you see in the toolbar shortcut menu, however. To find and open them, right-click the toolbar area and click Customize. All the available toolbars in Excel are listed in the Toolbars tab; select a toolbar check box to show it.

Change toolbar buttons

We all have too many buttons on our built-in toolbars — and we differ on which buttons we want to keep and which we want to lose.

Remove and move buttons

The fastest way to get rid of buttons you never use is to Alt+click and drag the button away from the toolbar. Press and hold Alt while you drag the button into the worksheet; when you see the X next to the mouse pointer, drop the button.

You can move a button to a different toolbar by Alt+clicking and dragging the button and dropping it on another toolbar. You can also copy a

Inside Scoop

You can reset the configuration of built-in toolbars, but you cannot delete a built-in toolbar; you can delete a custom toolbar, but you cannot reset a custom toolbar's previous configuration.

button to another toolbar by Alt+clicking and dragging the button and pressing Ctrl (in addition to Alt) when you drop the button.

Add buttons

If the button you want to add to any built-in toolbar is part of the toolbar's built-in configuration, point to the arrow at the right end of the toolbar (the ScreenTip reads Toolbar Options); click the arrow, and point to Add or Remove Buttons; point to the toolbar name, and click the button name on the list that opens (see Figure 19.4).

If the button you want to add is not on a built-in toolbar (and many useful buttons are not), you must add it from the Customize dialog box.

To add a button from the Customize dialog box, right-click the toolbar area and click Customize. On the Commands tab (see Figure 19.5), select a category and drag the button from the dialog box to a toolbar.

Figure 19.4. Add or remove standard buttons from built-in toolbars by clicking the button name, or reset the original configuration by clicking Reset Toolbar.

Inside Scoop

To create a vertical separator line between two buttons, drag the right button a little more to the right and drop it (you can Alt+click and drag the button if the Customize dialog box isn't open). To remove a space, Alt+click and drag the button on the right over the separator line and drop it.

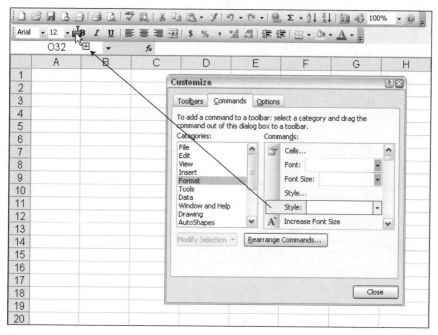

Figure 19.5. Drag the button to a toolbar.

Create custom toolbars

Rather than search through the Standard or Formatting toolbar for my special and custom buttons, I like to have a custom toolbar that carries my favorite buttons. A custom toolbar can be displayed by itself or fitted into the toolbar area alongside the other toolbars.

To create a custom toolbar, right-click in the toolbar area and click Customize. On the Toolbars tab, click New; in the New Toolbar dialog box, type a name for the toolbar and click OK.

A small empty named toolbar appears (see Figure 19.6). Now you get to fill it with buttons, using the techniques demonstrated earlier in this

> **Inside Scoop**
> Your custom toolbars can hold menus and menu commands as well as buttons.
> See the section "Customizing your menu bar" to learn more.

chapter. The new toolbar name appears on the toolbar shortcut menu when you right-click the toolbar area.

To delete a custom toolbar, open the Customize dialog box, click the toolbar name on the Toolbars tab, and click Delete.

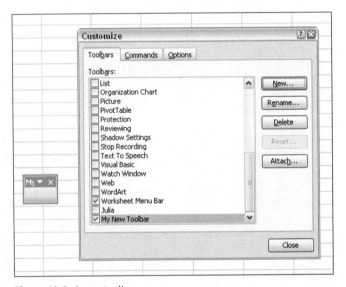

Figure 19.6. A new toolbar

Create custom buttons

Custom buttons are those you create to run macros you record or write. Chapter 21 covers recording and writing VBA macros. If you want to run a macro by clicking a button (which is a convenient way to run a macro), you need to add a custom button to a toolbar.

To add a custom button to a toolbar, right-click in the toolbar area and click Customize. On the Commands tab, scroll down the Categories list and click Macros (see Figure 19.7); in the Commands list, drag the Custom Button icon onto a toolbar.

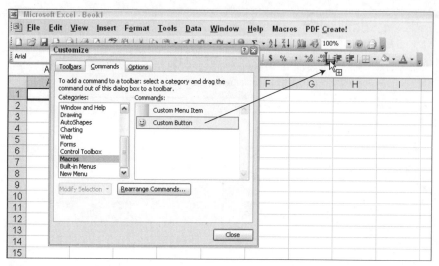

Figure 19.7. Creating a custom toolbar button to run a macro.

When the Custom button is on a toolbar, leave the Customize dialog box open. Right-click the button to format it and assign the macro (see Figure 19.8). You won't use the Customize dialog box, but it must be open when you want to work with the button.

The three aspects of the button you want to change are the name, the image, and the assigned macro.

- Type a name for the button in the Name box. The name is both the ScreenTip that appears when you point to the button, and the text in the button image if you choose to display text. The ampersand (&) makes a hotkey of the letter to the right of the ampersand — the letter you choose can't be a hotkey for any other command or button, so it's easiest to ignore the whole idea of creating a hotkey in the button name.

- For the button image, choose Default Style for a simple image, Text Only (Always) for the name alone, or Image and Text for both an image and the button name. I usually use Text Only (Always) because it's the easiest way to remember what the button does.

- If you want to give the button an image, either point to Change Button Image and click an image in the palette, or click Edit Button Image and paint your own image pixel by pixel.

- If you have recorded or written a macro to run from the button, click Assign Macro, click the macro name, and click OK.

Bright Idea

You can change any button or menu image or text — including all built-in buttons and menus — by using these same techniques. If a button isn't intuitive enough to remember, change it! (But keep in mind that any other people working at your computer will get lost.)

Display just the name

Name

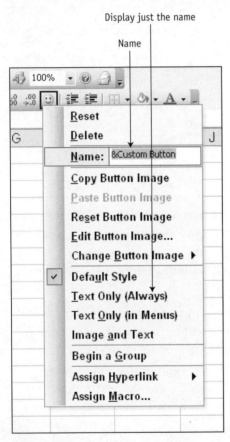

Figure 19.8. Customizing a custom button

My custom toolbar

Figure 19.9 shows my custom toolbar.

Figure 19.9. My custom toolbar

The buttons, from left to right, are:

- **Camera.** From the Tools category in the Customize dialog box; I use it to take linked pictures of cells to paste on other worksheets.

- **Visual Basic Editor.** From the Tools category in the Customize dialog box; I use it for quick access to my macros in the Visual Basic Editor.

- **Record New Macro.** From the Tools category in the Customize dialog box; I use it for quickly starting up the macro recorder.

- **Toggle Decimal.** A custom button that runs my macro to toggle fixed decimal entry on and off; the image is from the image palette (I show you the macro in Chapter 21).

- **Clear.** A custom button that runs my macro to clear everything in the selected range (a simple recorded macro runs the Edit ⇨ Clear ⇨ All command); the image is Text Only (Always).

- **Select Current Region.** From the Edit category in the Customize dialog box; I use it to select the table around the active cell (it does the same thing as Ctrl+A).

- **Select Visible Cells.** From the Edit category in the Customize dialog box; I use it when I hide rows and/or columns and want to copy and paste a range from the remaining visible cells (if you don't select visible cells, your copy-and-paste includes the hidden cells).

- **Toggle Grid.** From the Forms category in the Customize dialog box; I use this to toggle the gridlines on my worksheets on and off when I'm being artistic.

Customizing your menu bar

Customizing a menu bar is not an essential procedure for day-to-day operations in Excel, and when you begin moving menus and commands around, you can make Excel uncomfortably unfamiliar. But there are times when customizing menu bars is very useful; for example, when you want to run a macro from a menu command, or when you know you'll never use a particular menu command, ever, and want to remove it.

The menu bar is just another toolbar and can be moved, floated, and reshaped when floating.

To remove an entire menu from the menu bar, Alt+click and drag the menu off the bar.

Watch Out!

Menus and menu commands are application-specific, which means they are part of the Excel program rather than a workbook. If you share your computer with other users, warn them that you've made changes in the Excel program window.

If you drag a menu off of the menu bar and then change your mind, you must either painstakingly search out the commands to replace them, or restore the menu bar—and when you restore the menu bar, you lose all custom modifications you've made.

To restore the menu bar to its original configuration, open the Customize dialog box and click the Toolbars tab. In the Toolbars list, click Worksheet Menu Bar, then click Reset. Click OK when asked if you're sure.

Add a command to a menu

To add a command to a menu (either an existing menu or a new menu you create), open the Customize dialog box. On the commands tab, click a category and then drag the command you want from the dialog box onto the menu bar. Position the mouse pointer over the menu on which you want to place the command, and when the menu drops open, drag the command into position on the menu (see Figure 19.10).

If you want to add a command to run a macro, you must use the Macros category and Custom Menu Item command.

To format and/or assign a macro to a menu command, open the Customize dialog box (you won't use it, but it must be open), then right-click the menu command on the menu bar. Click Assign Macro, the macro name, and then OK.

Remove a command from a menu

To remove a command from a menu, open the Customize dialog box. Click the menu name to open it, and drag the command away from the menu.

Inside Scoop

Because the menu bar is just another toolbar, you see the same commands on the shortcut menus for both toolbar buttons and menu commands, and the shortcut menu commands work the same way. For menu commands, you only need the Name box and the Assign Macro command.

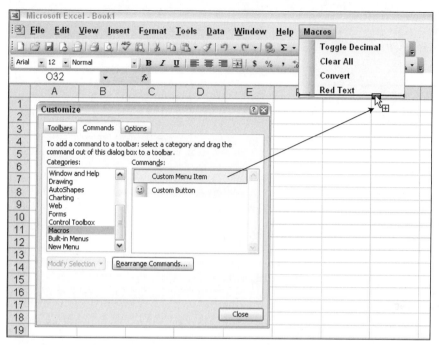

Figure 19.10. Drag a command to the menu, and when the menu opens, drag the command into position.

Create a new menu for the bar

To create a new menu for the menu bar (such as a Macros menu to hold commands you create to run macros you create), open the Customize dialog box. On the Commands tab, in the Categories list, click New Menu (at the bottom of the list), then drag the New Menu command from the Commands list onto the menu bar (see Figure 19.11).

When you drag a new menu to the menu bar, the nearest menu opens — pay no attention to the open menu while you drop the new menu on the menu bar.

With the Customize dialog box still open, right-click the new menu. Type a name for the new menu, and click in the worksheet to close the shortcut menu.

Finally, add commands to the new menu with the procedure in the earlier section "Add a command to a menu."

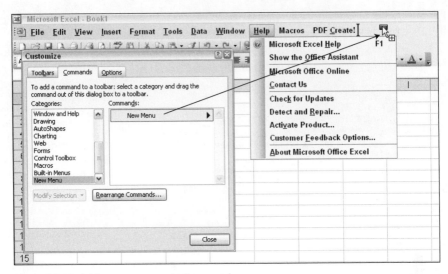

Figure 19.11. Adding a new menu to the menu bar

Just the facts

- Fill a monitor screen with the worksheet by choosing View ➪ Full Screen.

- Use the Zoom box on the Standard toolbar to change the worksheet magnification.

- Move toolbars to dock them or float them wherever they're most useful.

- Hide toolbars you don't need, and show them again with either the toolbar shortcut menu or the Customize dialog box.

- Change toolbar buttons to make the toolbars more useful.

- Remove a toolbar button by Alt+clicking and dragging it away from the toolbar.

- Add a toolbar button by dragging it from the Customize dialog box to the toolbar or create custom toolbars to hold just the buttons you want.

- Customize your menu bar to add custom menus and menu commands, especially to run macros.

GET THE SCOOP ON...
What worksheet controls can do ▪ The Forms toolbar
controls ▪ All worksheet controls ▪ List boxes and combo
boxes ▪ Option buttons and group boxes ▪ Scroll bars
and spinners ▪ Check boxes ▪ Button controls ▪ Labels

Adding Controls to a Worksheet

Worksheet controls give you another level of worksheet automation. Controls make a worksheet easier to use for users who are not proficient with Excel, and limit input values so the resulting data retains its integrity.

There are two kinds of controls in Excel: worksheet controls and ActiveX controls. Worksheet controls require no VBA programming, while ActiveX controls, designed to run VBA procedures and to be used in custom dialog boxes, are much more complex to set up.

Microsoft is very proud of its ActiveX controls and wants you to use them instead of the older worksheet controls, but for basic automation of worksheet functions, worksheet controls are much faster and easier to set up. The programming required to create and use both ActiveX controls and custom dialog boxes (called *userforms*) is beyond the scope of this book; if you want to pursue these topics, a good place to begin is my book *Master Visually Excel 2003 VBA Programming.*

I'm going to show you how to use worksheet controls (no programming required) to automate data input procedures in a worksheet.

What can worksheet controls do?

It's easier to show you what worksheet controls can do than to try to tell you. To begin this chapter, I'm going to show you two worksheets with functional controls in place and explain what's going on in each worksheet; after I show you what controls can do, I'll show you how to create the specific controls.

Worksheet controls are not designed to be stand-alone features; they're designed to work with formulas and macros, and they give a user an easy (and controlled) way to change the variables in formulas. A good example is shown in Figure 20.1. I've placed all of these controls in a single worksheet to show you the similarities between them; I discuss each of them in more detail in later sections.

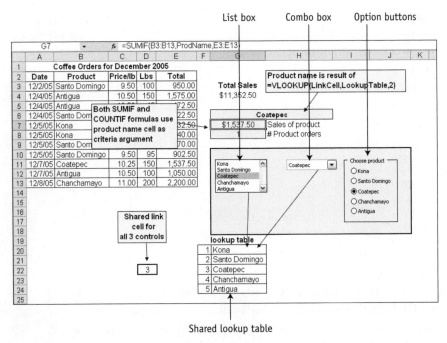

Figure 20.1. A worksheet using a list box, a combo box, and option buttons in a group box

List boxes, combo boxes, and option buttons all do the same thing: They allow a user to select one of a limited group of items. They don't enter the data itself into a cell; instead, they enter a number in a *linked cell*, a cell that's linked to the control, and the number in the linked cell is used by formulas in the worksheet.

Bright Idea

Hide the linked cell and the lookup table by positioning them far away on the worksheet or on a different worksheet, or by hiding the columns that contain the linked cell and the table.

(In this example, all three controls — list box, combo box, and option group — are sharing the same linked cell; you wouldn't normally do that, but I do it here for illustration purposes.)

Each control allows you to make a single choice from a limited list of choices; each choice puts a specific number in the linked cell (you cannot control what the numbers are).

Then you can use the number in the linked cell in formulas by referencing the linked cell in the formula. In this example, the cell with the product name actually contains a VLOOKUP formula; the formula looks up the linked cell entry in the lookup table, and returns the corresponding entry from the lookup table (see Chapter 5 to learn more about the VLOOKUP function).

The sales of product and # Product orders cells contain SUMIF and COUNTIF formulas that use the product name returned by the VLOOKUP formula as the criterion for summing and counting cells in the coffee orders list. It's all very inter-related and elegantly functional.

In general, to create a worksheet like the one shown above, follow these steps:

1. Create controls (and create a lookup table for a list box or a combo box).

2. Write a VLOOKUP formula for the product name (use cell link and lookup table in the formula).

3. Use the VLOOKUP result cell (the product name) in SUMIF & COUNTIF formulas.

The next example (see Figure 20.2) illustrates ideas for using spinners, scroll bars, and check boxes.

Bright Idea

Which controls you use for this kind of worksheet setup depend on your sense of aesthetics, but if the list of choices is very long, a combo box takes a lot less room on the worksheet than a list box or an option group.

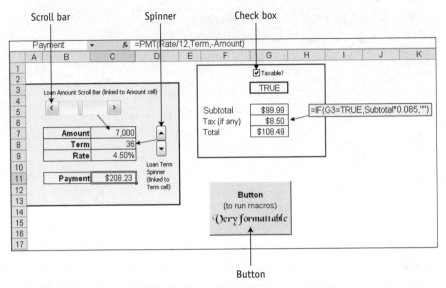

Figure 20.2. A worksheet using a scroll bar, spinner, check box, and button

In this worksheet, the spinner and the scroll bar change the values in the loan calculator (no formulas are involved in this example).

The check box in this example changes the value in the linked cell below it, switching between TRUE and FALSE. The Boolean values TRUE and FALSE are useful in an IF formula such as the tax calculation in the previous example (useful in an invoice).

The button control exists to run macros you record or write.

Now that you have a few ideas about how you can use worksheet controls, I'll tell you how to create each one.

The Forms toolbar controls

To create worksheet controls, right-click the toolbar area and click Forms. The Forms toolbar (see Figure 20.3) contains all the worksheet controls.

Figure 20.3. The Forms toolbar

Table 20.1 explains the buttons on the Forms toolbar, from left to right. A few of these buttons are not functional because they are left over from Excel 5, and Microsoft neglected to remove them. (But if by some extraordinary coincidence you are using Excel 5, in Windows 95 — or would that be 3.1? — those buttons are available; on the other hand, if that's true, why are you reading this book?)

Table 20.1. The Forms toolbar

Icon	Button	Purpose
Aa	Label	Text that provides information.
abl	Edit Box	Not functional.
xyz	Group Box	Groups option buttons into functional groups; also provides visual grouping of related controls of any kind.
	Button	Runs a macro when clicked.
☑	Check Box	Enters TRUE or FALSE into a linked cell.
◉	Option Button	Enters a number into a linked cell; all option buttons in a group box share the same linked cell and only one option button in a group can be selected.
	List Box	Displays a list of items from which the user can choose one.
	Combo Box	Displays a drop-down list of items from which the user can choose one.
	Combination List-Edit	Not functional.
	Combination Drop-Down Edit	Not functional.
	Scroll Bar	Increases or decreases a value within a range.
	Spinner	Increases or decreases a value within a range.

continued

Table 20.1. *continued*

Icon	Button	Purpose
	Control Properties	Opens the Format Control dialog box — same as right-clicking a control and clicking Format Control.
	Edit Code	Opens the Visual Basic Editor for writing or editing VBA code for the control. You can run macros by clicking worksheet controls.
	Toggle Grid	Turns the worksheet gridlines (and userform grid marks) on and off.
	Run Dialog	Not functional.

All worksheet controls

All worksheet controls have some things in common. They can be

- Moved, resized, and reshaped
- Drawn repeatedly by double-clicking the button to make the controls "hot" (click the button again to turn the feature off)
- Overlapped, and sent to the back or brought to the front using the commands on the Draw button (on the Drawing toolbar)
- Grouped to move as a unit using the commands on the Draw button (on the Drawing toolbar)
- Aligned and distributed using the commands on the Draw button (on the Drawing toolbar)
- Snapped to worksheet gridlines with the Alt key
- Assigned macros
- Set up and made functional by right-clicking the control and clicking Format Control
- Deleted by right-clicking the control and clicking Cut

All controls can be formatted to some degree, at least to apply 3-D shading, and some can be formatted with colored lines and fills. When you open a control's Format Control dialog box, you see what formatting, if any, is available.

Hack

When you click a control, the control becomes active and responds to your click, even if it hasn't yet been set up. When you want to move or reshape a control, you must right-click the control, then click the control to keep it selected while removing the shortcut menu.

Like cells, all controls are locked by default, and when you protect the worksheet, you must unlock the control to keep it functional. Like cells, the Locked check box is on the Protection tab in the Format Control dialog box.

The Current value setting for all controls is used to set a default initial value when the control is used on a custom dialog box — ignore it for worksheet controls.

List boxes and combo boxes

List boxes and combo boxes on the Forms toolbar (that is, *not* ActiveX controls) are identical in function; they only differ in appearance. If your list of choices is short and you have the space, a list box is faster to use, but if the list is long or the available space is tight, a compact combo box with a drop-down list of choices is better.

Create a list box

To create a list box, follow these steps:

1. Create an input list, the list of items you want displayed in the control. The list can be anywhere on the worksheet or on a different worksheet.

2. Click the List Box button on the Forms toolbar, then either click or draw to create the control in the worksheet.

3. Right-click the new control, and click Format Control.

4. In the Format Control dialog box (see Figure 20.4), click in the Input range box and drag to select the input list from Step 1.

Bright Idea

List boxes and combo boxes can't enter the selected text items into a list; if your intention is to automate and control entries in a list, use the list-type Data Validation instead.

Input list

New list box

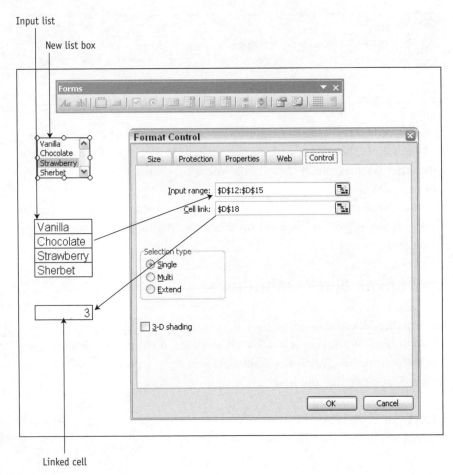

Linked cell

Figure 20.4. Setting up a list box

5. Click in the Cell link box, and then click a cell on the worksheet that will hold the numeric result of clicking a choice in the control.

6. Click OK, and the control is set up. You can use the value in the linked cell in formulas.

You can put the linked cell (from Step 5) anywhere you want; I suggest putting it out of view, either far away on the worksheet or in a hidden column along with the input range.

Create a combo box

To create a combo box, follow the previous steps, but click the Combo Box button on the Forms toolbar. In the Format Control dialog box (see

Hack

What if you discover a misspelled item in your list box or combo box? Just correct the spelling in the input list.

Figure 20.5), there's a Drop down lines box that governs the length of the drop-down list.

When you first click OK in the Format Control dialog box, no entries appear in the new combo box. Don't worry—when you click the arrow and select an entry for the first time, the list appears.

You can set any number you like to control the length of the list. If you make the list shorter than the number of items in your input range, the drop-down list has a scroll bar; if you make the list longer than the number of items in your input range, the list has white space at the bottom.

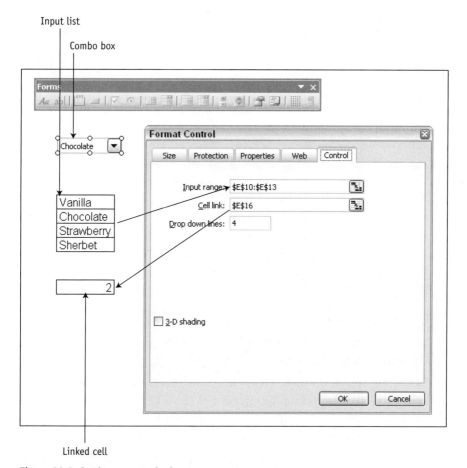

Figure 20.5. Setting up a combo box

Option buttons and group boxes

Option buttons allow a user to select one of a group of two or more choices, just like list boxes and combo boxes. Option buttons work together in a group; all the option buttons on a worksheet are in the same *logical group*—they share the same linked cell—unless you create separate groups of option buttons by placing them in group boxes.

You can put any controls you want in a group box to visually segregate them—but the real function of a group box is to create distinct logical groups of options buttons. In other words, all option buttons within a group box are part of the same logical group and share the same linked cell, but are not connected to any other option buttons on the worksheet.

Create option buttons

To create option buttons, follow these steps:

1. Click the Option Button button on the Forms toolbar, and then click in the worksheet to create the new control.

2. Drag to select the text in the new option button, and type a new label.

3. Repeat Steps 1 and 2 to create more option buttons (see Figure 20.6).

Figure 20.6. Creating and naming option buttons

4. Drag the option buttons into roughly the arrangement you want.

5. Show the Drawing toolbar and click the Select Object button. The Drawing toolbar is covered in Chapter 14.

6. Lasso the option buttons. When they are all selected, use the Distribute and Align commands on the Draw button (on the Drawing toolbar) to arrange the buttons neatly. Then click the Select Object button to turn it off.

Bright Idea

Option buttons are one of the worksheet controls you can format with fill colors and colored borders. Formatting options are on the Colors and Lines tab in the Format Control dialog box.

7. Right-click any button and click Format Control.

8. In the Format Control dialog box, on the Control tab (see Figure 20.7), click in the Cell link box, and then click a cell in the worksheet. Click OK to finish — all the option buttons in a logical group automatically share the same linked cell.

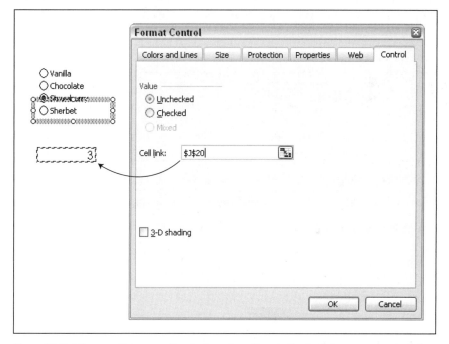

Figure 20.7. When you link one option button, the others in the logical group are automatically linked.

Inside Scoop

The first option button you create displays the number 1 in the linked cell, the second displays the number 2, and so on. If you move the buttons around, they keep the same linked cell numbers based on the order in which they were created.

Create a group box

If you only have one logical group of option buttons on a worksheet, there's no need for a group box (unless you want one because it looks good). But if you want to use option buttons for two or more sets of choices, you need to place each logical group of option buttons inside its own group box.

You can create the group box after you create the option buttons; either draw the box around the buttons or drag the buttons into the box, or you can create the group box first and create the option buttons inside it. Either way, Excel knows there are option buttons within a group box.

To create a group box, click the Group Box button on the Forms toolbar, and either click or draw the box in the worksheet. Drag to select the group box name and type a new name (see Figure 20.8).

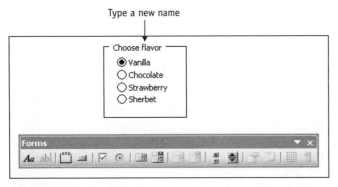

Figure 20.8. Creating a group box

There's nothing to link in a group box, but if you want to apply (or remove) 3-D shading, right-click the box and click Format Control; the 3-D shading check box is on the Control tab.

Scroll bars and spinners

Scroll bars and spinners are nearly identical—both change the integer value in a cell when the user clicks the arrows in the control. Both have

Bright Idea

If you move your group box and option buttons, you risk losing the perfect alignment and distribution you created. To maintain the layout, group them: Click the Select Object button on the Drawing toolbar, lasso the box and buttons, and click Group on the Draw button menu.

Hack

If linked cells are locked and the worksheet is protected, the linked cell values can't be changed and the controls won't work. Instead, put the linked cells else where, set the displayed cells =*cellref* of the real linked cells, unlock the real linked cells, and then protect the worksheet.

minimum and maximum values, and both control the increments by which the values change. The only functional difference between the two is that in a scroll bar the user can also make a large jump in value, by clicking within the scroll bar instead of clicking an arrow.

The linked cells for scroll bars and spinners can be used directly in the worksheet, as illustrated in the loan calculator in Figure 20.2, as well as hidden for use in formulas (as is common with option buttons and list boxes).

Create a spinner

To create a spinner, click the Spinner button on the Forms toolbar, then click or draw a spinner control in the worksheet. Right-click the new spinner and click Format Control.

In the Format Control dialog box (see Figure 20.9), click the Control tab.

In the Minimum value and Maximum value boxes, set the minimum and maximum values for the spinner to put in the linked cell (the values must be integers greater than zero).

In the Incremental change box, type the increment by which the spinner changes the linked cell value (for example, in the example illustrated at the beginning of this chapter, the spinner changes the value of the loan term cell by 12 because loan terms are commonly in 12-month increments).

Finally, click in the Cell link box and then click the linked cell on the worksheet. Click OK, and the spinner is functional.

Spinners can only be created vertically, so don't bother trying to draw a horizontal spinner control.

Create a scroll bar

To create a scroll bar, click the Scroll Bar button on the Forms toolbar, then click or draw a scroll bar control in the worksheet. Right-click the new scroll bar and click Format Control.

Watch Out!

You cannot set a maximum value higher than 30,000. If you try, Excel won't allow you to proceed.

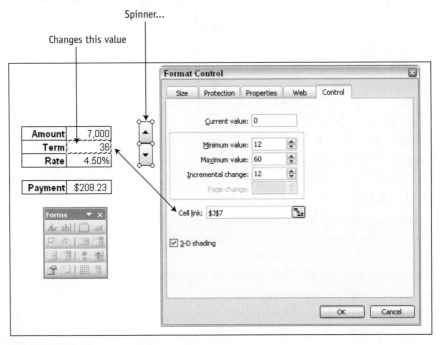

Figure 20.9. Setting up a spinner

In the Format Control dialog box (see Figure 20.10), set the minimum and maximum values for the scroll bar to set in the linked cell, and set the incremental change by which clicking the scroll bar arrows changes the value in the linked cell.

In the Page change box, set the incremental change for the linked cell value when the user clicks in the center of the scroll bar (not on the arrow buttons).

Inside Scoop

In a scroll bar, the width of the scroll bar makes a difference in the size of the arrow buttons. Drag a side handle to make the width smaller pixel by pixel, and the size of the arrows in the scroll buttons will suddenly jump to a reasonable size.

Scroll bar...

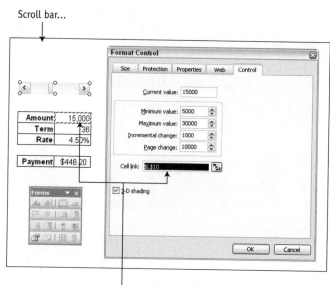

Changes the value in this linked cell

Figure 20.10. Setting up a scroll bar

Finally, click in the Cell link box and then click the linked cell on the worksheet. Click OK, and the scroll bar is functional.

To make a scroll bar horizontal, you must draw it that way (you cannot change the orientation after the control is created).

Check boxes

A check box toggles between TRUE and FALSE in the linked cell. You can use the linked cell result in any formula or activity that requires a true/false, yes/no, or on/off input.

A check box can take the place of two option buttons, because both a check box and a group of two option buttons offer the user a choice between two options.

To create a check box, click the Check Box button on the Forms toolbar, and click or draw a check box in the worksheet. Drag to select the text and type a new label, then right-click the new check box and click Format Control.

In the Format Control dialog box (see Figure 20.11), click in the Cell link box, then click the linked cell on the worksheet. Pay no attention to the Values options—they set a default initial value for the check box if you use it in a custom dialog box.

Bright Idea

You don't have to use linked cells with check boxes; you can use unlinked check boxes as visual reminders in a worksheet, such as a project checklist, and mark the check box to indicate that a task has been accomplished.

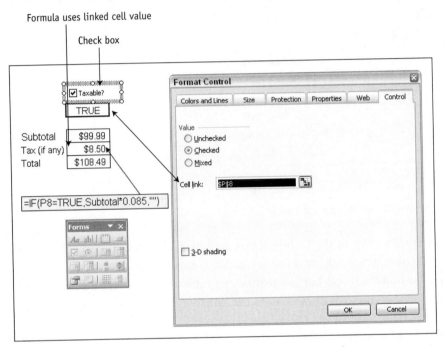

Figure 20.11. Setting up a check box control

Button controls

Button controls exist only to run macros and are limited to running macros on the worksheet where they exist. I don't mean to disparage them, however; I like button controls and use them often.

To create a button control, click the Button button on the Forms toolbar, then click or draw a button in the worksheet.

As soon as you release the mouse button, the Assign Macro dialog box appears listing all the macros available to this workbook (see Figure 20.12). Click the macro name you want, and click OK.

While the button is selected, drag to select the button text and type your button label.

Bright Idea

While you cannot change the color of a button control, you can format the text in a button as much as you want using the text formatting buttons on the Formatting toolbar.

Button

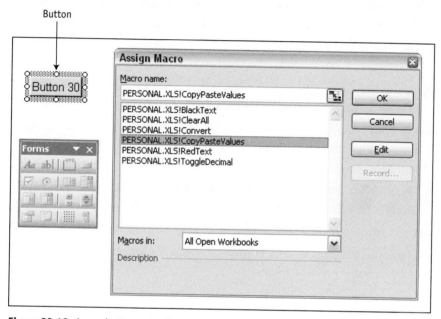

Figure 20.12. A new button control needs a macro.

If you need to change or edit the macro assigned to a button control, right-click the button and click Assign Macro. The Assign Macro dialog box opens, and you can either assign a different macro or click the Edit button to open the Visual Basic Editor to edit the existing macro.

Labels

Labels are completely passive and not at all formattable. They're designed for labeling controls on a custom dialog box; they're not of much use on a worksheet. I suggest using a normal text box (on the Drawing toolbar) instead.

If you want to create a label, click the Label button on the Forms toolbar, and click or draw the label in the worksheet. Drag to select the label text and type your own text.

Just the facts

- Automate your worksheets quickly and easily using controls on the Forms toolbar (the controls on the Control Toolbox toolbar are similar but more complex).

- List boxes, combo boxes, and option buttons all do the same job — they put a sequential integer value into a linked cell.

- Use the linked cell values in formulas to automate procedures on a worksheet.

- Group option buttons in a group box control to separate them functionally from other option buttons on the same worksheet.

- Use scroll bar and spinner controls to change the value in a linked cell, and use the changeable linked-cell value in worksheet features and formulas.

- Use a check box to toggle the value in a linked cell, and use the linked-cell value in worksheet formulas.

- Use button controls to run macros you've written or recorded.

- Combine features, controls, and formulas for an elegant, automated, bulletproof worksheet.

GET THE SCOOP ON...

Introducing macros ■ Recording a macro ■ Running a macro ■ Exploring the Visual Basic Editor ■ Editing a macro ■ Deleting a macro ■ Setting macro virus protection

Using Macros to Automate Repetitive Work

Macros are programmed procedures that are written using the Visual Basic for Applications (VBA) programming language. The words *macro* and *procedure* are used interchangeably.

Macros are a useful way to automate repetitive procedures in Excel and are actually a lot of fun once you get past any initial confusion barriers. This chapter barely scratches the surface of VBA; mostly I teach you how to use it in the simplest possible way to program short procedures and get you past the "programming is hard to learn" obstacle that stops most folks from exploring it.

I focus on the types of simple VBA procedures that I use most often, written by recording a procedure with the macro recorder and sometimes lightly editing that procedure to make it more fully functional and useful.

I won't discuss VBA programming language or writing your own code from scratch — that's beyond the scope of this book (and beyond the interests of most Excel users). If you're interested in pursuing VBA in more detail, try my book *Master Visually Excel 2003 VBA Programming*.

Introducing macros

Macros are programmed procedures written in VBA language and are the same whether you record them or write them directly.

463

Chapter 21

When you create a macro, you must choose a storage workbook. Macros are stored in three places: in the workbook in which you create them, in a new workbook, and in the Personal Macro Workbook.

- **This Workbook.** If you store a macro in This Workbook (the workbook in which the macro is created), it is available to all open workbooks as long as the workbook in which the macro is stored is open. This is a good option if you want to send a workbook and its associated macros to another user, because the macros stored in the workbook go along with the workbook file.

- **New Workbook.** If you store a macro in a New Workbook, Excel creates a new, unsaved workbook and stores the macro there regardless of which workbook you record the macro in. You must save the new workbook to save the macro, and (like the This Workbook option) the macro will only be available when the new workbook is open.

- **Personal Macro Workbook.** If you store a macro in the Personal Macro Workbook (nearly always my choice), the macro is available all the time to any workbook you have open. The Personal Macro Workbook is a file named PERSONAL.XLS (which is created the first time you store a macro there), is saved in the XLSTART folder in your Microsoft folders, and is hidden. Every time you store another macro in the Personal Macro Workbook, the macro is added to the existing Personal Macro Workbook. The Personal Macro Workbook opens whenever you start Excel, but you won't see it unless you deliberately unhide it. These macros are available to any open workbook, but only in your copy of Excel, and they don't travel with other workbooks.

Before I discuss recording and writing macros, open the Visual Basic toolbar (see Figure 21.1). Right-click in the toolbars area and click Visual Basic. I use four of those buttons in this chapter.

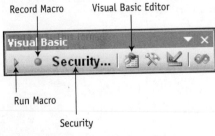

Figure 21.1. The Visual Basic toolbar

Watch Out!

Macros in your workbooks wake up the security settings, which is Excel's built-in protection against malicious viruses you might receive in workbooks sent to you. See the section "Setting macro virus protection" to learn how to work with and around the security settings.

Table 21.1 explains the buttons on the Visual Basic toolbar.

Table 21.1. The Visual Basic toolbar

Icon	Button	Function
▷	Run Macro	Opens the Macro dialog box; click the name of the macro and click Run.
○	Record Macro	Starts the macro recorder.
Security...	Security	Opens the Security dialog box; check or change your security settings.
	Visual Basic Editor	Opens the Visual Basic Editor window.
	Control Toolbox	Opens the Control Toolbox toolbar (not covered in this book).
	Design Mode	Switches the workbook into design mode for Control Toolbox controls (not covered in this book).
	Script Editor	Opens the Web scripting feature (not covered in this book).

Recording a macro

Recording a macro (which records all your actions) is an easy way to automate tedious and repetitive tasks without having to write code or understand programming language. Macros can be very short and quick to record, and I often create them just to save a few mouse clicks.

Before you start the recorder, it's a good idea to run through all the steps you want to record—like a rehearsal—to prevent mistakes while recording.

Record a simple macro

To record a macro, follow these steps:

1. Click the Record Macro button on the Visual Basic toolbar (or choose Tools ⇨ Macro ⇨ Record New Macro if the toolbar isn't open).

2. In the Record Macro dialog box (see Figure 21.2), name the macro. Macro names (like cell and range names) must begin with a letter and are limited to 255 characters. They cannot have spaces, but can have letters, numbers, and underscore characters.

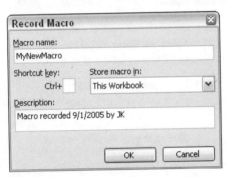

Figure 21.2. Record a new macro.

3. If you want a keyboard shortcut (it's optional), click in the Shortcut key box and type a letter. Your keystroke will be Ctrl+*yourkey*.

   If it's the same as an existing keystroke (such as Ctrl+C), the macro keystroke overrides whatever action the existing keystroke performs. You can get around this by typing Shift+*yourkey*—the macro keystroke will be Ctrl+Shift+*yourkey*.

4. In the Store macro in box, click the down arrow and select a storage workbook (see Figure 21.3). Then click OK.

Figure 21.3. Select a storage workbook for the macro.

Hack

If you inadvertently override a built-in keystroke that you need, you can get the original built-in keystroke back: Either delete the macro, or change the macro's keyboard shortcut (see the section "Run a macro with a keystroke").

5. The Stop Recording toolbar appears (see Figure 21.4), and the recorder is recording all your actions. Notice the Record Macro button changes to Stop Recording while you record.

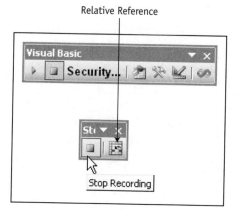

Figure 21.4. The Stop Recording toolbar has two buttons: Stop Recording and Relative Reference.

6. Perform the actions you want the macro to perform. You can use both the mouse and the keyboard. In this example, I choose Edit ⇨ Clear ⇨ All because I want the macro to perform those actions for me with a single click.

Don't be in a hurry — there's no clock running when you record a macro, and when you take your time, you're less likely to record errors. Also, if you misspell an entry, just fix the spelling while you're recording.

7. Click the Stop Recording button to stop the macro recorder.

Bright Idea

Use the recorder to make longer macros easier to write by recording smaller subprocedures and then copying and pasting them together in the Visual Basic Editor.

The macro is finished. Because I want this particular macro to clear everything (formats, contents, and comments) from whatever range I select before I run the macro, I don't select a range while recording — the only actions I record are the command clicks.

Record a macro with relative references

When you record a macro that involves selecting a cell, the macro records an absolute reference for the selected cell and always selects that same cell. Sometimes that's good — for example, when you want a macro to write the current date in the upper-left corner of a worksheet — but sometimes you want the macro to make an entry in a cell with a relative reference, a cell that's always a specific distance away from the active cell.

The Relative Reference button on the Stop Recording toolbar makes the relative reference selection possible.

To record a relative reference selection, start recording a macro, and when you're ready to select the relative reference, click the Relative Reference button on the Stop Recording toolbar (see Figure 21.5). Click the relative-reference cell, and then click the Relative Reference button again to stop recording relative references.

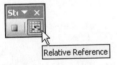

Figure 21.5. Record relative references.

For example, suppose you want the macro to enter a formula in the cell four rows below the active cell, no matter where the active cell is when you run the macro. Start recording the macro, click the Relative Reference button, click the cell four rows below the active cell, type your formula, and press Enter. Then click the Relative Reference button again.

If the recorded macro does what you want, you need never look at the code the recorder writes; but when you begin looking at code in the Visual Basic Editor, you see how relative references are written in Visual Basic code.

Hack
You cannot undo any action performed by a macro. If a macro does something in a workbook that you need to undo, you have two options: Undo the damage manually, or close the workbook without saving it.

Record a macro to select the last cell

Suppose you want a macro to write a sum formula at the bottom of a list, but you never know how long the list is going to be. You don't need to know any VBA programming to write a macro to select the cell at the bottom of a list—all you need to do is record a macro with a special keystroke.

Select a cell in the list and start the macro recorder. Then press Ctrl+Down Arrow. The active cell jumps to the last cell in the column. It doesn't matter if relative references are on or off because the recorder writes the same code for both—Selection.End(xlDown) .Select—and the macro selects the cell at the bottom of the list no matter how long the list is or where the starting point is.

When you run the macro, start with the active cell near the top of the column, then let the macro jump to the bottom of the list and continue with your recorded macro actions.

Running a macro

The whole point of a macro is to make tedious procedures quicker and less tedious, so you'll want to run a macro in the most convenient way. Some macros are most conveniently run from a toolbar button (available in every workbook as long as the toolbar is open); other macros—those you use often—are most conveniently run from a keystroke; rarely used macros might be most conveniently run from a menu command; and macros intended to be used on a single worksheet are always conveniently run from a graphic object on the worksheet.

Run a macro with a keystroke

To run a macro with a keystroke, type the keystroke you entered when you recorded the macro.

If, however, you didn't enter a shortcut key when you recorded the macro, or if you wrote a macro without using the recorder and you want to run it with a keystroke, you can add one at any time.

To regain the use of a built-in keystroke after inadvertently overriding it with a macro keystroke, use the following steps to change the keystroke; when the macro keystroke is no longer overriding the built-in keystroke, the built-in keystroke is automatically restored.

To add or change a macro shortcut key, click the Run Macro button on the Visual Basic toolbar (or choose Tools ⇨ Macro ⇨ Macros). Click the macro name in the Macro dialog box, and click the Options button. In the Macro Options dialog box (see Figure 21.6), type a shortcut key, and click OK.

Click Cancel to close the Macro dialog box, and test your shortcut key.

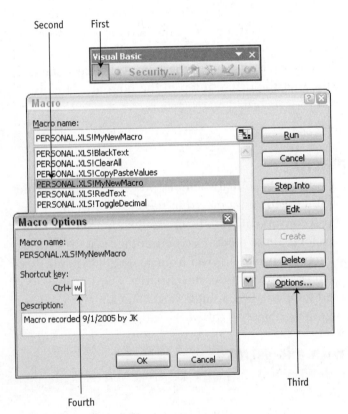

Figure 21.6. Add or change a macro shortcut key.

Attach a macro to a toolbar button

To run a macro from a toolbar button, add a custom button to a toolbar (see Chapter 19), and with the Customize dialog box open, right-click the Custom button. In the shortcut menu, click Assign Macro.

Hack

If you don't see the macro name, check the Macros in box — it should read All Open Workbooks.

In the Assign Macro dialog box (see Figure 21.7), click the macro name and click OK.

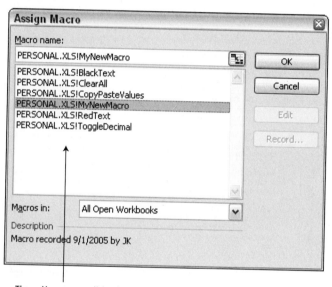

These Macros are all in the Personal Macro Workbook

Figure 21.7. Assign a macro to a custom toolbar button.

Attach a macro to a menu command

Attaching a macro to a custom menu command is exactly like attaching a macro to a custom toolbar button; create the custom menu command (see Chapter 19), and with the Customize dialog box open, right-click the custom menu command. In the shortcut menu, click Assign Macro.

Attach a macro to an object

Attaching a macro to any graphic object is a lot like attaching a macro to a custom toolbar button or menu command: Right-click the object and click Assign Macro. In the Assign Macro dialog box, click the macro name and click OK.

Exploring the Visual Basic Editor

I'm not going to go into the Visual Basic Editor very deeply—that's for another book to do—but I'm going to get you familiar enough with the Visual Basic Editor to edit your recorded macros comfortably.

Figure 21.8 shows the Visual Basic Editor, which opens in its own program window.

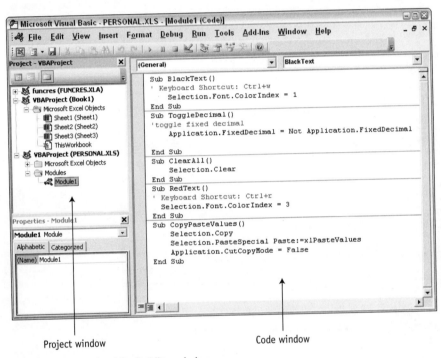

Project window   Code window

Figure 21.8. The Visual Basic Editor window

The Project window

The Project window (also called the Project Explorer window) is structured like the file tree in Windows Explorer. Each entry in the Project window is called a *node*. The top nodes, in bold font, are open *projects*—a

Inside Scoop

In my Project window, the funcres project (the Funcres.xla file) is displayed because I have the Analysis Toolpak installed (because I like having the Convert function always available). If you don't have the Analysis Toolpak installed, you won't see this project.

VBA project is the container for all the VBA code in a workbook, and the workbook name is in parentheses next to the project name.

All projects are initially named VBA Project (*workbook.xls*), as seen in Figure 21.9. After you record your first macro, the Personal Macro Workbook is created, and it has a project node — VBAProject (PERSONAL.XLS) — in the Project window. Projects for every open workbook (and only for open workbooks) are listed in the window.

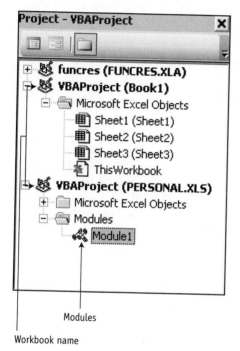

Figure 21.9. The Project window

Below each project node are the folder nodes for Excel objects (the workbook and the sheets in the workbook) and modules. Each sheet object and the workbook object can hold procedures that are triggered by specific workbook or sheet events, such as sheet activation or workbook opening.

Inside Scoop

You can rename the project — right-click the project name and click VBA Properties, then type a new project name — but it's completely unnecessary when you're a beginner in VBA.

To collapse or expand the list of Excel objects for a project, double-click the project name.

Modules

Modules only appear when you create VBA procedures (macros) for them to hold. A project can contain multiple module folders; Excel creates a new module every time you open a workbook and record a macro (but all the macros you record during a single Excel session are written to the same new module).

You can combine procedures (macros) from several modules into the same module by copying and pasting the routines from one module to another.

To display the code for a specific module, double-click the module. Macros in the open module appear in the Code window.

The Code window

The Code window (see Figure 21.10) displays all the routines and sub-routines for the open module (or other Excel object).

For our purposes, the important parts of a macro are the Sub line, the End Sub line, statements, and comments.

The Sub line

Every macro begins with a Sub line. *Sub* is a keyword that signals the beginning of a macro and is followed by the macro name (which you typed when you recorded the macro) and a pair of open parentheses.

If you must change the macro name for some reason, follow the macro naming rules and don't delete the parentheses. When you change a macro name, every object that depends on that name (such as objects to which you attached the macro) will be inoperative until you attach the new macro name.

Inside Scoop

The Procedure View and Full Module View buttons in the lower-left corner of the Code window switch between listing all of your macros and listing them one at a time. In Procedure View, select individual macros from the Procedure list box in the upper-right corner of the Code window.

Bright Idea

Use the recorder to learn what the code is for specific procedures (record the procedure and then read it in the Visual Basic Editor).

Procedure list box

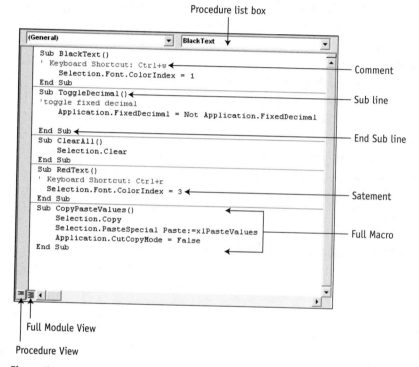

Figure 21.10. The Code window

The End Sub line

Every macro closes with an End Sub line. *End Sub* is a keyword that signals the end of the macro — don't mess with it.

Statements

Statements are the individual steps a macro follows — these are the parts you can edit or write yourself. Indents in statements are only for ease of reading and editing the procedure.

Comments

Comments (colored green and preceded by an apostrophe) are informational and don't affect the macro at all. Some are entered by the macro recorder, but you can erase them, edit them, and enter your own at will.

Any line preceded by an apostrophe becomes a green comment when you press Enter, and you can enter comments wherever you like (on their own lines, at the ends of statements, and so forth). Many programmers enter comments at the end of almost every statement, as a quick reminder of exactly what that statement is intended to do, so that later they can find and fix bugs in the code more quickly.

In Figure 21.10, I entered the keyboard shortcut comments myself, because if you don't create keyboard shortcuts when you first record the macro (which I didn't), the macro recorder doesn't write a keyboard shortcut comment. I created the keyboard shortcuts later—using the Macro dialog box Options button—and then wrote the reminder comments myself because I tend to forget keyboard shortcuts that I don't use every day.

The Visual Basic Editor Standard toolbar

In the Visual Basic Editor Standard toolbar (see Figure 21.11), the only important buttons for our purposes are View Microsoft Excel, Save, Run, and Reset. Those buttons are explained in Table 21.2.

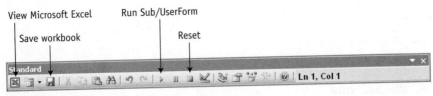

Figure 21.11. The Visual Basic Editor Standard toolbar

Table 21.2. Visual Basic Editor Standard toolbar buttons

Icon	Name	Function
![icon]	View Microsoft Excel	Switches you back to the Excel program window (the same as clicking the Microsoft Excel button in the taskbar). The Visual Basic Editor window stays open, and you can return to it quickly by clicking the Microsoft Visual Basic button in the toolbar or by clicking the Visual Basic Editor button on the Visual Basic toolbar.

Icon	Name	Function
💾	Save *workbookname*	Saves both your current changes in the Visual Basic Editor and the workbook. Whether you're in the Excel window or the Visual Basic Editor window, whenever you save one, you save both.
▶	Run Sub/UserForm	Runs the macro in which the cursor resides. Click anywhere in the macro code, then click Run Sub/UserForm to run that macro.
■	Reset	This button is for problems. If you run a macro and there's a bug, the Visual Basic Editor wants you to respond before it goes any further. The Reset button stops the whole process of running the macro and removes the yellow highlighting from the statement in error. If all you do is record macros and do some light editing, you'll probably never need the Reset button.

Editing a macro

After you record a macro, a little minor editing can make it even more useful. For example, I use a macro to turn on fixed-decimal entry by recording Tools ⇨ Options ⇨ Edit tab, Fixed decimal check box, OK. That's five clicks, and my macro performs it in a single click. But after I turn fixed-decimal entry on, I need to turn it off again — so I edit the macro into a toggle that turns the fixed-decimal setting on and off by clicking the same button.

Create a toggle macro

Any macro that turns on a feature that has only two settings — on and off — can be easily turned into a toggle macro. All you do is edit the macro to read "whatever this setting is, make it the other."

To make a macro into a toggle macro, follow these steps:

1. Record the macro.

2. Open the macro in the Visual Basic Editor (Figure 21.12 is my recorded fixed-decimal macro).

3. Replace the keyword *True* with the keyword *not*. (Don't type capital letters; if you spell the keyword correctly, Excel properly cases the word when you're done with the statement.)

Hack

If you get a Compile error and the statement turns red, click OK and ignore the red color. All will be normal when you finish the statement.

4. Copy the first part of the statement and paste it to the right of the keyword *not*. Be sure you type a space between the keyword and the pasted text.

5. Click at the end of the statement and press Enter. The finished toggle macro is shown in Figure 21.13.

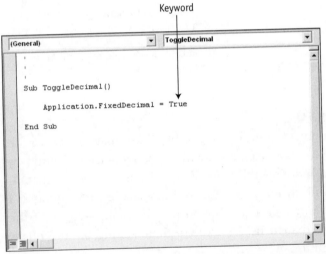

Figure 21.12. My fixed-decimal macro — the keyword, *True*, is blue.

Now you can test the macro: Maximize your Excel window, and then resize the Visual Basic Editor window smaller so you can see the Excel status bar below the Visual Basic Editor (see Figure 21.14). Click in the macro and then click the Run Sub/UserForm button on the Visual Basic Editor toolbar repeatedly — you see the word FIX (which indicates that fixed-decimal entry is on) appear and disappear in the right end of the Status bar every time you run the toggle macro.

Now all you need to do is attach the macro to a custom toolbar button and the toggle macro is always available.

Changed keyword

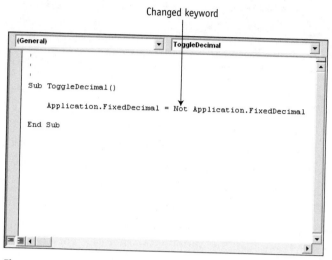

Figure 21.13. The keyword *Not* tells Excel to change this setting to its opposite.

Run the macro

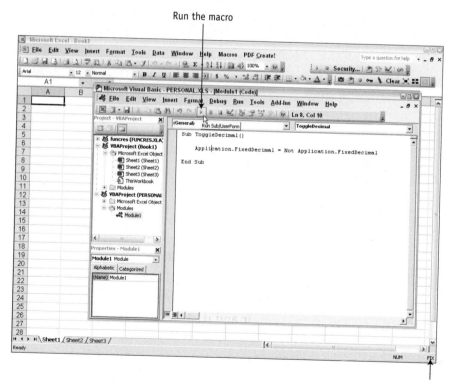

Fixed-decimal entry on

Figure 21.14. The Excel and Visual Basic Editor windows displayed together.

Hack

If you delete statements from a macro, or make any other changes, and suddenly the macro doesn't run or is buggy, click in the macro and press Ctrl+Z to replace or undo whatever you did. Press Ctrl+Z until the macro is returned to its original working condition, and start editing again.

Fix errors in a macro

If you record a macro to enter a text string in a specific cell, and discover later that the text string was misspelled or you need to change the specific cell where the entry was made, you don't need to re-record the macro. These are simple errors that you can edit in the macro.

1. Open the macro in the Visual Basic Editor (Figure 21.15 is a macro that enters a company name in the upper-left corner of a worksheet).

2. Type any changes you need as if you are typing in a Word document. In this example, I fixed the spelling error ("Statioery" to "Stationery") and changed the cell reference — Range("B2") to Range("A1"), and the active cell movement to the next cell down, Range("A2"), as shown in Figure 21.16.

3. Run the macro. If it works, save the macro and workbook (click the Save button in either the Excel window or the Visual Basic Editor).

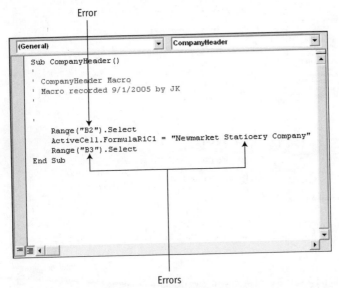

Figure 21.15. This macro has three errors — a misspelling in the text string, and the wrong cells.

Corrected

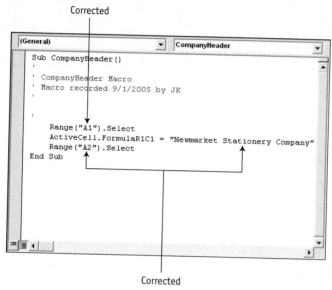

Corrected

Figure 21.16. The edited macro

Deleting a macro

After learning to use the macro recorder, you'll have experimental and test macros you don't need.

To delete a macro that's not in the Personal Macro Workbook, click the Run Macro button in the Visual Basic toolbar, click the macro name, and click Delete. When asked if you want to delete the macro, click Yes.

If the macro is in the Personal Macro Workbook, you must unhide the Personal Macro Workbook before you can use the Macro dialog box to delete macros.

Unhide the Personal Macro Workbook

To delete a macro that's in the Personal Macro Workbook, choose Window ⇨ Unhide; in the Unhide dialog box (shown in Figure 21.17), click PERSONAL.XLS and click OK. The Personal Macro Workbook is unhidden and is displayed in the Excel window (it is, or should be, empty). Now, click the Run Macro button on the Visual Basic toolbar, click the macro name, and click Delete. When asked if you want to delete the macro, click Yes.

Inside Scoop
You can use this method to delete a macro in the Personal Macro Workbook without unhiding the Personal Macro Workbook: If you work in the Visual Basic Editor and want to delete a macro, select the entire macro (from the Sub line to the End Sub line) and press Delete.

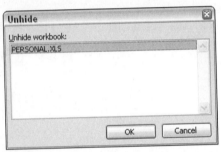

Figure 21.17. Unhiding a hidden Personal Macro Workbook

Hide the Personal Macro Workbook

To keep the Personal Macro Workbook hidden to protect it, be sure the Personal Macro Workbook is active (you should see PERSONAL.XLS in the Excel window title bar), and choose Window ⇨ Hide. After making any changes to the Personal Macro Workbook (such as storing a macro there), when you close Excel you may be asked to save the Personal Macro Workbook — click Yes.

Setting macro virus protection

A macro virus is a macro that can do some damage to a workbook — such as overwrite text or delete sections of data — when you perform an action that triggers the macro to run. Most macro viruses also spread to other workbooks on your computer or network, and if you don't realize you have one, you can unknowingly send it to others in e-mail and infect their computers.

Watch Out!
Always use a good antivirus and firewall program (don't rely on the Windows firewall). Be forewarned – there are some antivirus programs that are so zealous they can cripple your ability to work, and others that just aren't quite up to snuff. I like Norton AntiVirus by Symantec.

Because macro viruses spread so easily, Excel has protection built in that warns you if a macro is present before you open the file. This is a good thing that's also very annoying because Excel can't distinguish between dangerous macros from computer crackers and your own benign macros.

Fortunately, you can change the macro security settings to suit your comfort level. To change your security setting, click the Security button on the Visual Basic toolbar (or choose Tools ⇨ Macro ⇨ Security); click a security level (see Figure 21.18); and click OK.

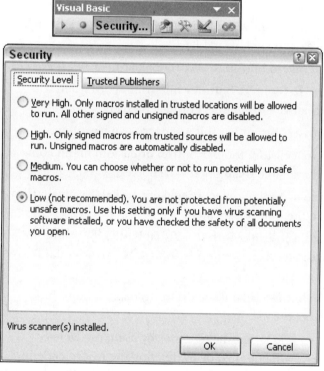

Figure 21.18. Set a security level you're comfortable with.

- **Very High.** Allows only macros from trusted locations to run and disables all others, even if they're signed.

- **High.** Allows only signed macros from trusted sources to run and disables all others. To run your own macros, you must have a digital signature and set it up as a trusted source.

- **Medium.** Warns you when you open a workbook that contains a macro and gives you the opportunity to enable or disable all macros in the workbook before you open it.

- **Low.** Allows all macros to run without any warnings. This is the setting I use because I rely on a good antivirus and firewall program, and I hate the intrusion of warnings about my own macros.

This book doesn't cover digital signatures and trusted sources — those subjects are thoroughly covered in other books that focus on VBA.

Just the facts

- To make macros easier, show the Visual Basic toolbar — right-click in the toolbar area and click Visual Basic.

- Click the Record Macro button to record a macro.

- Click the Relative References button while you record when you want to record relative movements of the active cell.

- Run a macro with a shortcut key if it's a macro you use often.

- Attach a macro to a custom toolbar button or custom menu command to make it available to all open workbooks.

- Attach a macro to a graphic object to make it available only on the worksheet where the object is located.

- Open the Visual Basic Editor with the Visual Basic Editor button on the Visual Basic toolbar, or choose Tools ⇨ Macro ⇨ Visual Basic Editor.

- Edit macro code in the Visual Basic Editor to make it more functional or to correct errors.

- Delete a macro you no longer need either by using the Delete button in the Macro dialog box, or by deleting the macro code in the Visual Basic Editor.

- Set the macro security level you're comfortable with in the Security dialog box.

Appendixes

PART IX

Glossary

Absolute reference   A cell reference that specifies the exact address of a cell. An absolute reference takes the form $A$1, $B$3, and so on.

Activate (Chart)   Select a chart for editing or formatting. To activate a chart sheet, click the sheet tab. To activate an embedded chart, click the chart.

Active cell   The selected cell. You can enter or edit data in the active cell.

Active sheet   The sheet that you are currently working on. When a sheet is active, the name on the sheet tab is bold.

Active window   The window that you are currently using or that is currently selected. Only one window can be active at a time, and keystrokes and commands affect the active window.

Add-In   Add-Ins are files that can be installed to add commands and functions to Excel.

Address   The location of a cell on a sheet. The cell address consists of a row address and a column address, such as F12, in which F is the sixth column on the sheet and 12 is the twelfth row on the sheet.

Argument   Information you supply to a function for calculation. An argument can be a value, reference, name, formula, or another function.

AutoComplete   An automated means of quick data entry that maintains data integrity; when you begin to type an entry that is similar to other entries in the column, Excel completes the entry for you (if that's not the entry you want, continue typing).

AutoCorrect   An automated means of quick data entry that corrects spelling mistakes; any misspelling that's listed

487

in the AutoCorrect dialog box is automatically corrected as you type. You can also use AutoCorrect to enter long phrases for you when you type an abbreviation.

AutoFill   AutoFill creates a series of incremental or fixed values on a worksheet when you drag the fill handle with the mouse.

Axes   Borders on the plot area that provide a frame of reference for measurement or comparison. On most charts, data values are plotted along the Y axis and categories are plotted along the X axis. On a typical column chart, the X axis is the horizontal axis and the Y axis is the vertical axis. Pie and Doughnut charts have no axes, Radar charts have a single central axis, and Scatter charts have two value axes. Some 3-D charts have three axes (X, Y, and Z) for values, categories, and series.

Boolean   Only two possible values: True or False. Any object or function that returns the values On/Off, Yes/No, I/O, and so forth is returning Boolean values. Check boxes are a worksheet control that returns only Boolean values (True/False).

Button control   A button that initiates an action when it is clicked.

Cell   The intersection of a column and a row.

Cell format   The visual aspect of a cell in a worksheet — number format, color, borders, and so forth.

Cell reference   The set of row and column coordinates that identify a cell location on a worksheet. Also referred to as the cell address.

Chart   A graphical representation of worksheet data. A chart can be embedded (an object on a worksheet) or it can be a chart sheet (a separate sheet in the workbook). Charts are linked to the data they are created from and are automatically updated when the data changes.

Chart area   The entire region surrounding the chart, just outside the plot area. When the chart area is selected, uniform font characteristics can be applied to all text in the chart.

Chart object   An embedded chart that is not selected and active. A chart object behaves like other graphical worksheet objects.

Chart sheet   A sheet in a workbook that contains only a chart.

Chart text   Text in a chart is either linked to worksheet data or unlinked. Unlinked text (for example, axis and chart titles, text boxes, and trend-line labels) can be added after creating a chart, then edited, formatted, and moved. Linked text (for example, legend entries, tick-mark labels, and data labels) is created from text or values in the source data.

Chart toolbar   The toolbar that contains buttons for the most common chart procedures.

Chart type   A chart type is a specific kind of chart. All Excel chart types are based on these basic chart types: Area, Bar, Column, Line, Pie, Doughnut, Radar, XY (scatter), 3-D area, 3-D bar, 3-D column, 3-D line, 3-D pie, 3-D doughnut, or 3-D surface. Each chart type has at least one subtype that is a variation of the original chart type.

ChartWizard   A series of dialog boxes that guides you through the steps required to create a new chart (or modify settings for an existing chart).

Check box control   A control that turns an option on or off; click to select the check box to turn the option on, and click to deselect the check box to turn the option off.

Circular reference   A formula that refers to its own cell, either directly or indirectly. Formulas containing circular references can be solved if iteration is turned on (choose Tools ⇨ Options, and click the Calculation tab).

Clipboard (Office or Windows)   A temporary holding area for data that is cut or copied. The data remains on the Clipboard until you clear the Clipboard or quit Excel. You can paste data in the Clipboard to another location, worksheet, workbook, or application.

Code window   The Visual Basic Editor window in which macro code is displayed, written, and edited.

Column   A vertical range of cells. Each column is identified by a unique letter or letter combination (for example, A, Z, CF).

Combo Box control   A text box with a drop-down list box. It is similar to a list box control (you can select a choice from the list), but it takes less room on the worksheet. (This book discusses only combo boxes that are not ActiveX controls.)

Command bar   Any toolbar or menu bar that holds buttons or menus/commands for performing actions or starting features.

Comment   A note that adds supplementary information to the data in a specific cell, without being a part of the worksheet.

Comparison Operator   A mathematical symbol used to compare two values (such as, =, >, <, =>, =<, <>).

Conditional formatting   Cell formatting that depends on the value in the cell.

Constant   A cell value that does not start with an equal sign. For example, the date, the value 345, and text are all constants.

Constraints   Limitations placed on a Solver problem. Constraints can be applied to changing cells, the target cell, or other cells directly or indirectly related to your problem.

Criteria   A set of search conditions used to find data in filters and queries. A criterion can be a series of characters you want matched, such as "March," or an expression, such as ">300."

Cursor   The flashing vertical line that shows where text is entered (for example, in a cell during in-cell editing). Also referred to as the insertion point.

Custom sort order   A non-alpha, non-numeric sort order, such as Low, Medium, High, or Monday, Tuesday, Wednesday. You can use one of the built-in custom sort orders or create your own choosing Tools ⇨ Options and the Custom Lists tab.

Data form   A temporary data entry form in which you can see, change, add, and delete records in a table one at a time. Display the data form for a list or table by choosing Data ⇨ Form.

Data label   A label that provides additional information about a data marker in a chart. Data labels can be applied to a single marker, an entire data series, or all data markers in a chart. Depending on the chart type, data labels can show values, names of data series (or categories), percentages, or a combination of these. They may be formatted and moved, but not sized.

Data marker   A bar, area, dot, slice, or other symbol in a chart that represents a single data point or value originating from a worksheet cell. Related data markers in a chart comprise a data series.

Data point   An individual value plotted in a chart that originates from a single cell in a worksheet. Data points are represented by bars, columns, lines, pie or doughnut slices, dots, and various other shapes. These shapes are called data markers.

Data series   A group of related data points in a chart that originates from a single worksheet row or column. Each data series in a chart is distinguished by a unique color or pattern. You can plot one or more data series in a chart, except for a pie chart, which is limited to one series.

Data source   The source of raw data for a chart, PivotTable, or query.

Default startup workbook   The new, unsaved workbook that is displayed when you start Excel. The default startup workbook is displayed only if you have not saved any workbooks in the XLSTART directory.

Delimiter   A hidden character, such as a space, tab, or paragraph mark character that separates rows (records) of data into columns (fields). When you import data from a text file such as a Word document, delimiters in the imported text determine how the imported text is parsed, or separated, into columns.

Dependent worksheet   A worksheet that contains a formula, PivotTable, or chart that draws values from another source. When two worksheets are linked, the dependent worksheet relies on a source worksheet for values. When you link a worksheet to a document in another application, the dependent worksheet relies on that source document for values.

Dependents   Cells with formulas that refer to (draw values from) the active cell.

Destination area   In a Consolidation, the range of cells you select to hold the summarized data. The destination area can be on the same worksheet as the source data, or it can be on a different worksheet.

Dialog box   A dialog box appears when you choose a command that requires additional information. It may include areas in which you type text or numbers, and view or change settings for options related to the command.

Discontiguous selection   A selection of two or more cells or ranges that do not touch each other (also known as noncontiguous or nonadjacent).

Docked toolbar   A toolbar that is attached to the top, bottom, or side of the program window.

Dynamic list   The new Excel 2003 list feature that adds AutoFilter buttons to the list headers and a Total row with a SUBTOTAL formula at the bottom.

Dynamic range   A range definition that changes as you add or delete rows and/or columns of data. The formula =OFFSET($A$1,0,0, COUNTA($A:$A),COUNTA($1:$1)) defines a dynamic range that begins in cell A1.

Embed   The process of creating or copying an object into another document. Objects can be embedded between documents within the same application, or between documents in different applications if both applications support the embedding process. An embedded object maintains a connection to its original application, so that you can open the original application and edit the embedded object by double-clicking the object.

Embedded chart   A chart object that has been placed on a worksheet. When a chart object is selected, you can move and resize it; when it's activated, you can select items and add data. You can also move, format, and resize items in the chart, depending on the item. Embedded charts are linked to source data and are updated when the source data changes.

Empty text   Text without characters, or null text; for example, a pair of quotes with nothing between them ("").

Enter   You manually enter data in a cell when you type and then press Enter, Tab, or an arrow key, or click in a different cell. Using any of the non-typing data entry techniques, such as AutoFill, AutoCorrect, AutoComplete, and Pick From List, also enters data in a cell.

External reference   In a formula, a reference to a cell, range, or named area in a different worksheet or workbook.

Field   A column in a database. Each field (column) in a database contains a unique category of data, and each cell in a database shares a common characteristic with other cells in the same field (column).

Fill color   The background color of a cell or a graphic object.

Fill handle   The small black square in the lower-right corner of the selected cell or range. When you position the mouse pointer over the fill handle, the pointer changes to a black cross. Drag the fill handle to copy contents to adjacent cells or to create a series. Right-dragging the fill handle displays a shortcut menu.

Filtering   Hiding all data that doesn't meet specific criteria.

Floating toolbar   A toolbar that is not docked at the edges of the application window. A floating toolbar stays on top of all Excel windows within the program window.

Font   A collection of letters, numbers, and special characters that share a consistent and identifiable typeface, such as Arial or Times New Roman.

Font color   The color of characters displayed in a cell.

Forms toolbar   The toolbar that holds the buttons for creating worksheet controls (not ActiveX controls).

Formula A sequence of values, cell references, names, functions, or operators that is contained in a cell and produces a new value from existing values. A formula always begins with an equal sign (=).

Formula bar A bar above the worksheet in which you type or edit values and formulas in cells or charts; displays the formula or constant value from the active cell or object.

Function A built-in formula that uses a series of values (arguments) to perform an operation and returns the result of that operation. You can use the Function Wizard to select a function, fill in the arguments, get help with the function, and enter it into a cell.

General number format General is the default number format for all cells on a new worksheet. In the General format, Excel displays numbers using integer format (for example, 125), decimal fraction format (for example, 125.42), or scientific notation (for example, 125E+07) if the number is longer than the width of the cell. The General format displays up to 11 digits, numbers are right-aligned, text is left-aligned, and logical and error values are centered. When you enter data into a cell formatted as General, Excel usually assigns another built-in format (such as Date) based on what you enter.

Global A setting or procedure that applies throughout a worksheet, workbook, or document. For example, if you click Replace All in the Find and Replace dialog box (to replace all instances of a specific word in a worksheet or document), you run a global find-and-replace procedure.

Goal seek A tool for finding the input value a formula needs in order to return a specific result. You can enter your goal value, select the variable that you want to change, and then let Excel find the input value that returns your goal result.

Graphic object A line or shape (button, text box, ellipse, rectangle, arc, picture) you draw using the tools on the toolbar, or a picture you paste into Excel.

Gridlines (Chart) Lines on a chart that extend from the tick marks on an axis across the plot area. Gridlines come in various forms: horizontal, vertical, major, minor, and combinations. They make it easier to view and evaluate data in a chart.

Group In an outline or PivotTable, one or more detail rows or columns that are adjacent and subordinate to a summary row or column.

Group box control   A control composed of a bordered area containing a group of option buttons, only one of which can be selected at a time. A group box serves to segregate groups of option buttons from other option buttons in a worksheet or form, as well as visually segregating controls for easier reading.

Handles   Small black squares located around the perimeter of selected graphic objects, chart items, or chart text. By dragging the handles, you can move, copy, or resize the selected object, chart item, or chart text.

Hardcode   Specific, nondynamic data or settings that will not change, such as specific numbers in a formula or VBA procedure. See *Static.*

Hyperlink   Word, phrase, or icon that is a link to another file or Web page; when you click a hyperlink, the linked file or Web page opens. Hyperlinks are usually colored and underlined.

Insertion point   A flashing vertical line that shows the text entry point. Also known as the cursor.

Iteration   Repeated calculation of the worksheet until a specific numeric condition is met. When iteration (choose Tools ⇨ Options, and click the Calculation tab) is turned on, Excel can solve formulas containing circular references. Also, Goal Seek and the Solver add-in use iteration to solve problems.

Keyword   A VBA programming word that has a specific meaning in the Visual Basic Editor, such as Not, True, False, Sub, and End Sub. Keywords, when spelled correctly, appear in blue in completed statements in a macro.

Label control   A worksheet control consisting of text you provide for the user, including control names, instructions, and cautions.

Legend   A box containing legend entries and keys that help to identify the data series or categories in a chart. The legend keys, to the left of each entry, show the patterns and colors assigned to the data series or categories in the chart.

Link   A data connection between a dependent worksheet (the worksheet that uses the data) and a source worksheet (the worksheet in which the original data resides). Because of the link, the dependent worksheet is updated whenever the data changes in the source worksheet. You can link graphics, text, and other types of information between a source file and a dependent file.

Linked picture   A picture object that's linked to a specific range of cells or to a specific part of a file in another program. A linked picture is dynamic; it always reflects (or can be updated to reflect) the current contents of the source range or file.

List   A range of cells containing data that is related to a particular subject or purpose. The terms table and list are used interchangeably. (Similar but not to be confused with the new Excel 2003 "list," which I refer to as a dynamic list.)

List box control   A worksheet control that displays a list of items from which a user can choose a value.

Logical group (option button control)   A group of values that's exclusive to a group of option buttons. When option buttons are not enclosed in a group box control, all the option buttons on the worksheet are part of the same logical group; when option buttons are enclosed in a group box control, those grouped option buttons are part of a logical group that's separate from the rest of the worksheet.

Macro   A sequence of VBA commands in a module. You can write or record a macro, then run the macro to automate your work. A macro can be assigned to a shortcut key, button, or object for easy use.

Mixed reference   In a formula, a combination of a relative reference and an absolute reference. A mixed reference takes the form $A1 or A$1, where A is the column cell address and 1 is the row cell address. The dollar sign ($) denotes the absolute portion of the reference.

Module   The part of a workbook's VBA Project in which general macros are stored. All recorded macros are stored in modules, and macros written without the recorder are usually stored in modules. Macros attached to worksheets, workbooks, controls, and userforms are not stored in modules; instead, they are attached to the specific object.

Moving average   A sequence of averages computed from adjacent points in a data series. In a chart, a moving average smoothes the fluctuations in data, thus showing the pattern or trend more clearly.

Name   A unique identifier you create to refer to one or more cells, a formula, or an object. When you use names in a formula, the formula is easier to read and maintain than a formula containing cell references.

Named formula   A formula that's given a name in the Define Name dialog box; a formula name can be used in place of a lengthy formula in a cell, and is the only means of redirecting a linked picture to alternate pictures.

Nested functions   Functions that serve as arguments within other functions/formulas; the inner (contained) functions are called *nested*. Functions can be nested seven levels deep in a formula.

Nested subtotals   Multiple levels of subtotals within a table that provide additional levels of detail.

Node (Visual Basic Editor)   The icon in the Project window with which you navigate to code in a specific part of a VBA Project.

Normal style   The style used by all cells on worksheets until another style is applied.

Option button control   A button for selecting one of a group of mutually exclusive options. Place two or more option buttons in a Group Box to group them and segregate them from other option buttons in a worksheet.

Outline   A summary report of worksheet data that contains up to eight nested levels of detail data and summary data for each level of detail. The user can change the view of the outline to show or hide as much detail as needed.

Page change (scroll bar control)   The incremental jump in value produced by clicking in the middle of a scroll bar instead of on one of the scroll buttons.

Pane   Panes allow you to view different areas of a large worksheet simultaneously. You can horizontally or vertically split a window into two panes or split a window both vertically and horizontally to display four panes, and you can freeze panes to keep some data frozen in view while you scroll through the rest of the worksheet.

Parse   To separate imported data into discrete columns in a worksheet. Parsing is accomplished by setting delimiter characters during the text import process.

Password   A secret word or expression that prevents access to a protected item by unauthorized users.

Personal macro workbook   A hidden workbook that contains macros that are available every time you start Excel and in every open workbook. When you record a macro, you can choose to save it into your personal macro workbook.

Pick from list   An automated means of quick data entry that maintains data integrity; when you right-click a cell and click Pick From List, you see a list of all the entries in that column, and can click an entry to enter it in the cell.

Picture   A linked image of a range of cells. When the contents of the cells change, the picture or image also changes. Take a picture of a selected cell or range using the Camera tool (in the Tools category in the Customize dialog box).

PivotTable   An interactive worksheet table that summarizes data from existing databases, lists, and tables. Use the PivotTable Wizard to specify the database, list, or table you want to use, and to arrange the data in the PivotTable. Once you create a PivotTable, you can reorganize the data by dragging fields and items.

PivotTable column field   A field that is assigned a column orientation in a PivotTable. Items associated with a column field are displayed as column labels.

PivotTable data area   The part of a PivotTable that contains summary data. Values in each cell of the data area represent a summary of data from the source records or rows.

PivotTable data area label   In a PivotTable, the cell in the upper-left corner that identifies the source field for the data area and the function used to calculate the values of cells. For example, a data label for a data area calculated using the default summary function in the Sales field reads "Sum of Sales."

PivotTable data field   A field in a source list or table that contains data you want summarized in a PivotTable. A data field usually contains numeric data, such as statistics or sales amounts, but it can also contain text values. Data from a data field is summarized in the data area of a PivotTable.

PivotTable detail item   An item associated with an inner row or column field in a PivotTable.

PivotTable field   A category of data that is derived from a field in a source list or table. For example, the Year field in a source list or database becomes the Year field in a PivotTable. Items from the source list or table, such as 2004, 2005, and so on, become subcategories in the PivotTable.

PivotTable grand totals   Total values for all cells in a row or all cells in a column of a PivotTable. Values in a grand total row or column are calculated using the same summary function used in the data area of the PivotTable.

PivotTable item   A subcategory of a PivotTable field. Items in a PivotTable are derived from unique items in a database field or from unique cells in a list column. In a PivotTable, items appear as row, column, or page labels.

PivotTable page field   A field that is assigned to a page orientation in a PivotTable, in the upper-left corner above the PivotTable. Only one item in a page field is displayed in a PivotTable.

PivotTable row field   A field that is assigned a row orientation in a PivotTable. Items associated with a row field are displayed as row labels.

PivotTable subtotal   A row or column that displays the total of detail items in a PivotTable field, using a summary function you choose.

Plot area   The area of a chart in which data is plotted. In 2-D charts, it is bounded by the axes and encompasses the data markers and gridlines. In 3-D charts, the plot area includes the chart's walls, axes, and tick-mark labels.

Precedents   Cells that are referred to by the formula in the active cell.

Precision   The number of digits Excel uses when calculating values. By default, Excel calculates with a maximum of 15 digits of a value (full precision). If Precision As Displayed is selected (choose Tools ⇨ Options, and click the Calculation tab), Excel rounds values to the number of digits displayed on the worksheet before calculating. Numbers in General format are always calculated with full precision, regardless of the Precision As Displayed setting.

Print area   The area of a worksheet that is specified to be printed.

Print titles   Worksheet rows and/or columns that are printed at the top or left of every page. For example, if you select row 1 for a print title, row 1 values are printed on the top of every page. If you select column A for a print title, column A values are printed in the left column of every page. Print titles are part of the worksheet, not in the margin like headers and footers.

Procedure (VBA)   See *Macro*.

Project (VBA)   See *VBA Project*.

Project window   The Visual Basic Editor window in which the object, module, and userform nodes for each open workbook are listed. You navigate to the code in different parts of a VBA Project by double-clicking nodes in the Project window.

Query definition Information that Microsoft Query uses to connect to and determine which data to retrieve from a data source. A query definition can include table names, field names, and criteria. A query definition is sent to a data source for execution in the form of a Structured Query Language (SQL) statement.

Query In Microsoft Query, a means of finding the records that answer a particular question you ask about the data stored in a data source.

Range Two or more cells on a sheet. Ranges can be contiguous or non-contiguous.

Record A single row in a list or table. The first row of a table usually contains field names, and each additional row in the database is a record. Each record in the table contains the same categories (fields) of data as every other record in the table.

Reference The location of a cell or range of cells on a worksheet, indicated by column letter and row number. For example, B2 and C3:D4 are references.

Reference style The method used to identify cells in a worksheet. In the A1 reference style, columns are lettered and rows are numbered. In the R1C1 reference style, R indicates row and C indicates column, and both rows and columns are numbered.

Reference type The type of reference: absolute, relative, or mixed. A relative reference (for example, A1) in a formula indicates the location of the referenced cell relative to the cell containing the formula. An absolute reference (for example, $A$1) always refers to the exact location of the referenced cell. A mixed reference (for example, $A1; A$1) is half relative and half absolute.

Refresh Update a pivot table or a query.

Regression analysis A form of statistical analysis used for forecasting. Regression analysis estimates the relationship between variables so that a new variable can be predicted from existing variables.

Relative reference Specifies the location of a referenced cell in relation to the cell containing the reference. A relative reference takes the form A4, C12, and so on (no dollar signs).

Result cell   A cell on the worksheet that is recalculated when a new scenario is applied.

Result set   The set of records that results from running a query.

Route   Send a workbook through e-mail to one or more other users, and have the workbook send itself to the next person on the list (or back to you) when the current user sends it to the next recipient.

Row   A horizontal set of cells. Each row is identified by a unique number.

R-squared value   In regression analysis, a calculated value that indicates how valid the correlation between two sets of data is for interpolating or extrapolating new data points.

Scale   In a chart, the scale determines what value tick-mark labels are displayed on an axis, at what intervals the values occur, and where one axis crosses another. You can make changes to an axis scale by choosing Format ⇨ Axis and clicking the Scale tab.

Scenario   A named set of input values that you can substitute in a worksheet model to perform a what-if analysis.

Scenario manager   A feature that allows you to create, view, and summarize scenarios.

Scroll bar control   A worksheet control that looks like a scroll bar, used for changing a displayed value in specified increments.

Scroll bars   The shaded bars along the right side and bottom of the Excel window. With the scroll bars, you can scroll from top to bottom in a long sheet, or from side to side in a wide sheet.

Scroll lock   With Scroll Lock on, the arrow keys move the active sheet, column by column and row by row, rather than moving the active cell within the worksheet.

Secondary axis   In a chart with more than one series, a secondary axis allows you to plot a series or a chart type group along a different value axis, so that you can create two different value scales in the same chart.

Sheet tab shortcut menu   A shortcut menu containing commands relative to Excel sheets. To display the sheet tab shortcut menu, right-click a sheet tab.

Shortcut menu   A menu that shows a list of commands relative to the selected item. To display the shortcut menu for an item, right-click the item.

Solver An add-in program that calculates solutions to complex problems based on adjustable cells, constraint cells, and, optionally, cells that must be maximized or minimized. You must install the Solver add-in before you can use Solver.

Sort key The field name or criteria by which you want to sort data.

Sort order An arrangement of data based on value or data type. An ascending sort order sorts text from A to Z, numbers from the smallest negative number to the largest positive number, and dates and times from the earliest to the latest. A descending sort order is the opposite of an ascending sort order, except for blanks, which are always sorted last. If you choose a custom sort order, an ascending sort order is the order in which the items appear in the Sort Options dialog box.

Source data for PivotTables The list, database, or table used to create a PivotTable. Source data can be an Excel list or database, an external data source such as a dBase or Microsoft Access file, Excel worksheet ranges with labeled rows and columns, or another PivotTable.

Source worksheet The worksheet referred to by an external reference formula. The source worksheet contains the value used by the external reference formula.

Spinner control A worksheet control composed of a pair of arrow buttons for increasing or decreasing a displayed value in specified increments.

Split bar The horizontal or vertical line dividing a split worksheet. You can change the position of the split bar by dragging it, or remove the split bar by double-clicking it.

Standard font The default text font for worksheets. The standard font is the default font for the Normal cell style. You can change the standard font by choosing Tools ⇨ Options, and clicking the General tab.

Startup directory A directory named XLSTART in which you save workbooks or other files that you want to open automatically when you start Excel. Templates placed in this directory are not opened automatically, but are listed in the New dialog box (displayed by choosing File ⇨ New).

Static An entry that is not dynamic (that is, does not change when data in the worksheet changes). For example, a formula that calculates a specific tax rate (rather than referencing a cell that contains the tax rate) calculates a static tax rate argument. See *Hardcode.*

Status bar   The bar at the bottom of the screen that displays information about the selected command or tool, or an operation in progress.

Structured query language (SQL)   A language used for retrieving, updating, and managing data.

Style   A named combination of formats that can be applied to a cell or range. If you redefine the style to be a different combination of formats, all cells to which the style was applied will automatically change to reflect the new formats. A style can include (or exclude) formats for number, font, alignment, borders, patterns, and protection.

Summary function   A type of calculation that you direct Excel to use when combining source data in a PivotTable or a consolidation table, or when inserting automatic subtotals in a list or database. Examples of summary functions include Sum, Count, and Average.

Table   Data about a specific topic that is stored in records (rows) and fields (columns). Also known as a list.

Target cell   The cell that you want Solver to set to a minimum, maximum, or specific value by adjusting the changing cells defined in the problem. The target cell should contain a formula that depends, directly or indirectly, on the changing cells.

Template   A workbook that you create and then use as the starting point for new workbooks. Template filenames end in .xlt.

Text box   A rectangular graphical object in which you can type text.

Tick marks   In a chart, small lines that intersect an axis like divisions on a ruler. Tick marks are part of and can be formatted with an axis.

Tick-mark labels   Labels that identify the categories, values, and series in a chart. They come from and are automatically linked to cells in the worksheet selection. They can be formatted like other chart text.

Title bar   The bar across the top of the main application window that contains the program name, Microsoft Excel, and the active workbook name.

Toolbar   A bar on which buttons reside. You can rearrange any toolbar or create new toolbars by adding, deleting, or rearranging buttons.

Trendline   A graphical representation of a mathematical trend in data. Trendlines are used to study problems of prediction, also called regression analysis.

Trendline label   Optional text for a trendline, including either the regression equation or the R-squared value, or both. A trendline label may be formatted and moved; it cannot be sized.

Unattached text (floating text)   Text that is not linked to a chart object and can be moved anywhere on the chart. A text box is an example of unattached text.

VBA (Visual Basic for Applications)   VBA is the programming language for Microsoft Office programs.

VBA Project   The container for all the VBA code in a specific workbook.

Web query   A query to extract data from a Web page into an Excel worksheet. As long as the Web page doesn't change, the data can be refreshed as often as you like without rebuilding the query.

Wildcard character   A character (? or *) that stands in for one or more other characters in search criteria when finding or filtering data. An asterisk (*) represents any number of characters. A question mark (?) represents any single character in the same position as the question mark. To search for a literal question mark or asterisk, precede it with a tilde (~). For example, to search for an asterisk, search for ~*.

Workbook   An Excel file. It contains at least one worksheet or chart sheet.

Working directory   The directory that Excel first makes available to you when you choose File ⇨ Save As or File ⇨ Open.

Worksheet   The primary document you use in Excel to store and manipulate data. A worksheet consists of cells organized into columns and rows, and is always part of a workbook.

X axis   The category axis in a chart. On most charts, categories are plotted along the X axis. On a typical column chart, the X axis is the horizontal axis.

XY (scatter) chart   A 2-D chart that has numeric values plotted along both axes, rather than values along one axis and categories along the other axis. This type of chart is typically used to analyze scientific data to see whether one set of values is related to another set of values.

Y axis   The data axis in a chart. On most charts, data values are plotted along the Y axis. On a typical column chart, the Y axis is the vertical axis. When a secondary axis is added, it is a secondary Y axis.

Recommended Resources

Books

These are books about Excel that I use and find useful.

Excel Hacks — 100 Industrial-Strength Tips and Tools

A great accessory book once you get a handle on Excel. Lots of stuff you already know, but there are gems in this book (and things you didn't know you wanted to do) waiting to be discovered.

Microsoft Excel 2002 Visual Basic for Applications Step by Step

A great course in beginner Excel VBA programming. Don't let the version 2002 throw you — VBA has not changed since Excel 2002.

Master Visually Excel 2003 VBA Programming

My beginner-to-intermediate level book about VBA programming in Excel. Good for a nonscary, easy-to-follow introduction to VBA in small bites, and a quick reference for simple-but-important VBA procedures such as conditions and loops.

Appendix A

Excel for Scientists and Engineers

A great book that focuses on data analysis, number-crunching, and "what-if" scenarios. Written for scientists and engineers, but lots of non-scientists and nonengineers find it extremely useful, even if they're not Excel masters. Out of print, but you can find it from used booksellers online (expensive now because it's so terrific).

Excel 2003 Bible

A compendium of all things Excel 2003, in great detail and very well written. The Bible covers the more in-depth topics that this book doesn't cover.

Internet sites

Here's a selection of Web sites that are safe, free, and full of interesting stuff for Excel, Windows, and more.

Google

www.google.com

This is my home page because I use it so much. It's not just for shopping — you can Google words for definitions, computer drivers to find updates, phone numbers to locate and research people, and just about anything else you can think of.

Excel 2003 Review (and Excel in general)

www.j-walk.com/ss/excel/xl2003.htm

John Walkenbach's Excel site, which includes a great review of the disappointments in the Excel 2003 upgrade (with which I totally agree), but more useful are the loads of tips, oddities, and minutiae you can access from the navigation pane on the left side of the Web page.

FOLDOC (Free Online Computing Dictionary)

http://foldoc.doc.ic.ac.uk/foldoc

This is a great Web site for quickly looking up computer terminology and acronyms.

OnlineConversion.com

www.onlineconversion.com

If you think the Excel CONVERT function is too much trouble (it's in the Analysis Toolpak add-in), give this Web site a try. It converts just about anything to anything else (more than 5,000 units and 50,000 conversions).

Microsoft

http://office.microsoft.com

This is the Microsoft site for all things Microsoft, including downloads of extra stuff and updates for your Microsoft programs.

Annoyances.org

www.annoyances.org

The Annoyances site has long been a good place to find fixes for annoying things in all versions of Windows.

Build Creative Worksheets

I find Excel most useful when I combine features and formulas to create functionality that goes well beyond what any single feature can accomplish. In this appendix, I show you how to create three real-life worksheets (worksheets I created for myself and for clients): a checkbook calculator (that I use at least weekly), a time-log that gives the user a very quick way to track actual hours worked, and a presentation worksheet in which you can switch charts by clicking option buttons.

You probably won't need any of these specific worksheets, but they are full of ideas you can adapt for your own worksheets.

All the features in these worksheets have been covered elsewhere in this book, and I won't be leading you step-by-step through features covered elsewhere (although there are a couple of macros that I didn't cover in Chapter 21 that I tell you step-by-step how to write).

Checkbook calculator

I'm one of those people who has a meltdown if my checkbook isn't balanced. I used to calculate running balances on an empty worksheet, but then I designed this worksheet (see Figure B.1) just for balancing my checkbook. It's dedicated, easy to get to, and quick to use.

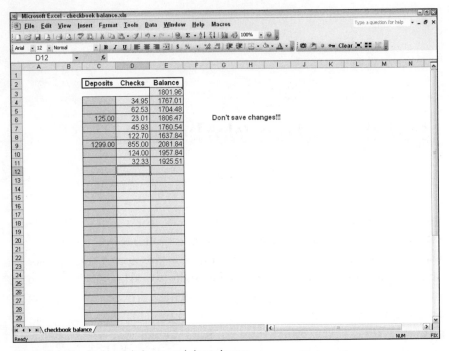

Figure B.1. My checkbook balance worksheet, in use

This single-worksheet workbook uses formulas to calculate the running balance, and macros to turn fixed-decimal entry on when the workbook opens and turn fixed-decimal entry off when the workbook is closed. It also uses a macro to close the workbook "quietly," without saving changes or asking you to save changes, so that every time you open it you get a clean, ready-to-use worksheet.

When I open this workbook, it opens with fixed-decimal entry on; I start by entering the current balance in the topmost cell in the Balance column. Then I enter all my check and check card amounts in the Checks column, and deposits in the Deposits column (I don't bother with dates — this is just a temporary record for balancing my checkbook). Because fixed-decimal entry is turned on, I never type the decimal

> **Watch Out!**
> Never save changes when you use this worksheet; if you save changes while you work in the worksheet, the workbook won't open clean and ready to use the next time you open it.

Bright Idea

To keep your eyes focused on the correct number as you read down a long list of numbers, select the entire column of numbers, and press Enter to move the highlighted active cell down the column as you transcribe each number. The highlighting helps draw your eyes to the correct cell.

point—just the numbers. Be sure to type the zeroes when you enter a whole-dollar amount.

When I finish entering the check and deposit amounts from my checkbook, I transcribe the numbers from the balance column back into my checkbook.

When I finish balancing my checkbook, I close the workbook. I don't ever save it while I work in it—my "Don't Save Changes" note reminds me not to—and when I close it, I'm not asked to save. When the workbook closes, a macro turns off fixed-decimal entry in Excel.

Build the worksheet

Okay, now that you know what this worksheet does, I'll show you how to build it.

1. Enter the table headings and format the first few rows (see Figure B.2). Leave the row below the headings blank (the first cell below the Balance heading is where you enter the starting balance each time you use the worksheet).

Figure B.2. Enter table headings.

2. In the second row below the headings, in the Balance column, enter the formula **=IF(AND(ISBLANK(D4),ISBLANK(C4)),"",E3-D4+C4)**, as shown in Figure B.3. The formula reads "If the Checks cell and Deposits cell to the left are both blank, display nothing, otherwise calculate the Balance cell above minus the Checks cell to the left plus the Deposits cell to the left."

This running balance formula uses relative references, and this particular formula assumes that the table is positioned on the worksheet as shown in Figure B.3, with the table headers beginning in cell C2. If your table is positioned elsewhere, you need to modify the references in the formula.

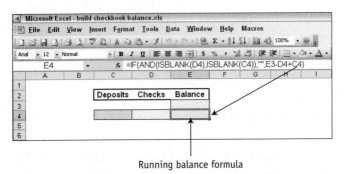

Running balance formula

Figure B.3. This formula calculates a running balance when data is entered in either of the other two columns.

3. Use AutoFill to fill the formula down the column (make the list as long as you like).

4. Use Format Painter to paint the formatting from the second row (borders, colors, whatever you choose) down the length of the list.

5. Make yourself a reminder comment in the starting Balance cell, and a Don't Save Changes reminder entry on the worksheet, as shown in Figure B.4.

6. Save the workbook and give it a memorable name, such as Checkbook Balance.

Bright Idea

The list length is changeable; when you use the worksheet, if you need to make the list longer, just use AutoFill and Format Painter to make it longer. When you close the workbook without saving, the list returns to its original length.

7. Enter a starting balance and a few checks and deposits to test the formulas, then delete the test data (be careful not to delete the formulas in the Balance column).

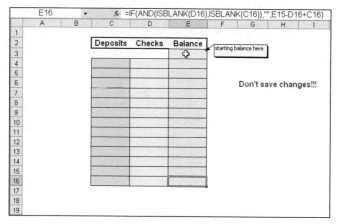

Figure B.4. Add reminders to the worksheet.

Write the macros

The workbook needs two short macros that cannot be recorded, only written. They turn on fixed-decimal entry when the workbook opens; when the workbook closes, they turn off fixed-decimal entry and close the workbook "quietly" without saving.

1. Open the Visual Basic Editor.

2. In the Project window (see Figure B.5), you should see the VBA Project for this workbook. Open the Microsoft Excel Objects node to display the This Workbook node, and double-click This Workbook.

3. In the Object list box above the Code window (see Figure B.6), select Workbook. A Workbook_Open macro starts for you automatically. Any statements you write in this macro run automatically every time the workbook opens.

Watch Out!

Don't make any changes in the Private Sub Workbook_Open line. If you change anything in this line, the macro won't work.

Workbook name

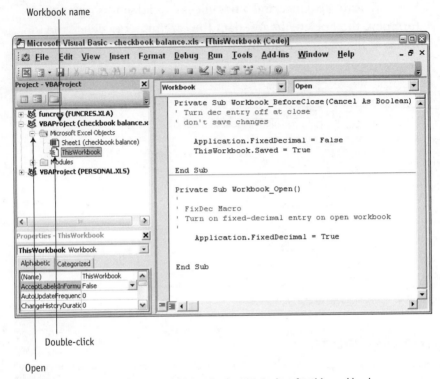

Double-click

Open

Figure B.5. Open the This Workbook object in the VBA Project for this workbook.

Object list box

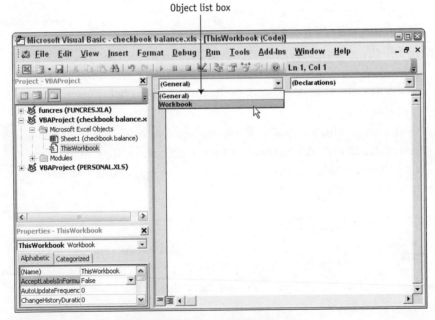

Figure B.6. Select the Workbook object in the Object list box.

4. Click in the line between the Sub line and the End Sub line, and type the statement **Application.FixedDecimal = True** (see Figure B.7).

When you type the statement, the Visual Basic Editor helps by giving you AutoLists of appropriate objects for whatever you typed. For example, type **application.** After you type the period, an AutoList appears. Type **fix**, and the AutoList jumps to FixedDecimal. Double-click FixedDecimal — the list enters FixedDecimal and disappears. Type the equal sign (=) and another AutoList appears. Double-click True and click away from the line to finish the statement.

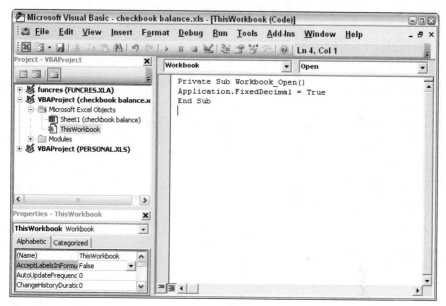

Figure B.7. This macro turns on fixed-decimal entry when the workbook opens.

5. Open the Procedure list box (see Figure B.8), and click BeforeClose. The Private Sub Workbook_BeforeClose(Cancel As Boolean) macro appears at the top of the Code window.

Inside Scoop

You can give yourself more room to work by pressing Enter to create new blank lines in the macro; blank lines don't affect the macro at all. And you can type the entire statement yourself and ignore the AutoLists — they are helpful but optional.

Watch Out!
Don't make any changes in the Private Sub Workbook_BeforeClose(Cancel As Boolean) line. If you make any changes in this line, the macro won't work.

Procedure list box

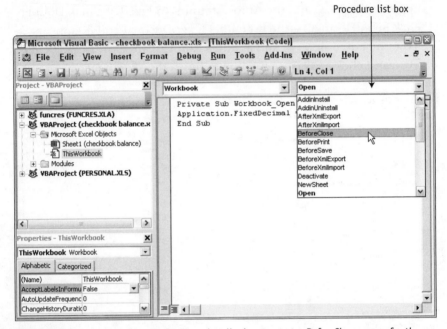

Figure B.8. Select BeforeClose in the Procedure list box to start a BeforeClose macro for the workbook.

6. In the BeforeClose macro, enter two statements:
   Application.FixedDecimal = False and **ThisWorkbook.Saved = True**
   (see Figure B.9).

   These statements turn off fixed-decimal entry and close the workbook without asking you to save just before the workbook closes.

7. Click the Save *workbook* button on the toolbar, and close the Visual Basic Editor.

8. Test the worksheet. Enter a starting balance and some checks and deposits, and then close the workbook (without saving or deleting data).

9. Open the workbook again. It should open clean, with fixed-decimal entry turned on.

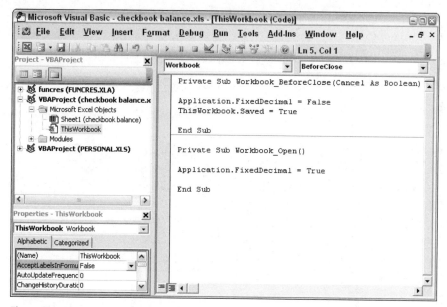

Figure B.9. These two statements run just before the workbook closes.

One last thing to make the worksheet easy to open quickly: Place a shortcut to the workbook on your desktop. Open the folder where you saved the workbook, and right-click-and-drag the workbook icon from the folder to your desktop. When you release the mouse button, select Create Shortcuts Here on the shortcut menu.

Time-log template

I have a client who is an independent contractor and needs to keep precise records of the time he spends on the job. He wanted a worksheet in which he could click to mark ten-minute time blocks or click to unmark them, and have the worksheet automatically total his marked time blocks for each day and for the week.

Yes, he could just type an **X** in cells in a worksheet grid and total them with COUNT formulas, but that was too much trouble. He wanted

Inside Scoop

In this worksheet, I must use the arrow keys to select cells beneath the check boxes; I can't click to select cells because they are completely covered by the check box controls (which is unavoidable but also protects the underlying cell values).

to just click with the mouse to mark and unmark, and have everything else automatic.

Shown in Figure B.10 is my solution (and he likes it).

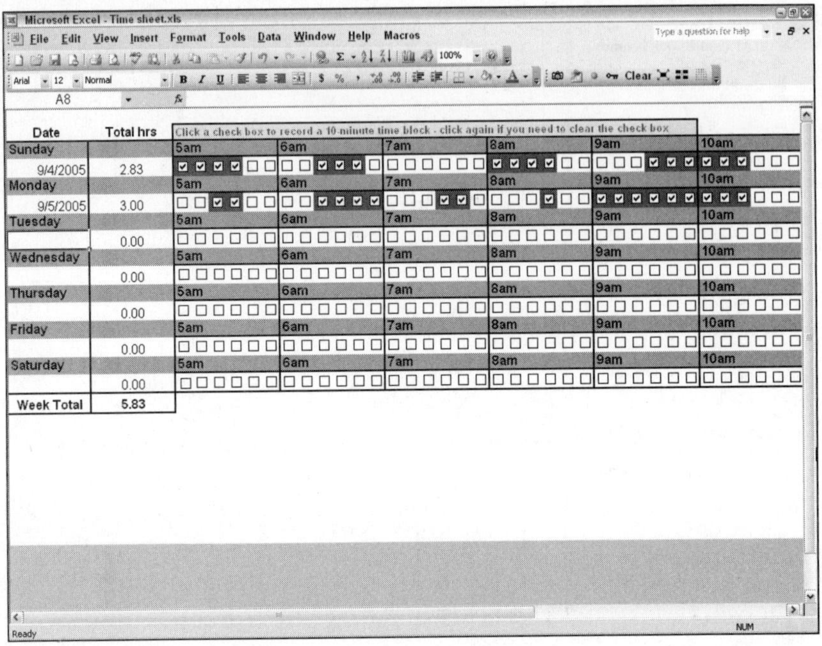

Figure B.10. Click a time block to mark it or unmark it.

There's no VBA programming involved in this worksheet—just formulas, check boxes, and conditional formatting.

Each check box is linked (and fitted) to the cell directly beneath it, and each cell is conditionally formatted to turn red when the value is TRUE (see Figure B.11) but returns to uncolored when the value is FALSE.

The formulas that total each day's hours are COUNTIF formulas that count the number of cells that have the value TRUE and multiply that count by 0.166667 (which is the date/time serial number value for ten minutes). The weekly hours total sums the daily hours totals.

The cells beneath the check boxes, the cells for entering dates, and the cells with formulas are unlocked so that their values can change, and then the worksheet is protected so that the check boxes cannot be inadvertently selected and moved.

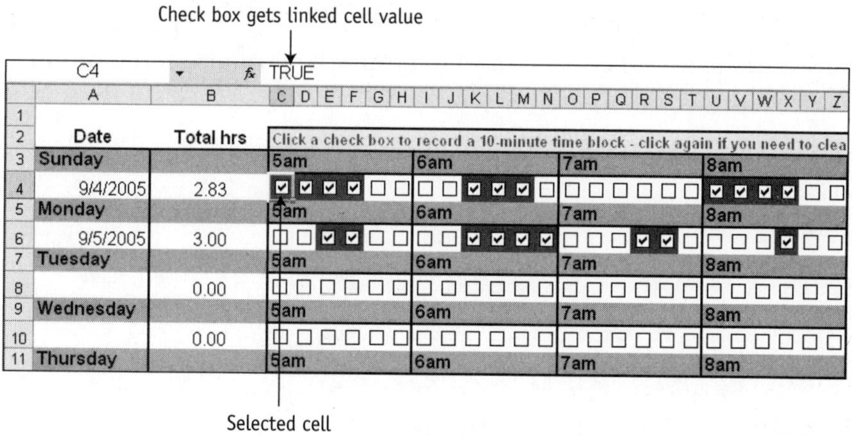

Check box gets linked cell value

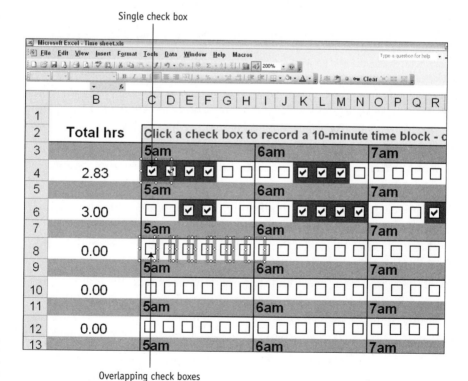

Selected cell

Figure B.11. Marking the check box turns the linked cell beneath it red.

Figure B.12 shows a close-up view of the relationship between the check boxes and the cells whose values they control.

Single check box

Overlapping check boxes

Figure B.12. Each check box is centered over the cell beneath it (the control borders overlap one another).

To create this worksheet, follow these steps:

1. Set up the worksheet grid in which you write formulas and position check boxes, as shown in Figure B.13.

	A	B	C	D	E	F	G	H	I	J	K	L	M	N	O	P	Q	R
1																		
2	Date	Total hrs																
3	Sunday		5am						6am									
4	<enter dates>																	
5	Monday		5am						6am									
6																		
7	Tuesday		5am						6am									
8																		
9	Wednesday		5am						6am									
10																		
11	Thursday		5am						6am									
12																		
13	Friday		5am						6am									
14																		
15	Saturday		5am						6am									
16																		
17	Week Total																	
18																		
19																		
20																		
21																		
22																		

Figure B.13. Set up the grid for all the components of your worksheet, enter headers, and apply fill colors to cells.

2. To each time-segment cell, add a check box (see Figure B.14). If you use small cells like the ones shown, you need to create the check box away from the cell, delete the label, and resize it as small as possible. Link the check box to the cell and then move it into position over the cell.

   Move each check box into alignment by "snapping" it to the worksheet grid by pressing Alt. This is a good way to get all the check boxes positioned perfectly over their linked cells and aligned with each other.

3. Repeat Step 2 for every cell that needs a check box. It's tedious, but there's no faster way to do this because every control must be linked individually to its own cell.

   To speed up the process, make one check box, delete the label, resize it perfectly, and then copy it repeatedly to make matching check boxes. They still must be linked individually to their cells and moved into position, but copies make it a bit faster.

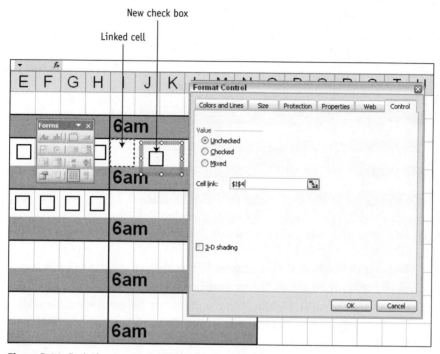

Figure B.14. Each time-segment cell gets its own check box.

4. To total the hours for each day, enter the formula =(**COUNTIF** (*reference range,***TRUE**))**time serial* in a day total cell. The reference range is all the time segments in a day, and the time serial is whatever's appropriate for your time segments, for example, 10 minutes, 30 minutes, and so on. Use relative references and copy the formula to all the day total cells (see Figure B.15).

   To determine the appropriate time serial for a period of time, enter a time segment in a cell (such as 00:20 for 20 minutes), and then format the cell with the Number format General.

5. Write a SUM formula in the weekly total cell. Because the weekly total is more than 24 hours, the cell needs the custom format [h]:mm to display the full number of hours.

Bright Idea

Once you make a worksheet full of linked check boxes like this, save it as a starter workbook for other workbooks you might want to create in the future, so you won't have to do the tedious linking more than once.

Daily total hours formula

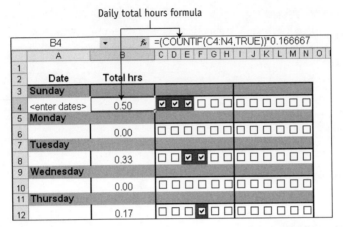

Figure B.15. Write the formula once, with relative references, and copy it to the other cells.

6. The next procedure is conditional formatting to make the cells below the marked check boxes highly visible and to hide the display of TRUE and FALSE behind the check boxes. Select the entire set of linked cells and conditionally format them to be a vibrant cell color and the same color font when the value is TRUE, and for the cell and font to be white when the value is FALSE (see Figure B.16).

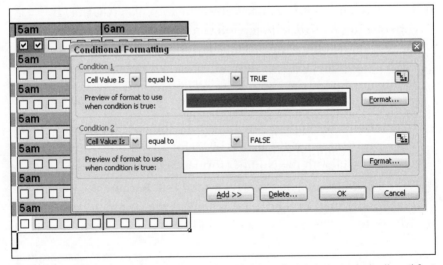

Figure B.16. The marked cells and font are colored bright red, and the unmarked cells and font are colored white.

7. The last piece of the puzzle is protection. You don't want the check boxes inadvertently selected or moved, and you don't want the cells behind the check boxes to be easily selected by clicking. All the cells that change value — the cells behind the check boxes and the cells with formulas — must be unlocked, and then the worksheet protected.

Here are a few final bright ideas for the worksheet:

- Enter instructions for use in the cells below the grid in the worksheet.

- Turn the gridlines off so the worksheet looks more polished.

- Save a copy of the workbook as a template, at least in your machine, so if other users break their copies of the workbook you have another workbook immediately available to send them.

- Make several copies of the worksheet in a workbook, and use a new worksheet for each time period (date each worksheet on its sheet tab).

- To reuse a worksheet, print it to save the data, then unprotect it and drag to select all the cells underneath the check boxes (start the drag outside the grid, and continue the drag across the entire grid of controlled cells), and press Delete to delete all the TRUE/FALSE entries.

- Make the worksheet look like a custom program. Hide all the columns and rows outside the grid (select the unused columns all the way to the edge of the worksheet, and hide them; do the same with the rows below the worksheet).

Chart presentation

Figure B.17 shows an example of using worksheet controls in a presentation worksheet. Option buttons (or a list box or a combo box) display a variety of charts with a click.

Hack

This is a somewhat complex procedure that intertwines several features. I suggest you follow the steps and figures exactly the first time you try this; after you get a handle on it, you can make changes with less opportunity for confusion. Refer to earlier chapters for guidance when you need to.

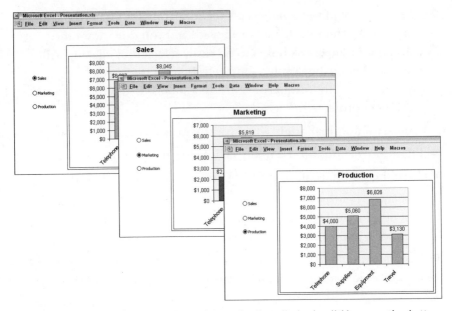

Figure B.17. A great presentation idea — change the chart display by clicking an option button.

In the worksheet shown in Figure B.18, option buttons, formulas, charts, and the Camera button work together to make a worksheet that the most unsavvy Excel user can use, and that makes an easy-to-switch presentation. The charts are switched using linked pictures and a named IF formula.

To create the previous worksheet:

1. Create all the embedded charts you want to display. Locate them off the viewable screen on the presentation worksheet or on another worksheet in the workbook.

2. Position each chart precisely over a specific range of cells (press Alt when you move or resize a chart to "snap" it into position over cells).

3. Name the range of cells beneath each chart (use simple, identifiable names, because you'll be using these names in a formula).

Bright Idea

Choose Format ⇨ Column ⇨ Width to make sure all the columns beneath your charts are exactly the same width. This ensures that the chart pictures on the presentation worksheet are exactly the same size (if you don't do this, the chart pictures appear to jump around when you switch charts).

Range name   Camera button

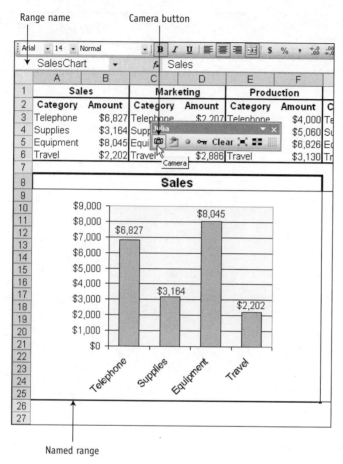

Named range

Figure B.18. This named range includes a cell with a chart title.

4. Use the Camera button (from the Tools category in the Customize dialog box) to take a picture of the cells beneath just one chart. The Camera button takes a picture of selected cells; any graphical objects on top of those cells are included in the picture.

5. Switch to the presentation worksheet, and click where you want the upper-left corner of the chart to appear. Position the chart picture object exactly where you want all the charts to appear (you'll be switching charts with option buttons, and they all appear right where you position the first picture).

6. Create option buttons — one for each chart — and label them according to the chart they switch to (see Figure B.19).

Hack

How do you select cells when you've covered them perfectly and completely with a chart object? Either use the arrow keys and Shift key to select all the cells beneath the chart, or move the chart, select the cells, take the picture (or name the range), and then reposition the chart perfectly over the cells.

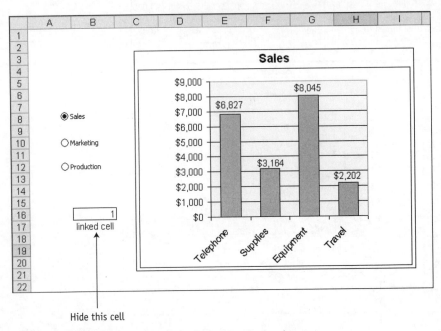

Hide this cell

Figure B.19. Create option buttons to switch charts in the picture.

7. Name the linked cell (you'll use the linked cell name in a formula). In this example, the linked cell is named LinkCell.

8. Create a named formula that uses the linked cell name and value, and the named cell ranges beneath the charts, to select each chart. In this example, the formula named Choice (see Figure B.20) is =IF(LinkCell=1,SalesChart,IF(LinkCell=2,MarketingChart, ProductionChart)).

Bright Idea

For illustration, the linked cell is displayed on this worksheet, but in a real-world worksheet, you want to hide the linked cell (under the picture would be a good place).

This IF formula is nested two levels deep (it has two IF(levels), and can display three results. Because an IF formula can be nested up to seven levels deep, you can use up to eight LinkCell values in the formula by adding more nested IF levels into the main IF formula.

9. Click the picture object. In the Formula bar, delete the formula and type this new formula: *=formulaname* (use the formula name you defined in Step 8) and press Enter. As shown in Figure B.21, the picture uses the named formula =Choice to select the named range to display.

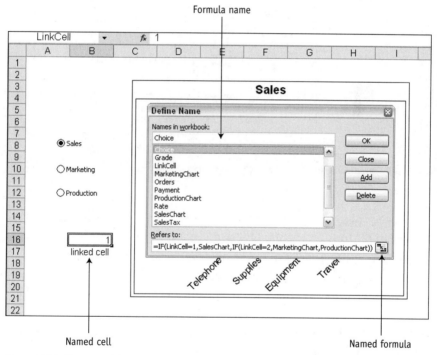

Figure B.20. The named formula will be used in the picture object. Each different value in the LinkCell results in a different named range displayed in the picture object.

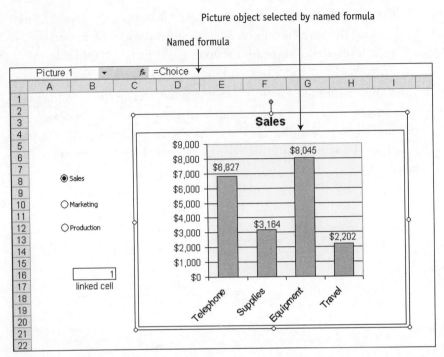

Figure B.21. The picture displays a named range selected by the named formula and linked cell value.

10. Click a cell in the worksheet (to deselect the picture), and click option buttons to test the new presentation worksheet.

When the worksheet is functional, try these ideas for polishing : Dress up the presentation by hiding row numbers, column letters, gridlines, the Formula bar, sheet tabs (choose Tools ⇨ Options and click the View tab), and all unnecessary toolbars. Color the background cells, use borders, and make the worksheet look like a custom application rather than an Excel workbook.

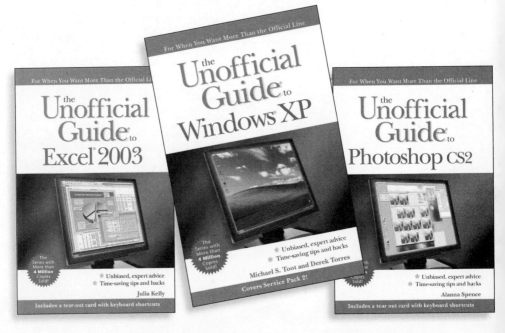